920 - St634f   147152

Stoddard

Famous American women

DATE DUE

MY 9			
MY 13 76			
FEB 15 1979			

ST. CLOUD PUBLIC LIBRARY

GREAT RIVER REGIONAL LIBRARY
St. Cloud, Minnesota 56301

FAMOUS
AMERICAN
WOMEN

By the Author

FAMOUS AMERICAN WOMEN

FROM THESE COMES MUSIC:
Instruments of the Band and Orchestra

SYMPHONY CONDUCTORS OF THE U.S.A.

FAMOUS AMERICAN WOMEN

*

BY

Hope Stoddard

ILLUSTRATED WITH PHOTOGRAPHS
AND PRINTS

THOMAS Y. CROWELL COMPANY

New York

Grateful acknowledgment is made to the following for permission to reprint from copyrighted material:

Doubleday & Company, Inc., for material from *Susan B. Anthony: Her Personal History and Her Era* by Katherine Anthony. Copyright, 1954, by Katherine Anthony.

W. W. Norton & Company, Inc., for material from *The Greek Way* by Edith Hamilton, 1930, and from *Edith Hamilton: An Intimate Portrait* by Doris Fielding Reid, 1967.

Charles Scribner's Sons for material from *This Was a Poet; a Critical Biography of Emily Dickinson* by George Frisbie Whicher, 1938.

Copyright © 1970 by Hope Stoddard

All rights reserved. Except for use in a review, the reproduction or utilization of this work in any form or by any electronic, mechanical, or other means, now known or hereafter invented, including xerography, photocopying, and recording, and in any information storage and retrieval system is forbidden without the written permission of the publisher. Published simultaneously in Canada by Fitzhenry & Whiteside Limited, Toronto.

Manufactured in the United States of America

L.C. Card 73-87158

1 2 3 4 5 6 7 8 9 10

To the memory of my mother

CONTENTS

Jane Addams	*1*
Louisa May Alcott	*12*
Marian Anderson	*24*
Susan B. Anthony	*36*
Ethel Barrymore	*48*
Clara Barton	*59*
Mary McLeod Bethune	*71*
St. Frances Xavier Cabrini	*81*
Mary Cassatt	*90*
Willa Cather	*101*
Agnes de Mille	*111*
Emily Dickinson	*124*
Dorothea Dix	*136*
Isadora Duncan	*149*
Amelia Earhart	*162*
Mary Baker Eddy	*173*
Margaret Fuller	*181*
Lillian Gilbreth	*193*
Martha Graham	*201*
Edith Hamilton	*211*
Oveta Culp Hobby	*218*

Contents

Malvina Hoffman	225
Helen Keller and Anne Sullivan	234
Dorothea Lange	245
Susanne Langer	255
Mary Lyon	263
Margaret Mead	275
Edna St. Vincent Millay	287
Maria Mitchell	295
Harriet Monroe	305
Constance Baker Motley	314
Lucretia Mott	325
Rosa Ponselle	336
Eleanor Roosevelt	347
Florence Sabin	361
Margaret Sanger	372
Margaret Chase Smith	387
Gertrude Stein	399
Harriet Beecher Stowe	410
Harriet Tubman	421
"Babe" Didrikson Zaharias	431
Index	441

ACKNOWLEDGMENTS

This book could not have been written without the assistance of a number of individuals and facilities. The Newark (New Jersey) Free Public Library became my second home during the book's preparation, the stacks open to me, the members of the staff generous with suggestions. The Library at the Margaret Sanger Research Bureau at 17 West 16th Street, New York City, gave me access to otherwise unobtainable material on Miss Sanger's life. The Department of Photography of the Museum of Modern Art in New York City, John Szarkowski, director, provided me with important records of Dorothea Lange's career.

Various experts helped me with their suggestions. Artist Louis Lozowick indicated changes in the Mary Cassatt biography, which gave greater precision to the passages describing her art. John F. Whicher, son of the late George Frisbie Whicher, who wrote *This Was a Poet; a Critical Biography of Emily Dickinson*, examined the chapter devoted to the poet's life. Julia Sabine of the Art and Music Department of the Newark Free Public Library, made valuable suggestions concerning the biography of Susanne Langer. For many of the items in the Mary Lyon biography, I am indebted to Sydney R. McLean, Ph.D., Professor Emeritus of English, Mount Holyoke College.

Friends and relatives of some of the women discussed helped me with the biographical pieces. Ethel Barrymore Colt Miglietta, daughter of Ethel Barrymore, read over her mother's biography and made pertinent suggestions. Jane Callaghan, secretary to Lillian Gilbreth, gave generously of her time to assist me. Marguerite Johnston, of the Houston *Post*, was of much help in my preparation of the biography of Oveta Culp Hobby. Paul Taylor, social science professor at the University of California, reviewed the chapter about his late wife and partner in his projects, Dorothea Lange.

Finally I want to thank Elizabeth Fischer, former English teacher in California schools, who read my manuscript in its roughest state, smoothed out some of the worst dents, and assembled the bibliographies.

FAMOUS AMERICAN WOMEN

JANE ADDAMS

JANE ADDAMS: Born in Cedarville, Illinois, September 6, 1860. Died in Chicago, Illinois, May 21, 1935. Father: John H. Addams; mother: Sarah Addams. She was the youngest of a family of eight.

*

Hull-House, Chicago's first settlement house and the country's most famous one, was opened, in the words of its founder, Jane Addams, because "If it is natural to feed the hungry and care for the sick, it is certainly natural to give pleasure to the young, comfort to the aged, and to minister to the deep-seated craving for social intercourse that all men feel." She did not think of it as an organization, however. For her it was a matter of individuals: the burglar who broke into Hull-House one night—she told him to come back in the morning and they would have work for him; the ex-trapeze performer—she saw that he got a job suited to him, as window cleaner at Hull-House; the little bride, who came to Hull-House because her husband had beaten her for losing the wedding ring. Thus Miss Addams helped the needy and united the community. Through her, the great influx of immigrants who arrived in Chicago during the eighties and nineties was given a pattern for living and was shaped into an American community.

*

HER mother died when she was a baby. As a child she was not strong. She had a spinal defect which was to cause her trouble all her life. But her father, who was a Quaker and a member of the state legislature for sixteen years, insisted on her seeing life whole and facing it courageously. She once asked him how it happened that some people had good things and some didn't, and he told her that some inequities "might never be righted," so far as clothes and such went, but that they need not occur in things that "really mattered—in education and religion, for instance." Later she wrote that he "drew me into the moral concerns of life."

She thought of herself as "an ugly, pigeon-toed little girl whose crooked back obliged her to walk with her head held very much upon one side." But a chance meeting with her father in town one day made her stop grieving about her looks. He met her on the main street and, obviously pleased to see her, tipped his hat low as if she were a grand lady.

After a childhood with the whole countryside to play in, she went for four years to Rockford (Illinois) Seminary. On the death of her father, she had a siege of illness and the doctors advised a trip abroad to recuperate. Her stepmother—her father had remarried when Jane was eight—a woman of much social distinction, hoped to introduce her stepdaughter to society. But dress shops and drawing-room chatter did not appeal to Jane.

Two incidents on her trip did impress her. Late one Saturday night, from the top of a sight-seeing bus in East London's slum district, she saw an auction of vegetables. Here rejects from ordinary markets, put up for last-minute sale before a Sunday deadline made selling illegal, brought together under the street's flaring gas lamps "huge masses of ill-clad people, clamoring, hands outstretched, around the hucksters' carts . . . bidding their small coin, for food already unfit to eat." One man, having had his purchase slung at him, sat on a curbstone "tearing the cabbage-head with his teeth, unwashed and uncooked as it was."

Then from a hotel window in Germany she saw a line of

brewery working women crossing the town square through the snow, carrying on their bent backs in huge wooden tanks a scalding brew which at the least misstep slopped over onto their faces. She noticed on their reddened skins white scars, the results of previous scaldings. After that she went down to a breakfast "for which I had lost my appetite."

It was on a second trip to Europe in 1887–1888 that another event brought her to the point of decision: a bullfight in Madrid, which she attended with a group of friends, one of them Ellen Starr, later to be her colleague at Hull-House. Although she saw five bulls and many more horses slain in the most brutal fashion, she felt toward the whole spectacle merely a scholarly interest—it was a survival of the gladiatorial combat. Later, in her hotel room, however, she had a revulsion. This entire period of travel, she decided, instead of being a preparation for life, had become a dreamer's retreat. She figured that women had been given the advantages of higher education too suddenly. "Somewhere in the process of 'being educated' they had lost that simple and almost automatic response to the human appeal . . . ." She decided that the very next day, whatever happened, she would begin to carry out, if only by talking about it, a plan she had formulated.

So in the morning she confided to Miss Starr, "with stumbling and uncertainty," that she would like to rent a house in a part of a great city "where primitive and actual needs are found." This way she could learn from life itself, could replace mere dreams by actual living. Miss Starr listened eagerly, said she would like to go in with her friend on such a project. They continued talking as they boarded the train, and before they had reached the next stop in their itinerary, the plan had become, although still hazy in detail, "convincing and tangible."

When Jane Addams headed for East London again, she visited Toynbee Hall, a settlement house, and studied their means of assisting the poor. Then she returned to America and, with Miss Starr, started a search which centered on the large immigrant area of Chicago.

Their choice finally narrowed down to a well-built structure on Halsted Street, standing in a section lined with small shops, saloons, and ready-made clothing establishments. The foreign-born had congregated there in crowded rat-infested tenements. The streets were indescribably dirty, the paving miserable, the stables foul. Hundreds of houses were not connected with the street sewer.

The house they chose stood well back from the street and was surrounded on three sides by porches. Wide halls and open fireplaces gave it a sense of spacious comfort. They went to its owner, Helen Culver, who told them she would lease it to them rent free. And so they took over Hull-House.

They furnished it with works of art which they had collected in Europe and with some good family mahogany pieces. When they finally were settled, Miss Addams felt she had come home.

In that year, 1889, social work had only begun to be a subject of intensive study. Four years later, at Chicago University, it was first to be incorporated in a college course. So in Hull-House the teachers and the taught, the helpers and those helped, combined in a search for ways of aiding each other. It might be called a school, for certainly there were classes in art, music, dressmaking, cooking, millinery, even college extension courses. It might be called a clubhouse, for there were women's clubs, men's clubs, boys' clubs, children's clubs, social clubs, social science clubs, working people's clubs, the Friendly Club, the Eight-Hour Club, the Shakespeare Club, Circolo Italiano, the Women Necktie Workers Club. It might also be called a charity-dispensing organization, since thousands of dollars went out of it and into the hands of the needy.

But at first it was simply a way of getting acquainted with the neighbors and of making them acquainted with each other. People began wandering in, curious, open-minded, eager. Working mothers found that they could leave their children in safe hands there, with a midday meal and amusement—all this provided for five cents a day. Many small children, let loose on the streets while their mothers were at work in factories, found their way there by themselves. Almost the first week a group of girls joined a "reading party," and listened absorbed to George Eliot's novel *Romola*. On the very first New Year's Day a party was staged for older people, carriages being provided to pick up those who could not walk. Every Thursday evening a free public lecture was given, with a well-known speaker.

While the people learned, so did Jane Addams. Once she directed one out-of-work applicant to a canal-digging project, despite his contention that he could not do outdoor work. When he contracted pneumonia, she was made to realize that one must never make hard and fast rules.

They started a dietetic kitchen, had well-balanced meals, scientifically prepared. But it didn't work out. So they turned it into a coffee house, with quantities of coffee from immense coffee urns and thousands of thick roast beef sandwiches dispensed. It was a success from the start.

The little children who came to the kindergarten in the morning were followed by older children in afternoon clubs, and these, in turn, made way for the educational and social adult groups, occupying every room in the house every hour of the day.

The Jane Club, a boarding arrangement for girls, developed into a residence accommodating fifty members. A house for men was opened across from Hull-House. The gymnasium and the coffee house were put in another building and they supplemented each other nicely. The Children's House developed from a little cottage on a side street to a building especially designed for its use. Another structure, Bowen Hall, was used for dancing parties with soft drinks dispensed in the lobby.

In the first building to be erected especially for Hull-House the second floor was carefully constructed and lighted for art exhibits. Arts, by their very universality, Jane Addams decided, could be an excellent means of communication. A "Labor Museum" was fitted up to display old crafts: spinning wheels, basketry, weaving. It served to highlight the accomplishments of the older people from overseas.

At Hull-House Theater, plays—*Snow-White, Puss-in-Boots*—were presented for and by the very young. The older people acted in plays by Shakespeare, Molière, and Schiller, even when these entailed long hours of rehearsal.

Concerts were given every Sunday afternoon. Musicians donated their services as performers and as teachers. A chorus and a band were formed. The Music School, opened in 1893, was housed in a quiet court.

With all possible saving and scraping and contriving—"We cooked the meals and kept the books and washed the windows"—the project would have bogged down had not Jane Addams had a way with people. Her solicitude brought aid not only in services but in gifts of money and land. A Chicago man, fond of athletics, chose to build a gymnasium for the boys. Another Chicagoan gave five thousand dollars for the art gallery. Jane Addams convinced still others that the success of the Jane Club justified the erection of a building for its sole use. Several blocks of dilapidated houses were torn down and a playground built in their place. On July 31, 1889, she wrote to one of her friends, Mary Rozet Smith, "The playground this year is a fine affair, the willows wave in the breeze, likewise clover; the children . . . play in the sand, build block houses, and the mothers sit in the shelter and sew . . . quite like a story book. My fund is up to $65,150."

And so this smallish, quiet-faced woman, who favored soft grayish blue colors in her dresses, wrote letters, addressed meetings, moved about Hull-House, watching, advising. She tramped up flights of stairs in tenements to visit ailing school children, answered calls to wash newborn babies, talked to the troubled, nursed the sick. She had to readjust all her living habits. "Any student tendency to sit with a book by the fire was of necessity definitely abandoned."

She also worked through civic channels. After agitating without effect for proper garbage removal, she put in a bid for herself as garbage removal agent. This bid was thrown out on a technicality, but it led to her being appointed by the mayor as garbage inspector of the ward. Her insistence on increasing the number of wagons, on making landlords provide proper receptacles, and on cleaning away the debris accumulated through the years—a long forgotten pavement was found under eight inches of refuse on one street—brought down the death rate of the ward from third in the city to seventh.

She swung into the wider orbit of social legislation. At the very first Hull-House Christmas party several little girls refused candy, saying simply they worked in a candy factory and "couldn't bear the sight of it." On one of her house visits she saw a child of four sitting hour after hour on a low stool beside her mother, pulling out bastings. She started investigations of the child labor laws and the sweatshop systems. She publicized her findings: "An unscrupulous contractor regards no basement as too dark, no stable loft too foul, no rear shanty too provisional, no tenement room too small for his workroom." When a boy who attended the Hull-House gymnasium was killed by a factory machine simply because it lacked a guard, she began to agitate for safety measures in factories. She obtained temporary charge of the young boys arrested on trivial offenses, thus preventing their being jailed. She and her colleagues conducted careful investigations into the proportion of tuberculosis cases among working children and factory women. Support for deserted women, insurance for dependent widows, damages for injured operators, were other causes for which she agitated

She was an adept public speaker. Before the child labor law was passed in Illinois in 1903, she addressed benefit societies, church groups, social clubs, night after night for three straight months. She was expert at dealing with hecklers. Once when a group of extremists inferred she was "all right now," but just to wait till she was "subsidized by millionaires," she answered that she had no idea of being "subsidized by millionaires," but neither did she propose "to be bullied by workingmen." "I shall state my honest opinion without consulting either of them," she said. The crowd of radicals burst into applause.

In July 1905 she became a member of the Chicago Board of Education. She was elected the president of the National Conference of Social Work in 1909, the first woman to be chosen for the post. The same year, President Theodore Roosevelt called her to the White House for a conference on dependent children. In 1910 she became vice president of the National Woman's Suffrage Association and made speaking tours on women's behalf through New England and the Middle West. She believed women's intuition was "an accurate perception of truth and justice."

Her talks published in popular magazines widened her audiences, as did her books: *Hull-House Maps and Papers*, written with her colleagues in 1895; *Democracy and Social Ethics* (1902); *The Spirit of Youth and the City Streets* (1909); *Twenty Years at Hull-House* (1910); *A New Conscience and an Ancient Evil* (a study of prostitution, 1912); *The Long Road of Woman's Memory* (1906).

Her trips to Europe were now working tours—to consult with Tolstoy, the great novelist and labor reformer, on his theories regarding comradely relationship with the humblest; to visit labor leaders and social workers in England and on the Continent.

She became an avowed pacifist. "It is easy to kill a man. It is not easy to bring him forward in the paths of civilization," she reminded her audience at the Universal Peace Congress in Boston in 1904. In her book *Newer Ideas of Peace* she summed up her convictions: "I believed that peace was not merely an absence of war, but the nurture of human life, and that in time this nurture would do away with war as a natural process."

In 1914—when World War I was declared the United States was as yet uncommitted—she tried harder than ever to bring her peace projects before the people. In 1915, with Carrie Chapman Catt, she called together a Woman's Peace Party and was elected its national chairman. Also in that year she headed the commission selected to seek an end to the war, at the first International Congress of Women held at The Hague. She visited representatives of the various nations, both neutrals and belligerents, seeking ways toward peace. When in February 3, 1917, relations with Germany were broken off, she was one in a committee who conferred with President Wilson—to no avail. During the war years she was connected with the Department of Food Administration and collected food in the United States for European nations, both neutrals and belligerents, including German children. Hull-House was the scene of many "send-off" dinners for those going overseas. She remained through all inflexibly committed to the cause of world peace. The Woman's Peace Party was kept open in a downtown office building in Chicago.

In May 1919, before the peace treaty had been signed at Versailles, women from twenty different nations gathered to attend the Women's Peace Conference in Zurich. Jane Addams at the time pointed out some of the dangers to permanent peace—for instance the subjugation of the conquered—contained in the treaty. (Time has proved her correct.) At the same meeting she "ventured to assert that war is not a natural activity for mankind, that large masses of men should fight against other large masses is abnormal, from both the biological and ethical point of view."

The name of the organization was changed to the "Women's International League for Peace and Freedom" and she was elected its first president.

In 1920 Miss Addams helped to found the American Civil Liberties Union. Its purpose was to contest all attempts of the courts "to violate the right of free speech, free press and free assembly." In 1922 she published her book *Peace and Bread in Time of War*, an account of women's work for peace.

She suffered a heart attack in 1926 and went to live with her friend Louise de Koven Bowen. In 1929 she resigned as president of the Congress of the Women's International League for Peace and Freedom, but was immediately elected honorary president for life. Her book *The Second Twenty Years at Hull-House*, covering the period from 1909 to 1929, appeared in 1930. This year, too, she received an honorary LL.D. degree from the University of Chicago. What was perhaps the most treasured honor came to her in 1931: She was corecipient with Nicholas Murray Butler of the Nobel Peace Prize.

On May 18, 1935, it became apparent that she must undergo surgery. Mrs. Bowen came to her room where she was quietly reading to tell her, "Jane, the ambulance will be here in an hour." Miss Addams replied, "That's all right, for that will give me time to finish this book." Three days after the operation she died in Chicago's Passavant Hospital.

Hull-House has been her memorial. "The Settlement," she

once said, "is an attempt to relieve the overaccumulating at one end of society and the destitution at the other . . . It must be grounded in a philosophy whose foundation is on the solidarity of the human race, a philosophy which will not waver when the race happens to be represented by a drunken woman or an idiot boy."

BIBLIOGRAPHY

ADDAMS, JANE, *A Centennial Reader*. New York: The Macmillan Company, 1960.
———, *Second Twenty Years at Hull-House, Sept. 1909 to Sept. 1929; with a Record of a Growing World Consciousness*. New York: The Macmillan Company, 1930.
———, *Twenty Years at Hull-House; with Autobiographical Notes*. New York: The Macmillan Company, 1910.
BOWEN, LOUISE HADDUCK, *Open Windows; Stories of People and Places*. Chicago: Ralph Fletcher Seymour, 1946.

LOUISA MAY ALCOTT

LOUISA MAY ALCOTT: Born in Germantown, Pennsylvania, November 29, 1832. Died in Roxbury, Massachusetts, March 6, 1888. Father: (Amos) Bronson Alcott; mother: Abigail (May) Alcott; sisters: Anna, Elizabeth, and May.

*

Louisa May Alcott made girlhood, its problems, its urges, its fulfillments, real. Since her books first appeared, adolescence has had a place in the world of books. At least eight of her books are still widely read here in America, and are popular in translations in twelve foreign languages. *Little Women* has been made into a successful drama and was twice filmed.

*

So forthright and vivid is the portrayal of the March family in *Little Women* that many who have read it are convinced they already know about the Alcott family, which formed the basis for these sketches. But for all this is an autobiographical novel—one of the best of its genre—it shows only one side of this interesting family. The real Alcotts were far more complex and far more problem-weighted than the characters in *Little Women*.

Louisa, even in her childhood, was not the flyaway tomboy pictured as Jo in *Little Women*. She was a discerning and purposeful young lady, given to highjinks, it is true, but soberly aware of the family situation to which she was born.

Moreover, she was determined to alter it. She knew her father was considered by many of the neighbors a ne'er-do-well and a freak. But she was aware, too, of his greatness. Thomas Carlyle has described him as "The good Alcott, with his long, lean face and figure, with his grey worn temples and mild radiant eyes, all bent on saving the world by a return to acorns and the golden age . . . a kind of venerable Don Quixote whom nobody can even laugh at without loving." It was as such she loved him, but this did not keep her from realizing his drawbacks.

When she was eleven years old, her father brought about a situation which might have meant tragedy for the family. They were then living in "Fruitlands," a farm near the town of Harvard, Massachusetts, where some six to a dozen philosophers (they came and went) and their families were engaged in an experiment in "Con-Sociate" living. They were followers of transcendentalism, which meant they had turned away from materialism, believed that pure thought could accomplish miracles, and trusted in man's Godlike nature. Winter was coming on, and the philosophers had been so busy discussing their beliefs that they had not had time to tend to the crops. Once, when an easterly storm had come up, Louisa's mother, Abba, had marshaled the three older daughters, and "harnessing herself and them to clothes-baskets and receptacles, hurriedly devised from bed sheets," had dragged the grain to shelter.

Things came to such a pass that one of the philosophers, Charles Lane, tried to persuade Louisa's father to enter a nearby community made up of Shakers, a thrifty sect who always had bursting granaries. But Louisa's mother discovered that the Shakers did not respect family ties, that they separated couples already married, that, even in death, they had one burial plot for the men and one for the women. She steadfastly refused to go along with the experiment. Lane was irritated. Her "peculiar maternal love blinds her to all else," he complained.

It was at this juncture that Abba called a family counsel. Louisa could not have been aware of all the fine points of the discussion, but she did grasp the main issue: Was her family to stay together or was it to be separated? Afterward up in her little attic bedroom she got out her journal and wrote in it, "I was very unhappy, and we all cried. Anna and I cried in bed, and I prayed to keep us all together"; and further, "I wish I was rich . . . and we were all a happy family."

Fortunately the crisis at Fruitlands was resolved peaceably by the father. "My faithful wife, my little girls—they have not forsaken me. They are mine by ties that none can break. What right have I to leave them alone?"

But plainly the Con-Sociate experiment was a failure. Something had to be done. Abba took steps. She sold a "silver piece" and with the money arranged to rent a part of a neighbor's house in the nearby town of Harvard. Then she and her husband and the little girls piled the household utensils and furniture on an ox-sled, the children clambered on top, husband and wife walked on ahead, and the family left Fruitlands forever.

As they jogged along, Louisa went over other moves they had made: from her birthplace, in Germantown, Pennsylvania, to Philadelphia; from there to Boston (she could just barely recall going on a big steamer then); and after that to three different places in Boston. Next—when she was seven—they had gone to Concord, and when she was ten, to Fruitlands. They'd moved in a cart that time, too, and she had sat on top. A bust of Socrates had gone along with them, and here it was still, on the move.

All these moves—and there were to be many more of them, mostly in vain attempts to find stable teaching arrangements for Bronson Alcott—might have had a disintegrating effect on the family had not Abba been such a wise wife, mother, and manager. Always the children were made to feel a part of the homemaking, proud to be able to help with the washing, sweeping, and cooking, with the firewood collecting, berry picking, and wall mending. Work for the good of all, they were made to believe, was as enjoyable as running in the field, jumping off high beams in the barn, having theatricals, and journeying over the hillsides with scrip and staff, pretending they were characters in the book *Pilgrim's Progress*.

At Hillside, in Concord, Massachusetts—this was three moves after Fruitlands and Louisa was thirteen—Bronson Alcott got into the thick of the transcendentalist movement. He contributed articles to *The Dial* magazine and communed with a wide circle of like thinkers: Emerson, Thoreau, Hawthorne, Channing, Ripley, Peabody, Parker. When Robert Owen, the famous British social reformer, came to America in 1845, he visited the Alcotts at Hillside, and the whole galaxy of transcendentalists were invited there to meet him. Mrs. Alcott wrote her brother, "Though unfeasted and unpledged our guests left us feeling that the true hospitality was love and intelligence."

Emerson, already famous as a philosopher and writer, lived just down the road and became Louisa's mentor and friend. She liked to visit his library, was given books by him. She wrote him passionate little notes (but never sent them), left wild flowers at his study door, and often stood under his window reciting verses, but in so low a voice not even the birds could hear. She wrote at his death, years later, that he had done more for her than he knew "by the simple beauty of his life, the truth and wisdom of his books."

At Hillside Louisa had a long-held wish granted: a room of her own, with a desk by the window. Here she composed her dramas, which she and her sisters acted out in the barn. She also set up as a dressmaker for dolls, "with my sign out and wonderful models in my window. All the children employed me, and my turbans were the rage of the town." But, though this brought her plenty of goodwill, it brought her very little money.

When, on her fourteenth birthday, her mother gave her a pen accompanied with a verse beginning, "Oh may this pen your muse inspire/When wrapt in pure poetic fire . . ." Louisa began to write down the stories she had been telling Ellen, the young daughter of Emerson. These later were to be published in her book *Flower Fables*.

But the family was getting deeper and deeper into debt. Bronson was no more able to make a living at Hillside than elsewhere. If a lecture realized a dollar or two, he was likely to give it away. A group of Boston women, "The South End Friendly Society," wanted someone to do charity work for them. They asked Mrs. Alcott if she would like the work. She would, and the family moved back to Boston, to live there in various locations for six years while Mrs. Alcott, now forty-eight, distributed food and clothing to the poor, solicited money from the rich, and ran an employment office at her home, for all of thirty dollars a month. Anna and Louisa helped out by getting together a school in the front parlor of their home, and for a brief, awful period Louisa even "went out to service"—brought water from the well, dug paths in the snow, split kindling, made fires, sifted ashes for her employer, but balked at blacking his boots. At the end of the eight weeks of work she received exactly four dollars. She was later to use this episode in her story "How I Went Out to Service."

During this period Mr. Alcott made a lecture tour in the West. When he came home—but let Louisa tell it—"We were waked by hearing the bell. Mother flew down, crying, 'My husband!' We rushed after, and five white figures embraced the half-frozen wanderer who came in hungry, tired, cold, and disappointed, but smiling bravely and as serene as ever. We fed and warmed and brooded over him, longing to ask if he had made any money; but no one did till little May said, after he had told all the pleasant things, 'Well, did people pay you?' Then, with a queer look, he opened his pocketbook and showed one dollar, saying with a smile that made our eyes fill, 'Only that! My overcoat was stolen, and I had to buy a shawl . . . but I have opened the way, and another year shall do better.' " Mrs. Alcott answered, "I call that doing *very well*. Since you are safely home, dear, we don't ask anything more." Louisa wrote further: "Anna and I choked down our tears, and took a little lesson in real love . . . the look that the tired man and the tender woman gave one another. It was half tragic and comic, for Father was very dirty and sleepy, and Mother in a big nightcap and funny old jacket."

Next Mrs. Alcott took in some immigrants as free lodgers, and the Alcotts all caught smallpox from them. "We had a curious time of exile, danger, and trouble. No doctors, and all got well," wrote Louisa.

They next moved to High Street in Boston, where as part of her charity work Mrs. Alcott took in "lost girls, abused wives, friendless children, and weak or wicked men." Louisa was teaching. "Father doing as well as a philosopher can in a money-loving world."

Then something miraculous enough to please even a transcendentalist occurred. Louisa began making money from her stories. Llewellyn Willis, a young friend of the family (he is part of the composite picture of Laurie in *Little Women*), took Louisa's story "The Prince and the Fairy" to the *Boston Olive Branch*, a Methodist newspaper, and sold it for five dollars. That was sign enough for Louisa. Now, writing hour after hour in the Pinckney Street garret (they had moved again), she finished, sent out, and sold stories at five, six, ten dollars apiece. She completed *Flower Fables*, her first book, in 1854. An edition of sixteen hundred copies sold nicely, but she realized only thirty-two dollars from it. She gave a copy of the book to her mother on Christmas Day: ". . . you will accept it with all its faults . . . and look upon it merely as an earnest of what I may yet do . . . I hope to pass in time from fairies and fables to men and realities."

The family in 1855 went to live in a friend's house in Walpole, New Hampshire, where "Father can have a garden; Mother can rest, and be near her good niece; the children have freedom and fine air."

But leisure was not for Louisa. In November she decided to go to Boston alone. She was now twenty-two, handsome, with a wide forehead, thick brown hair parted in the middle and netted up in a large knot at the back. Her lips and chin were firm. She had no time for fun, no time for romance. She was too busy trying to write salable stories.

In Boston she wrote "A Sister's Trial," got six dollars for it, and ten dollars for a story titled, "Genevieve." She did sewing jobs, obtained a position as governess to an invalid girl, read to the elderly, went to lectures by William Makepeace Thackeray, and to literary gatherings at the home of the preacher Theodore Parker. In late 1856 she got her first silk dress that was not a hand-me-down and went to New Year's parties in it.

But the family in Walpole sent word that Mrs. Alcott had nursed some children with scarlet fever, and that Louisa's sister Elizabeth had come down with it. The house in Walpole was damp and drafty, and they had decided to move back to Concord in hopes this would benefit Elizabeth, who had seemingly recovered from scarlet fever but remained weak. With Louisa's help they got together enough money and moved in October 1857 near Town Hall in Concord. But Elizabeth grew worse. On the morning of March 14, 1858, at three o'clock, the family gathered around the bed of this, the youngest daughter of the house. She opened her eyes, looked from one to another, said contentedly, "All here!" and sank into unconsciousness. Soon after, she died.

In July the family moved to Orchard House (near Hillside), which was to be the setting for *Little Women*. This move, as well as medical expenses, had put the family heavily in debt. So off Louisa went again to Boston, where she tutored, took in sewing, and of course wrote. She got twenty-five dollars for a story. She sent word to Anna, "I shall get a second-hand carpet for the little parlor, a bonnet for you, and some shoes and stockings for myself."

Then came 1860, the "Year of Good Luck," as Louisa called it. It started in November 1859 when she got fifty dollars for a story in the *Atlantic Monthly* magazine. Shortly after that she was paid seventy-five dollars for "Cinderella." Emerson invited her to his classes—"A great honor as all learned ladies go." At her sister Anna's wedding on May 23, when Emerson kissed the bride, Louisa noted, "I thought that honor would make even matrimony endurable." To top all these good things, in 1860 her father was appointed superintendent of schools in Concord, not a well-paying job—that would be asking too much—but one that brought him honor.

In April 1861 war was declared. Louisa longed to help. She tried running a kindergarten but gave it up. She got thirty dollars for a story, "King of Clubs." Finally she volunteered as a nurse, was accepted immediately, and in December 1862 started off for the Union Hospital at Georgetown, near Washington, D.C. She was thirty years old now, had been carefully reared. Suddenly she was plunged into over-crowded, evil-smelling wards. These days were described in her journals: "Up at six, dress by gaslight—poke up the fire—cold damp dirty, full of vile odors from wounds, kitchens, wash-rooms, and stables . . . . Till noon I trot, trot, giving out rations, cutting up food for helpless 'boys,' washing faces, teaching my attendants how beds are made or floors are swept, dressing wounds . . . dusting tables, sewing bandages, keeping trays tidy, rushing up and down after pillows, bed-linen, sponges, books, and directions . . . . Dream awfully and wake unrefreshed . . . ." After six weeks of this she fell ill of typhoid pneumonia and was taken home to Concord by her father. For three weeks she was delirious. One of her dream-fantasies she has recorded was that their home had no roof.

The letters she had sent home from Georgetown were published by *Commonwealth* newspaper as "Hospital Sketches" and later appeared in book form. This showed her what her forte was: writing of real events, of real people.

This also brought her a market. In October 1861 she wrote, "A year ago, I had no publisher, and went begging my wares; now *three* have asked me for something, several papers are ready to print my contributions." In January 1864 she could write: "I find I have earned by *writing* alone near *six hundred dollars* since last January, and spent less than a hundred for myself, which I am glad to know."

In 1865 she managed to squeeze in a short trip to Europe, as companion to an invalid lady. It was there she met a young Pole, Ladislas Wisniewski, and was escorted around Paris by him. But when debts called her home, she told her "Laurie" farewell.

Among the publishers who were now seeking her out was Thomas Niles of Roberts Brothers. "I think, Miss Alcott, that you could write a book for girls," he had told her. And now when the family needed funds badly, she decided to try. By the end of June 1868 she had written the first twelve chapters of *Little Women*, and by July had handed in the whole 402 pages of handwritten manuscript. "I plod away, though I don't enjoy this sort of thing. Never liked girls or knew many, except my sisters; but our queer plays and experiences may prove interesting, though I doubt it."

When he saw the completed manuscript, Mr. Niles had doubts, too, but decided to publish it anyway. It came out in October 1868 and was an immediate success. Everyone read it, lawyers between cases, commuters between coaches, housewives between chores, and of course young ladies, because no proper mother would think of letting a birthday or Christmas go by without presenting her daughter with it.

Little Women paid all the Alcott family's outstanding debts. Not only that but a new furnace was installed; Mr. Alcott's books were rebound in fine leather; the parlors were redecorated; new carpets were laid on the floor. Louisa wrote, "Now I feel as if I would die in peace. My dream is beginning to come true." She added, though, "I was tired with my hard summer, with no rest for the brain that earns the money."

Little Women brought money, but seemed to have robbed her of her health. "Cough and weariness keep me from working as I once could fourteen hours a day." The almost constant ache in her legs sent her from one doctor to another. In January 1870 she lost her voice for a period. In October, just before her thirty-eighth birthday, she went to Boston to work there away from the "dampness and worry" of Concord.

In 1870 she went again to Europe, but "Laurie" was no longer on hand to be her swain. When she received word of the death of Anna's husband, John, she felt a resurgence of her old vigor if not of the old magic. She began writing *Little Men* so that "John's death may not leave Anna and the dear little boys in want." She finished *Little Men* in Europe and sent it to the publishers. By the time she returned, the book had been published, and had had an enormous advance sale.

Now she was a celebrity, but she found it more and more

difficult to use her "writing brains." However, in the summer of 1876 she wrote *Rose in Bloom,* and in September sent her sister May to Europe to continue her art studies. In 1877 she wrote *Under the Lilacs,* then returned to Concord to nurse her mother. That long-struggling lady died November 25.

Then, by another sad twist of fate, May, who had married in Europe and given birth to a daughter, died. She left word that her child be put in Louisa's care. So on September 18, 1880, the baby, Lulu, was brought to America and Louisa had another charge.

She rented a house in Boston with trees in front. Her father was pleased with his room, and Lulu was delighted with her big sunny playroom. Anna and her two sons came, too. The boys were "in clover." But because of her writing commitments and her deteriorating health, she could no longer take full charge of Lulu. The child came more and more under the supervision of Anna. Louisa got into the habit of spending her summers at the Mountain House near Princeton, Massachusetts, where she could write when she wished and rest when she needed to.

She had become interested in the Woman's Rights Movement and wrote a friend, "Let us hear no more of 'woman's sphere' from the State House or pulpit—no more twaddle about sturdy oaks and clinging vines. Let woman find out her own limitations, but in heaven's name, give her a chance! Let the professions be opened to her. Let fifty years of college education be hers. And then we shall see what she can do!"

In December 1886 she went to stay at a retreat at Dunreath Place, in Roxbury, Massachusetts. The next year she completed plans for officially adopting her nephew, Anna's younger son, John, so that her estate could be properly settled in the male line. In the midst of a renewal of old aches and pains she put together one of her most fanciful books, *A Garland for Girls.*

Her father's health began to fail rapidly, and on a visit to him she was so distraught by worry that, returning home, she forgot to wear her fur coat. She reached Roxbury chilled and in the morning complained of a violent headache. When her father died on March 4, she was too ill to be told. She herself died two days later. She was fifty-five.

BIBLIOGRAPHY

CHENEY, EDNAH D., ed., *Louisa May Alcott: Her Life, Letters and Journals*. Boston: Little, Brown and Company, 1889.

MEIGS, CORNELIA LYNDE, *The Story of the Author of Little Women: Invincible Louisa*. Boston: Little, Brown and Company, 1933.

SALYER, SANFORD, *Marmee, the Mother of Little Women*. Norman: University of Oklahoma Press, 1949.

WORTHINGTON, MARJORIE, *Miss Alcott of Concord: A Biography*. New York: Doubleday & Company, Inc., 1958.

MARIAN ANDERSON

MARIAN ANDERSON (FISHER): Born in Philadelphia, Pennsylvania, February 27, 1903. Father: John Anderson; mother: Anna (Ricker) Anderson; sisters: Alyce and Ethel; husband: Orpheus H. Fisher.

*

On Easter Sunday, April 9, 1939, seventy-five thousand people—senators, members of the President's Cabinet, clerks from government bureaus, porters, janitors, icemen, salesmen, office workers—crowded about the steps of the Lincoln Memorial in Washington, D.C. The crowd flowed down along the plaza in a great semicircle, and completely surrounded the reflecting pool of the Washington Monument. They came to register their indignation at a flagrant act of discrimination: the refusal of the Daughters of the American Revolution (D.A.R.) to allow Constitution Hall to be used by Negro singer Marian Anderson for her concert in Washington, D.C. The whole nation had become involved in the controversy, and to absolve itself, practically the whole nation had gathered here or at their radio sets to hear Marian Anderson sing in this open-air concert at the Lincoln Memorial.

All eyes were fixed on the platform, eager and sympathetic, when a figure, small in the great distance, came forward. Marian Anderson stood silent as if listening for a moment, and then was heard that voice, rich, deep, glorious—a voice unique in the annals of song. Contemporary commentators called this "the greatest single event in the slow march of the American Negro to full equality as a citizen." From this moment Marian Anderson was to be a symbol of her race's emergence.

*

MARIAN Anderson grew up, as she says in her autobiography, *My Lord, What a Morning*, "not knowing when I did not sing." As a small child, while her mother worked in the kitchen, she would sit at the table, pretending it was a piano, beating out a sort of rhythm, and making up a vocal accompaniment. By the time she was six, she was singing with the choir in church. She would learn all four parts of the hymns to fill in for absent singers. By the time she was ten she was singing solos in church. It was all invaluable training, both for developing her marvelous three-octave range, and for accustoming herself to public appearances. The church, proud of its young singer, took up collections now and then for her lessons. When she was eight, her father, an ice-and-coal man, who himself liked to sing bits of "Asleep in the Deep," bought a secondhand piano for the family. There was no money for piano lessons, but Marian picked out little tunes herself and soon, with the help of a cardboard chart, could name the notes. She bought a violin with money she earned scrubbing neighbors' steps, and learned to play it, after a fashion, too.

Though luxuries were scarce in those days, she did not feel deprived. "Warm and cozy" was the way she described her life then. Her mother, who had been a schoolteacher in Virginia, was a good friend to her children. "She never lifted her voice to us in anger . . . She guided us by her example . . . . We were aware that she had a strength beyond the energies of her small body. We believed as she did because we wanted the same kind of haven in time of storm."

When Marian was twelve, her father died, the family

moved to her grandmother's home, and her mother went out to work as a cleaning woman at Wanamaker's Department Store. Marian helped out by occasionally serving as assistant artist at church concerts and, under church auspices, at affairs outside. "I would come home from school, try to scramble through my lessons and do whatever chores I was expected to attend to, and then I would run out to fill my engagements . . . hurry from the YMCA to the YWCA to a Methodist or Baptist or Episcopal church. I might appear at three different places in an evening." In time she was earning all of five dollars a performance. She gave her mother two dollars, her sisters one each, and kept one for herself.

Once she sang in her church as assisting artist to Roland Hayes, one of the outstanding Negro singers of the day. He took the trouble to go to her home and tell her grandmother, an imposing lady, part Indian, that Marian should start studying voice professionally.

Her high school principal, at the South Philadelphia High School for Girls, suggested Giuseppe Boghetti, an outstanding voice instructor in that city, as a teacher. At first Boghetti said he could not accommodate any more pupils, but when he heard her sing "Deep River," he changed his mind. The problem of how to pay for her lessons was solved when the church members arranged a benefit concert, which realized six hundred dollars.

Her singing engagements now spread out to include colleges and other institutions. Her accompanist, Billy King, was soon doubling as her manager, keeping a card catalogue of schools, colleges, and halls where she was asked back annually. Her fees crept up to ten dollars, to twenty dollars, and finally to fifty dollars a concert. She and her mother and sisters moved from her grandmother's to a house of their own, with three rooms downstairs—a living room, a little dining room, and a shed kitchen—and two rooms upstairs, besides a sort of studio for herself, fixed over from a lean-to. "We contracted to buy furniture on the installment plan . . . . I was incredibly happy."

In 1922, at a reception held after a concert in Wilmington, Delaware, Marian Anderson first met the man she was later to marry, Orpheus H. Fisher. He called on her again when he came to Philadelphia—he was taking courses there preparatory to becoming an architect—and they began to see each other often. But then he went to New York. "I cried when he left," she notes in her autobiography, "but one gets swept up in a career . . . has time for little else. Presently, though, we knew that someday we would be married . . . . Our wedding did not take place until 1943. It was worth waiting for."

Then came 1923, a year she marked down as her "dark" year. She gave a concert at New York's Town Hall, but only a scattering of people showed up. The critical comments were unfavorable, spoke of "unevenness," lack of surety. She returned to Philadelphia feeling lost and defeated. She stopped going regularly to Mr. Boghetti's studio. But she couldn't give up. She kept turning over in her mind the *reasons* for her lack of success. Why had some songs failed to get across? Why had she not made her points? She had let the small audience discourage her. She had not made the most of her voice. And here she showed the quality, her analytical judgment, that was to help her toward success.

One day Mr. Boghetti told her of a competition for singers. The winner would get a chance to appear at New York's Lewisohn Stadium with the New York Philharmonic. He coached her for it carefully. At the time of the contest, a blistering August day, nearly fifty young singers (reduced from three hundred through local run-offs) met at Aeolian Hall in New York. Mr. Boghetti had gone with her, and noticing that she was placed late on the program (No. 44) and thinking the judges would be weary by that time, he advised her to go right on singing even if they gave her the signal to stop. But there was no such signal. They let her sing the aria "O mio Fernando" from *La Favorita* right through. Then one of them called down from the balcony: "Has No. 44 another song?" She had. They let her leave the concert hall without comment, but when she got back to Philadelphia word came through that she had won.

Her Lewisohn Stadium appearance, August 26, 1925, marked the start of her professional career. "A remarkable voice . . . astonishing vocal powers displayed," wrote critic Francis Perkins in the New York *Herald Tribune*, "a voice in a thousand . . . or shall we say ten thousand or a hundred thousand? . . . a notable feature was its entire naturalness."

From then on she sang in large halls as well as in churches and clubs. Her ability to communicate with her audiences increased. She was receiving $350 a concert, and in special cases $500. So the happy day came when she could call up Wanamaker's and tell them that her mother would not be coming back to work there anymore.

In 1929 she sailed to England for further study, but the person with whom she was to study became ill. After some student appearances in London's Wigmore Hall and at the Promenade Concerts, she returned to America. Then came another trip, this one financed by the Julius Rosenwald Fund. She headed for Germany, there to receive coaching in the singing of *Lieder*—German art songs—and in languages. Through lesson contacts, she was launched on a tour of Norway, Sweden, Denmark, and Finland. Serving as her accompanist was the Finnish pianist Kosti Vehanen, who gave her interpretative suggestions and stage pointers. She would try to remember, after concerts, audience reactions to specific songs and passages in songs, and then examine the music to see which phrases could be done more effectively.

Her Scandinavian tours comprised hundreds of concerts between 1930 and 1934. One critic named the furor she created "Marian Fever." She sent generous amounts of money home, purchased all the music she wanted (and had it bound in leather), and bought the clothes she needed to appear at her best on the platform.

She visited the Finnish composer Sibelius, and when she had sung some of his songs he strode to her side and gave her a hearty hug. He had invited her to "coffee" but now he called out to the kitchen, "Bring champagne!" This was no coffee occasion. Later he dedicated his composition "Solitude" to her.

The next stop in her travels, London, she found difficult. The most the reviewers would say was that she showed "possibilities." But Paris was another story. There they came in droves to hear her. She was at first shy of these sophisticated and highly critical audiences. Her accompanist, Mr. Vehanen, relates that, after taking a few steps onto the stage one night and seeing the glittering audience in the packed house, she backed off, took a deep breath, then walked on again, slowly, in her gold lamé gown. Those who have seen her walk across a platform—the calm nobility of her stride, the fine lift of her head—will agree that her entrance thus into Parisian musical circles must have been most effective. She had inveigled her mother into visiting her in Europe, and there, up front, the little woman sat, a snug, beaming figure.

Just before her third concert in Paris, on June 16, 1935, the American impresario Sol Hurok noticed a poster advertising "The American Contralto" and decided to take in the concert. After the first number, he says, he was booking her mentally for a whole year ahead. His actual procedure was a bit more restrained. At intermission he suggested that she see him the next day at his office. Miss Anderson had heard of him as a courageous and astute promoter of talent, and when he told her, "I think I can do something for you in America," she felt she had reached a milestone in her career.

Before she went back to America, Miss Anderson made a tour of Europe. In Rome the hall was so crowded that people had to sit on the stage. In Vienna, as she sang Bach's "Komm' süsser Tod," many members of the audience wept. In Salzburg, Toscanini came backstage to compliment her.

It would have been understandable if Miss Anderson had decided to remain in Europe. She had seldom been made conscious there of discrimination because of her race. True, a concert bureau in Germany had turned her down after she had failed to declare herself "pure Aryan." But with this exception she had stayed at hotels, gone to seashore resorts, eaten at restaurants, made purchases in stores, quite like any other member of society. It was only during her tours in America that she had had so often to depend on friends' kindness for lodgings, had been assigned to "Berth 13" (a euphemism for the train's drawing room in lieu of a real sleeper), had been refused restaurant service. And she couldn't help remembering that when she had tried to register as a student at a conservatory in her home town, the registrar had looked at her coldly and said, "We don't take colored." But Miss Anderson tells us she never had a thought of not returning to America. "I had gone to Europe . . . to reach for a place as a serious artist, but I never doubted that I must return. I was—and am—an American."

Her return to her native country came when Hurok arranged a concert for her on December 30, 1935, at New York's Town Hall. Critic Howard Taubman summed up the reaction of the audience, in *The New York Times* the next day: "Let it be said at the outset Marian Anderson has returned to her native land one of the great singers of our time!" He described her voice as "a contralto of stunning range and volume, managed with suppleness and grace." It is ironic that even on this occasion she was unable to get accommodations at a midtown hotel, but had to stay in Harlem, relatively far from the concert hall.

High praise, far from making her giddy, brought her sober thoughts. After the debut "I got out my music," she writes. "I studied the songs I had sung, examining my singing in retrospect to check where I had not done as I would have liked and where a point had been exaggerated or undervalued. Here was a song that should have begun more softly and ended more powerfully. There was another that had not been all of a piece . . . in some places I had touched too lightly on the essential feeling, missing its depth . . . . I resolved to be more careful."

Gradually her engagements in America increased, crowding out those overseas. In 1936 she made a tour of the United States and Europe (in Leningrad they shouted for her song "Deep River"). In 1937 she made a home tour again plus a tour of South America. In 1938 she sang seventy recitals in the United States. During a tour of the southern states Howard University conferred on her an honorary Doctorate of Music. In 1939–1940 she sang ninety-two concerts in seventy United States cities between November and June, following which she sailed on her first trip to Hawaii. By now her regal walk would have been recognized by passersby in almost any large city in America, and her resonant voice on any radio broadcast, at the first turn of the dial.

Then suddenly fate called on her to take on a further role: that of protagonist of her race. Hurok, after booking her for concerts in most of the principal cities of the United States, had decided that the nation's capital was the next logical city and that Constitution Hall, where the symphony concerts were regularly presented, was the logical place. But the D.A.R. (Daughters of the American Revolution), owners of the hall, refused to permit the concert, giving as their excuse the trouble over segregated seating arrangements that ensued years before when they had booked Roland Hayes. Miss Anderson was filling dates in San Francisco, was, in fact, on her way to the concert hall there, when she first saw displayed on a newsstand a paper with the headlines, "Mrs. Roosevelt Takes Stand—Resigns from D.A.R." By the time she had reached Washington, Miss Anderson's case had become a national issue. Ministers preached sermons on it; high-placed citizens signed manifestos; the New York conductor, Walter Damrosch, issued a protest in the name of the nation's musicians. Senator Robert F. Wagner of New York called it "The most challenging issue confronting American democracy." The D.A.R. in a Texas city bought up a whole block of two hundred tickets for a forthcoming Anderson concert as a rebuke to the Washingtonians.

Then, as a national protest, a people's committee arranged an open-air concert at the Lincoln Memorial. Miss Anderson admits she had qualms—she doesn't like a lot of show. But "I could see that my significance as an individual was small in this affair. I had become, whether I liked it or not, a symbol, representing my people. I had to appear . . . . I could not run away from this situation." Secretary of the Interior Harold Ickes, speaking just before she appeared, told the multitude, "Genius draws no color line. She has endowed Marian Anderson with such a voice as lifts any individual above his fellows, as is a matter of exultant pride to any race. And so it is fitting that Marian Anderson should raise her voice in tribute to the noble Lincoln, whom mankind will ever honor."

So she sang—sang in spite of nervousness such as she had rarely experienced. She sang as she had never sung before, sang the National Anthem, "Ave Maria," the "Gospel Train." At the end, to calm the tumult of applause, she told them, "I thank you from the bottom of my heart again and again."

Marian Anderson

Some twenty-five years later Marian Anderson was asked how she felt about the D.A.R.'s affront. "I forgave the D.A.R. many years ago," she said briefly. "You lose a lot of time hating people."

Not too long after this she was invited to the White House, there to meet the visiting King and Queen of England. She has also sung at the White House for President Truman and President Roosevelt, and at the inaugurations of Presidents Eisenhower and Kennedy. Sweden's *Litteris et Artibus* medal and Finland's Order of the White Rose have been conferred on her. Eleanor Roosevelt bestowed on her the 1938 Joel Spingarn Medal of the National Association for the Advancement of Colored People. The Republic of Liberia presented her with the Order of the African Redemption. With the ten thousand dollars she received as the Philadelphia Award of 1941 (the Bok award, given annually to outstanding inhabitants of that city) she established cash scholarships, ten annually, for aspiring young singers.

During World War II she gave a benefit concert, January 7, 1943, in the once-prohibited Constitution Hall—on the D.A.R.'s invitation, the proceeds going to United China Relief. In 1944 she set a record when war bonds to the amount of $1,700,000 were purchased as admission to a concert she gave at Carnegie Hall. Her cross-country schedule now included singing in the camps, the hospitals, the war factories, the shipyards. In 1950 she appeared in Germany under the auspices of the occupation authorities.

Then, in her late forties, came her engagement by the Metropolitan Opera Company. She was asked to sing the part of Ulrica (a Negro fortune teller) in Verdi's *Masked Ball*. She at first demurred, "I was no longer going out of my way to sing high notes above the staff." But Dimitri Mitropoulos, who auditioned her, told her "When you know it, it will go." The period of training "caused the blood to race through me with new meaning." On the night of the opening, January 7, 1955, close to two thousand telegrams arrived. When the curtains parted on the second scene, and she was revealed as a witch-like figure bent over her magic brew, a thunderous applause sounded. Here again she was a symbol: the first Negro to be heard in the company's seventy-one-year history. She was asked back to the Met the following season. Her entrance there has opened the way for other members of her race to sing at the Met and with other opera companies.

In 1955 she toured Israel (she endowed a fellowship fund in Tel Aviv to be awarded annually to talented young musicians), and in 1957 she went on a tour of the Far East for the State Department: the Philippines, Vietnam, Burma, Thailand, Malaya, and India. She talked directly to the people—backstage, in club gatherings, out on the street. Did they feel oppression could be brought to an end? Did they look forward to a bettering of conditions? A television program of the trip was presented in the United States during Christmas week of that year. On her return she received a State Department Citation: "You have brought credit to your country." In 1958 she was assigned to the Trusteeship Committee of the United Nations, a group that handles matters relating to the status and well-being of inhabitants in territories under United Nations trusteeship. In 1963 President Johnson presented her with a Freedom Medal for her work at the United Nations and abroad.

A tour of the world in 1964 ended with her farewell concert in New York City, April 18, 1965. "A significant epoch in American culture came to an end," wrote Harold Schonberg of *The New York Times*. "Miss Anderson stood as a symbol for the emergence of the Negro . . . . Those who remember her at her height can never forget that big resonant voice, with those low notes almost visceral in nature, and with that easy, unforced ascent to the top register. A natural voice, a hauntingly colorful one, it was one of the vocal phenomena of its time."

In 1966 President Johnson appointed her to the National Council on the Arts. (Created by Congress in 1964, this committee recommends how money should be allocated to develop the arts.) In her private life she has received the Merit Award of the New York Youth Committee for her work with underprivileged children in Harlem: visiting schools and orphanages and speaking to the children. When not at these duties or filling lecture dates, or dates with symphony orchestras as narrator for Copland's "A Lincoln Portrait," she lives happily with her husband on their farm in Connecticut. She believes that life is good, and that one can make it better. She has proved this in her own life—has become a symbol not only of a race emerging through difficulties but of an artist come into her own after overcoming obstacles of formidable dimensions.

BIBLIOGRAPHY

ANDERSON, MARIAN, *My Lord, What a Morning; an Autobiography*. New York: The Viking Press, Inc., 1956.

VEHANEN, KOSTI, *Marian Anderson, a Portrait* (written with the Collaboration of George J. Barnett). New York: McGraw-Hill Book Company, 1941.

SUSAN B. ANTHONY

SUSAN B. ANTHONY: Born in Adams, Massachusetts, February 15, 1820. Died in Rochester, New York, March 13, 1906. Father: Daniel Anthony; mother: Lucy (Read) Anthony; brothers: Daniel Read and Jacob Merritt; sisters: Guelma Penn, Hannah, Mary Stafford, and Eliza Tefft.

*

Susan B. Anthony was one of those lucky individuals whose special abilities dovetailed perfectly with the needs of the age. Or we might put it, the age itself was lucky. For just as the Gold Rush began, territories became states, schools sprouted up everywhere, slaves were freed, she came into prominence to fight for women's rights. She was as integral a part of the surge forward as the covered wagon or the Erie Canal.

*

SUSAN Anthony was born into the Quaker community—exceptional in those days for giving equal scope to men and women. Her aunt was a famous preacher who spoke at Quaker meetings throughout the country. At home Susan heard discussions against slavery—Quakers were not allowed to hold slaves—for temperance and for the right of women to be heard in good causes, even in public places. Her father, a cotton manufacturer, appreciating her quick mind, gave her his constant support and sent her to what for that day was a progressive school, where the girls could learn geography and languages, as well as needlework and the three R's.

Susan B. Anthony

When she grew older her father lost his cotton mill as a result of the panic of 1837, and she was faced with the problem of making a living. Girls in those days were offered almost no outlet into full adulthood save through marriage or teaching. She turned down offers of marriage. Later she wrote: "When I was young, if a girl married poverty, she became a drudge; if she married wealth, she became a doll. Had I married at twenty-one, I would have been either a drudge or a doll for fifty-two years. Think of it!"

So she taught school for $2.50 a week, was governess in the home of a merchant in Fort Edward, New York, and when she was at home over the holidays—the family moved to a farm near Rochester, New York, when she was nineteen—helped with the housework. Her diary records: "Did a large washing . . . . Spent today at the spinning wheel . . . . Baked 21 loaves of bread . . . . Wove three yards of carpet . . . . Got my quilt out of the frame last 5th day . . . . The new saw mill has just been raised; we had twenty men to supper on the 6th day and 12 on the 7th day." Interesting people came to her father's house, and the conversations dealt with moot topics of the day. Susan Anthony rushed between the kitchen and the dining room, torn between her desire to take part in the discussions and to present a well-cooked meal.

When she was appointed principal of the girls' department in Canajoharie Academy in New York, she joined the Daughters of Temperance Society there and was made its secretary. She spoke at Temperance Daughters' suppers and lined up halls and churches where meetings were to be held.

One July day in 1848 she noticed an item in the Canajoharie paper—a report on a Woman's Rights Convention held in Seneca, New York. It reconvened a week later in Rochester and her family attended. On a trip home shortly thereafter she heard about it from them. She learned the convention had advocated better education for women, wider industrial opportunities, equal pay for equal work, the right of women to hold property and retain wages, the right to free speech on public platforms, and, of all things, the right to vote.

Susan Anthony now began to find her schoolroom walls unbearably confining. She spent her leisure time visiting towns around Canajoharie to form new branches of the Women's Temperance Society. She was invited to larger temperance conventions. Returning from one, she passed through the town of Seneca Falls, and her hostess for the night, Mrs. Amelia Bloomer, introduced her to another woman's rights advocate, Elizabeth Cady Stanton. Mrs. Stanton in turn invited Miss Anthony, in the summer of 1851, to meet Horace Greeley, the famous journalist and reformer, at her home for a discussion on coeducation. Miss Anthony's range was widening.

On September 8, 1852, again on the invitation of Mrs. Stanton, who liked her "honest Quaker manner," she went to her first Woman's Rights Convention, held in Syracuse. What she heard there convinced her women should have the vote. As the laws stood then, women were getting a bare pittance, much less than men, for a hard day's work, were unable to collect and control their own earnings, were deprived even of their children in case of divorce. Her way seemed clear: She would devote her life to the cause of woman's enfranchisement.

She got a sample of the difficulties involved when she attended a Teachers' Convention in Rochester, August 3, 1853. To her "grief and indignation" she noticed that the men, far in the minority, took over the meeting, and did all the discussing, while the women sat in silence at the back. An argument arose over why teachers were a less respected group than lawyers, doctors, and ministers. Susan Anthony stood up and addressed the chair: "Mr. President." If an explosion had occurred right there in the hall it could not have produced a greater effect. There was a long silence, while all faces were turned in her direction. Finally, the chairman asked, "What will the lady have?" "The lady," said Miss Anthony, "would like to speak to the question." Then, for a half hour, while she remained standing, her hands tightly clasped to hide their trembling, the men debated on whether such an innovation should be allowed. A vote was finally taken, among the men, with a very small majority indicating that she would be allowed to speak.

"It seems to me you fail to comprehend the cause of the disrespect of which you complain," said Susan. "Do you not see that so long as society says woman has not brains enough to be a doctor, lawyer, or minister, but has plenty to be a teacher, every man of you, who condescends to teach, tacitly admits before all Israel and the sun that he has no more brains than a woman?" Then she sat down.

This speech broke up the meeting. After the hasty adjournment the men stood around in little huddles discussing the unheard-of thing. Some of the women conspicuously avoided Miss Anthony, even drew their skirts away as they passed. Others, however, congratulated her on her courage. From then on, she was looked to as a champion of women teachers in New York State.

During this period the issue of property rights for women came up before the state legislators in Albany. Miss Anthony and her coworkers braved the blizzards of a New York winter, and in a ten-week house-to-house canvass (she practically invented this means of publicity) collected six thousand signatures on a petition asking that married women be given the right to their own earnings. In 1854 she spoke, in her clear contralto voice, before the state legislators. Women must have a right to the money they earn and the children they bear, she insisted.

But another national problem was crowding the woman question into the background. As western territories became settled, the question, "Shall they enter the union as slave states or free states?" became paramount. Miss Anthony became a speaker for the Anti-Slavery Society. By her very presence on speakers' platforms she promoted the cause of women.

Many of the towns she went to in the Middle and Far West had never before been visited by a woman speaker, and people came in wagonloads from miles around to hear her. If they first came out of sheer curiosity, as they would have come to see a dancing dog, they remained to listen respectfully. Her clear logic, her fiery hatred of injustice, her quick wit, kept the audiences alert.

She had an answer ready for every question. Once the Abolitionist speaker Rev. A. D. Mayo threw out the remark, "You are not married; you have no business to be discussing marriage." "Well, Mr. Mayo," she replied, "you are not a slave, suppose you quit lecturing on slavery." It was later, during the Kansas campaign for women's suffrage, that Horace Greeley put the question to her, "Miss Anthony, you know the ballot and the bullet go together. If you vote, are you ready to fight?" "Yes, Mr. Greeley," was Miss Anthony's famous reply, "just as you fought in the late war—at the point of a goose quill."

Like all abolitionists, she believed immediate and unconditional emancipation was the only ethical solution. She said so even when those who hoped the Civil War would end in a stalemate caused mobs to break up Anti-Slavery Society meetings by throwing rotten eggs, demolishing benches, extinguishing lights, sprinkling pepper on stoves.

In Syracuse the hall was taken over by a crowd of roughnecks brandishing knives and pistols. In New York City after the meeting the mobsters dragged a hideous effigy of Susan through the streets and burned it in a public square. Such mob takeovers Susan cheerfully chalked up as an asset: "A hundred unmolested conventions would not have made a tithe of the sympathizers this one diabolical mob has done."

In Albany, New York, the mayor was determined to maintain order. He planted plainclothes policemen throughout the hall, set himself on the platform with a revolver across his knees, and in a firm voice told Miss Anthony to begin. She was not interrupted.

When such disturbances made her lecture dates fall off, she went back to the Rochester farm and threw herself into housekeeping. "Quilted all day but sewing seems to be no longer my calling . . . . I stained and varnished the library bookcase today, and superintended the plowing of the orchard . . . . The last load of hay is in the barn; all in capital order . . . . Fitted out a fugitive slave for Canada with the help of Harriet Tubman . . . . The teachers' convention was small and dull. The woman's committee failed to report. I am mortified to death for them. Washed every window in the house today . . . . Put a quilted petticoat in the frame . . . . Commenced Mrs. Browning's 'Portuguese Sonnets.' "

The Civil War created new opportunities for women. Now they not only took in boarders, made quilts, did sewing, ground the corn, got in crops, and cared for the livestock, but also went to work in factories—textile, clothing, shoe—and into printing and cigar-making. In some cases they traveled to battlefields to care for the wounded. But while the women were engrossed in war work, the New York legislature, April 10, 1862, quietly took away from mothers their lately acquired right of equal guardianship over their children and that of control of the minor children's property on the husband's death. As Miss Anthony said, "Twenty thousand petitions—a hard year's work—and now all is lost!"

After the war she again went full force into lecturing, mostly through the regular circuit bureaus. Year after year she traveled up and down the country. She did not mince words. "The facts prove that, by all the great fundamental principles of our free government, not only married women but the entire womanhood of the nation are in 'a condition of servitude,' as surely as were our Revolutionary fathers when they rebelled against King George." "What is a slave? A person who is robbed of the proceeds of his labor; a person who is subject to the will of another." And, "By the laws of almost every State in this Union today, North as well as South, the married woman has no right to the custody and control of her person." And referring to women's place in the labor movement: "Your own interest demands that you should seek to make women your political equals, for then, instead of being, as now, a dead weight to drag down all working men, a stumbling block in their path, a hindrance to their efforts to secure better wages and more favorable legislation, the working women would be an added strength, politically, industrially, morally."

On the last day of 1871 she noted in her diary, "Left Medicine Bow at noon, went through deep snow cuts ten feet in length . . . . Reached Laramie at ten P.M. Thus closes 1871, a year full of hard work, six months east, six months west, of the Rocky Mountains: 171 lectures, 13,000 miles of travel; gross receipts $4,318; paid on debts, $2,271. Nothing ahead but to plod on." That year (1871) in the newly devised Fifteenth Amendment (enfranchisement of slaves) the word *male* was first used to define voters. It showed that the men on Capitol Hill were beginning to realize the force of the woman's rights movement and to put up guards.

Then Miss Anthony had an inspiration. One bright fall morning she simply went to the polls and *voted*. That is, having previously registered—this aroused only an amused reaction on the part of officials—she went to the polling place near her home in Rochester, and before the astonished guards could prevent her, cast her vote. Shortly thereafter she was arrested at her home and taken to court by a much embarrassed officer of the law. (He refused to put handcuffs on her.)

Her trial was "fixed" from beginning to end. She was not allowed to testify in her own behalf. The jury was not allowed to retire to consider the verdict, was simply instructed to pronounce her there and then "guilty." By other maneuverings she was prohibited from carrying her case to the Supreme Court. As Miss Anthony's biographer, Ida Husted Harper, puts it: "If Miss Anthony had won her case on the merits, it would have revolutionized the suffrage of the country and enfranchised every woman in the United States. There was a pre-arranged determination to convict her. A jury trial was dangerous, and so the Constitution was openly and deliberately violated."

But Miss Anthony made a victory of defeat. When the judge, after sentencing her, asked her if she had anything to say, she said yes she had. "Your denial of my citizens' right to vote is the denial of my right of consent as one of the governed," she said, "the denial of my right of representation as one of the taxed, . . . the denial of my sacred right of life, liberty, property . . . . A commoner in England, tried before a jury of lords, would have had far less cause to complain than I, a woman, tried before a jury of men."

When the penalty was announced ($100 fine and the costs of the prosecution), Susan said very quietly: "May it please your Honor, I shall never pay a dollar of your unjust penalty. All the stock in trade that I possess is a $10,000 debt, incurred by publishing my paper, the *Revolution*, four years ago, the sole object of which was to educate all women to do precisely as I have done, rebel against your man-made, unjust, unconstitutional forms of law, that tax, fine, imprison, and hang women, while they deny them the right of representation in the government; and I shall work on with might and main to pay every dollar of that honest debt; but not a penny will go to this unjust claim. And I shall earnestly and persistently continue to urge all women to the practical recognition of the old revolutionary maxim, that 'Resistance to tyranny is obedience to God.'"

Indignation over the machinations of the trial swept the country. Across the nation people sent her sums of money to pay the costs. From this time on Susan B. Anthony was an honored prophet in her own land.

She made good use of her added influence. At woman's rights conventions she was now making the motion: "*Resolved:* That a committee of three be appointed to wait before the President and remind him of the existence of one half of the American people." She herself appeared both before the President of the United States—several Presidents, in fact, through the course of time—and before sessions of the Congress. She lectured in any states where the suffrage question was about to be voted. The halls were invariably sold out.

A Mrs. Starrett, who entertained Miss Anthony at one stop in her Kansas tour, has written: "At the gate I met a dignified Quaker-looking lady with a small satchel and a black and white shawl on her arm. Disarmed by her genial manner and frank, kindly face, I led the way into the house and said I would have her stay to tea and then we would see what further arrangements could be made. While I was looking after things she gained the affections of the babies and seeing the door of my sister's sick-room open, she went in and in a short time had so won the heart and soothed instead of exciting the nervous sufferer, entertaining her with accounts of the outside world, that by the time tea was over I was ready to do anything if Miss Anthony would only stay with me."

As late as 1894 this seventy-four-year-old woman had two states to tour almost simultaneously: New York with a Constitutional Convention coming up, and Kansas with a suffrage amendment pending. She shuttled back and forth between the states and managed also to cover all sixty counties of New York. Her ceaseless lecturing—seventy-five to one hundred lectures every year during a sixty-year career—brought a nationwide change of attitude toward the woman question. The response of the public at two fairs, seventeen years apart, illustrates this change. At the Philadelphia Centennial in 1876 the National Woman Suffrage Association was denied any official recognition—no displays, no program placement. But at the World's Columbian Exposition in Chicago in 1893 the World Congress of Representative Women was given a whole building in which the achievements of women throughout the world were exhibited. Speeches were given all over the building, sometimes as many as eighteen simultaneously. But whatever lecture it was, even the mention of Susan B. Anthony's name brought forth bursts of applause. If she herself gave a speech, the police were employed to break the jam of those crowding to see and hear her. At seventy-three she had come to be recognized as "the mother of us all."

Her extreme old age found her a revered personality throughout the world. Her strong face, her keen blue-gray eyes looking out through gold-rimmed spectacles, her gleaming white hair, her red shawl, became symbols of high purposefulness. The days of ridicule and denigration were over.

The high point of her career, in her own opinion, came when she went to Berlin in 1904 to the convention of the International Council of Women, which, meeting at regular intervals, gave excellent opportunities for registering gains made by women. This important body had not yet committed itself to woman suffrage. Just prior to the 1904 meeting a suffrage committee (headed by Miss Anthony) had been formed, but had been kept in the background lest it foment opposition from Germany's conservative element. However, when the meeting opened, the presiding officer glanced over the platform and asked, "Where is Susan B. Anthony?" At the sound of that name everyone sprang up; the men threw their hats in the air; the women their handkerchiefs. The cheering lasted for fifteen minutes, with the name "Susan" sounding out again and again. But no Susan appeared. She would wait until the Council head had properly recognized her in her capacity as officer of the suffrage committee. That very week the International Woman Suffrage Alliance was formed as a separate organization with affiliates in Australia, Denmark, Germany, Great Britain, the Netherlands, Norway, Sweden, and the United States, and from then on full political freedom was the goal of women throughout the world.

In 1906 she went to the Baltimore convention of the National Woman's Suffrage Association in spite of the fact that shortly before she had suffered a slight stroke. Here her dearest wish was granted—a permanent fund was established to support the cause of suffrage. It so delighted her that she got out of her sick bed to go to Washington for a celebration of her eighty-sixth birthday. "The hammer may as well fall one time as another. I am going," she told her doctors, who had warned her against it. President Theodore Roosevelt sent his congratulations, but she answered this with, "When will men do something besides extend congratulations? I would rather have President Roosevelt say one word to Congress in favor of amending the Constitution to give women the suffrage than to praise me endlessly." And she closed her speech—the last one she was ever to give—with the words "Failure is impossible."

It was the Nineteenth Amendment (not the Sixteenth, as she had hoped) that gave the vote to women. This was in 1920, fourteen years after her death. But it was Susan B. Anthony, more than any other person, who laid the groundwork for this accomplishment.

BIBLIOGRAPHY

ANTHONY, KATHARINE SUSAN, *Susan B. Anthony: Her Personal History and Her Era.* New York: Doubleday & Company, Inc., 1954.

DORR, RHETA LOUISE, *Susan B. Anthony, the Woman Who Changed the Mind of a Nation.* New York: Frederick A. Stokes Company, 1928.

FLEXNER, ELEANOR, *Century of Struggle; the Woman's Rights Movement in the United States.* Cambridge, Mass.: Harvard University Press, 1959.

HARPER, IDA A., *The Life and Work of Susan B. Anthony; Including Public Addresses, Her Own Letters and Many from Her Contemporaries During Fifty Years; a Story of the Evolution of the Status of Women,* 8 vols. Indianapolis and Kansas City: The Bowen-Merrill Company, 1898–1908.

LUTZ, ALMA, *Susan B. Anthony; Rebel, Crusader, Humanitarian.* Boston: Beacon Press, 1959.

RIEGEL, ROBERT EDGAR, *American Feminists.* Lawrence: University of Kansas Press, 1963.

ETHEL BARRYMORE

ETHEL BARRYMORE (COLT): Born in Philadelphia, Pennsylvania, August 15, 1879. Died in Beverly Hills, California, June 18, 1959. Father: Maurice Barrymore; mother: Georgiana Drew Barrymore; brothers: Lionel and John Barrymore; husband: Russell Griswold Colt; children: Samuel Colt, Ethel Barrymore Colt, John Drew Colt.

*

Ethel Barrymore was for more than fifty years a reigning queen of the stage. She starred in more than two score Broadway productions and toured thousands of miles in one night stands across the country. Besides making a career for herself, she started her brothers John and Lionel on their distinguished acting careers. The three of them were known as "The Royal Family of the Theater."

*

IN her childhood Ethel looked for guidance to her grandmother, Mrs. John Drew. This regal lady, besides being one of America's first great actresses, was, during the period of Ethel's childhood, manager of a midtown theater in Philadelphia. "Home" to the child was her grandmother's house, and her early impressions were of the great golden sofa and the square piano in the parlor, the cavernous halls with their "alarming echoes," the nursery on the second floor, and the two attics, filled with an amazing assortment of articles left by generations of actors. Ethel's parents had a romantic glamour appealing to a child. Her father was one of the leading male actors of the day, and her mother was an accomplished actress. But Ethel and her brothers never thought of them as parents-in-charge to be looked to for day-by-day guidance. Most of the time they were on tour, and even when they were at the Philadelphia house they were scarcely different from the other visiting actor relatives, Ethel's famous uncles and aunts and cousins.

The three children did not lack discipline, but in this actors' household, even commands were given in quotes. If the children had to go to bed: "Stand not on the order of your going, but go at once." When they gulped their food they were told to eat "wisely and slowly," and when Ethel, who was shy, kept her eyes down when she spoke, they would use a phrase from the current play *Lady of Lyons*: "Look up, Pauline." Their grandmother Drew did not allow them to "utter"—as she called conversing at length in the presence of grown-ups—but this did not prevent them from "uttering" long and loud when they were alone together. Ethel, who liked to play the piano and read, did not join in most of her brothers' shenanigans: like "fishing" for gentlemen's hats, with long lines and hooks hung over the second story balustrade. But she was one of the cast when they put on *Camille* in an old barn at two-cents-a-head admission.

One glowing memory in her early childhood was the year or so she spent in England. Her father used a legacy left him by an aunt to take his wife and children to his native land, while he filled acting engagements in London. They lived in a cottage with a large garden, and had dogs and a monkey— the nearest the children and their parents ever came to experiencing a real home life together.

The children were back in America in time to go to school. Ethel started at the Convent of Notre Dame in Philadelphia. She enjoyed her convent school years. The sisters listened sympathetically to her problems, encouraged her in her love of music—she won a silver prize for playing a Beethoven sonata—and instilled in her a sense of responsibility. But at thirteen this good time came to an end. Her mother became seriously ill; the doctors diagnosed her case as advanced tuberculosis, and Ethel was chosen to accompany her to Santa Barbara, California, and look after her.

On her mother's death, Ethel took on the sad tasks of telegraphing her Uncle Sidney (her father was on tour and could not be reached), packing her mother's beautiful gowns—here was the only time the young girl broke down and cried—arranging to have the body sent home, and buying her own ticket for the eight-day journey back east. Before she started, she put up her hair and bought herself a long black dress. Because she had no money for a pullman berth, she sat up all the way. She kept saying to herself: "Next month I'll be fourteen. Next month I'll be fourteen." She was grown up. Her childhood was over.

The theater in Philadelphia had ceased to make money, and this meant that her grandmother must go on the road again. She was acting in Montreal when she sent for her granddaughter. Ethel had hoped to become a concert pianist, but now she put all this behind her. She would have to make her own living, and acting seemed the only way possible to her.

She was not even sure she could act. Nor was her grandmother. The latter, who was taking the part of Mrs. Malaprop in *The Rivals,* sat waving a fan very slowly as Ethel, playing the part of Julia, spoke her lines. Then at a certain point her grandmother laid the fan in her lap and gave a little nod. Everything was going to be all right.

Ethel played in *The Rivals* in Montreal and on a tour of eastern Canada and northern Maine. Sometimes, when there was a piano in the pit, she would play it between the acts. But when *The Rivals* closed, she had to return to New York—her grandmother had an apartment there—and for months trudged from agency to agency looking for a job. Finally she appealed to her Uncle Jack—John Drew, the "first gentleman of the American theater"—who asked his manager, Charles Frohman—he controlled theaters in large cities across the country—to look up something for her. Eventually a place was found for her as an understudy, and an understudy she remained for nearly four years.

During the tours—and in those days traveling filled about six months of every actor's working year—she lived in the poorest boardinghouse rooms, ate at the cheapest restaurants, or bought crackers and milk and made solitary lunches for herself in her room. But she liked the life, liked to study the characteristics of the various cities she visited, liked to go to concerts.

When she was in the midst of a tour of *Rosemary*, William Gillette, whose acting she had seen and admired, telegraphed her uncle he'd like Ethel to come to England to be an understudy in a production of *Secret Service*. When she got off the train at Waterloo Station in London, she felt as if she had come home. She soon had a chance at real acting. The young lady for whom she was understudy fell ill one evening, and Ethel took her part. She got good notices. But when this play closed, things looked bleak again. However, just before she was to return to America, in fact the very day of her farewell party, she won the lead part in a new English play, *The Bells*.

She made a success of it. Soon she was not only a well-known actress in England, but also a figure in the world of society. Word got back to America that she was the most talked-of beauty in London. "Practically all the staid gentlemen of London are about to jump out of windows for love of her," wrote one newspaper man. Her grandmother could say proudly, "My darling, beautiful granddaughter is the friend of the Duchess of Sutherland." Ethel was now eighteen.

Ethel Barrymore

With the death of her grandmother, Ethel Barrymore returned to America and took on another role—a permanent one, as it turned out—that of stabilizer in the ups and downs of her family. John Barrymore was only sixteen at the time, but already handsome, restless, and adept at getting into trouble. She got him enrolled in the Slade School of painting in London. A few years later it was her father who needed her help. He had suffered a mental breakdown, and she took him to a private hospital in Amityville, Long Island. Also she assumed all the expenses of the two years he remained there before his death. Not long after this she was paying her brother Lionel's expenses for two honeymoon years in Paris. No wonder Lionel later wrote of her, "Ethel, bless her, was always on hand when the chips were down."

She appeared with mild success in America during the next few years, and spent her summers on holiday in England. Then came her triumph. In February 1901, in New York, she portrayed Madame Trentoni in *Captain Jinks of the Horse Marines*—a play of society's goings-on in New York in the early 1870's—and the first-night audience stood up and cheered. A few nights after the opening her brother John and she were headed for the theater when he suddenly took her arm and pointed. There she saw her name flashed on the marquee. She had arrived.

In the years to come she would act the parts of an invalid wife, a marked-down Duchess, an old scrubwoman, a brisk business woman, a queen, an adventuress, a peasant girl, a nun, a school teacher. But the public, at least in the first twenty-five years of her career, would clamor for her most strenuously in society roles. She came dangerously near being "typed" in these parts. It was only her genius and good sense that saved her.

That summer she didn't go to England—*Captain Jinks* ran too long. After its New York season, the play toured all over the country. At one point, when one of the cast fell ill, she got her brother John in as a replacement. It meant a start for him. Then, when her manager, Charles Frohman, in his elation at her success, said he would give her a bonus, she told him she wanted it in the form of a part for Lionel. He found it for him: as the organ-grinder in *The Mummy and the Humming Bird*. Lionel made a hit—and so began his stage career.

Through several years filled with other successes—*The Country Mouse, Cousin Kate, Sunday, Lady Frederick*—with summers in England, where she met authors Hilaire Belloc, Gilbert Chesterton, Henry James, and Winston Churchill, Ethel Barrymore became the fashion. Girls all over America were imitating her dress, her hats, her hairdo (her hair was straight and she wore it straight), and her voice, low and melodious. Artist John Singer Sargent did a drawing of her. Painter Kenyon Cox, when he painted the face of "Justice," now in the Newark (New Jersey) Courthouse, used her as a model.

In 1909 she married Russell Colt, wealthy young friend of her brother John and a descendant of the famous inventor Samuel Colt. The wedding took place in Boston, where she was playing *Lady Frederick* and their honeymoon was the rest of the play's tour. During the next five years her three children, Samuel, Ethel, and Jackie, were born. No more than two hours after the birth of Jackie she called up her agent, Mr. Frohman, with the news: "I have a nice little boy." "It is impossible you are talking," he cried. Oh, she felt fine, she said, and would be in for a rehearsal "very soon." She was as good as her word—she appeared at the theater ten days after the birth.

Now she successively played in *Alice Sit-by-the-Fire, Mid-Channel, The Twelve Pound Look,* and *The Witness for the Defense. The Twelve Pound Look*, a one-act play, was to become her personal speciality. Whenever she had a free stretch of time for the next twenty-five years, she played it in vaudeville, and every time it proved a success.

Other successes—*The Scrap of Paper, Tante, Our Mrs. McChesney*—followed, and in 1916 she opened the day before Christmas in New York in the tragedy *The Lady of the Camellias.* ("I don't think I ever played in anything that I loved so much," she once said of this play.) This was followed by a light comedy, *The Off Chance.* Then came *Déclassée,* with the public relishing her in the role of a downgraded socialite. "Beg, borrow or steal, but get to the Empire Theatre!" wrote critic Heywood Broun. Firemen had to be called to help the police handle the crowds. On and on it ran, through that season and into the next, and then into the next. President Wilson, passing backstage, called to her, "It was beautiful, my dear. It was beautiful."

In 1920 her brother John showed her *Clair de Lune,* a play written by his wife, Michael Strange, and asked her to play in it. Perhaps because of the wordiness of the script, it was not a success. John wanted to give the apathetic audience a piece of his mind, but Ethel dissuaded him. Next she had a long run in the title role of *Mrs. Tanqueray.*

One day John appeared at her home in Mamaroneck, New York, on the verge of a nervous collapse. "Guess you'd better take me in." She did, and it was during that period that she put into his hands a small, inexpensive edition of *Hamlet.* "Jake, read the two soliloquies. You may enjoy them." He did. It took his mind off his troubles. It did more. It gave him the idea he would like to play this Shakespearean role. He was to become one of the world's most famous Hamlets.

It was 1922 and Ethel Barrymore was forty-three. She had been trouping for almost twenty-eight years. One thumbs through the mounds of yellowed newspaper clippings dating

Ethel Barrymore

from these years and realizes how exposed her life was. It was not only the publicity ensuing on her divorce—only a "legal" divorce, she said, and indeed she never married again—but also the headlining of her least activities, whether she sued a dentist for overcharging, bobbed her hair, or broke her ankle. Ironically, the pertinent things of her life—her endless rehearsals, seeing that her children were properly educated, her hobbies of playing the piano and reading—passed unnoticed.

The plays continued. She became progressively more sensitive in her interpretations. The first part of her role as Portia in *The Merchant of Venice*, she said, was like "algebra or a complicated fugue." In Shakespeare's *Hamlet* she played, opposite Walter Hampden, the role of Ophelia, the distraught young girl in love with the Mad Prince. But she conceived Ophelia not as a weak-minded young thing, but as a thoughtful person caught in a psychological impasse.

When playing *The Constant Wife* by Somerset Maugham, she decided that "Thinking, thinking—that is what acting is all about. It is the only thing in acting. The thought running through the person's mind is what the actor has to capture. You pounce on that thought; you reach out and grasp it and never let it go."

In 1928 the Shuberts—she had come under their management after Charles Frohman lost his life on the *Lusitania*—built a theater in her honor, and here she played the part of a nun in *The Kingdom of God*. Here, too, she began to direct her own plays. *Scarlet Sister Mary*, in which she starred and in which her daughter played the role of Seraphine (1930), was a famous mother-and-daughter combination of the era.

At first she stood aloof from Hollywood. Lionel said of her that she "scorned the cinema as a Metropolitan diva might scorn hog calling." But in 1933 she accepted the part of the Queen in *Rasputin and the Empress*, a film in which her two brothers also starred. Though it was not a historically authentic production, it was a gorgeous spectacle and a great box office success.

Now came a slowing down of her activities—some revivals, some radio work, these interspersed every so often with announcements of her "retirement." Then in 1938 Lionel told her about seeing the play *Whiteoaks* in London and thinking of her in connection with it. About the same time an English promoter asked her if she would be interested in playing the part of the 101-year-old woman in it. She said she'd be delighted—that that was exactly the way she felt. It went well. In her next play, *The Farm of Three Echoes*, she acted the part of a mere ninety-seven-year-old, and that went well, too. But in 1940 came her real comeback. She took the part of the plucky Welsh schoolteacher in *The Corn Is Green*, and proved that her age, far from dimming her abilities and audience appeal, could even brighten them. The play opened in New York November 26. She got eighteen curtain calls the first night. It played in the city until January 17, 1942—her longest engagement on Broadway—and then went on the road for a year, playing in about 145 cities, then going back and playing in many of them again. "Let's stop quibbling and just call it a masterpiece," wrote Brooks Atkinson. It was also a lifesaver, and she was the first to admit it. "The play and I were instant and terrific successes and, believe me, it was high time for that success. It came at a crucial moment of my life and made all the difference."

During this period she acted in the film *None but the Lonely Heart*, RKO paying all the actors' salaries in *The Corn Is Green* and making other reimbursements during the time she would have to break her stage tour. She won an Oscar for her work in this film.

After *The Corn Is Green* had finished its run, Ethel Barrymore moved to California, to live in a house surrounded by trees and flowers. She appeared occasionally on television and over radio. For several years at Easter she read the Passion Story, from St. Matthew, on the air.

In 1946 the American Academy of Arts and Letters tendered her the "beauty of speech on the American stage" award. But it was in 1949, on her seventieth birthday, that her friends gave a celebration in honor of "The Dowager Queen of the American Theater," a half-hour coast-to-coast radio program with President Truman, Bernard Baruch, Katharine Cornell, Eleanor Roosevelt, the Lunts, Herbert Hoover, Katharine Hepburn, and Somerset Maugham—altogether one hundred of her friends and admirers—taking part. "She had more friends than anyone I know," said Miss Hepburn, "but she's not a dear, gentle soul. . . . She has a trenchant wit . . ." Lynn Fontanne related, "When I came to America, you were among the first persons I met. I was an unknown actress and there was no reason that you should have said more than how do you do, but you did. You were kind and friendly and I've never forgotten . . ." Tallulah Bankhead called her "the most exciting actress, the most vivid personality I have ever seen on the stage."

In 1950 she received a scroll for her part in the third National Theater and Academy's *Album*, and in 1952 an honorary doctorate at New York University. Her last acting film role was in *Johnny Trouble*, a 1957 Warner release.

Even toward the end she read a great deal, played the piano, listened to good music. But it is said, on the very night she died, she had been listening to a baseball broadcast, a Dodgers-Braves doubleheader, and enjoying it hugely.

Ethel Barrymore

BIBLIOGRAPHY

Barrymore, Ethel, *Memories; an Autobiography*. New York: Harper & Brothers, 1955.
Barrymore, Lionel, *We Barrymores*, as told to Cameron Shipp. New York: Appleton-Century-Crofts, 1951.
Fowler, Gene, *Good Night, Sweet Prince* (the life and times of John Barrymore). New York: The Viking Press, Inc., 1944.

CLARA BARTON

CLARA BARTON (CLARISSA HARLOWE BARTON): Born in North Oxford, Massachusetts, on Christmas Day, 1821. Died in Glen Echo, Maryland, April 12, 1912. Father: Captain Stephen Barton; mother: Sarah Stone Barton; brothers: Stephen and David; sisters: Sally and Dorothy.

*

Clara Barton, whom posterity remembers chiefly as the founder of the American National Red Cross, was even more famous in her day as the first woman to stand "between bullets and beds," caring for wounded soldiers on the actual battlegrounds. "My business," she would say, "is staunching blood and feeding fainting men; my post the open field." To thousands in the Civil War, and later in the Spanish-American War, she was the embodiment of compassion. At seventy-four years of age, when she was administering Red Cross relief on a battlefield in Cuba, a soldier, among the wounded lying in the tangled grass, spotted her and shouted, "My God, boys, it's Clara Barton. Now we'll get something to eat."

*

THE youngest of five brothers and sisters, Clara never played with dolls. She was far too busy learning from her brothers how to drive nails straight, tie knots securely and ride a pony bareback, and from her mother and sisters how to sew, cook, make soap, and tend her small garden. "They were a family of teachers," she wrote later.

Clara Barton

She had her full quota of regular schooling, too—at four was carried on the shoulder of one of her brothers to the village school, and at eight was driven by her father in the carriage, her little trunk strapped behind, to a boarding school in nearby Oxford, Massachusetts. She called her slate her "favorite toy."

Instruction in practical nursing was added to her schooling when, at eleven, she was given full care of her brother David, during a siege of illness after a wall had collapsed on him at a barn razing. She still had time, however, for an occasional horseback ride on the Morgan her father had given her on her tenth birthday. And evenings, when the whole family gathered around the fireplace, they would listen to the war stories her father would tell, of when he had fought the Indians with "Mad Anthony Wayne." Always the value of loyalty was impressed on her. "I learned early that next to Heaven, our highest duty was to love and serve our country and honor and support its laws."

School was in session only part of the year, and as she neared her mid-teens, she felt she must have something to satisfy her need for service. (Her brother, recovered, no longer needed her nursing.) The only vocation for a woman in those days, aside from marriage, was teaching. So into teaching Clara went. For fourteen years (minus a year or two when she was herself a student in the Liberal Institute of Clinton, New York) she taught the three R's in various localities. At one time her brothers let her have an unused "picking room" at the mill they ran, and though it had only the doorway to let in light, it served very well as a classroom. Parents gladly left their children with her while they worked in the mill. In time she had some seventy pupils. Later her brothers built her a regular schoolhouse, with windows.

Her reputation as a teacher increased. She was offered a post in Bordentown, New Jersey, in a private school. In those days nearly all schools were private, with parents paying, if ever so little, for their children's instruction. No one seemed concerned about the many children who received no education at all. But Clara Barton kept noticing the ragged boys huddled on street corners and idling on rail fences, and was convinced they should have a chance at education, too. She talked the school board into her way of thinking and was made teacher of a "free" school. It became so popular that before long she had to have two assistants and enlarged quarters. A $4,000 building to seat six hundred students—a most ambitious project for the time—was planned. But with this expansion Clara was to be replaced by a male superintendent, and she herself was to become his assistant. Her pride would not let her accept this arbitrary demotion and she resigned.

During this period she had a siege of throat trouble and decided a climate farther south might cure her hoarseness. She fixed on Washington, D.C., because friends of the family lived there. Through their help she got work as a copyist in the Office of Patents. Washington was to be her center of operations for the rest of her active life.

Now her days took on a definite pattern: up at four or five; scrub the floors of her rooms; study some French; do some washing and ironing; be at the Patent Office by nine o'clock; work there until three; take documents home to work on far into the night.

But it was just as unusual for women to work in offices in those days as to be superintendents of schools, and the forces of opposition began to move in. When she was promoted to the position of confidential clerk to Judge Charles Mason, Robert McClelland, the then Secretary of the Interior, made objections. "There is such obvious impropriety in the mixing of the sexes within the walls of a public office," he wrote Mason, "that I am determined to arrest the practice." But her employer stuck by her, not only keeping her on but increasing her salary. However, when he himself had to resign because of a new administration, Clara went home to Oxford. Luckily, with still another administration, Abraham Lincoln's, she returned to her job. Soon she became a familiar sight in the city with her easy, firm-footed walk, her deep sympathetic voice, her courteous attentiveness to what was being said. When she felt something should be done and that she could do it, she would make herself heard at the very top. She had already taken as her motto: "What is nobody's business is my business."

The Civil War period had need of just such a person. When she saw the hordes of Union soldiers streaming into Washington, ragged, bloody, bedraggled, she went to her rooms and tore up old sheets to make bandages and handkerchiefs for them. She wrote to her friends at home, telling them that fruits, jellies, tobacco, nursing equipment, were in order. She had an insertion put in the popular Worcester newspaper, *Daily Spy*, explaining the needs. Sewing circles, church societies, relief committees, sent her supplies. She rented a warehouse and collected the donations there. She got her fellow lodgers to help her. After a day's work at the Patent Office, she would tramp up the hills to the encampment with supplies.

She began to plead for passes to get her through to the front lines. She said that among the fighters were many of her former pupils, that she would pay her own expenses, that she had already amassed large supplies for the use of the wounded. In those days it was unheard of for women to be allowed anywhere near the battlefield, even as nurses. But at last her persuasiveness won. A pass was issued to her, later to be extended to unlimited free transportation by train and steamboat.

The first battle site she reached was Cedar Mountain, near Culpeper, Virginia. When she appeared in front of a hospital near there, at midnight, with a four-mule team pulling a wagon laden with supplies, the attendants thought they were seeing a mirage. It was the beginning for her of a lifetime of working under terrible handicaps. She learned to housekeep in fields and woods, in tents and wagons; to make fires on open ground in the rain; to turn out seven hundred loaves of bread at a single breakfast; to serve soup from wash boilers; to ladle out coffee by the gallons. She learned to work against time; to stem bleeding by holding a tight thumb to the vein; to assist in operations in tents, barns, under the night skies; to hold a candle against the black darkness while a surgeon sawed off a leg, and to apply chloroform at the crucial moment. Once when a soldier was hit in the leg, she sprang to his side, tore off a strip of her petticoat, used it for a tourniquet, and held the bleeding portions in place until medical help came. Another time, just as she raised a soldier so that his lips could reach a cup, a bullet whizzed between her body and her arm, passing through the soldier's chest and killing him instantly. She never mended the rent made in her sleeve. Often she would see both armies "lying face to face along opposing ridges," and would wait till the last moment, then spring on horseback just before the enemy troops came rushing down the hill.

She wrote letters home for the men, prayed with them, closed their eyes in death. The soldiers, seeing her coming in her hoopless dark skirt and her plaid jacket, her brown hair held smooth under a kerchief, would set up a cheer. Once a battalion of tramping soldiers threw down their coats, Sir Walter Raleigh style, so that she could pass over a creek dry-shod.

She aided the wounded of both armies—a practice that often angered the Union officers. But she finally established the right of the wounded or suffering, irrespective of flag or uniform, to have all the aid humanity can give.

Clara Barton

The Civil War ended in the Spring of 1865, but she worked four years longer, as she said, "in the debris" of "the awful aftermath." Of the 315,555 graves of Northern dead reported by the Quartermaster of the Federal Army, only 172,400 were identified. All the bereaved families knew was that their sons did not come home. Finally her pleas for a chance to help reached Abraham Lincoln, and only a month before his assassination he issued a manifesto which was printed in periodicals throughout the nation: "Miss Clara Barton has kindly offered to search for the missing prisoners of war. Please address her at Annapolis, giving her the name, regiment, and company of any missing prisoner." This gave her the impetus to organize a nationwide search for missing soldiers. By May, 1865, she had compiled a list of 3,000 names of missing men arranged according to states. Regional newspapers published them; 20,000 copies were circulated and posted in conspicuous places. Sackfuls of letters came to her headquarters—letters of appeal, of information. She built her office force up to twelve. They searched burial records, prison lists, hospital charts. Through her work at the Andersonville (Georgia) National Cemetery, 13,000 men "lay honorably where relatives knew them to lie." During her whole lifetime her name was associated with the Bureau of Missing Men. "Ask Miss Barton," became a stock phrase.

During 1866, 1867, and 1868 she lectured in the Midwest, relating her experiences on the battlefield. Veterans, many of whom had survived through her ministrations, dotted the audience, as did women in mourning.

She faced the woman's rights question squarely. When a newspaper announcing her lectures claimed peevishly that listeners would not have "thrust upon them a lecture on women's rights after the style of Susan B. Anthony and her clique," Clara Barton had her own answer. After giving one of her rousing battlefield talks, she put the question to her audience, "Who opened the way [for me], who but the detested 'clique' who through years of opposition, obloquy, toil, and pain openly claimed that women had rights . . . [and] should have the privilege to exercise them . . . . Soldiers, for every woman's hand that ever cooled your fevered brows . . . you should bless God for Susan B. Anthony."

Her lecture work tired her even more than the battlefield. At one lecture she all but fainted and was advised by her physician to go to Europe for a rest. She sailed in August 1869, but it was not be a "rest." In Europe she was introduced to a new project, called the Red Cross.

The International Red Cross had been created by the Geneva Conference in 1864. The organization was to provide for the neutrality of those dispensing medical services, and for humane treatment of the wounded. Its emblem was the Swiss flag but with the colors reversed (a Red Cross on a white background) in honor of the Swiss writer who had first proposed the idea, Jean Henri Dunant. At the time Clara Barton heard of the Red Cross, twenty-two nations and the Papal States had signed themselves as members. (There are today over three times this number.) The United States Government had been asked to join but had refused. Most Americans were not even aware their country had been approached.

Now Miss Barton joined with other Red Cross workers abroad, helping sufferers in the Franco-Prussian War. She remained eight months in Strasbourg, instituted sewing work for women which not only saved the workers from penury but clothed thirty thousand persons, then transferred to Paris, where for two months she distributed money and clothing, all under the insignia of the International Red Cross.

On her return to America Miss Barton interested many individuals in the Red Cross. She visualized a "national headquarters" in America, flying the Red Cross flag, with state organizations and smaller relief societies branching out from it.

She gathered well-wishers and eager workers around her, including the young enthusiast Julian B. Hubbell, who began studying medicine on her advice and later became her chief field worker. Then she was ready to start buttonholing reporters, diplomats, generals. She made forays into key offices, left leaflets, importuned the Secretaries of the Navy and the Treasury, the United States Postmaster General, and finally the President of the United States. At first . . . failure all around. President Hayes thought joining the International Red Cross would constitute "an entangling alliance," under the Monroe Doctrine of foreign policy.

But when James Garfield became President, he greeted her with "We fought together in the Civil War, didn't we?" and introduced her to his Secretary of State, James G. Blaine. "The Monroe Doctrine was not meant to ward off humanity," Blaine decided—and so hurdled the "entangling alliance" difficulty.

But with Garfield's assassination she was again without a champion. His successor, President Chester Arthur, was less than enthusiastic. But Clara Barton was on the warpath now. She had five thousand copies of a pamphlet on the Red Cross printed and distributed. After a talk she gave before notables in Washington, Dr. Theodore D. Woolsey, ex-president of Yale University, publicly proclaimed he "could see not the smallest shadow of reason" for rejecting the proposal. It was a benign cause. It did not create embarrassing alliances.

She sat up nights constructing a Red Cross Constitution. It was all there—"neutrality of sanitary supplies, ambulances, surgeons, nurses, attendants . . . safe-conduct . . . a uniform badge." It emphasized emergency treatment of the wounded and relief in time of peace to victims of "national calamities such as floods, earthquakes, fires, hurricanes, droughts, epidemics." (This part was distinctly Clara's contribution.)

The Constitution was approved by a group meeting in her rooms in Washington on May 21, 1881. On March 1, 1882, President Arthur signed the document chartering the American Red Cross, and on March 6 it was ratified by the Senate. She was appointed the organization's president. That day Clara Barton wrote in purple ink in her diary—otherwise written in pencil—"I had waited so long and got so weak and broken I could not even feel glad."

The Red Cross had already been functioning, under Clara's auspices, on a local basis. The first local Red Cross unit was organized in Dansville, New York, in August 1881, and the cities of Rochester and Syracuse soon followed suit. So these Red Cross units were ready to give help when the Mississippi flood, early in 1882, inundated millions of acres of cotton and sugar plantations. In 1884, when the Ohio River overflowed its banks, Clara herself sailed down the swollen river in a chartered steamer, giving food to flood victims who leaned out of the second-story windows of houses along the way. In each town she distributed clothing, fuel, seeds, farm implements. Newspapers called her ship "the floating ark of 1884." Stimulated by her efforts, more local Red Cross societies sprang up.

Later that year she went as a delegate to the International Red Cross Conference in Geneva, and under her influence the "American Amendment"—to provide Red Cross relief in nonwar calamities—was added to the International Constitution.

In the 1880's the United States was hit by the Texas drought, a tornado in Illinois, a yellow fever epidemic in Florida, and the Johnstown (Pennsylvania) flood, to all of which Clara brought on-the-spot study and relief. In Johnstown she set up headquarters for five months in an abandoned railroad car, while she superintended the construction of several temporary buildings including a hotel.

By now Clara Barton and the Red Cross were becoming famous everywhere. (In 1892 the name "American National Red Cross" was officially adopted.) Artists sought to paint her picture, and magazines to print articles about her. Red Cross societies were spreading across the nation.

Age did not curtail her activities. When she was in her seventies, a hurricane devastated the Sea Islands off the coast of Georgia. She drove over the rice fields in a lumbering cart, walked miles to talk to the phosphate workers, visited the local stores and the Negro cabins, rationed food, formed sewing circles, distributed twenty thousand garments, handed out tools, bought nine hundred bushels of potatoes for planting—"We must not leave a race of beggars but teach them the manliness of self-support and methods of self-dependence"—and left the place in a better condition economically than before the catastrophe.

By the end of 1897 she had settled on a farm at Glen Echo, Maryland, if one can use the word "settled," for a person on the go as much as she was. In 1898 she was off again to the Spanish-American War, nurturing the soldiers on the battlefield. The Galveston hurricane and tidal wave (1900) saw her converting the Sante Fe building into a storehouse and workshop, calling for lumber, food, clothing, supplying a million and a half strawberry plants to get the farmers set up again—all on her own. But returning to Washington, she sensed dissatisfaction from the Red Cross administration. (The relief, they complained, should be more regularized.) Still, in 1902 at the Seventh International Red Cross Conference she was acclaimed, and the same year President Theodore Roosevelt had her by his side on the reviewing stand at the Spanish-American War Veterans Convention in Detroit. But at the age of eighty-three her work had become somewhat erratic, while the Red Cross administration had become highly organized.

Clara Barton

On May 4, 1904, she formally resigned her presidency. But as the Chicago newspaper *Inter-Ocean* put it, "Clara Barton cannot resign her place in the world as the one real, true representative of the Red Cross in this country." A new charter, January 5, 1905, transformed the American Red Cross from an individual-directed to a government-directed and -controlled enterprise.

Now she took as her cause the National First-Aid Association. But though she believed that it also, like the Red Cross, would become "time-honored," she never became deeply involved in its workings.

She loved her home in Glen Echo—"the hills, the trees and the birds, and the moon which always seemed to be shining there"—and spent a quiet few years, with trusted friends about her. When she died her remains were transported back to Oxford, Massachusetts. When the carriage driver in Oxford was told what his burden was, he threw up his hands. "Why my father was a Confederate soldier and at the battle of Antietam he was bleeding to death when Miss Barton found him and bound up his wounds in time to save his life."

BIBLIOGRAPHY

Barton, Clara Harlowe, *The Story of My Childhood*. New York: Baker & Taylor Company, 1907.
Barton, William Eleazer, *The Life of Clara Barton, Founder of the American Red Cross*, 2 vols. Boston: Houghton Mifflin Company, 1922.
Epler, Percy Harold, *The Life of Clara Barton*. New York: The Macmillan Company, 1915.

Clara Barton

Ross, Ishbel, *Angel of the Battlefield; the Life of Clara Barton.*
New York: Harper & Brothers, 1956.
Williams, Blanche Colton, *Clara Barton; Daughter of Destiny.*
Philadelphia: J. B. Lippincott Company, 1941.

MARY McLEOD BETHUNE

MARY (JANE) McLEOD BETHUNE: Born near Mayesville, South Carolina, July 10, 1875. Died in Daytona Beach, Florida, May 18, 1955. Father: Samuel McLeod; mother: Patsy McIntosh McLeod; sixteen brothers and sisters, she being third from the youngest; husband: Albertus Bethune; son: Albert.

*

Mary McLeod Bethune, the founder and for thirty-eight years the president of Bethune-Cookman College, was organizer and director of the Division of Negro Affairs of the National Youth Administration (NYA) and adviser to President Franklin D. Roosevelt on Negro affairs. She was founder of the National Council of Negro Women, for which she worked for over two decades.

*

EIGHT-year-old Mary Jane McLeod walked slowly down the road beside her mother to their three-room cabin, after they had delivered the wash at the big house. She kept thinking about the nice little white girl back there. After the girl had let her play with her doll, Mary Jane had taken up a book. "Put that down—*you* can't read!" the little girl had said, snatching the book from her hands. Late in life Mrs. Bethune was to tell reporters, "That did something to me. I thought, maybe the difference between white folks and colored is just this matter of reading and writing. I made up my mind I would know my letters."

So, out picking cotton with her brothers and sisters, she would snap off the blobs of white and toss them into the great sacks she dragged behind her, working to the rhythm of the phrase "I'm goin' to read, I'm goin' to read." When the family knelt in prayer mornings and evenings, and her grandmother thanked God for freedom, her mother thanked Him for letting them all be together, and her father prayed for a good cotton crop, Mary Jane pleaded, "Let me learn how to read, God. Let me learn how to read."

She took it as a direct answer to her prayers when a young Negro woman, Emma Wilson, showed up one day at their cabin. She said she'd come to South Carolina from the Presbyterian mission up north. She asked could any of the McLeod children attend the school she was starting in Mayesville. The father looked his children over and picked out nine-year-old Mary. But could they spare her at cotton-picking time, Mary Jane anxiously wanted to know. Her father said they could and would. So a few days later Mary Jane, in a freshly ironed gingham dress, took her pail of lunch and the new slate her father had given her and started walking the five miles to the school, a tiny room in a shack down by the railroad. Soon she could read the great family Bible at prayers, could go with her father to market and tell the weight on the scales as the bale was lifted from the beam, could help neighbors when they brought their accounting problems to her. She taught her brothers and sisters to read and write. "I made my learning, what little it was, useful every way I could," she explained later.

After six years, when Mary Jane had absorbed everything her teacher could teach her, came another sign of God's goodness. A Quaker woman, Mary Chrissman, living in Denver, Colorado, heard of the movement to educate the newly emancipated Negroes. She wrote to Scotia Seminary in Concord, North Carolina (one of the few schools for higher education for Negro girls), that she would like to donate one-tenth of her earnings as a dressmaker to pay for the education of a Negro girl. When the letter arrived, Miss Wilson, herself a graduate of Scotia, happened to be at the school, and suggested her student Mary Jane for the scholarship.

Thus, one fine October day, a very excited young girl boarded a train for the first time in her life. When she arrived in Concord she was met and taken to a three-story brick building with great shining windows. Inside she was shown to the second story—it was the first time she had ever climbed a staircase—and a small neat room that was to be her own. Thus began seven years of study, during which she not only took courses comparable to high school and junior college but also developed a sense of poise and a breadth of vision that were to aid her during her whole career.

Besides excelling in her class work, Mary McLeod was president of the literary society, head of the debating team, and a member of the school chorus. She also worked, as did all the pupils, at the school's household tasks—baking in the kitchen, scrubbing the floors, stoking the fires, waiting on table. Through the director's wife she got summer work (she couldn't afford the fare home), churning butter at the dairy farm, acting as house girl, as a children's nurse, and as a laundress. She sent money home to her parents.

She graduated on June 13, 1894. On July 5, five days before her nineteenth birthday, she entered the Mission Training School of the Moody Bible Institute in Chicago, Illinois, again on a Mary Chrissman scholarship. She hoped to become a missionary to Africa. At the Institute she was a missionary worker, traveling in their "Gospel Car," a train that went through neglected areas of the Middle West, helping to establish schools and church centers.

When she completed the one-year course, however, and applied to the Mission Board, she was told there was no place for her in the African mission. She was deeply disappointed, but pulled herself together. After a short time at home, where she assisted her old teacher, Miss Wilson, in the Mayesville school, she was sent by the Presbyterian Board to Haines Normal Institute, a school set in the midst of the slums of Augusta, Georgia. Here the school's guiding spirit, Lucy Laney, helped Mary McLeod to see that "Africans in America need Christ and the school just as much as Negroes in Africa."

In Augusta, in addition to her work as an eighth-grade teacher, she collected homeless urchins from the back streets and alleyways, washed them, gave them clothes from the missionary barrels, and started a Sunday school to teach them the Bible stories, and guide them in religion. In time the Sunday school numbered a thousand youngsters.

Her zeal brought her other teaching assignments. By 1903 she had taught in schools in Sumter, South Carolina; Savannah, Georgia; and Palatka, Florida.

While teaching in Savannah, she met and married Albertus Bethune. Until his death in 1919 her husband helped her in various ways in her work. Their son, Albert, was born in 1899.

She had always wanted to start a school of her own. But where? When she was teaching in Palatka, she went on periodic exploring trips to find a possible place. The city of Daytona Beach, some fifty miles to the southeast, was becoming a popular vacation resort, with railroad tracks going down, hotels going up, and many Negroes, both local and from outside, finding work with the railroad gangs, as part of construction crews and as kitchen help. During the day their children, with no schools provided for them, were left mostly to their own devices. Dump heaps and street corners were their only playgrounds. Here seemed a good place for her to begin. She found a four-room cottage for rent, and moved in. She rounded up five little girls whose parents were willing to pay fifty cents a week tuition. She combed hotel refuse piles for broken furniture, old crockery, bits of cloth. She dragged in packing boxes for desks and turned baskets upside down for chairs. She begged at back doors for a broom, a lamp, a few pennies. Her own people would call after her, "There goes the beggar!"

But she got her school. The Daytona Educational and Industrial Training School for Negro Girls opened on October 3, 1904, with a thanksgiving service in which she sang, in her full rich voice, the hymn "Leaning on the Everlasting Arms," and recited the Twenty-third Psalm.

Using for pencils charred splinters from burnt logs, and for ink mashed elderberries, she taught the children, mothered them, washed them, begged materials to make dresses and underwear for them. To earn money she baked sweet potato pies on an old stove she had rigged up, and sold them to workmen along the railroad tracks. Soon she had ten pupils, then fifteen, then twenty-five. Some of them she took in tuition-free. Parents sometimes left their children with her overnight, and she stuffed corncob sacks with dried Spanish moss for mattresses. Next she was offering evening classes for adults who had never before had a chance to learn even reading and writing. Eagerly they came, these track workers, janitors, street cleaners.

Her pupils soon outgrew the school's small quarters. She decided she must have a building of her own. On the edge of the town was a piece of land used as a dump. She bought it for two hundred dollars—five dollars down and the balance within two years—and with her pupils' help, got rid of the debris. Then she rounded up masons, carpenters, mechanics, and plasterers, many of them the fathers of her pupils or the adult class pupils themselves, who were happy to put in a few hours' work evenings, against their and their children's tuition.

As the building began to creep up, she looked through the

society columns of the Florida newspapers for possible sponsors. She picked out wealthy tourists from the North, one of them James N. Gamble of Procter and Gamble, another Thomas White of the White Sewing Machine Company. Then she simply bicycled to their offices and won them over with her persuasiveness. Gamble gave her $150 as a start. White, not unreasonably, wanted to know, "Where is the school of which you wish me to be trustee?" "In my dreams," Mrs. Bethune staunchly replied. She took him to the site and showed him the foundation work and the walls with gaping window holes. They had stopped work temporarily for lack of materials. White wrote out a substantial check and left, but was back soon with the carpenter and the mason. After that he paid the workers, saw that bathrooms were installed, bought sheets and pillow slips, had one of his sewing machines sent up. "I've never invested a dollar that had greater returns," he said later.

The four-story building, "prayed up, sung up, and talked up," was opened in 1907, as soon as the roof was completed, as a school for girls. It was fittingly called Faith Hall. Over the entrance was carved, "Enter to Learn," and on the inside over the same door, "Depart to Serve."

But Mary Bethune's work had just begun. Here were 250 girls who had to be clothed and fed. "I rang doorbells and tackled cold prospects without a lead," she said. "I wrote articles for whoever would print them, distributed leaflets, rode interminable miles of dusty roads on my old bicycle, invaded churches, clubs, lodges, chambers of commerce. If a prospect refused to make a contribution, I would say, 'Thank you for your time.' No matter how deep my hurt, I always smiled. I refused to be discouraged, for neither God nor man can use a discouraged person." Her keen, kindly eyes, her wide smile, her strong jaw, her mighty stride, her very being, bespoke accomplishment. Her power to inspire generosity was prodigious.

She spoke about her school in hotels, halls, and on pleasure boats, taking along a quartet of her girls in their neat blue skirts and white middy blouses to sing spirituals. On the invitation of C. C. Mellour, owner of the largest music store in Pittsburgh, she spoke in various homes and halls in that city. Philanthropists in New York City and farther north gave her opportunities to make personal appeals in their homes. In 1909 she attended the Conference of the National Association of Colored Women, at Hampton Institute, Virginia, and asked, "May I have five minutes to talk about my school?" She made those five minutes tell.

Every year some new school building or facility appeared: Mr. Mellour bought the field opposite her school and turned it over to her so that the girls could raise vegetables. He donated a piano and the students made music Sunday afternoons —with adults, both white and black, attending. A frame cottage was rebuilt into a $5,000 hospital with an operating table, instruments, two beds, sheets, blankets. That was in 1911. By 1914 she had a fully equipped twenty-bed hospital for her people. Through bazaars, selling the vegetables, eggs, and butter from their own farm, and the baskets, brooms, woven rugs, beadwork, made by the girls, the school soon netted about $5,000 annually.

In 1916 there was a new administration building, White Hall; in 1922, a dormitory, Curtis Hall. In 1925 the school became coeducational, having merged with a men's college, Cookman Institute. It was thenceforth known as the Bethune-Cookman College. In 1934 a Science Hall and a New Faith Hall were erected. In 1940, at the thirty-fifth anniversary of the school's founding, Mrs. Eleanor Roosevelt came as the principal speaker. She later wrote in "My Day," a syndicated newspaper column, "Until I went over the plant I never realized what a really dramatic achievement this junior college is. It administers to the needs of 100,000 Negroes from Daytona, south, and it takes 250 students. The object is to train leaders who will return to their communities and serve their people in whatever line of activity they have chosen as a life work. Thirty-five years ago Mrs. Bethune began with five little girls. The first land was bought with the first five dollars earned. This land up to that time had been part of the city dump, a portion of the city known as 'Hell's Hole.' "

By 1947 Bethune-Cookman was a full four-year coeducational college, highly rated throughout the country. By 1954, with an enrollment of 794 students and a faculty of 42, it was called the most potent factor in the growth of interracial goodwill in America.

The college was, however, by no means the sole focus of Mrs. Bethune's enterprise. During World War I she went with three white women on a Red Cross recruiting tour, through Maryland, Virginia, and Pennsylvania. As head of the Florida chapter of the Red Cross she set in motion relief work, when in 1928 a hurricane swept over central Florida. Under the Hoover Administration she took part in the National Commission for Child Welfare.

It was during President Roosevelt's administration that she really branched out. He had inaugurated the National Youth Administration (NYA), "to prevent human erosion among America's young citizens who are on the fringe of economic and social security," and in 1935 appointed her as a special consultant, on the advice of the chairman of the executive committee. This chairman had heard Mrs. Bethune make an impassioned plea for her people earlier that year when she was awarded the Joel E. Spingarn gold medal, given annually by the National Association for the Advancement of Colored People "for the highest and noblest achievement of an American Negro." Later the President made Mrs. Bethune administrator of a new department, the Office of Minority Affairs, afterwards called the Division of Negro Affairs.

During these years she traveled all over the United States in behalf of the National Youth Administration, visiting NYA centers, inspecting new projects, giving talks, arbitrating difficulties. In one year alone she traveled forty thousand miles, visiting sixty-nine centers in twenty-one states. She saw that more and more appointments of Negroes were made in various agencies until practically every government office had a Negro consultant. To her goes much of the credit that under NYA more than 150,000 Negro boys and girls were given a chance to go to high school, more than 60,000 a chance to attend college. She was the guiding hand in setting up a special fund whereby students who were denied graduate facilities in their own states could be granted scholarships at such Negro universities as Howard, Atlanta, and Fisk, as well as at northern colleges. During the eight years she was with NYA, Mrs. Bethune received honorary degrees from Lincoln University, Bennett College, Tuskegee Institute, Howard University, Atlanta University, and Wiley College.

In 1935 she formed the National Council of Negro Women, whose membership, comprising almost all the Negro women's clubs of the country, was to represent many groups: civic, church, labor, educational, professional. Its goal was to improve opportunities on every front: housing, working conditions, standards of living, education. As its president for fourteen years, she assumed the leadership of Negro women in America. During World War II she became special assistant to Oveta Culp Hobby, commanding officer of the Women's Army Auxiliary Corps (WAAC). She selected Negro girls for the first Women's Officers Training School. In 1942 the Women's Army for National Defense (WANDS) made her a general, and on official occasions she wore a uniform with four stars on the shoulder. That year she also was recipient of the Thomas Jefferson Gold Medal Award, presented by the Southern Conference for Human Welfare for "outstanding service in the field of human welfare."

Mary McLeod Bethune

By the mid-forties she was the recognized leader of the women and youth of her race in America. Hundreds of her students at Bethune-Cookman, who had been graduated with full college degrees, were now spreading out through the South to be nurses, school teachers, managers of hotel staffs, dieticians, directors of private businesses.

She had once said, "My love, my heart, my very life's blood flows at Bethune-Cookman College." So when she was in her late seventies, she turned again to her school. She went to live in the house built on the campus for her by her friends, "The Retreat." There her life came to an end. She left a will and testament addressed to her people, which read in part: "Personally and racially, our enemies must be forgiven . . . our aim must be to create a world of fellowship and justice where no man's color or religion is held against him," and she added, "Our children must never lose their zeal for building a better world."

BIBLIOGRAPHY

EMBREE, EDWIN ROGERS, *13 Against the Odds*. New York: The Viking Press, Inc., 1944.
HOLT, RACKHAM, *Mary McLeod Bethune; a Biography*. New York: Doubleday & Company, Inc., 1964.
NATHAN, DOROTHY, *Women of Courage*. New York: Random House, Inc., 1964.
PEARE, CATHERINE OWENS, *Mary McLeod Bethune*. New York: Vanguard Press, Inc., 1951.

ST. FRANCES XAVIER CABRINI

ST. FRANCES XAVIER CABRINI (MOTHER CABRINI): Born in a village adjoining Lodi, in Lombardy in what is now northern Italy, July 15, 1850. Died in Chicago, Illinois, December 22, 1917. Father: Agostino Cabrini; mother: Stella Cabrini. She was the youngest of thirteen children.

*

Sixty-seven institutions—orphanages, hospitals, girls' schools, colleges, hostels—distributed over three continents, came into being through Mother Cabrini's solicitude during her lifetime. Nearly two thousand nuns and five thousand children came to look on her as their spiritual mother. These stand as testimony to the abundant faith and courage as well as to the sheer business acumen of this woman, the first American who, through papal proclamation, was declared a saint.

*

WHEN Frances (or Cecchina, as she was called) was a child, Italy had not yet become a unified nation, and at intervals Austrian soldiers occupied her native Lombardy. But in her peaceful home among the hills she heard little of the noise of battle. Instead she would listen enraptured to the sound of the bells of the village church, or she would wander happily in the meadows. Impressed by the prayers of her mother—the family would gather evenings around the log fire for religious worship—she would fill little boats with violets and set them floating in the stream, pretending they were missionaries sailing for foreign lands. She would dress up her dolls as nuns and send them on imaginary missions. When she was about seven, she had a mystical experience. She felt as though she were "wrapped in light and was in Heaven." After that she made a vow: She would devote her life to God's service.

At thirteen she was sent to a boarding school of the Daughters of the Sacred Heart, a short distance from Lodi, and, after five years of study there, received her teachers' diploma. She substituted for an ailing teacher in a neighboring village, and then, through the suggestion of the rector of the parish, went to help organize an orphanage for girls in the nearby town of Codogno. Two years later, on October 15, 1874, she and two young girls from the orphanage became novices, that is, went into training to be nuns. Soon after, five other orphans followed them into the novitiate. In 1877, when she was twenty-seven, she took the final vows.

In 1880 the orphanage was ordered dissolved because of mismanagement by an administrator, and the new nuns were without a home. "Why don't you form a missionary order of your own?" suggested the Bishop of Lodi. Accordingly, on November 10 Mother Cabrini moved with seven or so other nuns into an empty warehouse that had formerly been a Franciscan friary. The sisters gathered together the simplest of furniture, ate at a bench, and, lacking a lamp, went to bed in the dark. When the house was enlarged, they did some of the bricklaying themselves. This was the beginning of the religious order that came to be known as the Missionary Sisters of the Sacred Heart, and the beginning of Mother Cabrini's life of organizing groups for service, finding quarters for them, getting them into working order and enlarging their spheres of usefulness.

In 1887 Mother Cabrini had started affiliates of her missionary order in several adjacent small towns. The next branching out, she decided, should be to the city of Rome. So this provincial nun, who had engaged till then in only small undertakings, journeyed to Rome, and by her powers of persuasion not only was granted an audience with a representative of the pope but was instructed to found a kindergarten and a school for the poor in Rome itself. Aside from small church grants to start her off, the financing was to be her own concern.

She had not only to set up the schools but also to staff them. To get furniture she went every day to public auctions. Later, when orphans began to arrive, she and her nuns cut up some of their own clothes to make dresses for them. Once her schools were going smoothly, she decided to petition the pope again. This time she obtained a personal audience with His Holiness. She asked to be allowed to go to foreign lands as a missionary.

Her request came at just the right time. In the 1880's and 1890's poor Italian immigrants in America were exploited, not only by Americans of long standing, but by their own *padrones*—opportunists who, while they found menial jobs for the illiterate immigrants and wrote letters home for them, also exacted from them exorbitant fees. A lack of unity among the immigrants themselves—they spoke several different Italian dialects—complicated the situation. Clearly Italian-speaking priests and sisters were needed to take charge of homeless children, to give hospital care, to start schools. So when Mother Cabrini knelt before Pope Leo XIII, he had already decided that an order of Italian nuns should be sent to America. Mother Cabrini's persuasiveness did the rest. She was to go with a group of her Sisters of the Sacred Heart to give aid to Italians now settled in the United States.

Within four months after landing in New York, on the last day of March 1889, Mother Cabrini had collected four hundred destitute children and was begging enough money and materials to keep them sheltered and fed. Up and down Mulberry and adjacent streets in downtown Manhattan she and her nuns went, baskets on their arms, into little stores, street stalls, banks, basement saloons, gathering up not only small cash donations but canned tomatoes, strings of onions, preserves. A New York newspaper commented, "For some weeks past . . . Sisters of Charity have been seen visiting every portion of Little Italy, climbing up narrow steep stairs, going down into foul cellars . . . . Few of them speak English. At their head is Mother Frances Cabrini, a woman with great eyes and a winning smile. She knows no English but she is in earnest." They started a school in a church, one class in the choir loft, another under it, a third in an alcove off the sacristy, instructing two hundred children daily. Meanwhile Mother Cabrini was learning, too, getting a working knowledge of English.

She had been able to take children off the streets and give them a place to play and learn, but she felt they should be seeing trees and blue skies, should be playing in the fields rather than in dark streets. So in July 1890 she transferred the orphanage to a site up the Hudson River in the Catskills, called West Park. Its buildings, which were being vacated by a group of Jesuits, could house three hundred children. This became the American "Mother House" of the Sacred Heart novitiate.

Two years after she had come to the United States, the Church called on her for another difficult task. Mother Cabrini sailed with a group of sisters to Nicaragua in Central America and took charge of a hospital there. In a few months she was back, having left some nuns in charge. Next she brought into being the Columbus Hospital in New York City, by renting two adjoining houses, paying the rent for a month from fifty dollars that Archbishop Corrigan had given her, and buying beds through the generosity—fifty dollars each—of four other philanthropists. Doctors gave their services gra-

JANE ADDAMS

Courtesy Chicago Historical Society

LOUISA MAY ALCOTT

Wide World Photos

Metropolitan Opera Archives

MARIAN
ANDERSON

SUSAN B.
ANTHONY

Engraved by G. E. Perine & Co.
New York Public Library Picture Collection

Theatre Magazine, 1906
New York Public Library Picture Collection

**ETHEL
BARRYMORE**

CLARA BARTON

*Mathew Brady
Library of Congress*

MARY McLEOD
BETHUNE

ST. FRANCES
XAVIER CABRINI

Courtesy Mr. and Mrs. Richman Proskauer

A self-portrait by
MARY CASSATT

WILLA CATHER

AGNES DE MILLE

EMILY DICKINSON

DOROTHEA DIX

ISADORA
DUNCAN

Dance Collection
New York Public Library

tis; others donated surgical instruments, a writing desk, an ambulance. The Italian consul offered to pay a flat sum for the care of sick sailors from Italian boats. The sisters themselves were the nurses, and for the first few weeks, lacking enough beds, they slept on the floor.

Now during a two-year period she founded another Columbus Hospital in Brooklyn, an elementary school soon to have eight hundred pupils, and a boarding school for girls in upper Manhattan, the Sacred Heart Villa. This school was particularly dear to her heart and is today known as the Mother Cabrini High School. The saint's body lies buried in the chapel.

The Church next sent her to New Orleans, where many Italians had settled, most of them in miserable circumstances. Here she bought a whole tenement house, cleaned it, and turned it into a convent. At first all the cooking had to be done outdoors on a brick oven, with a bench for a table. Scrawny children stood around hopefully waiting for scraps of food. The sisters had to beg water from door to door because their pump water, from the Mississippi, was dangerous to drink. They baptized and cared for sick babies, provided schooling, comforted the dying. The St. Phillips Street Convent, as it was called, became a social center as well as a mission, a meeting ground for Italian immigrants.

Then Mother Cabrini went back to New York, where the first Columbus Hospital was enlarged. (It was officially incorporated by New York State in 1895.) Next she set out for South America, the following year opening a school in Buenos Aires, Argentina. The next few years she continued founding and staffing schools—renting two adjacent shops in upper Manhattan and transforming them into a school, starting dressmaking classes in lower Manhattan, taking an empty shop in Newark, New Jersey, and making it over into a school.

At the turn of the century Mother Cabrini was back in Europe, starting homes for nuns and orphans in Italy, Spain, and England. In 1903 she was again in America, this time heading for Denver, Colorado, where she started a school for underprivileged children and also a farm outside the city to raise vegetables to feed them. When asked who would tend the farm crops, she said, "Why our sisters will. They are nearly all women from the country and know about such things." In Denver she and her nuns visited the coal mines, went down the shafts in the plunging cages, walked through the tunnels, visited the miners' families in their shacks.

After Denver it was Arlington, New Jersey, where Mother Cabrini dedicated an orphanage, then back to Chicago to found a hospital. She bought the North Shore Hotel, a solid imposing building facing Lake Michigan, and paid for it by soliciting donations from local Italian-Americans. She hired workmen and supervised them in the rebuilding process—was in effect the contractor. When the neighborhood's residents, fearing a "free" hospital would lower property values, cut the water pipes and otherwise sabotaged the enterprise, she and her nuns moved into the unfinished building and began to accept patients at once. "They are not likely to murder helpless patients and the sisters in their beds," she surmised. The persecution ceased from that day.

Back and forth, back and forth, she went across the American continent, spotting good sites, raising money, starting construction, checking on institutions already founded: to Seattle to start a small orphanage and a parochial school; to New Orleans again (yellow fever raged there and the nursing nuns were in great demand); to Los Angeles, which she traversed on foot, trying to find the best location for an orphanage (she got one started on Sunset Boulevard); then to Burbank, where she bought a huge tract of land on which to build a "preventorium" against tuberculosis.

While she was in Los Angeles in 1905, the twenty-fifth anniversary of the founding of her Missionary Sisters occurred, but she said she was too busy, the celebration would have to wait. Others did celebrate, though, and with cause. Since her first arrival in New York the Sacred Heart houses had grown to fifty (in eight different countries) and the number of sisters to almost a thousand. The Italian government officially praised her, and on a later visit to Italy the Queen of that country (it was then a monarchy) decorated her.

These accomplishments were founded in a remarkable personality. Gazing at some oil magnate or real estate millionaire, Mother Cabrini would say, "You had dreams, when you began. Well, I have dreams, too." She would say, "In asking you for something, I am conferring a privilege upon you." And as a privilege they took it, handing over their donations totaling thousands and tens of thousands of dollars. As for covering ground and sea, she might well have had wings. A new building for an orphanage in New Orleans, a visit to Spain to open another orphanage, a school started in Rio de Janeiro, Brazil—these were all the work of one year, 1907.

In 1909 Mother Cabrini adopted America as her country, taking the oath of citizenship in Seattle, Washington. It wasn't long after this she opened an extension of the Columbus Hospital in Chicago and commissioned an architect to design a ten-story building in New York for the expanded Columbus Hospital there. Next came an annex for her orphanage in Denver, land purchased for setting up a convent in Los Angeles, and in Seattle a beautiful site acquired for building what was later to be called the Cabrini Memorial School. Back in New York State she bought a building for an orphanage near Dobbs Ferry and supervised the necessary alterations.

On July 3, 1914, a Jubilee Mass was held for her at Dobbs Ferry, at which the Italian government awarded her a medal and seventy thousand lire in recognition of her work.

St. Frances Xavier Cabrini

In her sixty-fifth year Mother Cabrini returned to Seattle and founded a home for boys. By April 21, 1916, she had "scraped together" $10,000 for a down payment on the Perry Hotel there, redoing it as a sanatorium for electric therapy and other remedial treatments. But her own health had begun to fail. When she returned to Chicago, on Easter Day 1917, the sight of the frail little figure leaning on a cane brought tears to the eyes of the nuns who met her. She was ordered to take restful rides in the country, but here, too, she managed to get in some useful work, spotting a suitable farm to supply her hospital and school. In November she had to take to her bed. Still, on December 21 she was doing up little packages of candy for the children in the Italian school on Erie Street. The following day she left this world.

In 1938, twenty years after her death, Mother Cabrini was beatified. That is, the Roman Catholic Church decreed that she had attained a sanctity that entitled her to public honor. Eight years later she was canonized—declared by ecclesiastical authority to be a saint. On this latter occasion Cardinal Mundelein, archbishop of Chicago, in a radio broadcast said of her: "When we contemplate this frail little woman, in the short space of two-score years, recruiting an army of 4,000 women under the banner of the Sacred Heart of Jesus, dedicated to a life of poverty and self-sacrifice, fired by the enthusiasm of the crusaders of old, burning with the love of their fellowmen, crossing the seas, penetrating into unknown lands, teaching peoples and their children by word and example to become good Christians and law-abiding citizens, befriending the poor, instructing the ignorant, watching the sick, all without hope of reward or recompense here below—tell me, does all this fulfill the concept of Catholic Action, practiced by a modern saint?"

BIBLIOGRAPHY

Borden, Lucile, *Francesca Cabrini: Without Staff or Scrip.* New York: The Macmillan Company, 1945.

Cotter, Maire, *Westward by Command.* Cork, Ireland: The Mercier Press, Ltd., 1947.

Di Donato, Pietro, *Immigrant Saint; the Life of Mother Cabrini.* New York: McGraw-Hill Book Company, 1960.

Maynard, Theodore, *Too Small a World; the Life of Francesca Cabrini.* Milwaukee: Bruce Publishing Company, 1945.

MARY CASSATT

MARY (STEVENSON) CASSATT: Born in Allegheny City, Allegheny County, Pennsylvania, May 23, 1845. Died in Mesnil-Théribus, France, June 14, 1926. Father: Robert Simpson Cassatt; mother: Katherine Kelso (Johnston) Cassatt; brothers: Alexander Johnston, Robert Kelso, Joseph Gardner; sister: Lydia Simpson (a sister, Katherine Kelso, and a brother, George Johnston, died in infancy).

*

Mary Cassatt, outstanding American artist of the Impressionist school, exercised a stronger influence on American art collecting than probably any other individual of her day. Since her death her pictures have become increasingly in demand. In May 1965, at the first transatlantic televised art auction ever held, with the pictures projected to New York from London via the Early Bird communications satellite, Mary Cassatt's *Maternité*, a pastel, was purchased for $35,000. In 1966 the United States government issued a commemorative postage stamp in her honor.

*

BORN, as she once put it, "with a passion for line and color," Mary Cassatt's first experience with professional portraiture probably occurred when she was ten years old. Her father, a well-to-do American, living at the time in Europe, had commissioned the artist Baumgaertner to do a group portrait of four members of his family. In this picture father and children are gathered around a chessboard. Robert and his father are intent on their game, but Mary is shown full face, looking straight ahead out of the picture. Slender face, pointed chin, firm mouth, sleek hair drawn back in side pigtails, she is intently watching the artist as he sketches the picture. It is as if she were already finding this work of creation more interesting than any other activity.

When her parents headed homeward in 1855, taking three of their children with them—young Robert had died during the sojourn, and Alexander stayed on in Germany to finish his schooling—Mary carried in her memory, beside the incident of the portrait group, the bright colors of the boulevards of Paris, and the pageantry of Louis Napoleon's coronation.

In America it was a life more free in some ways, more circumscribed in others. The Cassatt family was a restless one, living in rapid succession in Allegheny City, Pittsburgh, Hardwick, Philadelphia, West Chester, back to Philadelphia, then to Cheyney, about fifteen miles west of that city. Wherever Mary was, she enjoyed galloping horseback over the Pennsylvania hills. When Alexander returned from Germany, he took a few months before matriculating at Rensselaer Polytechnic Institute in Troy, New York, to go on cantering expeditions with her. She was his favorite sister, because she "was always ready for anything." Gardner, the younger brother, was preparing to become a banker. As for Mary, she was expected to do what her older sister, Lydia, did—what all properly brought up young ladies in those days did—some tending of flowers outdoors and arranging of them indoors, a little embroidery, some idle strumming at the keyboard, and an exchange of social calls. But Mary had other ideas.

She wanted to go to Rome to study art, but the Civil War, coming just then, made travel difficult. Besides her father thought it a "preposterous" idea. Why should a young lady whose livelihood was assured go galavanting off to Europe to train herself to be an artist? Then Mary said she wanted to enroll at the Pennsylvania Academy of Fine Arts in Philadelphia. Her father at last gave his grudging consent to this, and she became an art student there—spent four years copying mediocre paintings and plaster casts before she could finally win her father over to letting her study abroad.

She stayed in Paris more than three years, attended art classes, made short trips into rural France, where, as she wrote home, "costumes and surroundings are good for painters." Yet she remained an amateur. When the Franco-Prussian War forced her to return home, she tried painting her two-year-old nephew, Edward, but the picture only showed her technical immaturity. When on a brief visit to Chicago she lost all her European sketches in the great fire of 1871, she had almost a sense of relief. Now she could begin again with a clean slate. She decided to return to Europe.

When she arrived in Parma, Italy, in 1872, she wrote home enthusiastically that she was "going to school to Correggio." This Italian master had been dead over three hundred years, but she had advanced enough by now to be able to gain an insight into his creative processes by studying his canvases.

From Parma she went to Rome, and from there in 1872 submitted her first picture (*Pendant le Carnaval*, a group on a balcony) to the Paris Salón, an annual exhibit in which artists all over Europe vied for representation. It was accepted. This gave her confidence. After Rome it was Spain, where she studied the works of Velásquez and painted two pictures: *The Offering of the Panal to a Toreador*, which was accepted by the Paris Salón in 1873, and *The Toreador*, a study in deep reds, greens with bright silvers and blues to give contrast. The latter is considered by connoisseurs the best of her early works.

At the Prado Museum in Madrid she was so excited by the rich, colorful paintings of the Flemish artist Peter Paul Rubens that she headed for Antwerp, Belgium, his home city, where many other of his paintings were exhibited. She stayed in Antwerp all summer.

Her mother came over to be with her, and she now began what was to be a lifelong habit: using members of her family as models. This was natural. She had always been a family person, thoroughly involved in home happenings. It was also natural that later her father, after he retired from his brokerage business, and her sister Lydia as well as her mother should come to live with her in Paris. She was to devote much time through the years not only to painting them but to nursing them through various illnesses.

Paris was a challenge. One day on a street of art shops she saw in a window some pastel drawings by the artist Edgar Degas. She was struck as if with the discovery of a new world. "I used to go and flatten my nose against that window and absorb all I could of his art . . . . It changed my life. I saw art then as I wanted to see it."

This interest became reciprocal the following year when Degas saw her *Madame Cortier* (a study in blacks and whites) at the Paris Salón. "There is someone who thinks as I do," he decided. Finally a mutual friend, Joseph Tourny, took him to see her. It was the beginning of a long and productive friendship between these two artists, one living a Bohemian life, the other living austerely with her family, but both withdrawn from society and both dedicated to their work. While not her teacher, he was her guide, leading her toward conciseness of approach in her art, delineation of movement by simple means, abhorrence of extraneous effects. He was instrumental in introducing her into the group of independent artists called "The Impressionists," who sought to achieve a greater naturalism by rendering the play of light on the surface of objects—the flicker on leaf, wave, flower, or face—through such means as paint applied in tiny dabs of pure color, side by side with outlines somewhat blurred, to give a luminosity to the whole canvas.

She welcomed Degas's invitation to exhibit with the Impressionists, the more so since she had ceased to submit her work to the Paris Salón. She had become suspicious when the conservative judges refused a picture she had submitted to the Salón in 1875. She suspected them of arbitrarily favoring dark backgrounds and decided to test them out. The following year she resubmitted the picture with darker background shades painted in. So altered, it was accepted. Such biased judgments were not to her liking and she turned from the Salón.

A painting of hers was included in the Fourth Exhibition of the Impressionists (1879): *La Loge,* a glowing picture of a young girl in a box at the opera, its pinks, reds, oranges vying with each other for a luminous effect. It was purchased by a friend of Degas's. The financing of the exhibition was on a cooperative basis; so when this one closed with a profit of 6,000 francs, each of the participants was allowed 439 francs. Frederick Sweet writes in his biography that Mary's father, who had joined the family in Paris, could at last write to their son, a railroad executive, "She is now known to the Art world as well as to the general public in such a way as not to be forgotten again as long as she continues to paint." During this year she was also included in an exhibition in America, which was shown at the Pennsylvania Academy, at the National Academy of Design in New York, and in Boston.

The Cassatts in Paris were now living on a relatively modest legacy bequeathed by an uncle. Alexander (Aleck) sent money for "extras"—a carriage for his mother who had heart trouble, and payments now and then on expenses entailed by their country residence. The other members of the family, both those near at hand and those visiting them periodically, continued to serve as Mary's models: her sister Lydia for *The Cup of Tea, Woman and Child Driving*, and *Lydia Knitting in the Garden*; Mrs. Cassatt for *Reading Le Figaro*; and the Alexander Cassatts for various studies.

Because of her long years of studying art by examining paintings of old and new masters, Mary Cassatt had developed an extraordinary critical sense, as attested by the purchases she made for herself—Pissarros, Renoirs, Sisleys and Monets, when these now-famous artists were little known. She wanted others to share her finds. As early as 1873, she had begun to influence her wealthy friend Louisine Elder (later to be the famous collector Mrs. Henry O. Havemeyer) to buy works of the Impressionists. Then in 1881 her brother Alexander was also persuaded to invest in paintings of this group. On her advice he bought Monets, Renoirs, Pissarros, a Morisot, and, most important, *Ballet Class* by Degas. That America today is so rich in examples of the Impressionist School must be attributed in large measure to Mary Cassatt's enthusiasm and acumen.

When in the early eighties Paris suffered a financial crash, Mary Cassatt was able to help some of her artist friends by rounding up purchasers for their paintings. The famous collector Ambrose Vollard referred to her as "that generous Mary Cassatt" who "labored with frenzy for her Impressionist friends but who never pushed herself."

In the mid-eighties Mary Cassatt, on one occasion, herself acted as a model—and for Degas. His now famous *Portrait of Mary Cassatt* shows a trim figure in a brown dress, with a tan hat with green trimmings, leaning forward in a chair. She is holding in her hands some photographs spread out like a "deal" of playing cards. The slender face, the firm mouth, and the pointed chin are still in evidence, but unlike her ten-year-old counterpart, she is now looking meditatively toward the floor as if her thoughts were inward, as if she had resolved her doubts and now held her career and her success within herself.

Paris had accepted her fully. Her slim figure with the extremely well-tailored outfit, crowned by a big hat with *aigrettes* (she was always extravagant about hats), was a familiar sight in the museums and at the dealers' shops. Her friends knew her to be temperamental and strong willed, but firmly disciplined in her habits. She would go to her studio every morning at eight o'clock and not leave it till daylight failed. She always wore a white blouse while painting.

Pictures by Mary Cassatt were included in the eighth Impressionists Exhibition, the last of the group's shows in Paris, May 16 to June 15, 1886. Her *Girl Arranging Her Hair*, adventurous in pose and design, won the praise of Degas. But even more important was the exhibition—310 Impressionist paintings—that opened May 25 at the National Academy in America, the first showing of that group in this country. Besides Monets, Pissarros, Renoirs, Sisleys, and others, there were two Cassatts: *Family Group* and *Portrait of a Lady*. Miss Cassatt did not come over for the event. She was extremely prone to seasickness, and besides was kept in Paris tending her mother, who had been ill for some time.

The year 1890 marked her turning to the theme for which she is most noted: mother and child studies. She had always enjoyed the company of children and would take her four nephews and nieces to nearby Versailles "in a great gig" and at her country place would supply a boat for the children to ride on the lake.

She posed children carefully, thoughtful of their comfort. When one of her nephews once rebelled and, according to accounts, spit at his aunt, she dissuaded his mother from punishing him and instead made a special trip to town to buy him a box of chocolates. It must have delighted one of her young models when she had someone read to him from *Huckleberry Finn* to keep him quiet. But when the narrative got underway, Miss Cassatt herself laughed so much at it that she could not go on with the painting. At her summer place she used mostly the local French peasant children, and charming or plain, painted them just as they were. J. K. Huysmans of the Paris press spoke of the "family life painted with distinction and love," and of the "penetrating feeling of intimacy" in her works.

From 1890 the influence of Japanese art—subtle color harmonies, simplicity of line, over-all floral patterns (flowered dresses and wallpaper)—began to be apparent in her paintings.

At her one-man show in 1891 Degas told her that she had improved greatly, and this gave her spirits a boost. That year, too, she produced ten color prints of the highest quality.

Now she was kept busy painting a mural for the Woman's Building at the World's Columbian Exposition, held in Chicago in 1893. It represented woman in various symbolic activities (plucking fruits of knowledge, pursuing fame). When someone asked, "Then this is woman apart from her relations to man?" she answered staunchly that it was: "Men, I have no doubt, are painted in all their vigor, on the walls of the other buildings; to us the sweetness of childhood, the charm of womanhood; if I have not conveyed some sense of that charm, in one word if I have not been absolutely feminine, then I have failed."

No sooner had she sent away her mural than she began making selections for her second one-man show, held during November and December in 1893. This, far more ambitious than the first, had ninety-eight works.

Her father had died in 1891. Two years later Mary Cassatt and her mother moved into the Château de Beaufresne, at Mesnil, which she had purchased entirely from the proceeds of her pictures. She was to live there until her death. Violet Paget (Vernon Lee), the English writer, visiting there in 1895, wrote of it, in a letter to a friend: "I liked immensely being at Mesnil . . . there being . . . leagues of cloud and air; . . . The complete scheme of the eternal story told by mountains and rivers, the story of watersheds and sea . . . . And I liked the Louis XVI Château and the sort of white bareness of the rooms . . . . Miss Cassatt is very nice, simple, an odd mixture of a self-recognising artist, with passionate appreciation in literature, and the almost childish garrulous American provincial. She wants to make art cheap, to bring it within reach of the comparatively poor . . . ."

After her mother's death her brother Gardner's family came for a two-year stay in Europe. This kept Mary busy doing pastels of her young niece and nephew, one-and-a-half years old and nine respectively.

In 1898 she went to America—her first appearance there since leaving it twenty-six years before. But America was not ready for her even then. The Philadelphia *Ledger*'s report of the event gives an idea of nineteenth century America's artistic unawareness: "Mary Cassatt, sister of Mr. Cassatt, president of the Pennsylvania Railroad, returned from Europe yesterday. She has been studying painting in France, and owns the smallest Pekingese dog in the world."

At any rate the stay brought her commissions, and at a series of dinner parties arranged for her in Boston, she urged Americans to collect Impressionist paintings.

Then a few years later, in 1901, she joined the H. O. Havemeyers on a tour of south Europe. It was really a hunting trip, with the big game great works of art. Mrs. Havemeyer, who wanted to purchase paintings for her mansion in New York, and Mary Cassatt trailed masterpieces in the dusty corners of art museums and collectors' shops in Italy and Spain, going to some twenty cities. They found works by Veronese,

Mino de Fiesole, Filippo Lippi, Goya, Van Dyke. The rediscovery of El Greco's *Assumption*, now in the Chicago Art Institute, was entirely Mary Cassatt's feat, since the Havemeyers were all for rejecting the painting.

Prizes offered to her and refused by her marked the year 1904. A Lippincott Prize of $300 offered by the Pennsylvania Academy and the $500 Norman Wait Harris Prize were refused with the explanation that her membership in the Impressionist group precluded prize-taking, since their very existence had been a protest against such singling out. She also refused to serve as a juror for an exhibition at the Pennsylvania Academy. But she was happy at having four of her pictures included in the Seventeenth Annual Exhibition of the Art Institute of Chicago, and even happier at being made Chevalier of the Legion of Honor in France. With quiet satisfaction she wrote a friend, "It is hard to get the honor awarded to a woman." She accepted the honorary presidency of the Art League of Paris and occasionally gave talks there to the American girl students. Her simple earnestness was inspiring.

But she was nearing her seventies, and times and tastes were changing. With the advent of cubism in painting, she found herself in an alien art world.

It was hard also to bear the knowledge that her eyesight was failing. She could at first get about—she sailed again to America in 1908 and went to Egypt in 1911—but in 1912 she developed cataracts on both eyes and her traveling days were over. One-man shows of her works were now regular events in Paris. In 1914 the Pennsylvania Academy gave her the Gold Medal of Honor "awarded for eminent services to the Academy." But she could not attend these functions. When Degas died in 1917, she managed to get to his funeral. She wrote a friend, "His death was a deliverance, but I am sad. He was my oldest friend here and the last great artist of the nineteenth century. I see no one to replace him."

Mary Cassatt

When friends and relatives began again visiting her from America after World War I, they found her a querulous old lady, sparse, determined in her views. She could not condemn severely enough the American students who, she said, were loafing their lives away in the cafés of Paris. They should be up at daybreak working in their studios as she had done. She clung to the nineteenth century idea of impeccable manners. As for her blindness, she took that in stride. She would say, "There are ten thousand blind in France . . . an individual case seems of little account." She would enjoy *objets d'art* by tactile means, and she still insisted on cutting her roses herself. She had long had diabetes and had become very weak, but was served faithfully by her housekeeper and companion of forty-five years, Mathilde Vallet, by a cook, a maid, and a chauffeur, Armand Delaporte. She was leaning on his arm when she died on June 14, 1926.

BIBLIOGRAPHY

CARSON, JULIA MARGARET, *Mary Cassatt*. New York: David McKay Company, Inc., 1966.

SWEET, FREDERICK ARNOLD, *Miss Mary Cassatt, Impressionist from Pennsylvania*. Norman: University of Oklahoma Press, 1966.

WILLA CATHER

WILLA (SIBERT) CATHER: Born near Winchester, Virginia, December 7, 1873. Died in New York City, April 24, 1947. Father: Charles Cather; mother: Mary Virginia (Boak) Cather; brothers: Roscoe, Douglas, James, John (Jack); sisters: Jessica, Elsie. Willa was the eldest of the children.

※

Willa Cather was one of our great short-story writers and novelists. As a very small child, when her parents would try to help her put on her clothes or climb up and down in her high chair, she would insist, "Self-alone, self-alone!" So in her writing she dealt in themes that were her very own and used them in her very own way. Usually these subjects derived from her younger days. Though she was to shuttle all over the world, she kept the earlier surroundings clearest in her inner eye. As she has Jim Burden say, in her book *My Ántonia*, "Whenever my consciousness was quickened, all those early friends were quickened within it, and in some strange ways they accompanied me through all my new experiences."

※

AT ten years of age Willa Cather moved with her family from staid and conventional Virginia to the wide open plains of Webster County, Nebraska, where the scattered houses seemed to cling to the prairie sod as if, as she described them in her novel *O Pioneers!* "trying not to be blown away." Her father thought at first he would be a rancher, but found the pioneering life on the plains too strenuous and moved after a year to nearby Red Cloud, a thriving little town (population 2,500), which, as a railroad center, managed to support a cluster of small businesses. He started one himself, dealing in loans, mortgages, and insurance.

But eleven-year-old Willa had learned from her months on the plains the joy of riding on her pony over the grasslands along sunflower-bordered roads and buffalo trails, and now she continued her visits to the old women in the sod houses of the Norwegian and Bohemian communities and heard them tell about the ways and doings of the Old Country and their hopes for the New. "I always felt," she once related to H. W. Boynton of the *New York Evening Post*, "as if they told me so much more than they said—as if I had actually got inside another person's skin." They also brought her emotions into play. "No child with a spark of generosity," she was to write, "could have kept from throwing herself heart and soul into the fight these people were making to master the language, to master the soil, to hold their land and to get ahead in the world."

She made friends with the neighbor children in Red Cloud, played circus with them in their huge barn, or went on picnics and on snake hunts with them. But she went by herself to gather wild flowers. She would get whole armloads of them: "They were so lovely and no one seemed to care for them at all." She would visit the trees individually to see how they were doing. Their life on the plains seemed so hazardous.

When she was thirteen, she and her playmates built a little town of their own in the back yard, and called it "Sandy Point." They used packing boxes for stores, setting them up along the "Main Street," a graveled stretch reaching from hedge to hedge. Each child chose his own business and hung out his own sign. Willa was mayor as well as editor of "The

Sandy Point News," and so produced her first recorded "professional" writing.

At about fifteen she made up her mind to become a surgeon, and, trying to look the part, cut her reddish brown hair short and wore a boyish jacket. She gave her high school oration on vivisection. When she matriculated at the University of Nebraska in Lincoln, she still meant to pursue a medical career. But her ideas changed when an essay of hers, "The Personal Characteristics of Thomas Carlyle as Judged by His Writings," appeared in the March 1, 1891, issue of the newspaper the Nebraska *State Journal*. Though she had had nothing to do with its getting published—it had been submitted without her knowledge by her English professor—seeing herself in print changed her, as she later said, from a surgeon into a writer.

Before she graduated she had become not only editor of the undergraduate publication, *Hesperian*, but also a reporter for the Nebraska *State Journal*. In this latter job she interviewed actresses backstage, went to plays, wrote reviews—at a dollar a column for weekdays and four dollars on Sundays. It was just as well that her literary efforts were bringing in something. Her father's business was at a low ebb.

Back in Red Cloud with her B.A. degree Willa felt her "self-alone" motif must be somehow put into play. Going on botanical expeditions with her brother Roscoe, riding her pony across the plains, seeing her friends, even writing a regular newspaper column for the Lincoln, Nebraska, *Courier*—these were not enough. But how could she widen her horizon? The answer came when the management of the *Home Monthly*, having seen some of her critiques in the Lincoln paper, offered her an editorial job. This magazine, based in Pittsburgh, was dedicated to "more than half a million firesides." So she left the sunflowers, the pony rides, the picnics, the long talks in sod huts, and in 1896 went east to Pittsburgh,

Pennsylvania, there to struggle over the disciplines of editorial work—pasting up pages, reading proof, checking for inaccuracies, meeting deadlines. The one bit of excitement she allowed herself in this hard-driven life—she often worked till one o'clock in the morning—was chasing streetcars on her bicycle, on her way to work.

After a year with the *Home Monthly* she transferred to the Pittsburgh *Daily Leader*, the largest evening paper in Pennsylvania, and for four years read copy, rewrote articles, and handed in reviews of plays. But it was not this work, good experience as it was, that made her call Pittsburgh the birthplace of her writing. Rather it was the creative work that gradually began to absorb her.

After having a story published in *Cosmopolitan* magazine, "Eric Hermannson's Soul," she resigned from her newspaper job in 1901 and began teaching English and Latin in the Allegheny High School, hoping this would give her more time to write on her own. A pupil describes her during this period: "Her voice was deeper than is usual; she spoke without excitement, her manner was quiet, reposeful, suggesting reserves of energy and richness of personality." A place to write was provided when she was invited by a newfound friend, Isabelle McClung, daughter of a judge in Pittsburgh, to live in the spacious McClung mansion. Here, in a quiet room at the back, she could concentrate on her writing evenings and weekends.

Her stories began to appear regularly in the prominent literary magazines: *Lippincott's*, the *New England Magazine*, *Everybody's*, and *McClure's Magazine*. In the summer of 1902 she went on her first trip to Europe, sending back her written "impressions" to the Nebraska *State Journal*. There were articles on the studio of artist Sir Edward Burne-Jones, author A. E. Housman's lodgings, German poet Heinrich Heine's grave, ancient ruins in England. *April Twilights*, her first book of poems, was published in March 1903, after her return to America. During this whole period she was under the spell of Henry James's writings, shaped her phrases meticulously, made style her chief concern.

Her collection of short stories *The Troll Garden*, representative of this period, had appeared in *McClure's Magazine* serially, and the editor, S. S. McClure, now offered her a position on his staff. So in the spring of 1906 she traveled to New York. This city was to be the center of her activities for the rest of her life.

Her first assignment at *McClure's*, however, led her to Boston, on a two-year research stint to gather facts for an article on Mary Baker Eddy. Here also she made friends quickly, among them writer Sarah Orne Jewett, who had already won a reputation for stories about the seacoast of her native Maine. Miss Jewett advised her to write about people and places she knew and loved. The effect was to turn Miss Cather's attention back to the things she had cherished in her girlhood.

Miss Cather had returned to New York and been advanced to the post of managing editor on *McClure's* when she received a letter from Miss Jewett suggesting she give up her magazine work, because "when one's first working power (in writing) is spent, it cannot be regained." Miss Cather, however, did not leave *McClure's* until later, when she was in a financial position to do so.

Fortunately her editorial job did not pin her down to her desk. Mr. McClure, in fact, encouraged her to travel, to get new ideas, fresh slants. Accordingly, in 1909 she went to London, and every year during her time at *McClure's* she spent some months each summer back in Red Cloud, Nebraska. Her contacts in New York also were widening. She met authors Mark Twain and Edwin Arlington Robinson and actor George Arliss. Elizabeth Shepley Sergeant, who as a young writer came to the *McClure* office to submit a manuscript, later wrote of Miss Cather in her *Willa Cather; a Mem-*

oir, "I felt the freshness and brusqueness, too, of an ocean breeze. Her boyish, enthusiastic manner was disarming."

Finally Miss Cather saw her way clear to resign, and with the blessing of Mr. McClure, who even then was preparing to publish serially what was to be her first novel, *Alexander's Bridge*, turned in the spring of 1912 to her own writing as a full-time career. She was then thirty-eight. Her increased output immediately showed she had decided correctly. This year she was to write *O Pioneers!* the first of her novels in which she deals with a subject she considered her own. "I had been trying to sing a song that did not lie in my voice." This book, about Scandinavians and Bohemians, old neighbors of hers when she had lived on the ranch in Nebraska, was translated into many languages. A strong and beautiful descriptive novel, it gave her an international reputation.

To get a fresh outlook on life, she took, this year, a long pack-trip with her brother Douglas, starting from Winslow, Arizona, visiting Walnut Canyon, viewing the ruins of the cliff dwellers, and crossing into New Mexico.

On her return to New York City she took an apartment with a friend, Edith Lewis, at Number Five Bank Street in Greenwich Village. Here, in rooms hung with prints of Italian masters, which she had acquired in Europe, and with the coal fire casting warmer tones on the already colorful rugs, she had her "at homes" on Friday afternoons, attended by friends from Nebraska and Pittsburgh, by stage people, editorial people, musicians, writers. The Bank Street years (1912–1927) were her most prolific. Dating from them are, besides the completion of *O Pioneers!* her novels, *The Song of the Lark*, *My Antonia*, *Youth and the Bright Medusa*, *One of Ours*, *A Lost Lady*, *The Professor's House*, *My Mortal Enemy*, and *Death Comes for the Archbishop*. *The Song of the Lark* (1915) was a novel concerning the struggle of the daughter of a Swedish pastor in Moonstone, Colorado, to become an opera singer. "What I cared about," she wrote in an early preface, "was the girl's escape; the play of blind chance, the way in which commonplace occurrences fall together to liberate her from commonness." While working on this novel, she visited the singer Olive Fremstad in her home in Bridgton, Maine. Miss Fremstad was the model for the protagonist of *The Song of the Lark*.

Her novel writing was often preceded by visits to the land or to the persons she wrote about. Back in Red Cloud and environs in 1916, she remet Anna Panelka, whom she had known as a girl. *My Ántonia* was the result. This is the story of a daughter in an immigrant Bohemian family in Nebraska —her struggles with elements of nature within and without herself, all but untamable, but finally brought within the framework of contentment. In 1916 she also made a return visit to Taos, New Mexico—she had explored it on horseback the year before—and also spent time in Santa Fe—trips to be remembered when she wrote *Death Comes for the Archbishop* (1927). The year 1920—when *Youth and the Bright Medusa*, eight stories concerned with art and its irresistible and sometimes fatal attraction for the young, was brought out —she journeyed to Paris with Miss Lewis. It is of this year, when many unresolved issues of World War I were seething, that she wrote, "The world broke in two about 1920 and I belonged to the former half." She abhorred what she considered the materialism of the postwar United States.

In 1922 she took an old cottage on Grand Manan Island, off the coast of New Brunswick, Canada. While there, she wrote *One of Ours*. This book gained for her the Pulitzer Prize, though it was not by any means her best work. In 1922 she also gave a series of lectures on writing at the Bread Loaf School of English in Middlebury, Vermont. The gist of these lectures was that the writer must be so involved with his subject that he forgets his selfish interests entirely. In 1923, the year she wrote *The Lost Lady*, she was in Europe; in 1925, the year she wrote *The Professor's House*, in New Mexico. During this whole decade she still managed periodic trips to Red Cloud, Nebraska.

A glimpse of her is given by her biographer Elizabeth Shepley Sergeant at a dinner honoring Robert Frost on his fiftieth birthday. She remembers "Willa's large, impressive head, emerging from some rich low-necked gown with a touch of red that greatly became her." She adds, "Her lovely oval face brimmed with affection, her blue eyes gazed upon the hero of the evening as if he were a distant prospect, much admired." Miss Sergeant points out that "To both [Frost and Cather] the hardness of the basic struggle for existence was a long memory that purified their approach to the life of an artist . . . both like a rather bare and timeless world. Both were suspicious of their own emotional singing side, and imposed on it an elegant and sober line." As the party broke up, "she stood with stiffly regimented air," writes Miss Sergeant, "waiting for her furs, and bearing coldly with some bold critic who had tagged after her . . . . She never had the least little bit of small talk, not an iota of ease or light friendliness with a stranger who seemed intrusive."

In 1927 the demolition of the house on Bank Street (to make way for an apartment house) sent Miss Cather into hotel quarters for several years. Then she took an apartment with Miss Lewis on Park Avenue. These disruptions in her personal life were in some part counterbalanced by the great success of her novel *Death Comes for the Archbishop*, published in 1927.

Now came difficulties with which she was constitutionally little able to cope: the death of her parents; the sale of the family home in Red Cloud; and her own diminishing health. She began to seclude herself from the outer world. She refused to allow any of her books to be used in classrooms. After the failure of *A Lost Lady* as a movie, she refused to allow any more of her books to be filmed. The New Deal, the program instituted by President Franklin D. Roosevelt to promote economic recovery and social reform, threatened, she believed, the free activity of the individual. The 1930's were to her "the age of routine." However, this decade did see the publication of her books *Obscure Destinies, Lucy Gayheart, Not Under Forty,* and *Sapphira and the Slave Girl.*

In spite of her withdrawal, honors came her way. In the early spring of 1933 she was awarded the Prix Fémina Américain for her book *Shadows on the Rock* (1931). In 1938 she was elected to the American Academy of Arts and Letters. In 1944 she received the Gold Medal from the National Institute of Arts and Letters.

In 1941 she made her last long trip—across the continent to see her brother Roscoe in California. He died the following year, just as she finished *The Best Years*, written especially for him.

Though she was hampered in her movements now by a badly swollen wrist and had often to wear a leather or steel brace on it, she never lived the life of an invalid. She kept busy, walked, read, dictated letters. At her death in her seventy-fourth year, she had been readying another collection of short stories for the publishers, and one of them was lying unfinished on her desk. This collection, *The Old Beauty and Others*, was published posthumously in 1948.

BIBLIOGRAPHY

BENNETT, MILDRED R., *The World of Willa Cather*. New York: Dodd, Mead & Company, 1951.

BROWN, EDWARD KILLORAN, *Willa Cather, a Critical Biography*, completed by Leon Edel. New York: Alfred A. Knopf, Inc., 1953.

DAICHES, DAVID, *Willa Cather; a Critical Introduction*. Ithaca, New York: Cornell University Press, 1951.

LEWIS, EDITH, *Willa Cather, Living; a Personal Record*. New York: Alfred A. Knopf, Inc., 1953.

RANDALL, JOHN HERMAN, *The Landscape and the Looking Glass; Willa Cather's Search for Value*. Boston: Houghton Mifflin Company, 1960.

RAPIN, RENÉ, *Willa Cather*. New York: Robert M. McBride & Company, 1930.

SERGEANT, ELIZABETH SHEPLEY, *Willa Cather; a Memoir*. Philadelphia: J. B. Lippincott Company, 1953.

AGNES de MILLE

AGNES (GEORGE) de MILLE (PRUDE): Born in New York City. Father: William Churchill de Mille; mother: Anna George de Mille; sister: Margaret; husband: Walter Foy Prude; son: Jonathan.

✳

As a composer of dances, Agnes de Mille has been an innovator of the first order. There is hardly an American choreographer of the postwar generation but owes something to her. By including American folk dances in her ballet *Rodeo*, she gave new scope to American ballet. With her choreography of the famous musical *Oklahoma!* she widened the role of the dance in the theater, making it an integral part of the plot. Besides these things, she has raised the status of dancers as a class and improved their material condition. She has done all this working against great odds, especially in the early part of her career, when the dance was looked down on as a lesser art.

✳

As a child Agnes de Mille often pretended she was a knight, or Joan of Arc ready for battle. She built a "castle" in the empty garage, out of boxes, crates, sawed-off palm branches, and old furniture gathered from scrap heaps. Once, oh joy! her uncle, famous producer Cecil B. de Mille, sent her a bundle of "authentic fake wooden swords and spears," left over after completion of the movie *Joan the Woman*. She supervised mock battles, the neighbor girls serving as peasants and warriors. Sometimes they all took to the hills, which rose up from her very back door, and raced where the sage bushes smelled sweet after rains and the clouds seemed to touch the hilltops.

This all was in Hollywood, California. The family had moved there from New York when she was nine, so that her father, a playwright, could join forces with his brother Cecil in the young motion picture industry.

In contrast to the wild outdoor games, indoors there was rigid adherence to decorum. Agnes' mother, who was the daughter of the world-famous political economist Henry George, believed in discipline. Agnes was supposed to make every minute count. She practiced the piano diligently, read French aloud while her mother curled her hair, even said her prayers in French.

When she was ten, she was taken to see Pavlova, the greatest ballerina of the beginning of this century. "Across the daily preoccupation of lessons, lunch boxes, tooth brushings and quarrellings with Margaret," she writes in her autobiography, *Dance to the Piper*, "flashed this bright unworldly experience and burned in a single afternoon a path over which I could never retrace my steps." After the performance she went home, shut herself in her bedroom, and, using the brass rail at the head of her bed as a dancer's *barre*, rose "laboriously to the tips of my white buttoned shoes [and] stumped the width of the bed and back again." Her life from then on —through the tennis games she played with her father, through their conversations on books and the theater, through classes and homework—had a focus. She would be a great dancer. She gathered her gang together and put on dance pageants in the back yard. She did knee bends every night before going to bed. She begged for ballet lessons.

Her parents did not want her to go into the theater, certainly not on the ballet stage. But they were willing for her to take one private and one group dance lesson a week as good

Agnes de Mille

physical training. Her teacher, Theodore Kosloff, told her she had weak knees, was overweight, and too old to start. But she persisted and in time won his concession that she did show extraordinary talent for pantomime.

But the years of negativism on the part of her parents had their effect. When she was in her midteens, she gave up her lessons and stopped practicing at the homemade *barre*. One evening she told her father, "Pop, I've decided to give up dancing and go to college." He said he thought she had made a good decision.

That would have been that—except that in her sophomore year at the University of California a revue was put on for the benefit of student victims of a campus fire. She did a dance as a shepherdess, styling it after the paintings of Watteau. Then in her junior year she presented another dance about the close liaison of jazz and the jungle. (She was the jungle.) These brief moments on the stage brought back the old urges. She was graduated, having majored in English literature, *cum laude*, but shortly after, her father saw her practicing again at the *barre*. "All this education," he said, "and I'm still just the father of a circus."

Now events began to throw her more and more on her own resources. Her parents were divorced, and her mother, her sister Margaret, and she settled in New York City. Here Agnes de Mille, now twenty, started looking for a job, went to every agent on Broadway—with no success. She did not feel justified in paying three thousand dollars to a prominent agent for being "presented" in a series of New York concerts. She knew that, besides the concert fee, she would have the expense of studio rental, pianists' fees, lessons, and costumes. She did not like to make great dents in her mother's savings. (Today, even as then, dancers lose heavily in their first years and cannot break even on concerts.)

So it was a period of sporadic engagements at society parties, in movie houses, in nightclubs, wherever agents or friends could direct her. This hard time "didn't make me a better person," she was to say later. "It just made me angry." Nevertheless she did make a tour one autumn with dancer Adolph Bolm and performed three of her own pieces. She danced in a revival of the melodrama *The Black Crook*, in Hoboken, New Jersey, and arranged dances for this presentation. She shared a series of programs with the dancer Jacques Cartier, in New York City, and in the second concert stopped the show with her dance " '49." This was the first of her dances which she choreographed—that is "composed" as a creative entity—and one of the very first dances, with the possible exception of Ted Shawn's pieces, to make use of American folk material on the concert stage.

At this time, too, she got herself a dancing partner. Recommended by the dance critic John Martin, Warren Leonard came to her studio one morning, went through his paces, proved himself good for the job.

But this period in America led to nothing. Hoping for more solid success, she went in 1932 to Europe, danced in Paris, Brussels, Copenhagen, and London. In the latter city the British dance critic Arnold Haskell singled her out as "the first real idiomatic American dancer."

She could not begin to pay her own way with the proceeds from these recitals and was using up a good deal of her mother's money. But on the credit side she was acquiring the essentials of dance technique: finding out how to give pulse to the initial movement, how to make a single gesture establish a mood, how to curve it to the musical line, how to make the last downbeat tell.

She stayed in England for the next five years, with the exception of a sixteen-month interlude in America, financially profitable but artistically dispiriting. During these American months she did the dances for the Leslie Howard–Norma

Agnes de Mille

Shearer film *Romeo and Juliet*, only to see the dances cut to remnants in the final version. And she put on her dance *Harvest Reel* at the Hollywood Bowl, a performance that was a fiasco because it was invisible, an electrician having failed to push a master lever on signal. But she did manage to find time for some lessons with the great teacher Carmalita Maracci, and to do some teaching herself.

Back in England 1937-1938 she helped form with Anthony Tudor a ballet troupe called Dance Theater, in Oxford. Also in England she choreographed with notable success the Cole Porter hit *The Nymph Errant*, in which Gertrude Lawrence starred. All this time she was studying with Marie Rambert, who ran a ballet school and company in the Mercury Theater, owned by her husband, Ashley Duke. Most important of all, she plotted out a dance sequence which was later to form the groundwork for her ballet *Rodeo*. Yet, when she left for America in November 1938, ordered out by the British Government Home Office readying the country for war, she was burdened with debts and saw no means of getting free from them. It seemed all she had to show for the years of struggle since college were her costumes and her repertoire.

Her mother welcomed her to a studio on East Ninth Street in New York City. Here her books had been gathered together. A fire burned in the grate. Flowers had been sent by relatives. It was a good omen. This apartment was to be her home for eight years. Here each added bookshelf or dish was to be paid for by a new dance. Here she was to do the choreography for seven Broadway hits. Here she was to start her married life.

Her New York career began with sporadic engagements. The YMHA hired her to teach two classes a week. She danced in benefits for war victims. Some of her comic dances were so funny she had to slow them down to give the audience a chance to stop laughing in order to see the next point. She did a six weeks' engagement at the Rainbow Room nightclub. At last a solid engagement was offered. Richard Pleasant, who years before had observed her teaching a class in Hollywood, was now head of Ballet Theater and invited her into his group. (Today this is the famous American Ballet Theater sponsored by Lucia Chase.) The very first season Miss de Mille choreographed *Black Ritual,* the first ballet danced altogether with Negro dancers in a classic American ballet company.

Next she was lined up for a national tour, heading her own company (including Sybil Shearer, Katherine Litz, Joseph Anthony, Louis Horst, Trude Rittmann), by one of the great booking managers of this country, Lucius Pryor. Miss de Mille costumed her whole company, paid for composing, rehearsing, publicity material, pictures, and press books from $700 borrowed from Hollywood friends. Next, Mr. Pleasant asked her to choreograph a morality play, *Three Virgins and a Devil,* with herself dancing the lead. This was a smash hit.

These engagements came just in time. Hollywood, the Metropolitan Opera, and Broadway seemed closed to her. Her mother was ailing and she felt she should no longer lean on her for money. She felt she had become a problem to her family. She had almost decided to start as a saleswoman at Macy's Department Store—if they'd take her.

The famous Ballet Russe de Monte Carlo was, in 1941, touring from coast to coast. Because of the patriotic feeling engendered by the war, its head, Serge Ivanovitch Denham, decided to use an American ballet *by* an American. He asked Miss de Mille if she had anything. She shut herself in her room and within three days, working over the cowboy dance sequence she had created in London, produced a dance scenario, *Rodeo.* She sent it to Denham, was called to his office, and was told he liked it. But he wanted to have a clause inserted in the contract that would allow him to have final say on all points in the actual performance of the dance. She told him, "Never!" and implied if she went on with it, it was to be her work that was used and no other. She was to have the final say "on every artistic matter." With this statement, she says, "I came of age." The contract was made out and signed without the veto clause.

She had stipulated that composer Aaron Copland was to do the music. She explained to him the story of *Rodeo*—a cowgirl tries to get her man, the Head Wrangler, by dressing like a cowboy and showing her prowess at cowboy stunts, but manages only to annoy the cowhands and bring on the ridicule of the other women. The Champion Roper persuades her to come to a party dressed prettily. She trips into the dance in skirts, and the ballet ends with her happily pairing off with the man she has really loved all along, the Champion Roper. Copland had the music in her hands shortly, and then it was a whirling five months while the Russian dancers were taught how to dance and act "cowboy"—"We worked for four hours on a boy kissing a girl at a dance"—while the costumes were readied, while Miss de Mille herself underwent the rigors of training for her lead part as the cowgirl, and while she was completing the choreography.

It must be noted here that in group dancing it is impossible to work out all problems of choreography in the seclusion of one's room. Unlike the composer, who can give precise directives through notation and know they will be followed down to the minutest phrase, the choreographer must wait until the dance material—the actual bodies with their strengths and weaknesses—is in front of him before working out the complete pattern.

The dancers worked like fiends. They knew they had to. The Ballet Russe had to prove itself to America, where they had cast their lot. And they had stiff competition. Rumors drifted backstage that Ballet Theater was readying a dazzling repertoire that season. The dancers knew that the success or failure of the de Mille ballet would decide whether they were to continue as a company.

Rodeo was presented October 16, 1942, at the Metropolitan Opera House. As Miss de Mille explains in *Dance to the Piper*, she was acutely conscious that this event was the pivotal point of her career. "If it is possible for a life to change at one given moment, if it is possible for all movement, growth and accumulated power to become apparent at one single point, then my hour struck at 9:40 October 16, 1942. Chewing gum, squinting under a Texas hat, I turned to face what I had been preparing for the whole of my life."

The ballet had that combination of trigger quickness and drawling nonchalance that characterizes the cowboy's world. The audience applauded and shouted. There were twenty-two curtain calls. At the eighth, Miss de Mille saw the violinists in the orchestra pit beating their bows on their instruments and the other musicians standing, applauding—a rare sight and the sign of definite approval. Unmistakably it was an ovation. This success was followed by successes all along the tour route. "As American as Mark Twain," said Alfred Frankenstein in the San Francisco *Chronicle*. The Los Angeles audience, packed to the roof, went wild with excitement. But more than any critic or audience praise, Agnes de Mille treasured her father's words: "My daughter, you have come a long way. I am so proud."

Few realized then that *Rodeo*, uniting folk dance, modern dance, and classical ballet, would form a turning point in American ballet history, but they all realized that here was something they liked and wanted. Miss de Mille was besieged with offers from Hollywood. But she headed back to New York. In the enthusiastic opening night audience for *Rodeo* were composer Richard Rodgers, playwright and lyricist Oscar Hammerstein, and the Theater Guild staff. They were working on a new musical called *Away We Go*. Mr. Hammerstein hoped to use Miss de Mille and she signed a contract to choreograph the dances for the show. After the Boston run the name of the show was changed. When it opened on Broadway it was called *Oklahoma!*

The next few months were the most crucial of her life. Besides preparing the dances for *Oklahoma!*—it was presented in New York only five months after *Rodeo*—she was involved in plans for her coming marriage. It took place in June 1943, three months after *Oklahoma!* opened, when her soldier fiancé, Walter Prude, got his first furlough. In the interim, she was hard put to it to stick out rehearsals, with him away at a training camp in the Southwest. But she managed somehow to make the two motifs of her life synchronize.

With *Rodeo* she had been an innovator in the world of ballet. But with *Oklahoma!* she made a revolution on the Broadway stage—brought to an end the dance line routine of high kicks and mechanized movement, and gave in its place dance and plot smoothly integrated, choreography abetting the action. Twenty-five years later, in March 1968, a *New York Times* article by theater critic Walter Kerr, headed "In the Beginning Was *Oklahoma!*" stated, "*Oklahoma!* had a plot. It had to do with whether a boy would succeed in taking a girl to a picnic lunch. At the end of the first half this great issue was still unresolved, so unresolved that its emotional implications had to be danced out at great length in what remains the most exhilarating dancing—and, for that matter, the sexiest—ever devised for the American musical comedy stage."

The impact of *Oklahoma!* was instantaneous. The song "Beautiful Morning" sounded out via radios in restaurants, from cars passing on the highways, in shoeshine parlors. Full-skirted ginghams, street shoes made to look like ballet slippers,

Agnes de Mille

the ponytail hairdo, were the rage. The play ran for five years and nine weeks in New York City. A traveling road company played it for nine and a half years. It opened in London in April 1947 and ran for three and a half years there. It zoomed into Copenhagen, then into South Africa, Australia, and New Zealand. The last United States road company closed in December 1954. In 1955 it became a movie. A newly assembled all-star company was sent to Paris and Rome by the State Department as representative of our culture. In 1969 a company played all summer at the New York State Theater.

As for Agnes de Mille, her days of giving recitals and losing $300 to $1000 each time were over. She became the most sought-after choreographer on Broadway. In the winter of 1944 she had three musicals she had choreographed playing on the Great White Way at once: *Oklahoma!*, *One Touch of Venus*, and *Bloomer Girl*. In 1947 she staged the book and dances of an entire Broadway musical, *Allegro*, the first dance-director and the first woman ever to do so. Year after year they came, the musicals—*Carousel*, *Brigadoon*, *Gentlemen Prefer Blondes*, *Paint Your Wagon*—with dancing and plot inextricably intertwined. In *Carousel* whole scenes are portrayed entirely in dance. In *Brigadoon* the dances are the very substance of the show.

Not even Broadway was sufficient for Miss de Mille's talents. In 1944 she created *Tally-Ho* for the Ballet Theater group, and danced the part of the errant wife, "her tiny feet in little red shoes scarcely seeming to touch the ground." Other newspaper comments through the years—"an earthy quality," "comic genius," "half laughter, half tears" "sensibility of line," "a sense of humor"—show the many sides of her appeal.

Two successes marked the year 1948: the ballet *Fall River Legend*, a series of flashbacks in the life of Lizzie Borden of

Agnes de Mille

the famous murder case, and the direction of *The Rape of Lucretia*, an opera by Benjamin Britten. In the ballet *Harvests According* (1952) she leaned toward abstraction. In 1953–1954 she toured with her own dance company, the Agnes de Mille Dance Theater, covering 126 cities in twenty-six weeks, in a repertoire that included dances from *Paint Your Wagon, Brigadoon, Bloomer Girl,* and concert pieces. In 1955 she choreographed the movie version of *Oklahoma!* and the next year she herself danced in *Rodeo* when it was presented at Covent Garden, in London, England. Now she began her series of dance lecture programs over CBS-TV for *Omnibus* and Seven Lively Arts.

All through this period, with a growing son, a happy family life with much entertaining, and her own career expanding, she yet confesses herself on the horns of a dilemma. "If only I could choose," she says, "could live one way or another, cut my pattern clean—be like other women, simply a wife and mother, or, like great artists, sure and undivided. But all parts of me are set against each other."

Still she forged on. In 1962, the year she received the annual American National Theater and Academy (ANTA) award, she attended every single rehearsal for the revival of *Brigadoon.* In 1963 she choreographed her seventeenth Broadway musical, *110 in the Shade.* In 1965, when Ballet Theater celebrated its twenty-fifth birthday, she was represented with four ballets (more than any other choreographer), two of them new: *The Wind in the Mountains* and *The Four Marys,* and two revivals, *Frail Quarry,* a restaging of *Tally-Ho,* and *Fall River Legend.* She has done four works for the Royal Winnipeg Ballet: *Bitter Weird, Golden Age, Rehearsal,* and in 1969, *Fall River Legend.* She appeared in *Rehearsal* herself on tour and at Hunter College, New York, in 1965. In 1966 she was commissioned by Lincoln Center for the Performing Arts in New York to create major works for television. This year, too, she received the Capezio Award for service to the dance.

Active in legislation to improve the lot of the dancer both financially and socially, she has helped to repeal the New York State law making it illegal to dance on Sunday, and to get basic minimum salaries for dancers. As cofounder and president of the Society of Stage Directors and Choreographers she was possibly the only woman president of a labor union in the United States. In June 1969, she was invited as the guest of the Soviet government to be the only American representative on the panel of judges for the International Ballet Competition held in Moscow that month. She was a member of the first National Advisory Council on the Arts, appointed by the President of the United States. She holds eleven honorary doctorates. She writes extensively for magazines. Her books *Dance to the Piper, And Promenade Home*, and *Lizzie Borden, a Dance of Death*, besides being of high literary quality, are human documents of great appeal. Her textbook, *Book of the Dance*, is a standard in its field, as is her *To a Young Dancer*. These books have been translated into six languages.

So crowded is her present schedule, so rich her life, that if we can join the critics in saying, "In the beginning was *Oklahoma!*" neither we, nor they, can possibly predict what her future may hold.

BIBLIOGRAPHY

CLYMER, ELEANOR, and ERLICH, LILLIAN, *Modern American Career Women*. New York: Dodd, Mead & Company, 1959.

Agnes de Mille

DE MILLE, AGNES, *And Promenade Home* (autobiography). Boston: Little, Brown and Company, 1958.
———, *Dance to the Piper*. Boston: Little, Brown and Company, 1952.
MCCONNELL, JANE, *Famous Ballet Dancers*. New York: Thomas Y. Crowell Company, 1955.

EMILY DICKINSON

EMILY DICKINSON: Born in Amherst, Massachusetts, December 10, 1830. Died in Amherst, May 15, 1886. Father: Edward Dickinson; mother: Emily Elizabeth Dickinson; brother: William Austin; sister: Lavinia Norcross.

*

The children on their way home from school would see her kneeling in the yard on a red army blanket, pruning and weeding her flowers. She sewed well—made slippers for her father, a bookmark for a friend, stockings for all the members of her family. She won a prize for her "rye and Indian bread" at the Cattle Show held in Amherst in 1856. In these ways she did what proper women of her day were expected to do. She also wrote deathless poetry. Her pranks of grammar, her experiments in oblique rhymes, her verbalized nouns, the setting off of the stupendous against the minute, the terrible against the trivial, the similes that shake the very planks of the soul, even what was once considered her "morbidity"—these are now given universal acclaim. Today she is accounted one of the most readable, the most understandable, the most inspiring, poets of her own or any age.

*

HER home was the first brick residence built (by her grandfather) in Amherst, Massachusetts, then a little country town of four or five hundred families. The house had five chimneys, beautifully spaced windows and doorways, and balustraded stairways which led up to the second floor, where her bedroom and those of her parents and her brother and sister were. Her own little room had straw matting on the floor, white curtains at the windows, and a cherrywood bureau, where Emily tucked away her poems, one by one, as she wrote them. Just outside her window was a pine tree, so close that she would listen to its whispering at night.

The house had spacious grounds. Emily loved to wander along the garden paths and in the grove of oaks at the back. Her father was a rigid Puritan, and in his daily life, as lawyer, legislator, and treasurer of Amherst College, was, as she said, "too busy with his briefs to notice what we do." Still, he presented her with a shaggy dog, which she named Carlo and took with her on her walks. He also presented her with a piano and saw that she had lessons. He was a considerable figure in her life. "If father is asleep on the lounge, the house is full," she once said.

Emily and her younger sister, Lavinia, were close companions. Emily would confide secrets to her she would tell to no one else. Emily's older brother, Austin, shared with her a deep love of nature and books. He would bring home books of the more progressive sort, unlike the solemn legal and religious volumes in her father's library. Emily's mother was self-effacing, devoted to her husband, but often in poor health. Emily said once of her: she "does not care for thought."

After Emily graduated from Amherst Academy, her father sent her to Mount Holyoke Seminary, at South Hadley, founded just ten years before by Mary Lyon, famous advocate of higher education for women. Emily liked her classmates and they liked her—gathered around her at recess to hear her tell amusing stories. She also did well in her school subjects: history, English grammar, chemistry, physiology, algebra, astronomy. But she did not measure up in the religious practices then considered essential to proper living. It was not only that she did not believe in the current Calvinistic doctrine of Hell and "original sin." It was also a simple inability on her part to become convinced that she was "saved." Thus she was assigned, according to the rigid tenets of the day, to the category of those "without hope of God." This, to the authorities, was of graver concern than if she had failed in her studies.

When she was eighteen, her school days were over. Around this time she met Benjamin Franklin Newton, a young man who was serving his apprenticeship in her father's law office and who came often as a guest to the Dickinson home. He introduced her to a whole new world of books, unorthodox ones, for he was a searcher and a questioner. He gave her Emerson's *Poems*, this even before that great thinker had become widely accepted. Most important, he told her she was on the way to becoming a poet herself. When Newton went back to his home town, Worcester, to serve his apprenticeship in an office there, he wrote Emily suggesting special reading in philosophy, religion, and poetry.

It was well he offered her such outlets just then, because the walls of her brown brick house were becoming the backdrop for a round of household chores. She wrote a friend on May 7, 1850, that her mother was "still" an invalid and that her father and brother clamored for her cooking. And she did not like housework. At one time she said, "House is being cleaned. I prefer pestilence."

Five years after she had met Benjamin Newton, he died, a victim of tuberculosis. She described him as a friend "who taught me Immortality; but venturing too near, himself, he never returned." It was probably this loss that sent Emily Dickinson into the most spirit-deepening and sustaining relationship of her life. In April 1854, on the way home after a three week stay in Washington, D.C., where her father was serving as a member of Congress, she and her sister visited one of Emily's former schoolmates in Philadelphia. While there, she is believed to have heard a sermon by the Reverend Charles Wadsworth, pastor of the Arch Street Presbyterian Church, the most noted preacher in that city. She was probably introduced to him afterward and talked briefly with him. It is likely she poured out to him at the time her grief over her friend's death, and he must have lent an understanding ear. A letter still extant states he hopes he may be able to help her in her spiritual difficulties. At any rate, the impact of his personality on this shy young woman was instantaneous and permanent. She said of his preaching that he worked on his hearers and at the fitting moment dealt "one imperial thunderbolt that scalps your naked soul."

But the Reverend Wadsworth was stable in his profession; happily married; honored in his work. He was not geared to respond to her young fervency with anything but fatherly solicitude. Still their friendship, which lasted throughout his lifetime, served to widen Emily's intellectual and emotional horizons.

She came home to an outward turmoil that matched her inner mood. The tenant who since the early 1840's had been occupying the Dickinson ancestral home died, and in 1855 the family moved back into the house. She was not able to cope with the practicalities of packing, unpacking, and rearranging her effects. She spoke of a lost feeling, of being "out with lanterns looking for myself."

In 1856 Emily's brother, Austin, married Susan Gilbert, a long-time friend of Emily's. The couple settled down next door in a home built especially for them by Emily's father. The strong unity of the Dickinson family might have encouraged Emily in a tendency, which became evident about this time, to withdraw from the doings of the town. Whatever the cause, this once gay girl, participant in sleigh rides, sugaring-off parties, picnics, sewing circles, and sociables, gradually began to confine herself to a very small circle of friends and a very narrow round of activities. In this shrinking from the world, however, Emily was not unlike hundreds of other unmarried women of her day, who, hemmed in by the endless round of sewing, cooking, and cleaning, built a world of romance about some chance look, a handclasp, a sigh; except that, with Emily, circumstances gave substance to the dream. Her genius made it possible for her inner world to blossom in phenomenal fashion.

Early in 1860 the Reverend Wadsworth called on her. Probably unaware of the paramount part he played in her life, he decided, since he was visiting a friend in nearby Northampton, to drop in on the young lady he had advised in Philadelphia.

On entering the room where he waited, Emily noticed he was wearing mourning, and her reaction, as biographer George Frisbie Whicher points out, might have been to nourish a "wild illicit hope." In any case, she asked quickly, "Someone has died?" The delay of a split second in his reply, "My mother," might have stabilized the mood that had formed her question—his wife, had she passed away? Whatever wild hopes found a place in her mind at that time, it is certain that for the rest of her life she held herself as dedicated to him. She was to speak of him as her "dearest earthly friend," as "the fugitive whom to know was life." It is likely he called on her again the next year and told her of his impending departure for San Francisco, to take a pastorate there. "I had a terror since September I could tell to none," she later wrote a friend. Wadsworth sailed for his new pastorate May 1, 1862. The two did not see each other again for twenty years.

At the time of his departure, not surprisingly, Emily launched desperately into a sea of poetry. In 1862 she composed more than 360 poems, some 150 the next year, and more than 100 the next. She wrote them down on bits of paper, the margins of newspapers, the backs of envelopes. These poems already showed her gift for conveying the truth but conveying it "slant," and her genius for compressing similes: the sun rises "a ribbon at a time," a storm calls out "a strange mob of panting trees," trains "lick the valley up," wild flowers "kindle in the woods," clouds are "listless elephants," gentlewomen have "dimity convictions," frost is "the blond assassin." She assembled her poems into packets, folding and threading them so their pages turned like little books. In this year, too, she began her custom of dressing only in white. Lavinia, who was small like her sister, had the dressmaker fit Emily's dresses to herself, to spare this shy sister from embarrassment.

Emily craved the judgment of an expert on her poems. In the April 1862 issue of *Atlantic Monthly* magazine she saw a "Letter to a Young Contributor," penned by a well-known author and critic of the day, Thomas Wentworth Higginson. It contained an invitation to beginning writers to submit their works. Emily sent him some of her verses. "Are you too deeply occupied to say if my Verse is alive?" she wrote. "Could you tell me how to grow, or is it unconveyed, like melody or witchcraft?" She enclosed four of the poignant poems she was then writing: "Safe in their Alabaster Chambers," "I'll tell you how the Sun rose," "We play at Paste," and "The nearest Dream recedes unrealized." Higginson read them and was held by their freshness. He answered her note hopefully, wanted to hear more about her. This one bit of encouragement, she later told him, had saved her life.

From then on, Higginson became her teacher-friend, answering her letters—she wrote hundreds to him—giving her literary advice. But Higginson was hopelessly enmeshed in the literary formalities of his day. He felt she must change, must eliminate her peculiarities, before she published. Her verses, he said, were not conventional, were not suitable—he seemed to find it hard himself to put his finger on what was wrong with them. In any case, by June 1862, on the verdict of this chance-chosen mentor, Emily had become resigned to a life of poetic obscurity.

By then her withdrawal was almost complete. When her old friend Samuel Bowles returned in November 1862 from a summer in Europe, she remained in her room, only sending down a welcome home note.

During the following years, between stints of baking and sewing and gardening, she occupied herself with her jottings on scraps of paper. Only on rare occasions did she show herself to guests—an elflike creature, light of step, with eyes, as she herself described them, "like the sherry in the glass the guest leaves." Sometimes she would sit outside the parlor listening to conversations and to music, a dim blur of white in the hallway.

Letters poured from her pen—more than a thousand of them are extant today—letters to former schoolmates, to relatives, to acquaintances in Amherst. She felt there should always be a personal interaction in communications. When a friend once addressed a letter to both Lavinia and herself, she objected: "A mutual plum is not a plum. I was too respectful to take the pulp and do not like a stone. Send no union letters. The soul must go by Death alone, so, it must by life, if it is a soul. If a committee—no matter."

In her closest seclusion she was still an avid reader of newspapers. Current events, even macabre ones, interested her. She wrote a friend who was on a newspaper, "Who writes those funny accidents, where railroads meet each other unexpectedly, and gentlemen in factories get their heads cut off quite informally? The author, too, relates them in such a sprightly way, that they are quite attractive. Vinnie was disappointed to-night that there were not more accidents—I read the news aloud while Vinnie was sewing."

Emily Dickinson

Late in 1869 the Reverend Wadsworth returned from California to take up a pastorate in Philadelphia again, and their correspondence, if it had ever lapsed, was resumed. He did not at this time come to Amherst.

In the late summer of 1870 Mr. Higginson wrote that he would be in the vicinity and would like to see her, and Emily wrote back that she "would be at home and glad." That visit gave the world probably the best word picture we have of Emily Dickinson. In a letter to his wife, written shortly after the interview, he described her entrance: "A step like a pattering child's in entry & in glided a little plain woman with two smooth bands of reddish hair . . . in a very plain and exquisitely clean white piqué & a blue net worsted shawl. She came to me with two day lilies, which she put in a sort of childlike way into my hand & said 'These are my introduction' in a soft, frightened breathless childlike voice—and added under her breath, 'Forgive me if I am frightened; I never see strangers and hardly know what I say'—but she talked soon & thenceforward continuously—& deferentially —sometimes stopping to ask me to talk instead of her, but readily recommencing." She seemed to speak, he added, "absolutely for her own relief and wholly without watching its effects on her hearer." After the visit she wrote Higginson, "The vein cannot thank the artery."

One is glad that no echo reached Emily's ears of the letters Higginson wrote others, calling her "my partially cracked poetess," nor of the parodies some of his cowriters made of her literary style, using as copy parts of her letters to him. But he had his insights, too. Of her seclusion he wrote her, "Yet it isolates one anywhere to think beyond a certain point, or have such flashes as come to you—so perhaps the place does not make much difference."

Emily Dickinson's family pattern was disrupted in June of 1874 when her father died, and a year after when her mother suffered a paralytic stroke. Emily became her mother's nurse; and now, it seems, for the first time a feeling of closeness developed between the two. She wrote Higginson that "little wayfaring acts" filled her days. When he asked had she time for poetry, she answered, "I have no other playmate."

During the last decade of her life Emily Dickinson lived largely in the rush and surge of her own thoughts. On October 10, 1876, Helen Hunt Jackson, author of the widely acclaimed novel *Ramona* and a poet of ephemeral fame, made a special call on her—to ask if she might include a poem or so of Emily's in a collection she was making up, *A Masque of Poets*. Mrs. Jackson was a native of Amherst and the two had played together as schoolgirls. But now she was a world traveler, famous, twice married. She must have stood in surprising contrast to the slender spiritlike recluse. Mrs. Jackson, in a later letter, after apologizing for having told Emily she lived too much away from the sun, wrote, ". . . you seemed so white and moth-like [and] your hand felt like such a wisp in mine that you frightened me—I felt like a great ox, talking to a white moth and begging it to come and eat grass with me to see if it could turn into beef!" At this visit she did not obtain Emily's consent but it seems in the end Emily tacitly allowed Mrs. Jackson to go ahead with the printing so long as she was not apprised of the matter. So the poet of posthumous fame was included, if anonymously, among the "great unknowns" of the time. It was Emily Dickinson's poem, "Success," that was used.

Then in 1880 came what was perhaps the most heartwarming surprises of her life. One late afternoon in summer, when she was out tending her lilies and heliotropes, the doorbell rang and a servant answered. Lavinia, hearing the interchange at the door, told Emily in surprise, "The gentleman with the deep voice wants to see *you*, Emily" and disappeared. So Emily came indoors and went into the parlor. The Reverend Wadsworth was standing quietly near the door.

Emily Dickinson

The wisps of the meeting that later got into her letters tell only of her asking, "Why didn't you tell me you were coming, so that I could have it to anticipate?" and of his answering, "Because I did not know myself. I stepped from my pulpit to the train." When she asked him how long it had taken him to make the journey, he replied, with a head shake, "Twenty years." During the visit he spoke about his younger son, William, who, he said, reminded him of Emily. He was interested in such curious things—frogs, for instance. Emily said she always thought of frogs as her watchdogs. Wadsworth smiled. So the talk went. It was to be their last. Less than two years after, on April 1, 1882, her "dearest earthly friend" was dead.

Her mother, whom she had for seven years nursed devotedly, died on November 14 of the same year. In October of the following year, her favorite nephew, Gilbert, succumbed to typhoid fever, at the age of eight.

Judge Otis Lord, an old friend of her father's and a widower, would sometimes leave his legal practice in Salem and come to Amherst. He would stay at the inn there for a week or so and drop in on the sisters. He became the object around which Emily now wove the threads of her emotional life. She speaks of a book she sent him: "I was reading a little Book—because it broke my Heart and I want it to break yours. Will you think that fair?" When he became seriously ill, she sent word she had just been writing him a letter when "Vinnie came in from a word with Austin . . . 'Mr. Lord is very sick.' I grasped at a passing Chair. My sight slipped and I thought I was freezing." A helper around the grounds, Tom, came in "and I ran to his Blue Jacket and let my Heart break there . . . that was the warmest place. 'He will be better. Don't cry Miss Emily. I could not see you cry.'"

In 1883 Thomas Niles of Roberts Brothers Publishers asked Emily to submit a volume of her poems for publication, and Helen Hunt Jackson seconded his plea. "What portfolios full of verses you must have!" she wrote. "It is a cruel wrong to your 'day and generation' that you will not give them light." But when this letter came in late 1884, Emily Dickinson was already immune to such suggestions. On March 13 of that year Judge Lord had died. "How to repair my shattered ranks is a besetting pain"—and one day late in May she herself had had a nervous collapse. For the remainder of her life she would be a semi-invalid, stirring about her room, but scarcely ever leaving it.

She could still turn a charming phrase, however. Writing to her aunt, Elizabeth Currier, a month before her death, she said, "I haven't felt quite as well as usual since the chestnuts were ripe, though it wasn't the Chestnuts' fault." Then, on April 15, 1886, she wrote, as far as is known, her last complete letter. It was to a friend of Wadsworth's, and it described that last memorable meeting with him. "But the loved voice has ceased," it ended.

Nine of Emily Dickinson's poems were published during her lifetime, most of them in the Springfield *Republican* newspaper and anonymously. When her marvelous poem about a snake, "A narrow Fellow in the Grass," was published on February 14, 1866, her friend Samuel Bowles had only this comment to make: "How did that girl ever know that a boggy field wasn't good for corn?"

After Emily's death, Lavinia found in the small cherry bureau hundreds and hundreds of her sister's poems, carefully stitched into little booklets. She decided they must be brought to light. Finally, with the help of Mr. Higginson and Mabel Loomis Todd, Lavinia succeeded in having 117 of Emily's poems printed. Today more than 1,700 have been published. Emily Dickinson once wrote, "If fame belonged to me, I could not escape her; if she did not, the longest day would pass me on the chase." She also wrote a brief poem on fame:

"Fame is a bee./ It has a song—/ It has a sting—/ Ah, too, it has a wing." She at least had been spared its sting.

BIBLIOGRAPHY

CHASE, RICHARD VOLNEY, *Emily Dickinson.* New York: Dell Publishing Company, Inc., 1965.

DICKINSON, EMILY NORCROSS, *Letters,* edited by Mabel Loomis Todd, new and enlarged edition. New York: Harper & Brothers, 1931.

JOHNSON, THOMAS HERBERT, *Emily Dickinson: An Interpretive Biography.* Cambridge, Massachusetts: The Belknap Press of Harvard University Press, 1955.

SEWELL, RICHARD BENSON, ed., *Emily Dickinson; a Collection of Critical Essays.* Englewood Cliffs, New Jersey: Prentice-Hall, Inc., 1963.

WHICHER, GEORGE FRISBIE, *This Was a Poet; a Critical Biography of Emily Dickinson.* New York: Charles Scribner's Sons, 1938.

DOROTHEA DIX

DOROTHEA (LYNDE) DIX: Born in Hampden, Maine, April 4, 1802. Died in Trenton, New Jersey, July 18, 1887. Father: Joseph Dix; mother: Mary (Bigelow) Dix; brothers: Joseph, Charles Wesley.

*

Dorothea Dix revolutionized the status and treatment of the mentally ill the world over, popularizing the idea of institutional treatment for mental cases and making mental institutions themselves more humane and constructive. By the end of her life she could point to at least 123 asylums and hospitals built through her efforts.

*

DOROTHEA was born in a little hut in Maine, where her father and mother had been sent, shortly after their marriage, by her grandfather Dr. Elijah Dix, who owned vast tracts of land there. The bride was almost twenty years older than her husband, and was moreover considered unstable. Dr. Dix, senior, thought sending them away to this comparatively isolated region would force them to work out their problems for themselves.

It didn't turn out that way. In Maine her father took both to religious fanaticism and to drink. Before wandering off on his long preaching trips, he would have tracts printed up, and the young Dorothea would stitch them together, pushing the long needle in and out of the coarse paper till her small fingers ached. After her two brothers were born, and her mother had become a chronic invalid, she nursed her mother and cared for her young brothers.

Things were quite different when she went on brief visits to her paternal grandparents at the Dix mansion in Boston. Here she had her own little bedroom and good food to eat, and she often went with her grandfather on flower-studying walks or to see the bright bottles on the shelves of his apothecary shop. But she almost wished she was back in Maine when she heard her grandparents talk in low tones of how her father had been expelled from Harvard for marrying "that woman," and of how he had since gone "queer in the head."

When she was seven years old, her grandfather died, and the visits to Boston ceased—that is, until one day when she was twelve she suddenly appeared alone on her grandmother's doorstep. Whether her own father in a lucid moment had put her on the stagecoach, or whether she had just run away, she would never say. Anyway, her grandmother, though almost seventy, took care of her for two years, then sent her to Worcester to the home of her sister, Sarah Lynde Duncan, and her sister's daughter, Sarah Fiske. Here Dorothea became acquainted for the first time with carefree children, her young cousins. She told them stories as she had told her younger brothers stories back in Maine. An older cousin, hearing her, said she would make a good teacher. So, when she was only fourteen, Dorothea let out the hem of her skirt, brushed her red-brown hair smoothly back from her face to a knot in the back, and opened a "dame school" in a room over the bookstore on Main Street in Worcester. Here each child paid a small fee for the privilege of learning reading, writing, and arithmetic, and hearing, through her "stories," about the wonders of everyday life: the wind, the rain, rocks, stars, how flowers grow. Dorothea Dix was later to write a book called *Conversations on Common Things*, which became very popular as a textbook.

After teaching school for three years, she returned, a tall, slim lady with her most difficult years behind her, to her grandmother's in Boston. To prepare herself to teach more advanced grades, she borrowed books from the Boston library, had tutors for some subjects, and after two years of study started a school for older children in the gardener's cottage. Later, when the attendance increased, she transferred it to her grandmother's house.

During this period she joined the Unitarian Church and came under the influence of the great reformer Dr. William Ellery Channing, who was preacher there. During this period she also formed a friendship with Ann Heath, a shy girl, who was sympathetic with Dorothea's projects. They were to keep up a steady correspondence for fifty years, until Ann's death in 1878.

With the thought of aiding the poor children of the town, Dorothea approached her grandmother for permission to start a "charity school" in the hayloft over the carriage house. "Let me rescue some of America's miserable children from vice and guilt," she pled. At first her grandmother said no, the children would bring in diseases. Besides Dorothea was already teaching one school. But in the end she gave in. "Have your school for beggars, then!" Dorothea called the school, The Hope.

Teaching two schools, studying way into the night to keep ahead of her pupils, preparing school books—she wrote eight in five years—and, as her grandmother edged into her mid-seventies, helping to manage the household, Dorothea established work habits which were to be hers for life: up at four in the summer, at five in winter; working through the day; then writing letters often dated after midnight.

Dr. Channing and his wife invited her to spend summers as governess to their daughters, at their Rhode Island home overlooking Narragansett Bay. So for three summers Dorothea sat at the table of this intensely alive reformer, took walks with him, and absorbed his philosophy that all men should have an equal opportunity for self-culture, for progress in knowledge, for health, comfort, and happiness. He believed—and in his day this doctrine was revolutionary—"that the great end of government is to spread a shield over the rights of all."

Then in 1836, when she was thirty-four years old and had been school-teaching for some fifteen years all told, Dorothea suffered a nervous and physical collapse and was ordered off to Italy to rest and recuperate. But she did not get that far. Arriving in Liverpool, England, in a state of prostration, she was met by a friend of Dr. Channing's, Dr. William Rathbone, a well-known philanthropist, and was transported to his home near Liverpool. For eighteen months he and his wife were to care for her. She was, as she said, "adopted into this circle of living spirits." They did more than nurse her back to health. They introduced her to many of their friends, among them Samuel Tuke, builder of a modern mental hospital, The Retreat of York, where the mentally ill were provided with books to read and music to listen to. He told her of the terrible conditions of the insane in many parts of England—left without civilized comforts, thrown their food as if they were animals, put on display for a fee.

Recovered, at least partially, Dorothea returned to an America now changed for her. Her grandmother had died during her absence, and the money she had previously saved while teaching, plus her grandmother's legacy, brought her enough to live on.

For four years now she was a wandering invalid, searching for health, staying winters with friends in Alexandria, Virginia, and elsewhere in the South, and spending summers in boarding houses in Boston and thereabouts. Wherever she was she haunted libraries, looking especially for books on the treatment of the insane. In the Spring of 1841—she was thirty-nine then—she returned, restless and dissatisfied, to Boston. A young man was sent from the Channings to tell her someone was needed to read the Bible Sundays to a group of some twenty women convicts in the East Cambridge jail. She told him she would go herself.

In the early nineteenth-century paupers, criminals, and the insane were all confined together, as if all were equally guilty of crimes. It was generally believed that the insane were "possessed of devils," were perverted in their souls, were outside the human category. Jailers often thought of themselves as instruments chosen to punish these poor deranged people. But Dorothea had heard, at the church, more enlightened individuals talk of the awful conditions the insane suffered in dark caverns under the East Cambridge jail. So now, after reading the Bible lesson to the women at the jail, she asked the jailer's wife to show her the basement vault. Her own notes tell the story: "So terribly noxious was the poisoned air . . . that a considerable time elapsed before I was able to remain long enough to investigate . . . . The place had no light or ventilation . . . all was stone . . . [I saw] a human being on filthy straw . . . tangled hair fell about his shoulders . . . . emaciated to a shadow, an iron ring encircled his leg. 'In winter,' said the mistress, 'my husband rakes out sometimes of a morning half a bushel of frost, and yet he never freezes . . . . Sometimes he screams dreadful and that is the reason we had the double walls and had two doors instead of one; his cries disturb the house.'"

As Dorothea walked away, the phrase "and yet he never freezes" kept ringing in her ears. She went to Dr. Channing, who, after hearing her description, suggested she talk with three of Boston's prominent citizens: Horace Mann, educator; Charles Sumner, politician and statesman; and Dr. Samuel Gridley Howe, philanthropist. She told them she was sure that such things were happening all over Massachusetts and that the legislators should take steps in the matter. Mr. Mann pointed out that before anything could be done someone must visit the jails and almshouses in the state and present a report, all of which would take considerable time and money. Dorothea told them, "I intend to make the survey myself."

So, during the next eighteen months, at her own expense, Dorothea Dix traveled, notebook in hand, down back roads, along furtive paths, to outhouses, barns, sheds, stalls, visiting some five hundred jails, almshouses, and workhouses from the Berkshires to Cape Cod. She saw arms and legs pinioned, bodies cut with whiplashes, necks bowed beneath fetters. Evenings, by candlelight, she jotted down notes on her day's work: "*Dedham*—woman who seemed to be quite sane tied in a dark stall behind the almshouse. No one can recall why she had been put there; *Medford*—a man in a stall for seventeen years; *Shelburne*—an old naked man with his feet frozen off, the stumps in chains."

She had started out on her survey from the Channings' at 85 Mt. Vernon Street, and she came back there to find Mrs. Channing in mourning. Dr. Channing had died. It seemed almost as if he had been spared just long enough to convince her of her mission.

In a room at the back of Mrs. Channing's house she prepared her report. In those days such reports were called *memorials*, but the word had a special significance for her. Her report was to be a memorial to her friend's good influence. Presented to the legislature by member Dr. Howe, it read, "Gentlemen of Massachusetts: I have come to present to you the strong claims of suffering humanity. I come as the advocate of the helpless, forgotten, insane men and women held in cages, closets, cellars, stalls, pens; chained, naked, beaten with rods and lashed into obedience . . . ." The legislators were asked to vote funds to build a large state hospital.

When the memorial was publicized, the overseers of the

Dorothea Dix

almshouses denied inhuman treatment. Dorothea Dix wrote articles for the newspapers, the Boston *Advertiser,* the Boston *Courier,* describing the abuses. Readers said her statements were untrue, and anyway how could a decent woman allow herself to go to such places. "Such assertions must be fought," said Horace Mann. Politician Charles Sumner volunteered to check on several of the worst places. He returned with the terse report, which he sent to the newspapers: "I am obliged to state these facts untrue *only* to the extent that neither her words nor mine can convey an adequate picture of the suffering seen in these places. In the name of humanity I urge immediate passage of her bill now before the Massachusetts legislature." Dr. Howe again addressed the legislators: "Gentlemen, I move for resolves on the hospital bill. I move we vote two hundred thousand dollars to build an addition to the state hospital for the insane at Worcester." The bill passed the legislature in February 1843.

If Massachusetts could be made to care for its mentally ill, so could other states. Dorothea's future pathway now seemed plain before her.

Between June 1843 and August 1847 this slim lady, in her neat gray dress with the white collar and cuffs, a bonnet on her head, a shawl around her shoulders, and a rug to cover her knees, traveled a total of thirty thousand miles, from Canada to the Gulf of Mexico, from the Atlantic to the Mississippi, over rocky roads, through swollen streams, the horses struggling in water sometimes up to the carriage floor; by sidewheel steamer down the Mississippi River; in coastal packet boat along sea-bordered states; through dense forests and mosquito-infected swamps. She contracted malaria which was to continue to plague her for years. At inns, cockroaches crawled over her baggage and rats ran across her bed. In lonely junctions, in waiting rooms, she read books on mental diseases.

Dorothea Dix

She went into dungeons, stepped into barricaded cells where even the keepers feared to go. Then she called state legislators to the inn where she was staying and in her low gentle voice reported her findings. She studied their faces. She avoided the suave members who said nice things but voted against her bills. Instead she singled out the hard-bitten country members who dressed in homespun and thought straight thoughts. She told a group of hostile legislators gathered in her landlady's front parlor in Trenton, New Jersey, "Gentlemen, outside there is a cold wind blowing from the Delaware . . . . Gentlemen, you came up State Street in your greatcoats lined with fur. Some of you wore heavy capes and woolen shawls besides. Gentlemen, on such a night the insane poor in the Shark River poorhouse lie without heat, bedding, or covering in a shed penetrated by the wind." In a Raleigh, North Carolina, boardinghouse she told a group of legislators, "I am the hope of the poor crazed beings who pine in cells and stalls and cages, and waste-rooms . . . of hundreds of wailing, suffering creatures hidden in your private dwellings, and in pens and in cabins."

This "terrible reformer but gentle lady" caused fury in high places. On January 25, 1845, Joseph Dodd rose in the Senate of New Jersey and presented a resolution suggesting a thousand dollars be voted "to get Miss Dix across the Delaware and out of the state!" (A cartoon in the newspapers showed her being carried on a rail across the Delaware River.) However, in the end, Trenton built a hospital, which was to be copied as a model throughout the land.

One after another of the state legislatures responded to her appeal, enacting laws to build adequate mental hospitals and improving those already built: New Jersey and Pennsylvania in 1845; Illinois and Mississippi in 1847; Tennessee and North Carolina in 1848. Hospitals began to go up, laws to change. In 1849 she presented a report to the Alabama legislature, followed by one to the legislative assembly at Province, Nova Scotia, Canada. On February 25, 1852, she petitioned for a state hospital in Maryland. Following each successful campaign for a new hospital, she marked that state with a cross on a map she carried with her.

Before long, states were urging her to come. She laid out a regular pattern of travel, canvassing the South from autumn to the following spring and going north during the summer. Ann Heath provided her with home-sewn dresses—gray for traveling, black for special occasions. The railroads provided her with passes, refusing even to accept money for the trunk she sent ahead.

Early in 1848 she read of the government's practice of ceding vast tracts of federal land to the various states as they entered the Union, for the establishment of schools, reservations, and parks. All of 100,000,000 acres had been given away and there was still that much more to give. She petitioned Congress for an appropriation of 5,000,000 acres (later raised to 12,225,000) for the use of the mentally ill. An alcove was set aside for her in the Capitol building in Washington, D.C., where she could interview members of Congress and round up supporters. The bill, presented in June 1848, was referred to a "select committee"; was "deferred" (1849); was brought up again but was held over (1850); was passed by the Senate (1851); but there was not time that session to put it to the House. Then on March 8, 1854, after endless proddings of the legislators, the bill finally passed the House. Dorothea was jubilant. Now all that was needed was President Franklin Pierce's signature. But "after long and serious deliberation" the President vetoed the bill, maintaining that it violated states' rights. The House failed to raise a two-thirds majority to override the veto, and the bill went down to defeat.

Sick at heart, Dorothea Dix turned her thoughts toward her friends, the Rathbones. In September 1854 she secured passage

Dorothea Dix

on the *Arctic*, bound for Liverpool. After a visit with them she went in January 1855 to Scotland and began her investigations there. She stirred up such a storm—they took to calling her "The American Invader"—that a Royal Commission was appointed "to inquire into conditions of lunatic asylums in Scotland." Then she visited the islands of Jersey and Guernsey in the English Channel where the "Insanity Trade"—causing patients to be transported from England, where laws concerning their treatment were stringent, to the Channel Islands, where they were lax—had created terrible conditions. There Dorothea had the leader of the "trade" taken into custody, with an ensuing change in laws.

Then, after a vacation in Switzerland with the Rathbones, which she was to remember as the most delightful interlude in her life, she traversed most of Europe, beginning with France, examining and bettering conditions in hospitals and asylums. She obtained an audience with the pope, causing him to appoint a commission "to lay before us a plan for an asylum." In Vienna she pressed for a new asylum in Dalmatia, then part of Austria. Next, traveling counterclockwise through Greece, Turkey, Russia, Germany, Norway, and Holland, with reports made on each country, she arrived in England for another visit with the Rathbones before sailing for America in September 1856.

She was welcomed home by a flood of letters: "We need fresh extensions," "We must have another hospital," "Please decide on a location for our new hospital." She must get larger appropriations, take note of possible sites for further hospitals—was the soil right? was the water supply plentiful and pure? were the surroundings attractive? Her reports to the legislators kept her "swinging like a pendulum" between state capitals.

The Civil War caused a change in her activities. In 1861 she was appointed Superintendent of Nurses for the Union

Army, serving, as she had served in all her activities, without pay. She selected and assigned women nurses, set up base hospitals in barns and tents, opened infirmaries in converted churches, schools, private houses, arsenals, and warehouses. She traveled to Baltimore and New York to examine places already caring for the wounded; tore up carpets, scrubbed down halls, commandeered cots, tried to deal with lice, dysentery, measles. For four years, without a single furlough, this small woman, frail in health, over sixty, slaved until she began to lose that self-control she had so carefully cultivated. Her voice became shrill and demanding. Doctors, drunk on duty, were to be court-martialed; superior officers were bypassed while she tried to right a wrong. Nurses applying for jobs were warned they must be "plain in appearance, no hoops, and no ribbons." Louisa May Alcott, who served as a nurse under her, called her "a kind old soul, but queer and arbitrary." Miss Dix herself said tersely, "This is not the work I would have my life judged by." But she stuck to her job. The United States government, recognizing her services, ordered that a fine set of flags, "A Stand of Arms of the United States National Colors," be presented to her. In her turn, she collected $8,000 for a monument in the National Cemetery in honor of those slain in battle. Then she returned to the cause that had first place in her heart.

Asylums scattered across the land were now her "children," requiring her protection and care. "To have Miss Dix suddenly arrive at your asylum," said Dr. Isaac Ray of Providence, "and find anything neglected or amiss, was considered worse than an earthquake." She would taste the soup, turn over the mattresses, inspect the heating arrangements, study the bookkeeping, give induction talks to the new nurses, and have long conversations with the patients. "Get warm rugs and cheerful pictures . . . plant old-fashioned gardens . . . train ivy up those walls . . . ."

Dorothea Dix

But she was tired. In 1881 she went for a rest to her "firstborn," the hospital in Trenton. She was never to leave it. The board set aside a roomy and comfortable apartment for her, where she could look out on the great sweep of the Delaware River. One day, not long before her death, she wrote to her friend the poet John Greenleaf Whittier, "I have a notion to see a fountain for animals set up in Boston on Milk Street, where I have often seen the tired draft horses pulling heavy loads to the docks and having no place to drink." After her death the fountain was erected, and Whittier wrote the inscription:

> Stranger and traveler
> Drink freely and bestow
> A kindly thought on her
> Who bade this fountain flow . . .

BIBLIOGRAPHY

BAKER, RACHEL, *Angel of Mercy; the Story of Dorothea Lynde Dix*. New York: Julian Messner, Inc., 1955.

BROOKS, GLADYS BILLINGS, *Three Wise Virgins*. New York: E. P. Dutton & Company, Inc., 1957.

DIX, DOROTHEA, *Memorial Asking for an Appropriation for the state penitentiary*. Illinois Senate Reports, 1849.

———, *Memorial in behalf of the pauper insane and idiots in jails and poorhouses throughout the commonwealth: To the Legislature of Massachusetts*. Boston: Munroe & Francis, 1843.

Dorothea Dix

MARSHALL, HELEN E., *Dorothea Dix; Forgotten Samaritan.* Chapel Hill: University of North Carolina Press, 1937.
TIFFANY, FRANCIS, *Life of Dorothea Lynde Dix.* Boston: Houghton Mifflin Company, 1890.

ISADORA DUNCAN

ISADORA DUNCAN: Born in San Francisco, California, May 27, 1878. Died near Nice, France, September 14, 1927. Father: Joseph Charles Duncan; mother: Mary Dora (Gray) Duncan; brothers: Augustin and Raymond; sister: Elizabeth; children: Deirdre and Patrick; husband: Sergei Esenin.

*

Isadora Duncan was a pioneer in demonstrating, to a dance world constructed around formal ballet movements and gestures, that the dance should be an expression directly of the mind and heart. Her way of simple motion—running, walking and leaping on the stage—brought changes in every aspect of the dance as it was then known. Under her influence the modern dance began to incorporate more meaningful movements. She revivified an art that had become esoteric and precious. Floyd Dell wrote in his book *Women as World Builders* that, because of Isadora Duncan, "the body is no longer to be separated in the thought of women from the soul."

*

THE Pacific Ocean—the rhythm of the waves—gave Isadora her first idea of movement. The flight of bees, the floating of clouds, the whirling of leaves, the opening of flowers, absorbed her. As a child of six she would collect the babies in the neighborhood, line them up on the floor—they were too young to walk—and have them wave their arms like swaying flowers. When she herself was taken to ballet school, she was irritated by what she felt were artificial movements. Standing balanced on the toes seemed "against nature" and therefore ugly. She left after the third lesson.

But swaying flowers and stirring waves were only one side of Isadora's life. Going to school with an empty stomach and sitting in school through rainy days with soggy feet because her shoes were worn through and she had no rubbers were also a part. Once she found her mother crying—Mrs. Duncan was keeping the family together by teaching music lessons and doing whatever else she could—because the dozen mittens she had knitted had not been called for by the people who had ordered them. Isadora peddled them from door to door. Other problems were less easily solved. Isadora had read George Eliot's novel *Adam Bede* and pondered the predicament of the mother with the child born out of wedlock. She knew her own mother had given up her Catholic religion when she had divorced Isadora's father for desertion. Putting these ideas together, she came to the conclusion, as she says in her autobiography, *My Life,* that she would never marry, never put herself into any man's keeping, that she would bear children when and as it pleased her. In short, the dream she tried her whole life to realize was the attainment of freedom without responsibility, release without rules. As the writer Max Eastman put it, "She had confused caprice with independence."

When Isadora was twelve years old her father paid her family a visit and "lent" them a big house with a tennis court, a barn, and a windmill. For a while after this, things went swimmingly. Isadora and her older sister, Elizabeth, started a dancing school in the house. They taught "natural movements," beginning with children's play actions—skipping, runing, jumping—since these had been Isadora's own way of learning to dance. Her brother Augustin opened a theater in the barn. The plays they put on became so popular that the four children toured the Pacific Coast, giving performances, Isadora also doing dance bits. But the success was short-lived. The house had to be sold for debts (the buyers found much of the woodwork chopped away—had the family needed it for firewood?)—and then it was the same old story: begging grocerymen for advances, moving from one dingy house or apartment to another, as the landlords pressed them for the rent. Some twenty-five years later, when Isadora came to San Francisco on tour as one of the leading dancers of the age, she spent almost a whole day just visiting the various places in which she had once lived.

Wherever they went in those early days, however, the piano followed them, and always in the evenings Isadora's mother played Schubert, Chopin, Mozart, Beethoven, while Isadora composed dances to the music. Often she would improvise far into the morning.

When she was eighteen Isadora called a family council. They were getting nowhere in San Francisco. They must go east. So she and her mother—the others stayed on in San Francisco for a while—went to Chicago, where Isadora found work dancing at the Masonic Roof Garden, billed as "The Californian Faun." When after a few months they were joined by her brothers and sister, they all went to New York, where a theatrical producer got Isadora a part as a dancing fairy in *A Midsummer Night's Dream*. In New York, society took her up. She was so slim and so pretty that most of the matrons excused her bare arms and legs—shocking in those days—as sheer innocence. Sometimes she danced to poems of Shelley, read by her sister. She had a recital in Carnegie Hall with composer Ethelbert Nevin. He played his own works at the piano, while she interpreted them in dance.

But her engagements were sporadic. Isadora decided her real future lay in Europe. The family boarded a cattle boat in May 1899, under the name O'Gorman—to protect their true name for the footlights—and arrived in England with no cash but boundless enthusiasm to start them off. A few socialites who had seen her dance in America invited her to their soirées, and she met Charles Hallé, the son of the famous conductor. He arranged a series of "evenings with Isadora Duncan," at which she not only danced but made little speeches about the dance. J. Fuller-Maitland, the music critic of the London *Times*, advised her to "dance to good music rather than recited poetry." Meanwhile she haunted museums, stood entranced before Greek urns and medieval paintings.

But money was just as scarce in London as in America. In 1900 she and her mother settled in with her brother Raymond, who lived in the artists' quarter in Paris in a bare loft over the clackity-clack of a printing press. At this point it would have been hard for anyone to believe that Isadora was at the beginning of a thirteen-year rise to fame unparalleled until then by any American woman on foreign soil.

In Paris she gradually became a salon favorite. Dancing barefoot, dressed in gauzy veils, she was fresh to eyes accustomed to the heavily clothed ballet dancers of the day. Her speech-making was as revolutionary as her dancing. "My Art is just an effort to express the truth of my Being in gesture and movement," "I only dance my life." Seeing her "experiencing the music, not just dancing to it," many Parisians sent their children to her to be taught. Before long she had a large group of pupils. One of her later pupils, Irma Duncan—Isadora adopted her, hence the name—in her book, *Duncan Dancer*, gives a glimpse of Isadora's method of teaching. Isadora had chosen the Brahms song "If I Were a Bird" for interpretation. "I flew about the room as if I were a bird," writes Irma. "When I stopped, I saw 'that look' on Isadora's face. I was terrified. No, she explained, the song did not say, 'I am a bird,' it said, 'If I *were* a bird.' It meant, 'I wish I could fly to you, but I am earth bound.' . . . She demonstrated with beautiful gestures how the dance should have been done. She had really thought out the language of movement."

Isadora's first flight into Continental fame came through the assistance of Loie Fuller, an American who had already captured Paris with her scarf dances and who had Isadora accompany her and her troupe on tour. When they reached Vienna, Isadora was given a place on the program. Here the impresario Alexander Grosz spotted her and booked her for a tour on her own. News of her popularity soon bridged the Atlantic: "California Girl Succeeds," "Isadora Duncan Pleases Berlin in her Classic Dances." Late in 1902 an American journalist wrote from Munich to the St. Louis *Sunday Gazette*, "To the accompaniment of simple music . . . she glides quietly to her appointed place. Her dress is some soft gray stuff with printed blossoms. And now with wreathing arms and undulating body and bare twinkling feet, she endeavors to present us the vibrant atmosphere, the pulsing, ecstatic quickening of all life . . . . Never an abrupt movement, never a sharp angle."

After a trip to Greece, where she studied the classic lines of the dance, she was invited to Bayreuth by Cosima Wagner, widow of the great composer Richard Wagner and herself director of the Wagner festival in this German town. Isadora was to lead the dancing in one of the productions. Her slight figure in the flowing tunic with sandals on bare feet—she walked on the street so clad, too—attracted festival visitors in and out of the theater. But there were negative reactions. She tells in *My Life* of Frau Cosima sending one of her daughters to her "with a long white chemise, which she begged me to wear under the filmy scarf which served me for a costume. But I was adamant. I would dress and dance exactly my way, or not at all."

Dancing in Berlin, Germany, in December 1904, she attracted the attention of Gordon Craig, son of famous English actress Ellen Terry, and himself a revolutionary stage designer. The two fell in love. Years later, in a radio address, he recalled, "She moved as no one had ever seen anyone move before." Soon a fierce battle was raging "between the genius of Gordon Craig and the inspiration of my Art." She left him, at least temporarily, and, during the month of January 1905, went alone on a tour of Russia. Sergei Diaghilev, the famous ballet impresario, maintained, "She gave an irreparable jolt to the classic ballet of Imperial Russia." Prince Peter Lieven, ballet authority, said she "was the first to bring out in her dancing the meaning of music, the first to *dance* the music and not dance *to* the music." Michel Fokine, famous dancer and choreographer, seeing her, began to use Greek themes and flowing lyric movements in his dances.

Returning to Berlin (and to Gordon Craig), Isadora bought, from the proceeds of her tour, a large villa in Grünewald, a suburb of Berlin, took in some twenty students, and started a school of the dance. At least three of the original students were to survive the ups and downs of a pupil-teacher relationship with Isadora, and themselves become teachers of the dance.

Her school had only just started when she had to turn it over to her sister, Elizabeth, while she went to Holland to await the birth of her baby. In a little village there by the sea Gordon Craig visited her now and then, but she felt "miserable and defeated." Then on September 24, 1905, Deirdre—the name was suggested by Craig—was born, and Isadora felt repaid for all the months of inactivity.

She returned to her work. It was high time. Her school was in financial trouble and the only answer was for her to go on tour. By the spring of 1906 she was performing in the Scandinavian countries, in Holland, and in Germany. She led her students in their first public appearance, a matinée performance at the Kroll Opera House in Berlin. In 1907 she made another tour of Russia, and in 1908 a third, this time taking thirteen of her more advanced pupils with her. Then she visited London and was received enthusiastically there with her bevy of pupils who figured increasingly in her performance. But in America, where she went next—just nine years after she had left it in a cattle boat—she was less successful, at least at first. News of her extramarital relationships had reached across the ocean, and many sensation mongers felt cheated when they saw her simple dancing and the guileless interplay between her and her young students. But then Walter Damrosch, conductor of the great New York Symphony, saw her. She opened his eyes "to the significant connection between the art of music and dance." He invited her to perform at the Metropolitan Opera House with his own orchestra. From then on her American visit was a triumph. She went on to other large cities. In Chicago critic Harriet Monroe spoke of "the grace and loveliness of every movement, from her little round head to her lightly shifting bare feet; the game of ball and the crouching game of jackstones; all in fluttering gray chiffon draperies . . . . it was all a revelation of great art." She danced before President Theodore Roosevelt in Washington, D.C. At the end of December 1908 she sailed for Europe, promising to return the following year.

Now she had truly arrived. In Paris they jammed the theaters, fêted her, sketched and sculpted her, poetized and painted her. She "incarnated music in her dance," was "a flowing of movement into movement, an endless interweaving of motion and music." Author Max Eastman spoke of the world recognizing, "in that young, brave girl's beautiful body, running barefoot and half naked, running and bending, pausing and floating in a stream of music . . . an artistic revolution, an apparition of creative genius." Even the great Diaghilev streaming his own ballet productions across Europe could not dim her popularity.

She gathered her pupils together in Paris and decided to re-found her school there. But where to get the money? Then who should come backstage at the Gaieté-Lyrique but the tall handsome son of the Singer Sewing Company magnate. His name was Paris Eugene Singer, and he told her he wanted to help her finance her school. Now for a long time Isadora was to have no money worries.

The school project was held in abeyance for the time being, however. After her commitments at the Gaieté-Lyrique, a brief tour of Russia, and reappearances with Damrosch's orchestra in America in the late fall, she was back in Europe. While awaiting the birth of her son, Patrick—he was born May 1, 1910—she went with Singer on a Mediterranean cruise.

Now for several years Isadora had time to create new dances. Her popularity had widened. The bas-reliefs for the façade of the Théâtre des Champs Elysées were modeled after her, and so were the murals for that theater. She went on cruises with Singer. She basked on beaches. But her autobiography belies a state of pure happiness. She is reading her favorite poem, Whitman's "Song of the Open Road," to Singer and he is saying "What rot! That man could never have earned his living." She is "pondering the strange difference that divides life from art . . . wondering if a woman can ever really be an artist, since Art is a hard taskmaster who demands everything, whereas a woman who loves gives up everything to life." At Singer's château in England "with many bedrooms and bathrooms and suites, with fourteen automobiles in the garage and a yacht in the harbour," she found herself "positively desperate." So it was finally back to Paris, where she could be with her children and pupils again, and where she could give performances at the great theaters.

Early in the year she had created a new dance to the "Funeral March" by Chopin. So vivid was her portrayal that

Hener Skene, her accompanist, turned deathly pale and pleaded, "Never ask me to play that again." She did, however, at a performance in Paris, early in April 1913. On the nineteenth of that month her two small children tragically met their death in an automobile accident. After the funeral the grief-stricken Isadora left the house where they had been living and drove recklessly alone through Italy. She was finally persuaded to rest at the home of the famous actress Eleanora Duse. Here she went on lonely endless walks, thought of suicide, believed she would never dance again. Paris Singer, concerned for her health, belatedly bought a building for her school—the sixty-two-room Paillard Palace Hotel in Bellevue, a fifteen-minute ride from Paris—and promised her the wherewithal to keep it going. This gesture seemed to revive her. She brought six of her pupils from Berlin, some of them now ready to be teachers themselves. In Paris she again reigned a queen among artists and intellectuals.

But the start of World War I, in August 1914, changed all that. Isadora turned over the school building to the Red Cross for a hospital and in September sent her pupils to America, following them herself a month later.

Americans were now sympathetic toward her. A wealthy sponsor arranged for her to use a theater in New York City as an experimental Greek theater. She had rows of orchestra seats removed, covered the boxes with long draperies, and presented an English version of Euripides' *Iphigénie en Tauride*. She improvised on the stirring French anthem, "Marseillaise" —the audience stood and cheered this—and gave Schubert's "Ave Maria" with such poignancy that many wept.

But her curtain speeches stirred up trouble. She wanted to create a school of the dance in America, but she seemed bent on antagonizing the very ones who might have helped her. She railed at the "stingy millionaires." "My work is only appreciated by the people in the gallery because they are intelligent." Finally, leaving New York "to Philistine darkness" she sailed in May 1915 for Europe.

There was something pathological in her restlessness. She wrote later that after her children's deaths she had only one desire, "to fly—to fly . . . my life [since] has been but a series of weird flights from it all." So now she was in Paris, giving performances of new works; then she was off to South America, where she barely filled houses in Argentina, had a fair success in Uruguay, and triumphed in Brazil. Going back to Europe by way of North America she happened to meet Singer in New York, and a brief reconciliation led to his renting for her the Metropolitan Opera House, where she repeated her recent successes. Later that year she made a tour of the West Coast.

On her return to Europe in 1918 she went first to England and created more dances, "Les Funérailles" and "Bénédiction de Dieu dans La Solitude," both to the music of Liszt. She and her new accompanist, Walter Rummel, became deeply involved, toured the provincial towns of France, were off on tours of Switzerland and North Africa, returning to Paris by way of Italy.

Everywhere, all the time, she was begging funds for a new school. When she was presented with a laurel wreath after a performance in Greece ("You, Isadora, bring to us again the immortal beauty of Phidias"), she replied, "Ah, help me to create a thousand magnificent dancers to dance in this Stadium." At a London Philharmonic concert she was saying, "If you don't give me a school I will go to Russia with the Bolsheviks." A Russian official in the audience heard her and told her, "We will give you a school with a thousand children."

So to Russia she went. She and Irma Duncan—the only one of her former pupils who accompanied her—arrived in Moscow in the third year of the Russian Revolution. The Russians honored, acclaimed, trusted, and exploited her. They gave her a fine building and allowed her to select fifty children from hundreds of applicants. On the fourth anniversary of the Russian Revolution, November 7, 1921, the children made a surprise debut at the great Bolshoi Theater, coming onstage after Isadora had electrified the audience with her dancing of the song "Internationale." But then, with a change of policy, the government withdrew its financial support. The school became Isadora's personal responsibility. This meant she must tour again.

The agent Sol Hurok arranged a tour for her in America. To enable the Russian poet Sergei Esenin, who had become her lover, to accompany her to America, she married him, this in spite of her long-held principles. They arrived in New York in October 1922. Again she seemed bent on antagonizing her audience—for instance waving a red scarf from the stage and shouting, "This is Red: I am Red, too!" Boston closed its doors to her after her appearance there. Still, she exerted the same sway on lovers of the dance. Helen Tamaris, the famous dancer, who saw her last performance in the New York area, described it: "One moment in particular stunned me. She was dancing to *Pathétique*. She started on the ground, lying close to the floor, and it took a long time—the only physical action was the very slow movement which carried her from prone to erect with arms outstretched. At the finish, everyone was crying, and I was crying, too. . . ."

The tour across the Continent with her husband, who was habitually drunk, brawling, wholly irresponsible, became newspapermen's grist at every stop. The two returned to New York in a drift of concert cancellations, debts, scrapes, and lurid headlines. Paris Singer stepped forward to pay their passage back to Europe.

In Russia, in August 1923, she packed the Bolshoi Theater to the doors in eighteen consecutive performances. She made a tour of the Ukraine, pouring out money to whoever begged for it. In Moscow again, her purse entirely empty, she gave a last triumphant concert and left Russia, with praises ringing from every direction, but with her school now in other hands, with a government admittedly unprepared to support her, and with Esenin departed from her life forever. She reached Paris early in 1925. There she learned Esenin had committed suicide. She now faced a blankness such as she had never before encountered.

She had been commissioned to write her memoirs and this project gave some purpose to her life. While cajoling grocerymen, putting off landlords, wheedling restaurateurs, she managed to write or dictate, page by page, chapter by chapter, her autobiography. "It is mostly about my love affairs," she would say. "I wanted to write about my art mostly, but my publishers were not interested, and I needed the money desperately." She would add, "It's a crazed century that can only find interest in me as a female Casanova." In the summer of 1927 she handed in the manuscript. It was one of the first deeply self-revealing books by a woman seeking to solve the conflict between a career in art and a life of human expressiveness. It had a terrific impact on young artists. But Isadora was not to know this.

She was now becoming less and less mistress of her actions. She pulled herself together for a performance on July 8, 1927. At her dancing of "Ave Maria," many in the audience sobbed aloud. A month later, in Nice on the Riviera, she took a fancy to a small open low-slung racing car, and made an appointment to try it out. She stepped in beside the driver. The car jumped forward. The ends of a long red scarf which she was wearing became entangled in the back wheels, instantly tightened on her neck, and strangled her.

The whole world mourned the death of a great artist. A Copenhagen paper wrote, "In the realm of the arts she now belongs to the great fallen ones." The New York *World* eulogized, "This woman was one in a million. She was one of the greatest dancers we have ever seen or were like to see. For that, we were willing to humor her whims, to smile at them even, to honor her." The San Francisco *Chronicle* headlined: "Something Mighty Fine About Isadora."

But she herself had said it so much more simply in her lifetime: "I have only made movements which seem beautiful to me."

BIBLIOGRAPHY

BOLITHO, WILLIAM, *Twelve Against the Gods; the Story of Adventure.* New York: Simon & Schuster, Inc., 1929.
DELL, FLOYD, *Women as World Builders; Studies in Modern Feminism.* Chicago: Forbes and Company, 1913.
DUNCAN, IRMA, *Duncan Dancer; an Autobiography.* Middletown, Connecticut: Wesleyan University Press, 1966.
DUNCAN, ISADORA, *The Art of the Dance,* edited, with an Introduction, by Sheldon Cheney. New York: Theatre Arts, Inc., 1928.
———, *My Life.* New York: Boni & Liveright, Inc., 1927.
EASTMAN, MAX, *Heroes I Have Known; Twelve Who Lived Great Lives.* New York: Simon & Schuster, Inc., 1942.
MACDOUGALL, ALLAN ROSS, *Isadora; a Revolutionary in Art and Love.* New York: Thomas Nelson & Sons, 1960.
SCHNEIDER, ILYA ILYICH, *Isadora Duncan, The Russian Years.* New York: Harcourt, Brace & World, Inc., 1969.
TERRY, WALTER, *Isadora Duncan; Her Life, Her Art, Her Legacy.* New York: Dodd, Mead & Company, 1964.

AMELIA EARHART

AMELIA EARHART (PUTNAM): Born in Atchison, Kansas, July 24, 1898. Lost at sea over the Pacific, July 1, 1937. Father: Edwin Stanton Earhart; mother: Amy (Otis) Earhart; sister: Muriel; husband: George Palmer Putnam.

✳

Amelia Earhart was the first woman to fly solo across the Atlantic (1932) and the first person, man or woman, to fly 2,400 miles across the Pacific, from the Hawaiian Islands to the United States mainland (1935). She also established altitude and transcontinental speed records for the day. Her last flight in 1937 carried her all but around the world.

✳

As a child Amelia built a roller coaster starting from the ridgepole of the shed roof and ending in the yard. When on its first trip it crashed into a rail fence, she repaired it, and tried again, rerouting it. She constructed a "chicken trap" and captured a marauding hen in it. She explored the sandstone caves in the region. In the winter she took sled rides belly-buster down steep slopes, and in one spectacular dash catapulted her sled and herself beween the front and back legs of an ambling horse.

She spent summers at her grandmother's home in Atchison, Kansas. Winters she lived in a number of towns because her father, a railroad lawyer, had to relocate at intervals to be near his work. The family at times even accompanied him on

Amelia Earhart

his railroading, during which periods "home" was the private car of a train shuttling between points in the Middle West.

Amelia read much, but what she read often troubled her. It disturbed her, for instance, that in girls' books the heroines were relegated to comparatively inactive roles, could not follow "the shining paths of romantic adventure" as could boys. George Palmer Putnam, in his book *Soaring Wings*, quotes her as saying, "Who ever heard of a girl—a pleasant one—shipping on an oil tanker, say, finding the crew about to mutiny and saving the captain's life . . . with a well-aimed disabling pistol shot at the leader of the gang . . . . If girls read boys' books, they close the covers with, 'Oh dear, that can never happen to me—because I'm not a boy.'"

She attended four high schools before graduating in 1916 from Hyde Park High School in Chicago, then went on to Ogontz Preparatory School in Philadelphia. In 1919 she went to New York City to take a premedical course at Columbia University. In after-school hours she would go on tours of discovery in the underground passageways that connected the different buildings on the campus. On dark nights, having found a key to the roof stairway, she would crawl out over the dome of the university laboratory to the very top. She took not only the full quota of lectures and lab work at Columbia, but the full quota offered at Barnard College for girls, just across the way. (They didn't compare lists in those days, so the doubling went unnoticed.)

At the end of her first winter at Columbia she traveled to Long Beach, California, where her family now lived. Soon after arriving, she made a trip with her father to a nearby airfield. There an exhibition of stunt flying fascinated her. She begged him to let her ride in the small plane. By the time the plane was two or three hundred feet off the ground, she knew she had to fly by herself.

Now she begged for flying lessons, but her father told her,

no, it was too expensive. She rounded up a job with the telephone company and with what she earned took flying lessons after work and weekends. By 1921 she had completed her course, gone up "solo," and acquired the only flying license then issued: the Federation Aeronautique Internationale.

Next her family helped her buy a small sports airplane. She practiced stalls, spins, vertical drops. Before the year was over, she had established an altitude record for women by climbing her plane to 14,000 feet.

But her medical career had to be considered. In 1924 she sold her plane, bought a yellow sports car, and drove cross-country to the East and her studies at Columbia. She stuck to them painstakingly for several months. Finally, she was convinced that a doctor's life was not for her. In 1925 she enrolled at Harvard summer school with the idea of qualifying as a teacher. In 1926 she became a social worker at Denison House in Boston, directing the evening school for foreign immigrants and visiting them in their homes. Within a year she had become a staff worker with full charge of the prekindergarten section and director of the activities work for girls from five to fourteen. Then, with a social work career seemingly all set, she joined the Boston chapter of the National Aeronautics Association, "for the fun of it." It proved to be an opener into what was to be her real career.

Flying in those days was still in the "stunt" stage—was not taken seriously as a means of either passenger or mail transportation. It was considered dangerous, but exciting. People took chances. Landing in a cow pasture was relished both by the aviator and the farmer. It was "news." But women were loath to let their husbands and sons enter the flying field as a profession. And women aviators were about as scarce as women astronauts are today.

So it was fortunate that about this time Amelia was given an opportunity to show her courage by going on an extended flight. Mrs. Frederick Guest, sponsor of a projected goodwill flight between America, her native country, and England, her adopted country, was on the lookout for a likely passenger. Since the purpose of the flight was not only to promote friendship between the two nations but to advance the cause of women in aviation, she wanted an American girl "who would measure up to adequate standards of American womanhood." The Aeronautics Association list was consulted, and the searching committee, headed by George Palmer Putnam of G. P. Putnam's Sons, book publishers, came upon Amelia's name. They looked her up and subsequent conferences between the committee and her left the members favorably impressed. The young lady was enterprising. She had writing ability. This latter was important because G. P. Putnam wanted to have a book written about the flight. Amelia even looked a bit like Charles A. Lindbergh, who had made his daring transatlantic flight only the year before and whose book, *We*, which Mr. Putnam had commissioned, had been a best seller.

So Amelia Earhart was chosen. The plane, *The Friendship*, took off on June 17, 1928, with Wilmer Stultz as pilot, Louis Gordon as mechanic, and Amelia Earhart as passenger. Such was Stultz's skill that, after flying "blind" for twenty plus hours, eighteen of them over or between layers of fog, he was only one mile off course when the plane first sighted land. When they approached the British Isles, they were in doubt as to their exact location because their radio had gone dead. They flew on with their fuel so low that the engines were supplied only when they were flying level. They came to a channel, turned and flew along it to a village, and there let their plane down into the water, the *Friendship* having been fitted with pontoons. After several unanswered signals, one of which was Amelia waving a white towel, the sleepy town awoke to the fact it had visitors from afar, and a boat came out to welcome them. The next day the three flew to Southampton to be officially welcomed. This was the only part of the trip during which Amelia took a hand at the airplane controls.

When Amelia was met by Mrs. Guest at Southampton, the attention given her as the one woman member of the crew seemed to her disproportionate, considering her minor role during the flight. The whole enterprise had of course been arranged to popularize the idea of women entering the field of aviation. But it embarrassed her to have her name headlined in newspapers and she herself singled out for invitations to official affairs, when she had gone merely as passenger. She answered President Coolidge's congratulatory message with "Success entirely due great skill of Mr. Stultz."

After her trip back by steamship to America, she could have contentedly skipped the ticker tape parade in New York City and the crowd of admirers who mobbed her in Boston. But she did relish the chances the trip gave her to prove her abilities. She was asked to join the editorial staff of *Cosmopolitan* magazine as aviation editor—she held this job from 1928 to 1930—and was engaged to lecture throughout the country. She became a member of the staff of the pioneer air passenger line, Transcontinental Air Transport. Her job here was to promote the idea that flying was safe—that women should welcome air travel, should encourage their menfolk to travel so, and themselves be passengers. Later (1930–1931) she was vice president of this line. All the while she was busy mastering actual flying techniques. In 1929 her book about the transatlantic flight, *20 Hrs., 40 Min.*, came out.

This year, too, she placed third in a women's air race derby, beginning at Santa Monica, California, and ending at Cleveland, Ohio. The next year she set the women's speed record by flying 181 miles per hour. The business details of these ventures had, incidentally, been handled by Mr. Putnam. In fact Mr. Putnam was pretty much in evidence those days. Before long he asked her to marry him. She consented, with the stipulation that she be permitted to follow her own way of life, which meant, of course, a life in the air.

After the marriage, on February 7, 1931, her air activities even increased. In April she broke an altitude record (over eighteen thousand feet) in an autogiro, a forerunner of the helicopter. In May she flew about the country in this curious "flying windmill," under an arrangement with the Beechnut Packing Company.

Then one morning, hardly a year after her marriage, she looked across the breakfast table at her husband and asked quietly, "Would you *mind* if I flew the Atlantic—alone?" There was the marriage promise—so of course he told her, all right, if her heart was set on it.

Her solo flight began on the afternoon of May 20, 1932, at Harbor Grove, Newfoundland, and ended near Londonderry, Ireland, May 21, fourteen hours and fifty-six minutes later. It must be remembered, flights in those days were not like modern commercial flights, with every minute accounted for from the ground. Rather, they had to be guided almost entirely from within the plane itself. Moreover, there was no gear to tell the plane's position in the air—whether, for instance, it was right side up or upside down. When fog prevented a pilot from seeing the horizon, he had to fly very high to be sure to keep clear of the ground.

Amelia's flight had several handicaps, unexpected ones. About four hours out of Newfoundland she saw a tiny flame beginning to creep through a welded joint in the manifold ring. She couldn't turn back, for it would have been impossible to make a landing in the dark. Added to this harrowing discovery was the realization that her altimeter, the instrument that shows the height of the airplane above the surface of the earth, had suddenly failed. She nosed her plane up to the top of the clouds, only to find that in the higher altitude it was picking up ice. To get to warmer air, she came down where she could see the ocean, but the fog came so low she dared not remain there for fear of flying into the water. So she simply "ploughed through the soup" till dawn.

By morning the reserve fuel tanks had begun to leak. She sighted Ireland and decided to land at the nearest possible place. She spotted railroad tracks and reasoned they might lead to a city with an airport. So she followed along them. Instead of a city she found broad meadows and landed on one of these, after "scaring all the cattle in the country." Her arrival was a testimony to her nerve and her skill. She had flown two thousand miles of ocean with an altimeter out of commission and a part of the plane's mechanism ablaze.

Now the furor over her exploits was worldwide. While still abroad, she received the Certificate of Honorary Membership in the British Guild of Air Pilots and Navigators, an honor conferred only once before to a non-Britisher. Her plane was placed on public view in London. She was received in the French Senate and was decorated Chevalier of the Legion of Honor. King Albert I of Belgium bestowed on her the cross of the Chevalier of the Order of Leopold, a high honor.

When she returned to America in June 1932, the National Geographic Society gave her its special gold medal, with President Hoover making the presentation. She answered his speech with, "I think that the appreciation of the deed is out of proportion to the deed itself . . . . I shall be happy if my small exploit has drawn attention to the fact that women, too, are flying." Before a joint session of Congress she was awarded the Distinguished Flying Cross, becoming the first woman to be so honored. Editorials on her flying prowess appeared in newspapers from coast to coast. In 1933, on a visit to the White House, she piloted the First Lady, Mrs. Eleanor Roosevelt, on a flight over Washington, D.C. The flight was made on the spur of the moment, and both ladies were wearing party gowns. Amelia had long white gloves on her slim hands.

But for Amelia honors only meant she would try harder to deserve them. After a few months she began her horizon seeking again. Her book about her sky adventures, *The Fun of It*, came out in 1932. In August of that year she established the women's record for transcontinental flight from Los Angeles, California, to Newark, New Jersey, nonstop, 2,448 miles in nineteen hours and five minutes. Less than a year later, on July 7, 1933, she bettered her own record, flying the same distance in seventeen hours, seven minutes, and thirty seconds.

Then, in January 1935, she became the first person, man or woman, to fly solo from the Hawaiian Islands to the United States mainland. On the afternoon of January 11 she rolled her plane down a muddy runway at Sheeler Field in Hawaii and, through a steady downpour, climbed into the sky. She landed eighteen hours and fifteen minutes later in Oakland, California. When ten thousand Californians broke through police lines to get a closer look at her, they saw a face white with weariness. "I feel swell," she said firmly. Then, conscious of straggling locks about her face, "I'm a little tired—you will have to excuse me."

Three months later she was first to fly solo the air trail between Los Angeles and Mexico City. Three weeks after that, on May 8, she flew nonstop from Mexico City to Newark, New Jersey, another record-making flight.

Now came one of the most satisfying adventures of her life. She was engaged by Edward G. Elliott, president of Purdue University, as "Counsellor for Careers for Women," because he believed "she will help us to see and to attack successfully many unsolved problems." Here she talked with various student groups and counseled the senior, junior, and sophomore women on vocational opportunities. She said to them, "Sex has been used too much too long as a subterfuge by the inefficient woman who likes to make herself and others believe that it is not her incapability but her womanhood which is holding her back." She said, "A girl must nowadays believe completely in herself as an individual. She must realize at the outset that a woman must do the same job better than a man to get as much credit for it."

Fifteen thousand dollars was pledged by the trustees of the university and turned over to Amelia for the purchase, outfitting, and maintenance of a Lockheed twin-engined, ten-passenger aircraft—"my laboratory," she called it—in which she could have full scope in working out problems of navigation. The plane, of which she officially took possession on July 24, 1936, accommodated 1,204 gallons of gasoline, giving it a maximum flying range of 4,500 miles. This, the *Electra*, was to serve her well—but not for long. For its period of flight—and hers—was to end before she had rounded out another year.

It was on July 1, 1937, that the world paused to listen to news bulletins: "Earhart Plane Vanishes," "Amelia Down in Pacific," "Lady Lindy Lost!" "Search for Amelia Fails." Then came that day of waiting . . .

Of what exactly did this last adventure of hers consist? She had told reporters, "Well, I'm going to try to fly around the globe—east to west." The flight did begin westward, but this first try was unsuccessful. Taking off in Honolulu, the *Electra* crashed before it was well in the air. This was on March 20, 1937. Undaunted, Amelia Earhart had the *Electra* shipped to the United States for repairs and two months later, with the flight direction changed to east (because of a change in the weather pattern), took off again, this time from Oakland, California, eastward. She was the pilot and Fred Noonan was the navigator.

When they reached Miami, Florida, they decided that the plane should be lightened, and the trailing 250-foot wire antenna was removed, thus limiting the plane's ability to send out radio signals. On June 1 they took off for Puerto Rico. The next stop was Caripito, in Venezuela, and the next Paramaribo, in Dutch Guiana. Fortaleza and Natal in Brazil came next. Now, after flying over almost a thousand miles of jungle, they started over some 1,900 miles of the South Atlantic Ocean.

Amelia mailed back accounts from various stopping places, and these were later published in the book *The Last Flight*, arranged by Mr. Putnam. Jottings were: "Wheels down in Africa . . . bleak desert for many miles . . . . From Karachi on June 17 we flew 1,390 miles to Calcutta . . . . Black eagles came flying out of the sky at 5,000 feet . . . . The mountains of Java rose from the tropic sea . . . . Midway to New Guinea the sea is spotted with freakish islands, stony fingers pointing toward the sky. . . . This evening I looked eastward over the Pacific."

On July 2 came a wireless to the *Herald Tribune* from Lae, New Guinea: "Amelia Earhart departed for Howland Island at ten o'clock today beginning a 2,556-mile flight across the Pacific along a route never travelled before by an aeroplane." The plane never reached Howland Island.

As soon as word was received that the *Electra* was missing, Secretary of the Navy Claude Swanson ordered United States ships to comb the waters of the Pacific in the neighborhood of Howland Island. Carrier-based planes scanned 100,000 square miles of ocean. All the islands where they might have landed were searched. No trace of Amelia Earhart and Fred Noonan was ever found.

Their real fate may never be known. An RKO film (1943) portrayed a woman aviator as going on a mission for the United States and as having purposely crashed her plane when she learned the Japanese had discovered her whereabouts. In 1966 a book, *The Search for Amelia Earhart*, by Fred Goerner, related a plausible, but not fully proved, story of Amelia Earhart and Fred Noonan being captured by the Japanese and finally meeting death in a Japanese prison camp.

However, to Amelia Earhart all these surmises would have been extraneous to her life's purpose. She had believed in this flight around the world, as she had believed in her solo hops over the Atlantic and the Pacific. She so deeply believed these projects to be important that she had been willing to put her life on the scales against their accomplishment. We can be sure of one thing: the spirit of courage was with her to the end. In one of her letters "to be opened in case of death," she wrote: "Hooray for the last grand adventure! I wish I had won but it was worthwhile anyway. . . ."

BIBLIOGRAPHY

EARHART, AMELIA, *The Fun of It; Random Records of My Own Flying and of Women in Aviation.* New York: Harcourt, Brace & Company, Inc., 1932.
———, *The Last Flight,* arranged by George Palmer Putnam. New York: Harcourt, Brace & Company, Inc., 1937.
GOERNER, FRED G., *The Search for Amelia Earhart.* New York: Doubleday & Company, Inc., 1966.
PUTNAM, GEORGE PALMER, *Soaring Wings; a Biography of Amelia Earhart.* New York: Harcourt, Brace & Company, Inc., 1939.

MARY BAKER EDDY

MARY BAKER EDDY: Born in Bow, New Hampshire, July 16, 1821. Died in Boston, Massachusetts, December 3, 1910. Father: Mark Baker; mother: Abigail Barnard (Ambrose) Baker; brothers: Samuel, Albert, and George; sisters: Abigail and Martha. Marriages: George Washington Glover, Daniel Patterson, Asa Gilbert Eddy; son: George Glover.

*

Mary Baker Eddy was the initiator of the system of faith called Christian Science. She opened the First Church of Christ, Scientist, called the "Mother Church," in Boston, Massachusetts, in 1879. By 1950 more than three thousand branches of the Mother Church, twenty-two hundred of these in the United States and Canada, were flourishing. She was the author of the book used in the church services, *Science and Health with Key to the Scriptures*. Millions of copies have been printed. In her late eighties she founded *The Christian Science Monitor*, one of the world's great newspapers.

*

SHE was reared in a straight-laced New England household. Her family, especially her stern father, believed in the Puritan doctrine that man was born sinful and that therefore existence should be one long struggle of self-denial and privation. However his harshness was lessened with Mary, the youngest of his children, slight, pretty, and considered frail in health.

Mary attended school only sporadically. Her older brother, Albert, taught her when he was home on vacations from Dartmouth College. His death when she was eighteen was the first in a series of tragic losses in her life.

At twenty-two she married George Washington Glover, a friend of her brother Samuel, and went to live in his home town, Charleston, South Carolina. Six months later her young husband contracted yellow fever and died. She returned to her family in New Hampshire and not long after gave birth to a son, named George after his father. During the period of his babyhood she managed at intervals, in spite of poor health, to teach school and to write for local periodicals. Among the topics she chose to write about were the evils of the slave trade, as she had witnessed them firsthand in South Carolina.

On November 21, 1849, when she was twenty-eight, her mother, of whom she was very fond, passed away. The year after that her father remarried. After a period of living under these new family arrangements, she went to stay with her married sister, Abigail Tilton, in Tilton, New Hampshire. Since her health was still precarious, her six-year-old son was put in the keeping of Mrs. Mahala Sanborn, a former helper in the Baker household. The child soon came to look on the Sanborn home as his. When the Sanborns moved to the Far West, young George Glover went with them. Mother and son were not to meet again until he was a grown man with a family of his own.

Mary Baker's second marriage took place when she was thirty-two. Her husband, Daniel Patterson, a dentist, was a restless, unstable individual. He moved from one town to another, and his practice suffered. He absented himself from his wife for months at a time. Mary Baker again became ill.

The mid-nineteenth century in America was an era of searching into new psychic channels, of probing into new processes of the mind. The theories of transcendentalism, mesmerism, spiritualism, were the talk of the times, as exciting then as speculation about life on Mars is now. Behind it all was the dissatisfaction with the hell-and-damnation theories of Puritanism. So as the years passed by and her health remained poor, Mary Baker decided to consult a man widely spoken of for his "magnetic cures," Phineas P. Quimby, of Portland, Maine.

She traveled to Portland, was treated by him, and had long talks with him on his theories of mental suggestion. She said later he was able to cure by a "science not understood." After her return to Tilton, with her health regained, she stayed a short time with her sister. There was even a brief reconciliation with her husband. At last, though, it became clear that the marriage could not survive. They separated in the mid-sixties, and in 1873 were divorced.

Far from being an invalid now, Mary Baker was an assured and indefatigable worker for the new ideas she was formulating. A serious fall on a sidewalk on February 4, 1866, helped crystallize her beliefs. She was told by physicians she would never walk again. But "in two days," as she later wrote a friend, "I got out of bed alone and walked." Later she summed up the episode: "My immediate recovery from the effects of an injury . . . that neither medicine nor surgery could reach . . . was the falling apple that led me to the discovery how to be well myself, and how to make others so . . . . I gained the scientific certainty that all causation was Mind . . ."

During these years she became a visitor at various homes, offering housewives instruction in mental healing in return for their hospitality. Often there were other boarders at these houses, and with the mystic's intense desire to communicate, she would enter into discussions with them. Early in 1866 she became acquainted with Hiram S. Crafts, a boarder at a Lynn residence, and an exponent of the German philosopher Hegel.

Crafts had written an essay on Hegel's belief that the natural world, and with it mankind, is to be seen as a manifestation of a cosmic spirit. ("Mind is universal, the first and only cause of all that is."—Hegel) Mr. Crafts had many discussions with Mary Baker about the concepts of Hegel, Kant, Mesmer, and the transcendentalists. They would read each other's writings and make suggestions. Later she and Mr. Crafts opened a "healing office" in Taunton, Massachusetts. This venture was dissolved in August 1866.

In 1870 Richard Kennedy, whom she had met in Amesbury, Massachusetts, became a devoted advocate of her beliefs. The two decided to go to Lynn and set up a combination school and healing office. Kennedy was to be in charge of the healing, under Mary Baker's guidance, and she was to conduct the school. At first it worked out well. Mary Baker's teaching drew many pupils, and Kennedy became widely known for his cures. In 1872, however, the arrangement came to an end. Mary Baker, it seems, objected to Kennedy's practice of "laying on of hands." To her this smacked of mesmerism, a form of hypnotism, and a process she had by now abjured. She believed rather in the projection of thought as a curative measure.

Her years of introspection and discussion were producing a system of beliefs which she gradually embodied in a book, *Science and Health*. Matter, she believed, had no real existence. Sickness and evil were illusions which could be overcome. Christ came to rid the world not only of sin but of pain and death as well. Men and women could heal themselves and others if they arrived at true Christian consciousness. "The prayer that reforms the sinner and heals the sick," she stated in the first sentence of *Science and Health*, "is an absolute faith that all things are possible to God." With this concept she was ready to start on her career as a religious leader.

She carried her manuscript, *Science and Health*—it was 456

pages long—to the printers in September 1874. She was then fifty-three. It had taken her, as she said, "two and a half years of incessant labor" to write it. It was published in 1875, mostly at her own expense, though students helped her in the project. The first edition suffered from poor editing, and she had another prepared for the printer. She had the satisfaction of seeing, in 1881 and 1882, three good editions of one thousand copies each come off the press. *Science and Health* had begun its phenomenal sales record, which in time was to reach well into the millions.

During her stay in Lynn, eight students pledged themselves each to contribute ten dollars weekly for her to instruct them, to preach to them, and to take charge of Sabbath day services concerned with the "moral science called the Science of Life." Early in 1877 she and one of her disciples, Asa Gilbert Eddy, were married by a Unitarian minister. Eddy was to be a great help to her as a teacher and as a Christian Science practitioner. In August 1879 a charter was obtained for the "Church of Christ, Scientist," and on January 31, 1881, another charter was issued for a school, "The Massachusetts Metaphysical College," founded "for medical purposes, to give instruction in scientific methods of mental healing on a purely practical basis, to impart a thorough understanding of metaphysics, to restore health, hope, and harmony to man." For eight years she headed this school. During its existence approximately four thousand persons took the twelve-lesson courses.

In June 1882 Mary Baker Eddy suffered another personal loss, in the death of her husband. From now on she would forge her way alone.

Her area of influence was constantly widening. She had moved her church to Boston. Hundreds of her Metaphysical College students, returning to their homes all over the United States, were spreading the message of Christian Science. One student wrote Mrs. Eddy that within two weeks of graduation fifty students and patients had registered with her.

Mrs. Baker's teaching experience brought her not only the gratitude of many students but also lawsuits from some disgruntled ones. However, such suits seemed only to increase her prestige.

Her writing projects were influential in spreading her doctrines. The *Christian Science Journal*, the church's newspaper, which came out first in April 1883, proved a most effective means of making her beliefs known. *Science and Health* had a constantly widening audience of readers. In 1885 her book *Historical Sketch of Metaphysical Healing* was published, and in 1887 the books *Christian Science: No and Yes; Rudiments and Rules of Divine Science;* and *Unity of Good and Unreality of Evil*. All of these underlined her belief that mind was the all—that matter did not exist except as an "error."

In Boston in 1887 several church members opened a "Free Dispensary of Christian Science Healing" near the center of the city. This brought new converts. Her speaking engagements had an even greater effect. Appearing in Chicago before the National Christian Science Association in 1888, she spoke to such purpose that the whole audience rose and surged up on the platform, everyone struggling to touch her hand. Women raised their children and asked her to bless them. Many called out that they had been instantly healed of their ills. It was a climax in the career of this sixty-six-year-old woman. She has been described at this period in her life as a "slim, trim figure." Especially remarked were her "brightly shining eyes," and her "clear musical voice."

In the 1880's and 1890's Mrs. Eddy's popularity reached phenomenal proportions: students flocked to her courses; her sermons on Sundays and lectures on Thursdays were crowded to capacity. She wrote extensively, replying via newspaper articles to criticisms from the clergy and others. Her personal correspondence was voluminous. More than fourteen thousand of her letters are in the archives of the Mother Church.

Her home in Boston had become the meeting place for socialites and intellectuals. "Have you met Mrs. Eddy?" was a question to be answered, if one was "in the know," in the affirmative. Bronson Alcott, the transcendentalist, and father of Louisa May Alcott, after visiting Mrs. Eddy, wrote to her, "The profound truths which you announce, sustained by facts of the immortal life, give to your work the seal of inspiration—reaffirm in modern phrase the Christian revelations. In times like these, so sunk in sensualism, I hail with joy your voice, speaking an assured word for God and immortality, and my joy is heightened that those words are of woman's divinings." Clergyman and author Edward Everett Hale visited her and wrote that she had given him "more truth in twenty minutes than I have heard in twenty years."

On May 1894 the cornerstone of the present Mother Church in Boston was laid. Mrs. Eddy wrote instructions: "Hold your services in the Mother Church, December 30, 1894, and dedicate this church January 6. The Bible and *Science and Health with Key to the Scriptures* shall henceforth be the Pastor of the Mother Church. This will tend to spiritualize thought." She directed that a man and a woman should be readers: "one reading the Bible references and the other quotations from *Science and Health with Key to the Scriptures*, this reading to be done alternately." This made her church completely free from sex discrimination. She even spoke of "God, our divine Father and Mother."

In 1895 Mary Baker Eddy accepted the post of "Pastor Emeritus in perpetuity" of the Mother Church in Boston. In 1908, when she was eighty-seven, *The Christian Science Monitor*, one of the world's great newspapers, was founded, "to injure no man, but to bless all mankind."

In her extreme old age Mrs. Eddy lived in comparative isolation, choosing to be surrounded with only a very few persons of unquestioned loyalty. On her death, the congregation of the Mother Church, instead of hearing an out-and-out announcement of the fact, had a portion of a letter, which she had written years before, explaining her absence to students at the Metaphysical College, read to them: "You may be looking to see me in my accustomed place with you, but this you must no longer expect . . . . Rumors are rumors, nothing more. I am still with you on the field of battle, taking forward marches, broader and higher views, and with the hope that you will follow."

BIBLIOGRAPHY

BEASLEY, NORMAN, *Mary Baker Eddy*. New York: Duell, Sloan & Pearce, Inc., 1963.

DAKIN, EDWIN FRANDEN, *Mrs. Eddy; the Biography of a Virginal Mind*. New York: Charles Scribner's Sons, 1929.

EDDY, MARY BAKER, *Science and Health with Key to the Scriptures*. Boston, the Christian Science Publishing Society.

ORCUTT, WILLIAM DANA, *Mary Baker Eddy and Her Books*. Boston: Christian Science Publishing Society, 1950.

MARGARET FULLER

(SARAH) *MARGARET FULLER, MARQUISE OSSOLI:* Born in Cambridgeport, Massachusetts, May 23, 1810. Died in shipwreck off Fire Island, New York, July 19, 1850. Father: Timothy Fuller; mother: Margaret (Crane) Fuller. Eight brothers and sisters, two of whom died in infancy; husband: Giovanni Angelo, Marquis Ossoli; son: Angelo.

*

Margaret Fuller was the first woman editor of a large American newspaper. She was the most noted of American critics before 1850. She was considered one of the best conversationalists of her time. Her book on women's problems, *Woman in the Nineteenth Century*, laid the groundwork for feminism in the United States.

*

WHEN Margaret was four, her father, a lawyer and politician, and a member of the Massachusetts Senate, noted in his journal, "I devoted this evening to teaching Margaret her digits." By the time she was six, she was reading Vergil, Horace, and Ovid in the original Latin and was expected to translate them orally into English without hesitations. By sixteen she was reading French, studying Greek, and making forays into the field of metaphysics. Her father also supervised her conversation—her thoughts must be fully formulated before she spoke, and must come out without blurring or stumbling. Her mother, a self-effacing person, deferred to her husband in everything, even in this severe regime he set for their precocious eldest child.

However, with all her book knowledge, Margaret found it hard to keep up with her age-group in common sociability. At school she would insist on being ringleader, would start rumors, trying to pit one girl against another. When one day her schoolmates confronted her before the principal with her tales, Margaret began to defend herself. Then she suddenly stopped, flung herself down on the hearth, and beat her head against it again and again. For several days after this she refused to eat or speak. Then an understanding teacher told her she herself had had the same experience when she was young and explained to the child a few principles about getting along with others, quite as hard to master in their way as Greek or Latin. Margaret was always to remember her kindness. Five years later she wrote her: "Can I ever forget that to your treatment in that crisis of youth I owe the true life—the love of truth and honor?"

When she was sixteen, her father held a reception for his friend, President John Quincy Adams, when the latter was briefly in Cambridge. Since her mother was indisposed, Margaret acted as hostess, wearing an unflattering pink silk dress that made her look plumper than she was. She felt ill at ease. Later, recalling that evening, she wrote a friend, "I am wanting that intuitive tact and polish which nature bestows on some but I must acquire."

A distant relative, George Davis, came up from Cape Cod to Harvard College in Cambridge about then, and was welcomed into the Fuller household. She went into gales of laughter at his witticisms. For a young girl in that age of feminine restraint she was always overly responsive. After leaving Harvard, Davis went into a law office in Greenfield, Massachusetts, and soon became engaged to a young lady there. Then a friend of his, James Freeman Clarke, began instructing Margaret in German—in those days young college students, as a way of "dating," would spend evenings or whole vacations tutoring their young girl friends. Though he found her "inexhaustible in power of insight, and with good will 'broad as ether,' " he, too, was soon off for other fields—another disappointment for her.

With the defeat of John Quincy Adams and the election of Andrew Jackson as President in 1829, Timothy Fuller's political career came to an end. He bought a farm in Groton and took his family there. Margaret greeted her new home "with a flood of tears." After all, her friends were all back in Cambridge. Her father, to give her something to look forward to, told her he would see that she got a trip to Europe if she would prepare her young brothers for college. So it was Latin, English, geography, history five to eight hours a day. Besides this, since her mother was often ill, she did most of the sewing and a good deal of the housework. She also studied German, read Schiller, Victor Hugo, Disraeli, and her favorite, the German writer and philosopher Goethe.

In June 1835, on a short visit to Professor and Mrs. John Farrar—she had known them from her Cambridge days—she met at their home the young Ralph Waldo Emerson. She had been following his writings and sermons. Now, in her resolute way, she decided she would find a means of keeping up this acquaintanceship.

But, back in her home in the country, she faced unexpected responsibilities. Her father died suddenly of Asiatic cholera, and at twenty-five she, as the eldest child, became the virtual head of the family. Her dreams of going to Europe had to be put behind her. She saw no hope of getting married either. It wasn't only that she now had to find ways of supporting the family. She believed herself to be plain (her pictures do not show her so) and to be unable to attract men except on a scholarly basis.

Then, out of the blue, came an invitation (probably stemming from a suggestion she herself had made to the Farrars) for a three-week visit to the Concord home of Mr. and Mrs. Emerson. Of course she accepted. Emerson wrote his brother that "a most accomplished lady" was staying with them. "To see a very intelligent person is like being set in a large place; you stretch your limbs and dilate to your utmost size . . . her eyes, so plain at first, soon swam with fun and tides of superabundant life."

This visit led to a working out of other hopes. Another visitor at the Emersons', Bronson Alcott, invited Margaret to be a teacher of languages at his new Temple School, called "Institute of Spiritual Culture." She accepted and in the autumn of 1836 took a room with her Uncle Henry in Boston, within easy walking distance of the school. She also gave instruction in German and Italian to various private pupils and one evening a week read the philosophers Kant and Schelling in the original German to William Ellery Channing, already famous as a reformer.

When Alcott's school broke up—it was "too idealistic," people said—she went on to an even better position, as head of the new Green Street Academy in Providence, Rhode Island, with the astonishing salary, for the time, of one thousand dollars a year. In Providence she brought the student body closer to the teachers and started the practice of having visiting lecturers. (One of these, John Neal, spoke on women's rights and started her thinking in this direction.) On a visit to Boston she encountered an old friend, Samuel Ward, just back from Europe with a sheaf of his own paintings. Together they haunted art galleries.

In December 1838 she resigned her Providence post, and after winding up affairs at Groton and selling the house, moved her family to Jamaica Plains, not far from Boston. In the spring of 1839 she had her first book published, a translation of some of the conversations of Goethe. But she could not take satisfaction in this achievement. Her friend Samuel Ward wasn't visiting her any more, and she was shortly to hear of his engagement. Her sad postscript to this episode: "I have never really approached the close relations of life.... Those who live would scarcely consider that I am among the living."

By now she had developed the special interest in women's status that was to be her chief claim to fame. She believed that women were being handicapped by lack both of formal schooling and of openings that would allow them to make use of what learning they had. She decided to provide for an opportunity for women in this direction. On November 6, 1839, she called together twenty-five distinguished New England women—wives and daughters of Harvard professors, leading ministers, and writers—in Elizabeth Peabody's famous West Street bookshop in Boston, for the first of her "Conversations." The subjects ranged all the way from Greek mythology to "moral freedom." At one meeting the topic was "beauty." Each woman wrote down her definition of this elusive term and the definitions were then read aloud. A general discussion ensued. More important than what they talked about, however, was the fact that a group of women were coming together for intellectual stimulation. Such groups were to be the forerunners of women's study clubs, feminist conferences, colleges for women. One of the participants was the future women's rights leader Elizabeth Cady Stanton.

About this time Emerson introduced Miss Fuller to the Boston "Transcendentalists," a small group of individualists who believed human beings should always operate at their highest intellectual and spiritual potentials. A transcendentalist magazine was planned, and Emerson suggested Margaret Fuller as editor, a most unusual position for a woman to hold in those days. Her work on *The Dial*, as the magazine was named, brought her into the circle of the great minds of New England. Some of Emerson's essays and poems and Henry Thoreau's nature studies first saw the light of day in this magazine. Today copies of *The Dial* are collectors' items, prized on a par with first editions of great books. Margaret Fuller must be credited with maintaining the magazine at its high level. Sometimes she had to piece the issues out with her own writings. The October 1841 issue, for instance, went to press only because she herself wrote 85 of its 136 pages. Along with this work and her "Conversations," she was translating important works from the German. No wonder she wrote a friend, "I am tired to death of my own *earnestness* . . . . I long to do something frivolous—go on a journey, plunge into eternals somehow. I never can. My wheel whirls round again."

After two years Emerson took over the demanding editorship of *The Dial*, commenting, "Let there be rotation in martyrdom." Now she had more time to spend on her own writing. She had been turning over the matter of women's position in the social structure, and now prepared an article for *The Dial:* "The Great Lawsuit: Man Versus Woman—Woman Versus Man," which to this day is considered a trail blazer in the cause of women's rights. In it the author maintained that woman must fulfill herself as an individual apart from her relationship to man. Failure to do this had made woman "an overgrown child." "What woman needs is not as a woman to act or rule, but as a nature to grow, as an intellect to discern, as a soul to live freely, and unimpeded to unfold such powers as were given her when we left our common home." The article caused a sensation. The issue in which it appeared, July 1843, was the first in the magazine's history to be sold out.

When Horace Greeley, editor of the then most progressive newspaper in the United States, the New York *Tribune*, saw the article—his wife had attended Miss Fuller's "Conversations" and was praising her to the skies—he decided here was a woman to reckon with. His *Tribune* had many woman readers. He wished to attract more. Perhaps having a woman as assistant editor . . . . ? He asked her to take the position, and she accepted with alacrity.

The readers of the *Tribune* took a woman editor—the first on any great newspaper—in stride. But when, as an on-the-spot reporter, she visited prisons, mad-houses, and women's detention wards, and began writing about them, she was looked on as a sort of scandal. She also shocked some of the intellectuals, since she spared no feelings in her reviews of the works of Browning, Landor, Elizabeth Barrett, Shelley, Crabbe, Tennyson, Longfellow, Hawthorne, Poe, Emerson, Lowell. Poe, however, himself one of the chief critics of the day, called her articles "piquant, vivid, terse, bold, luminous."

In 1845 she had a chance at even more readers. Her book, *Woman in the Nineteenth Century*, an outcome of her previous article on "Man Versus Woman," was published in February on the *Tribune* press. It became the bible of feminists, the most talked-of book of the day. Copies reached the Far West, were pirated in London. Within a week of publication, with copies fifty cents each, a whole edition was sold, and eighty-five dollars, a great deal in those days, handed over to her in royalties. William Cullen Bryant, the editor of the New York *Evening Post*, wrote, "its language is pretty strong [but] the thoughts it puts forth are so important that we should rejoice to know it read by every man and woman in America." But adverse criticism almost drowned such praise. Because her text touched on such topics as prostitution, the double standard, and marital infidelity, she was pointed out as the author of "that book on women." Orestes Brownson, editor of the *Boston Quarterly*, wrote, "No person has appeared among us whose conversation and morals have done more to corrupt the minds and hearts of our Boston community." The

Broadway Journal made a personal attack: "Her most direct writing is on a subject no virtuous woman can treat justly. No woman is a true woman who is not wife and mother."

Meanwhile Miss Fuller, who was now living with the Greeley family, held court at their farm at Turtle Bay on the East River. She was also a guest at literary gatherings in New York. At one of the soirées she met James Nathan, a businessman and art lover. Soon they were going to concerts, operas, and museums together, as well as meeting at the homes of her friends. Notes began flying back and forth between them. She wrote: "I hung lightly as an air plant. Am I to be rooted on earth? Ah, choose for me a good soil and a sunny place!" "With awe I hear you assert power over me." But Mr. Nathan was shortly to leave for Europe on a business trip. Soon after came the announcement of his engagement to a German lady. Margaret Fuller came back to reality with a start.

Now she moved from the Greeleys', going first to Brooklyn Heights, and then to a little room in what is now Greenwich Village. She bought herself a fine gown, blond lace over Nile green silk, and began meeting the foremost authors, editors, publishers, poets, and scholars in New York. Of her, Edgar Allan Poe wrote, "The eyes blue-gray are full of fire . . . . The mouth when in repose suggests a profound sensibility and is even beautiful when moved by a slight smile; yet the upper lip habitually uplifts itself, conveying the impression of a sneer." He mentioned that she looked directly at you one moment, then away the next; also that she narrowed her eyes almost to the point of closing them.

In August 1846 she sailed to Europe as foreign correspondent of the New York *Tribune*. Now a steady flow of her comments and descriptions of people and doings came to the *Tribune* office: The poet William Wordsworth was "a reverend old man clothed in black and walking with cautious step along the level garden paths"; the writer Thomas Carlyle had "untamable energy that had given him power to crush the dragons," but "you cannot interrupt him . . . you are a perfect prisoner when he has once got hold of you." Emerson's letter introducing her to Carlyle had called her "our citizen of the world by special diploma," and Carlyle on his part described her: "Such a predetermination to eat this big universe as her oyster or her egg, and to be absolute empress of all height and glory in it that her heart could conceive, I have not before seen in any human soul."

From Paris she sent reports on the night schools for working people, on establishments for the feeble-minded, and on nursery schools where poor parents might leave their children while at work. She pleaded for such institutions in America. Her visit to the author George Sand lasted most of one day: "I have never liked any woman better . . . ." was her comment. She also met the Polish mystic Adam Mickiewicz, who gave her some advice. "You think that all you need is to express yourself in books," he insisted. "You exist as a ghost whispering to the living desires it is incapable of realizing itself." He added, "You need southern skies. Seek the society of Italians . . . . Think of yourself as a beauty! Say to yourself, *I am beautiful!* And bring from Italy all that you can of joy and health." So Margaret Fuller went to Italy.

There her destiny seemed to be waiting for her. After attending vespers in St. Peter's Cathedral in Rome, she was peering around nearsightedly for a cab when a young man came up and asked if he could be of service. In the end, he walked with her to her destination. He was Giovanni Angelo, Marquis Ossoli. When she left Rome, it was arranged that they would meet again.

After a short trip during which she met the Brownings in Florence—Elizabeth Barrett Browning later commented, "Was she happy in anything I wonder; she told me she never was"—she returned to Rome. Ossoli was there to welcome her. He explained then the difficulty in their relationship. She was a Protestant. He could not introduce her to his family, the members of which were traditionally in the service of the pope. Public marriage with a Protestant would mean he would be left without an inheritance. So their marriage, which is said to have taken place some time during this period, had to be kept a secret. Secret or not, it gave her poise. Her friends spoke of her new serenity, her self-possession.

With the beginning of the war for independence in Italy (the Austrians were being pushed back while Italian peasants fought over barricades in the streets) she knew she must leave Rome. She was pregnant. They found a quiet and secluded place near Rome, in Rieti, where she could await the birth of her child. Ossoli came every week bringing mail from America and journals with news, so that she could send in her material to the *Tribune*. As a captain in the national army, he was on call now to go north to fight against the Austrians. Luckily, however, his departure was delayed, and he was able to be with Margaret at the birth of their son, Angelo. But she could rest only a few days. She must go back to Rome, must continue to send in her reports. So, leaving the baby with a wet nurse, she went to join Ossoli who had gone ahead to prepare a place for her.

Soon the *Tribune* was getting reports in the highest tradition of journalism, written while the writer was all but under fire. When the National Assembly proclaimed Rome a republic and banners declared Mazzini president, she wrote of "this great radical thinker . . . . His socialism envisages neither class war nor any violation of property rights." A few days later, however, the Nationalist forces were routed. "We are alarmed by a tremendous Cannonade . . . the French entered the city walls . . . . The night of the 28th I sat with balls and bombs whizzing and bursting all about me . . . . I saw youths born to luxury who carried all their worldly goods in a kerchief . . . . I saw Garibaldi sitting his white horse like a medieval hero . . . . As foreign troops prepared to take over Rome, Margaret and Giovanni fled to Rieti and to their son. For a very brief time Margaret could now enjoy family life: "Ossoli loves me from simple affinity . . . loves to be with me, loves to serve and soothe me . . . ." Of her baby she wrote, "In him I find satisfaction, for the first time, to deep wants of my heart . . . . I wake in the night—I look at him. He is so beautiful and good, I could die for him!"

But money had to be earned. At the end of September 1849 they went to Florence, where the American colony took them in. During that winter Margaret worked on her history of the Italian Revolution, hoping to realize something from it. Friends and relatives in America were now appealing to them to come home, and she and her husband decided this was the only course.

In May 1850 they sailed with the baby for America, friends having lent them the money for the passage. The ship never reached harbor. It was wrecked in a storm off Fire Island, July 19, and sank in sight of the New Jersey coast. The baby's body was washed ashore. The bodies of Margaret and her husband were never recovered. Also lost was the manuscript of her "History of the Roman Republic," which she had hoped would prove her greatest work.

BIBLIOGRAPHY

Brown, Arthur Wayne, *Margaret Fuller*. New York: Twayne Publishers, Inc., 1964.
Chipperfield, Faith, *In Quest of Love; the Life and Death of Margaret Fuller*. New York: Coward-McCann, Inc., 1957.

Fuller, Margaret, *Woman in the Nineteenth Century*. New York: 1845.
Howe, Mrs. J. W., *Margaret Fuller, Marchesa Ossoli*. Boston: Roberts, 1886.
Stern, Madeleine Bettina, *The Life of Margaret Fuller*. New York: E. P. Dutton & Company, Inc., 1942.
Wade, Mason, *Margaret Fuller, Whetstone of Genius*. New York: The Viking Press, Inc., 1940.

LILLIAN GILBRETH

LILLIAN (MOLLER) GILBRETH: Born in Oakland, California, May 24, 1878. Father: William Moller; mother: Annie (Delger) Moller; five sisters, three brothers; husband: Frank Bunker Gilbreth. Twelve children: Anne, Mary, Ernestine, Martha, Frank, Bill, Lillian, Fred, Dan, John, Bob, Jane.

*

Lillian Gilbreth, the foremost woman industrial engineer of her day, incorporated the findings of psychology into industrial research, furthered the idea of fitting workers to jobs and jobs to workers, and was, with her husband, a pioneer in the search to eliminate useless motions in industry and in the home. The phrases "scientific management" and "efficiency expert" became common parlance through the Gilbreths' influence.

*

In the great house in Oakland, California, with its many servants, Lillian Moller grew up with her eight brothers and sisters. She thoroughly enjoyed playing in the garden and the woods surrounding the house. As she grew older, she also enjoyed looking after her little sister Josephine, who had been assigned to her special care in this closely knit family. She and the child were given the tower room, where Josephine's little crib was placed next to Lillian's bed. The room had a washstand, neatly screened off, a big closet, shelves for her many books, and a good study table. From the window on clear nights Lillian could see the lighthouse on the Farallon Islands.

When she attended the University of California, she did well in her studies, especially in English and psychology, and was chosen as the commencement day speaker for her class. Afterward she went on to do postgraduate work at Columbia University in New York. This was interrupted, however, by a trip abroad. Her father, who was a successful hardware merchant, wanted her to have every advantage.

It was while she was on a stop-off visit in Boston en route to Europe that she met her future husband, Frank Gilbreth. He was already a well-established contractor in charge of large building projects. He showed her through art museums in Boston, drove her about in his car, saw her off to Europe, and on her return met her at the dock. A little more than a year later they were married, October 19, 1904, in the Moller home. On the train back to New York City, where they were to begin their married life, Frank Gilbreth told his wife that he would want her to be his partner in his work, just as he himself would be a partner in raising the family. This arrangement would have startled many brides, but Lillian Gilbreth took it well in stride. And it was exactly the way things worked out.

Before long Lillian Gilbreth was accompanying her husband on his business trips: climbing scaffolding, inspecting brickwork, even learning to run a steam engine. Later, when he began to be employed as a consulting engineer by factories wanting to improve their means of production, he would take her for at least one trip to each plant. Then, while he worked on that project, he would bring his problems home to her each day and get her advice. She edited his writings, studied the innovations he introduced, and made contributions herself. In short, just as it had been planned, she became his partner.

After her marriage Lillian Gilbreth continued her graduate studies. Her husband suggested she devote her thesis to "The

Psychology of Management." When it was completed, she read it at a meeting of scientific experts at Dartmouth College. It gave a new slant to science in industry. In the move toward "efficiency," she pointed out, the human element had not received the attention it deserved. Industry would gain by the psychological approach. The handling of men—the endeavor to make them not only productive but happy on the job—this should be a part of management's production aims. No worker, she reasoned, likes to be in a job in which, say, he places one small item—a nut or bolt—in one position during the whole of his workday. Doing something he does not like inevitably slows down his work. She advocated making the worker a partner in the project, having him seek ways to alternate tasks and to vary ways of doing the same task. Thus he can make his own job interesting.

This new idea of applied psychology on the job made history in the engineering professions. From Lillian Gilbreth's pioneer work in this field evolved career suitability tests, fatigue elimination studies, and the idea of skill transference from one job to another.

Right from the start both Lillian and Frank Gilbreth set themselves steadfastly against the trend of making men the tool of their tools. As they mastered the complexities of engineering, selected the right materials for a product, devised ways and means of making the product better at lower cost, and designed new products, they consistently emphasized the fact that the tool is man's servant, invented for his aid, not the other way around.

As their children began arriving—the couple was to have twelve, six boys and six girls—the Gilbreths decided to move to roomier and quieter quarters. After their New York days they were to live successively in Providence, Rhode Island, and in Plainfield and Montclair, New Jersey.

The Gilbreths' laboratory workshop and business office

were incorporated in their home. It was a healthful intertwining of *motifs*—business and home, professional and personal. Almost from babyhood the children learned how to keep the extra large household running easily, with the older ones accepting responsibilities and teaching the younger ones to accept them also in the course of growing up. In short, all fifteen of the members of the family—Mr. Gilbreth's mother was part of the household until her death in 1920—lived like cooperative members of a going concern, as indeed they were.

Lillian Gilbreth's focal role in this household is described by two of her children, Frank and Ernestine, in their book *Cheaper by the Dozen*: "Mother had her first half-dozen babies at home, instead of in hospitals, because she liked to run the house and help Dad with his work, even during the confinements. She'd supervise the household right up until each baby started coming. There was a period of about twenty-four hours then, when she wasn't much help to anybody. But she had prepared all the menus in advance, and the house ran smoothly by itself during the one day devoted to the delivery. For the next ten days to two weeks, while she remained in bed, we'd file in every morning so that she could tie the girls' hair ribbons and make sure the boys had washed properly. Then we'd come back again at night to hold the new baby and listen to Mother read *The Five Little Peppers*."

Before they had been married ten years the "Gilbreth One Best Way" system had become famous in factories and offices throughout the country. They had also established the Gilbreth Summer School, where they taught scientific management to key people in key industries, and to teachers preparing to start management courses in colleges. During the crucial period of World War I, the motion study and time study charts, which the Gilbreths evolved in their laboratories, came to be considered a "must" in all well-run factories. The team, "Gilbreth, Inc.," was sought by companies all over the United States and in Great Britain.

Lillian Gilbreth

As the fame of their methods spread to Europe, Mr. Gilbreth's commitments increased. Calls for his advice poured in. He had been warned to go slow because of a heart condition. But when he was asked to speak in Prague at the First International Management Congress ever held, he plunged into preparations for the trip. On June 14, 1924, just three days before he was due to sail, Frank Gilbreth suffered a fatal heart attack. The Gilbreths had been married just short of twenty years.

Now the widow, at the age of forty-six, was faced with the dual role of carrying on her husband's work and keeping the family a "going concern." The "one best way" was now hers to explore alone.

Her immediate plan was to fulfill her husband's commitments in Europe. In Prague she presented the speech he was to have given. On its conclusion she was made an honorary member, as her husband was to have become, of the Masaryk Academy. When she returned, she again set up motion study courses in her home. Her classes were attended by some of the most prominent people in industry. Managers, at first wary of employing a woman as an on-the-spot consultant, preferred to have their best people get the benefit of the Gilbreth Method at her school. Later, however, they were glad to have her come to the factories to solve problems face to face with the workmen. She would say, "Now let's get together and find ways of making things easier for yourselves." And soon she would have the workers suggesting their own ideas.

She found further opportunities for service through, as she said, "the kitchen door." Her "efficiency kitchen," prepared for the Brooklyn Gas Company, was publicized in women's magazines. She and her students invented an electric food mixer and drew up blueprints for new types of electric stoves and refrigerators. Basic work concepts—"store the most-used utensils where you can easily reach them, dust and iron with both hands, use circular, rhythmic motions at a smooth, steady work pace"—have now become a part of the general practice of housewives.

She found time, too, for writing books: *The Quest of the One Best Way* in 1924; *The Home-Maker and Her Job* in 1927; *Living with Our Children* in 1928. She contributed to magazines and lectured at Harvard, Yale, Colgate, M.I.T., Michigan, Stanford, Purdue, and California State. She would illustrate her lectures with simple everyday examples. For instance, she would point out that, when one discovered a button missing on a boy's shirt, and finding a matching button was difficult, one could transfer the top button to the space, and use any same-sized button for the top, where it would not be seen. Colleges and universities, she stressed, should so teach that the gap between the campus and the great world outside would be bridged. Through her influence Gilbreth motion study courses and motion study laboratories were established in many colleges.

During the Depression of the 1930's the government asked her to head the women's work for the President's Emergency Committee. She directed women's clubs to make job surveys of their localities in a nationwide "Share the Work" program. Hundreds of reports on jobs needed in home repairs and maintenance were turned in and filled, giving employment to thousands.

From 1935 to 1948 she was professor of management at Purdue University, the first woman ever to hold such a position in an engineering school. She conducted "Home Economy" courses, with motion studies in dishwashing, bed-making, ironing. On Amelia Earhart's death, she also took over her position at Purdue as adviser on careers for women. During the same period she installed a new Department of Personnel Relations at the Newark, New Jersey, College of Engineering.

During World War II, when maximum efficiency in war

industries was often a matter of life and death, her time-saving and fatigue-eliminating methods became essential. In her work with the War Manpower Commission she helped set up rehabilitation programs for veterans deprived of the use of their limbs. Many of the disabled, once trained, were helped to find jobs in industry.

Honors and awards came her way from all parts of the world: the National Institute of Social Science's gold medal "for distinguished service to humanity"; the CIOS Gold Medal, highest prize given by the international association of management groups; the Washington Award, presented by engineers to a fellow engineer—in this case for the first time to a woman. At eighty-eight she was awarded the Hoover Medal for her "contributions to Motion Study and to recognition of the principle that management engineering and human relations are intertwined." The citation spoke of her "unselfish application of energy and creative efforts in modifying industrial and home environments for the handicapped, resulting in full employment of their capacities and elevation of their self-esteem."

Now in her nineties, she is still darting about the world on lecture tours in Asia, Australia, Europe, Canada, Mexico, as well as in the United States, a trim figure with twinkling eyes and a quick lightness in her step.

BIBLIOGRAPHY

GILBRETH, FRANK BUNKER, and CAREY, E. M. G., *Belles on Their Toes*. New York: Thomas Y. Crowell Company, 1950.
———, *Cheaper by the Dozen*. New York: Thomas Y. Crowell Company, 1948.

Yost, Edna, *American Women of Science*. Philadelphia: Frederick A. Stokes Company, 1943.
——, *Frank and Lillian Gilbreth: Partners for Life*, with a Foreword by A. A. Potter. New Brunswick, New Jersey: Rutgers University Press, 1949.

MARTHA GRAHAM

MARTHA GRAHAM: Born in Pittsburgh, Pennsylvania. Father: George Graham; mother: Jane (Beers) Graham; sisters: Georgia, Mary Hamilton; husband: Erick Hawkins (divorced).

✻

Martha Graham and the school she has founded are virtually synonymous with the modern dance. She has not only produced a technique of the dance, choreographed and taught it, but her disciples have gone out to fill the modern dance world. She has created 144 ballets, among them the finest dance works of the century. Dance critic Clive Barnes has called her "the most individual, the most important, and the most seminal native-born dance talent America has ever produced."

✻

MARTHA Graham's happiest childhood memories are connected with Santa Barbara, California, where her family moved from Pittsburgh when she was ten. There, Lizzie, the Irish nurse, who took charge of Martha and her two younger sisters, would think up plays and pageants "of the nowhere and off yonder," and would have the children make up dances to go with them. But Martha's "first dancing lesson," as she called it, came from her father, a physician specializing in mental ailments. "Martha," he told her, "never lie to me, for if you do I will know. Your body will tell me." And yet, even though he realized the significance of bodily movements, he did not want Martha to go to dancing school. He believed, as did almost everybody in those days, that dancing wasn't a proper career for girls.

When she was in her early teens, her father died. Her mother wanted Martha to do whatever would make her happy. The young girl knew that the only thing that would make her happy was dancing. She had gone to a performance by dancers Ruth St. Denis and Ted Shawn and later wrote of it, "Miss Ruth opened a door for me and I saw into a life." So now she enrolled in the Denishawn School of Dancing in Los Angeles, and for seven years was a part, first of the school as pupil and teacher, and then of the Denishawn Company.

According to the school's director, Ted Shawn, Martha Graham was at first "awkward, abnormally shy . . . She'd hover at the back of the stage, timorous, inhibited." But she soon changed. Agnes de Mille, who saw her some months later, remembers her "hurtling through the room to Schubert or sitting bare-legged on the polished floor with smoldering watchfulness."

At Martha's very first dancing lessons the school's musical director, Louis Horst, took note of her. Through some thirty years he was to follow her career, giving her at-the-right-moment suggestions, turn-of-the-road directions, and on-the-spot warnings. Miss Graham says of him, "His sympathy and understanding, but primarily his faith, gave me a landscape to move in."

After a year as a student she began to teach at the school. She also danced in vaudeville units the Denishawns sent throughout the country: performed tangoes with Ted Shawn, did Japanese flower arrangements with Ruth St. Denis. As she progressed, she was given the lead in an Aztec ballet, *Xochitl*, and went with the Denishawn Company on a European tour which lasted six months.

Louis Horst now advised her it was time to strike out on her own. A scout for theatrical enterprises suggested she come to the Greenwich Village Follies. So she entrained for New York City and for two years was a solo dancer with the Follies. During this "tinsel" period, as she calls it, she worked with standard themes, doing an Oriental dance, a Moorish dance, and a dance with a large veil. This period brought her money, but it also brought her acute dissatisfaction with herself. She remembered what her father had told her—that a person could not divorce himself from his body, that if he tried to, his spirit became alienated and he was lost. Like a nonbeliever worshipping in a church, prayers would not ring true, genuflections would have no meaning. She knew that tiptoe flights, willowy arm-wavings, breeze-wafted veils, were not for her. She must find a way to make her body express herself. But how?

After extensive "explorations of the landscape within," she decided to give up her lucrative job with the Follies and accept a teaching post at the Eastman School of Music in Rochester, New York. Louis Horst had meanwhile relinquished his post at the Denishawn School and was devoting himself to guiding her in her career. They appeared together at Eastman, prophets of a new era in the dance. Here, while she taught dance and stage movements for actors, she learned ways to develop her own dance idiom. With Horst's help as accompanist and mentor, she trained her body to move in different ways and in different contexts from any before attempted. "Life today is nervous, sharp and zigzag," she said later. "It often stops in midair. That is what I aim for in my dances." She insists she never started out to be a rebel. It was only that the emotions she had to express could not be projected through any of the traditional forms.

This was in 1925. The country was seething with unrest. All forms of art were undergoing a revolution. The theories of psychology were being used to extend the boundaries of poetry, music, painting.

Her debut dance concert in her new idiom occurred on

Martha Graham

April 18, 1926. A friend, Frances Steloff, contributed a thousand dollars to cover expenses. Louis Horst directed the orchestra. Connoisseurs of the dance, gathered at the Forty-eighth Street Theater in New York, witnessed Martha Graham's first foray into this new realm of the dance. They saw, through such dance sequences as "Three Gobi Maidens" and "A Study in Lacquer," desires and conflicts expressed through bodily movements. These critics agreed that something entirely new, a departure from all previous forms, had been witnessed.

Martha Graham continued her teaching. She joined the faculty of the John Murray Anderson–Robert Milton School in New York City. After 1928 she also taught at the Neighborhood Playhouse. In the early thirties, she founded the Martha Graham School of Contemporary Dance. Her classes were used as a laboratory for her stage works, and her stage works in turn were a means for attracting new pupils to her school —a sort of self-winding process, with herself as the key to the development.

Her dance company has been an outgrowth of her school. Through the years such notable dancers as John Butler, Merce Cunningham, Jane Dudley, Jean Erdman, Erick Hawkins, Stuart Hodes, Pearl Lang, Donald McKayle, Sophia Maslow, Norman Morrice, May O'Donnell, Anna Sokolow, Paul Taylor, Glen Tetley, and Yuriko have grown to maturity under her guidance and have gone on to independent careers.

Her first solo engagement with a symphony orchestra was also the result of a school affiliation. The Neighborhood Playhouse in 1929 was cosponsor, with the Cleveland Orchestra, at a performance of Richard Strauss's symphonic poem *Ein Heldenleben*. She danced to this and the publicity it brought led to her taking the part of the Chosen One in Leonide Massine's version of Stravinsky's *Le Sacre du Printemps*, played by the Philadelphia Orchestra.

Martha Graham

By 1930 she had begun using scores by such modern composers as Honegger, Křenek, Kodály, Toch, Villa-Lobos, Bartók, Schoenberg, Hindemith, Chavez, Lopatnikoff, and Varèse, and widening her horizons in other ways. She visited the American Indians in the sagebrush valleys of New Mexico and returned to create works which portrayed this ancient people through their rituals: "Primitive Canticles" and "Ceremonials." Horst began his collaboration with her as composer of musical settings, particularly of the primitive dances.

Now the whole country was beginning to take notice of this dancer whose technique conveyed the contemporary mood: sharp and dissonant movements, angular thrust of neck and shoulders, seeming pauses in mid-leap, kneeling, crouching, elbowing, lying, rolling—making the earth a partner to the dance.

In March 1932 she received a Guggenheim Fellowship, the first ever awarded a dancer, for a summer of study in Mexico. In 1933 she presented "Frenetic Rhythms," a sardonic commentary on the effects of jazz, and produced *Six Miracle Plays* for the Stage Alliance. She also assisted the famous actress Katharine Cornell in a production of *Lucrece*. She was now developing a dance-drama, as much theater as choreography. Her students were taught that dancing requires acting ability of a high order.

In 1935 she began her work at the Bennington (Vermont) College Summer School, presenting in her first workshop there *Panorama*, with a group of thirty-six dancers.

Over a decade beginning in the mid-thirties (her "American period") her works became peopled with figures of pioneers, colonists, Indians, and witches. Her creations dealt with migrations, homesteading, trailblazing, land breaking. The first of these works, *Frontier*, with its drive to explore, its yearning for new boundaries, its declaration of personal freedom, was to become her trademark.

In 1936 and 1937 Martha Graham made forty-two appearances across the country. Almost every year during the succeeding ten years she and the company toured extensively throughout the United States. In 1937 she danced for President and Mrs. Roosevelt at the White House. In 1939 she again received a Guggenheim Fellowship.

One of her most important works, *Letter to the World*, had its premiere at Bennington College August 11, 1940. In it she reveals the inner life of the poet Emily Dickinson by portraying each of the warring impulses of her nature as separate individuals: the young girl, happy, spontaneous; the ancestress, full of dreads and death wishes; the New England lady, gracious but inhibited; the young woman, searching for love, passionate and unrestrained. The men in Emily's life are portrayed as they appeared to the poet herself, within a framework of fantasy. Miss Graham has said that the pain she endured bringing this dance interpretation to completion was like the agony of a difficult childbirth.

Her costumes, which she designs herself, are as revolutionary as her movements. For *Lamentation* her garment was a tube of elastic purple cloth. Long flowing capes are used to symbolize qualities and values. The character Clytemnestra shows the magnitude of her vengefulness by the voluminous cape she offers Agamemnon. The unwieldiness of Tiresias' robe in *Night Journey* gives outward reality to his torment. In *The Lady of the House of Sleep* a cloak is swung over a woman to represent the wings of the angel of death. Shields, fans, swords, and other such objects are used symbolically.

She rehearses a new work with her full company and chamber orchestra. Right up to the hour of performance whole sections and dances may be changed. Between rehearsals her seamstress rips and restitches her costumes, working sometimes right through the night preceding the premiere.

In May 1944 Martha Graham opened an eight-day repertory season at the National Theater in New York. It was the first time since the days of the great ballerina Pavlova twenty years earlier that a dance company built around a single star had undertaken so extensive an engagement.

Her famous *Appalachian Spring* was first presented on October 30, 1944, at the Library of Congress under the auspices of the Coolidge Foundation. This tells the story of a young pioneer and his joyous, tremulous bride: their marriage, the hellfire and brimstone sermon at their wedding, the bride's soft dancing as if she could not believe his message, the groom's solemn joy—the preaching, the hoping, the pioneering, the praying, the loving—all portrayed in dance. This is one of the dances Miss Graham has chosen to restore, so that years later it is still being presented in her repertory season. The work of recalling the movements of a dance and teaching them to other solo dancers, she says, is so difficult that often she feels the result is not worth the effort.

As for the survival of her dance technique, there is no question of that. Agnes de Mille speaks of her technique as "probably the greatest addition to dance vocabulary made in this century, comparable to the rules of perspective in painting or the use of the thumb in keyboard playing. No dancer that I can name has expanded technique to a comparable degree. She has herself alone given us a new system of leverage, balance and dynamics. It has gone into the idiom . . . . Dancers for untold generations will dance differently because of her labors."

On September 4, 1949, Miss Graham married the man who was then her dancing partner, Erick Hawkins. But a family life in the ordinary sense was not for her and the marriage ended after two years.

On January 4 and 5, 1950, Martha Graham was soloist in a highly acclaimed performance of *Judith: Choreographic Poem for Orchestra*, by William Schuman, performed by the Louisville (Kentucky) Orchestra. She was later to dance this work at Carnegie Hall and still later at the dedication of the Benjamin Franklin monument in Berlin.

In 1952 her school was moved from lower Fifth Avenue to a red brick building at 316 East 63rd Street. It began to take on an international flavor, students coming to her from India, Korea, Thailand, Japan, England, France, New Zealand, Greece, Israel. The enrollment sometimes reached three hundred. Miss Graham's sister, Mrs. Georgia Sargeant, is the registrar. The school is one of the most revered in the dance world. It provides her company with a constantly fresh supply of dancers, and her dancers with teaching positions during the parts of the year when the troupe is not performing.

In 1954 the Martha Graham Company was off to Europe, opening in January at the Théâtre des Champs-Elysées in Paris, and after six performances going on to Norway, Sweden, Denmark, The Netherlands, Switzerland, and Italy. In 1955 she brought into her orbit Japan, the Philippines, Burma, Thailand, Java, India, and Iran. On the closing night in Tokyo fireworks were set off in her honor. When Paul Grey Hoffman, director of the United Nations Special Fund, presented her with the 1957 *Dance* Magazine Award, he spoke of her as "the greatest single ambassador we have ever sent to Asia."

In 1955 the B. de Rothschild Foundation began sponsoring an annual three-week season in New York of Martha Graham and her Dance Company. Meanwhile she appeared in shorter engagements in other cities. In 1957, through the help of the Pittsburgh radio-TV station WQED, the Mellon Foundation, and the B. de Rothschild Foundation, a film, "The Dancer's World," was completed. In the film she speaks briefly about what is required both physically and spiritually to become a dancer. It won the Peabody and Ohio State awards as well as awards from several European film festivals. Her dance *Night Journey*, made into a film, won awards at the Berlin, Edinburgh, Valencia, and American film festivals.

Martha Graham

In 1958 the three-act dance drama *Clytemnestra* was premiered. It is based on that tragic tale of the wife of the Greek warrior Agamemnon, who contrives her husband's assassination in reprisal for his sacrifice of their daughter as an offering to the gods. This, more than any of Martha Graham's dances, shows the close parallel between the dance as she conceives it and psychological analysis. Clytemnestra "dances" the ideas that go through her mind when she is dishonored in the underworld. Utterances of the subconscious, chantings of the inner spirit, sound out on the stage. In the end, through this process, catharsis comes as much to the audience as to the tragic figure on the stage.

When the president of Aspen Institute presented her with the Aspen Award of thirty thousand dollars in 1965, he said, "As a creative dancer, choreographer and company director she has probed deeply those dark recesses of the human spirit and expressed essential truths which have awakened others to a new appreciation of man's nature." Martha Graham's later works, *The Plain of Prayer, Cortege of Eagles,* and *Dancing Ground,* have similar implications.

In 1966 a Federal grant of $181,000 went to the Martha Graham Company, from the National Endowment for the Arts: $40,000 for the creation of two new works by Miss Graham, and a $141,000 matching grant to permit her to take her company on an eight-week tour of the United States. Her comment on hearing this news: "It destroyed despair." So that year, which happened to be the fortieth anniversary of her first appearance as a solo dancer, Miss Graham and her company toured the United States, visiting thirty cities. The whole nation is becoming personally cognizant of this taut figure with the high cheekbones, the huge deep-set eyes, the dark hair pulled straight back from the almost white face.

Martha Graham is now making a deliberate attempt to shift the focus from herself. Her company is, of course, an extension of her genius, but it is an extension which, she feels, must be made capable of supporting life separate from its source. Its members are remarkably gifted: Bertram Ross, Robert Cohan, Helen McGehee, Mary Hinkson, Matt Turney, Robert Powell, Clive Thompson, Noemi Lapzeson, Takako Asakawa, William Louther, Phyllis Gutelius, Moss Cohen, Judith Hogan, Diane Gray, Judith Leifer, Yuriko Kimura, Dawn Suzuki, Robert Dodson. Thus, by relaying her genius to others, Martha Graham is assuring the immortality of her great art.

BIBLIOGRAPHY

DE MILLE, AGNES GEORGE, *Dance to the Piper*. Boston: Little, Brown & Company, 1952.
LEATHERMAN, LEROY, *Martha Graham; Portrait of the Lady as an Artist*. New York: Alfred A. Knopf, Inc., 1966.

EDITH HAMILTON

EDITH HAMILTON: Born in Dresden, Germany, August 12, 1867 (during a visit by her mother, an American citizen). Died in Washington, D.C., May 31, 1963. Father: Montgomery Hamilton; mother: Gertrude (Bond) Hamilton; sisters: Alice, Margaret, Norah; brother: Arthur.

*

Edith Hamilton, famous classicist, author, and authority on the ancient Greek way of life, wrote the book *The Greek Way*, which has become a standard work on the subject. A few months before her ninetieth birthday she was declared a citizen of Athens, a rare honor. But it is more nearly accurate to say that for breadth of vision, for width of influence, for the extent to which her ideas have been assimilated, she was in her lifetime elected a citizen of the world.

*

EDITH had a lively childhood, making up games with her three sisters and eleven cousins on the ten acres of Hamilton property in Fort Wayne, Indiana. Together the children played Robin Hood, Knights of the Round Table, and the Siege of Troy (with the woodshed as a Greek camp). But even as a child Edith's chief love was reading, and not only in English, but in Latin and Greek. Her father was a lover of learning, who, because he was wealthy, had the opportunity to satisfy this bent. He set her to studying ancient languages when she was seven years old. She soon was absorbing books in Greek and Latin as easily as in her own tongue: stories of gods and goddesses and of mythological creatures, and conversations of the wise men who lived in Greece in the early days. As a thirteen-year-old she would read while she combed her hair in the morning, the book open before her on the dresser. When the children took long walks in the woods, she was elected the storyteller. Her mother, who believed in early study of modern languages, conversed with her children in French and employed servants who could talk with them in German.

In her young days Edith was moody, surprising in one who later developed so even a disposition. Summers, the family went to Mackinac Island in the straits between Lake Michigan and Lake Huron. There Edith liked to stand looking out over the stormy waters and feel they were answering her own stormy thoughts. Her sister Alice, her closest companion, was often mystified by these dark periods. Once, gazing at the lake, Edith intoned, "Gray as the sky the world lies before me." "You don't really feel like that?" Alice asked her. "Most of the time," Edith replied.

Winters, Edith and her younger sisters went to school at Miss Porter's in Farmington, Connecticut. But, though she liked the gentle way Miss Porter had of leading one into learning, it was not until later at Bryn Mawr College in Pennsylvania that she really got into her own scholarly stride. After completing her courses with the highest marks, she received both her B.A. and M.A. degrees there. As the outstanding student of her class she won a fellowship for a year of study abroad.

Her sister Alice accompanied Edith to Europe. They went first to the University of Leipzig, Edith to study the classics and Alice to study medicine. (Alice Hamilton was to become America's foremost expert in industrial diseases.) The sisters later transferred to the University of Munich. As the first

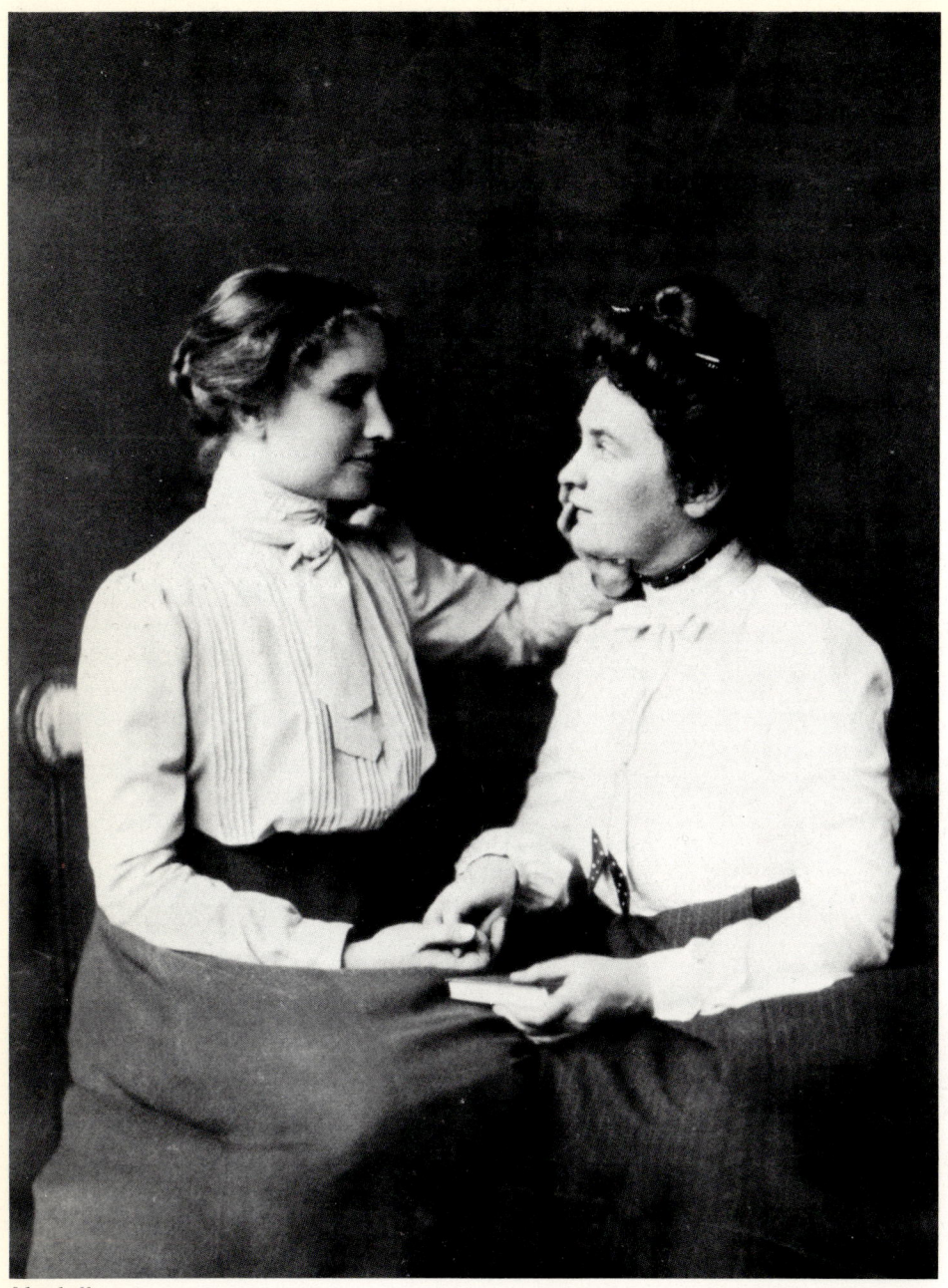

Marshall

*HELEN KELLER
and
ANNE SULLIVAN*

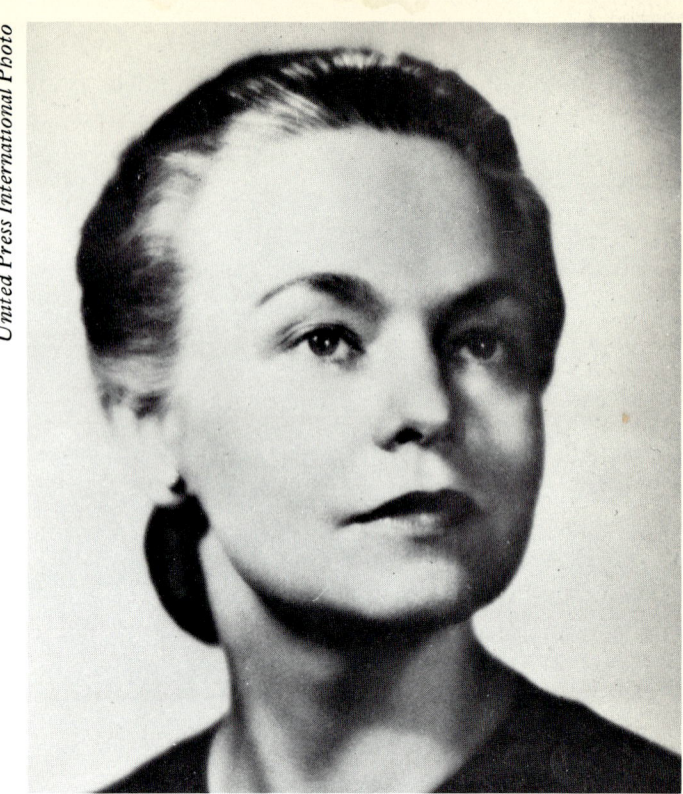

OVETA CULP HOBBY

MALVINA HOFFMAN

United Press International Photo

EDITH
HAMILTON

Wide World Photos

LILLIAN GILBRETH

MARTHA GRAHAM

*Dance Collection
New York Public Library*

MARY BAKER EDDY

McClure's Magazine, 1907
New York Public Library Picture Collection

MARGARET FULLER

Engraved in London from a portrait by Hicks
New York Public Library Picture Collection

United Press International Photo

AMELIA EARHART

Photo by Elliott Erwitt © 1966 Magnum Photos

DOROTHEA LANGE

SUSANNE LANGER

*Connecticut College
Photo by Philip A. Biscuti*

MARY LYON

MARGARET MEAD

woman student of the classics to be entered in this college Edith created a sensation. An elderly professor took her in tow on her first day, conducting her through throngs of curious male students. But there were problems to be met later. If she were seated in the main auditorium, she and a male student might have to share the same book! To keep her properly insulated, she was given a separate chair, on the lecturer's platform. And this is where she sat through the whole term, conspicuous but uncontaminating and uncontaminated. She wrote later of the period: "The head of the University used to stare at me, then shake his head and say sadly to a colleague, 'There, now you see what's happened? We're right in the midst of the woman question!'"

She would have liked to continue at Munich, but when a letter came from the dean of Bryn Mawr College, offering her the post of headmistress at Bryn Mawr preparatory school in Baltimore, she knew she must accept. Her father had lost much of his money and she would have to be finding work soon anyway. She returned to America. But in the fall of 1896, when her train pulled into Baltimore, she had to steel her nerves as for a vital encounter. "If I were put in charge of running this train," she told herself, "I could hardly know less how to do it than I know how to run the Bryn Mawr School."

She proved to be an excellent headmistress. In the twenty-six years she held the post, she not only made the Bryn Mawr School for Girls the largest and most popular one in Baltimore, but proved to hundreds of girls that a love of books can lead the way to a deeper, fuller life.

Her duties included talking with parents, attending teachers' meetings, and advising students. The architects, in constructing the school, had made provision for a gymnasium and a swimming pool, as well as for plaster casts of Greek statues in the entrance hall, but had forgotten to save any space for offices. So, seated on the back stairs with a student, she would go over a report card, item by item. Or she would make clear to a disappointed senior who had failed in her entrance exams to Bryn Mawr College—a "must" if the student was to be graduated from the school—that she knew she could pass them the next time if she worked harder. She would impress on another student that it was not hard work that was dreary but superficial work. She would go from room to room hearing recitations. Wherever she went she brought an air of nobility and dedication. As one student, Grace Branhan, put it, she seemed to have come "from some high centre of civilization, where the skies were loftier, the views more spacious, the atmosphere more free and open than with us."

Through her years at the school she also taught regular classes in Latin to seniors and on Sundays tutored in her home. Another student has stated that being able to read Greek in the original with Miss Hamilton was "the crowning intellectual experience of my life." She emphasized that any achievement entails hard work: "Nothing effortless was among the things the early Greeks wanted." Her motto, which soon became the students' motto, was Plato's "Hard is the good." And she could not repeat too often, "Responsibility is the price every man must pay for freedom. It is to be had on no other terms."

After twenty-six years as headmistress at Bryn Mawr School Miss Hamilton felt she had rounded out her teaching career. She retired in 1922 and purchased with some friends, the Reids, a summer place at Sea Wall, Mt. Desert Island, Maine. Here she was to spend practically every summer for the next forty years.

Her winter home was in New York City, where she moved with her friends' daughter, Doris Fielding Reid, in 1924, when she was fifty-seven. It was here that her career as a writer began. A group of her neighbors had been meeting to hear her talk informally about the ancient Greeks. Two members of the group, who were on the editorial staff of the magazine *Theatre Arts Monthly*, urged her to write down her ideas. After a great deal of prodding—"*Please* do not press me so. How would you feel if I were imploring you to attempt to become an opera singer?"—she did finally write an article on the Greek attitude. It developed into a series, and, published in the magazine, was so widely read that it led, in 1930, to the publication of her book *The Greek Way*.

The book made clear her credo: "In Greece there was a dominating ideal," she wrote. " 'Excellence' is the nearest equivalent we have to the word then commonly used for it, but it meant more than that. It was the utmost perfection possible, the very best and highest a man could attain to, which when perceived always has a compelling authority." Or, she says, "The special characteristic of the Greeks was their power to see the world clearly and at the same time as beautiful." Just before the book's publication she made her first trip to Athens. As she sat on the steps of the Parthenon, it was as though the Greek world, of which she had so long known the exact spiritual dimensions, its breadth, height, and depth, had now taken on physical dimensions.

The book began a brilliant writing career for Miss Hamilton. She went on to write: *The Roman Way* (1932), *The Prophets of Israel* (1936), *Three Greek Plays* (1937), *Mythology* (1942), *Witness to the Truth* (1948), and *Echo of Greece* (1957). Later a collection of her essays, *The Ever Present Past*, was published.

Like the Greeks, Miss Hamilton's life had a harmonious intertwining of emotional and intellectual activities. She helped bring up three children—a nephew and two nieces of Miss Reid's. One summer in Maine the children broke into the pump house and somehow managed to detach a pipe, creating an awful mess. Miss Hamilton and Mr. Reid spent the rest of the day mopping it up. That evening she exclaimed at the supper table how fortunate she was that her life was so full. Mr.

Reid burst out laughing. "That your life is fortunate is open to question," he said, "but that it is full, there is no doubt whatever."

In 1943, after she had lived in New York City for almost twenty years, she and Miss Reid moved to Washington, D.C. Miss Reid's position as vice president of an investment firm had been transferred there. At seventy-six Miss Hamilton was still quite prepared to begin a new life in a new home. To her house in Washington came distinguished visitors—author Isak Dinesen, historian Arnold Toynbee, poet Robert Frost, critic Stephen Spender—to partake of her wit, her wisdom, and her human understanding.

She began to give lectures. Criticizing slipshod methods of education, she would describe its current standard as "If at first you don't succeed, try something else." She wrote four of her books in Washington. These and her earlier books were translated into many languages. She was elected to the American Academy of Arts and Letters. Honorary degrees from Yale, Rochester University, Pennsylvania University, Goucher College, were bestowed on her. Yale University, granting her a degree, summed up her achievements: "By the sheer power of your books, you have become one of our great sources of adult education. Your scholarly love of Greek culture is no repining for a dead past, but a new dimension of depth and beauty in our civilization."

A few days before her ninetieth birthday one of the major events of her life took place. Her translation of Aeschylus' play *Prometheus Bound* was presented at the ancient theater of Herodes Atticus in Athens, and the Greek government invited her to attend the performance as its honored guest. So she and Miss Reid sailed for Greece. King Paul bestowed on her the Golden Cross of the Legion of Benefaction. At the performance, the mayor of Athens declared her a citizen of that city. In accepting the honor, this tall, spare woman, her

Edith Hamilton

white hair drawn smoothly back, told the audience, "It is impossible for me to express my gratitude for the honors shown me . . . . I am a citizen of Athens. I am a citizen of Athens, of the city I have for so long loved as I love my own country. This is the proudest moment of my life." Indeed it was a rare instance of actuality approaching the ideal: this ancient land, where she had lived in her imaginings for four-score years, this land of her girlhood dreams, of her college studies, of her teaching and of her writing, had now in very truth become her own. The occasion made headlines throughout the world.

In this same year, 1957, *The Greek Way*, twenty-seven years after its first publication, was chosen by Book-of-the-Month Club. The Chicago *Tribune* heralded her on her birthday, August 12, as "the wisest of womankind." In this and the following years awards came to her from all over the country. She wrote the introduction to *Dialogues of Plato*, gave lectures, traveled.

It was typical of her spirit that only a week before her death she said to Miss Reid, "You know I haven't felt up to writing but now I think I am going to be able to finish that book on Plato."

On her death, John Mason Brown wrote of her in *Saturday Review:* "Nobility of mind, character and spirit is rare indeed. Wisdom, true wisdom, is no less rare. Edith, one of the most human of mortals, was the radiant possessor of both."

BIBLIOGRAPHY

HAMILTON, EDITH, *The Greek Way*. New York: W. W. Norton & Company, Inc., 1930.

REID, DORIS FIELDING, *Edith Hamilton: An Intimate Portrait*. New York: W. W. Norton & Company, Inc., 1967.

OVETA CULP HOBBY

OVETA CULP HOBBY: Born in Killeen, Texas, January 19, 1905. Father: Isaac William Culp; mother: Emma (Hoover) Culp; second of seven children; husband: William Pettus Hobby; children: William, Jessica.

*

Oveta Culp Hobby first came to national prominence as head of the Women's Army Corps (WAC) in World War II. Under her leadership it became a full-fledged branch of the Army. Ten years later, as Secretary of the Department of Health, Education and Welfare, she became a member of President Eisenhower's Cabinet, the second woman in United States history—the first was Frances Perkins—to hold a Cabinet position. For many years she managed Texas' largest newspaper, the Houston *Post*.

*

IN her childhood Oveta and her young companions would stage make-believe battles—crusaders against wicked Ku Klux Klansmen. Always the crusaders won, and for reward stripped off the masks from the klansmen and made them "confess." But most of young Oveta's pleasures were of a milder sort. If she came home late from school, her mother could always guess exactly where she had been: curled up in the big leather armchair at her father's law office, listening to him and his friends discuss the ins and outs of legal questions. Or, if her father had no visitors, she might be poring over the

Congressional Record, with all the absorption most children give to reading about the adventures of Robinson Crusoe. Here she learned about the Red Cross relief sent to Galveston hurricane sufferers, about irrigation lessening the effects of drought, about the newly voted Sixteenth Amendment which empowered Congress to levy and collect taxes on incomes.

When her father was elected to the Texas State House of Representatives, he took this eager child of his along—she was then fourteen years old—to the state capital, Austin. There she would sit wide-eyed beside him during sessions of the house, while one faction of representatives stormily championed the League of Nations—President Woodrow Wilson had just submitted the Treaty of Versailles to the United States Senate after World War I—and another attacked it as unrealistic. She heard the Woman Suffrage Amendment debated. Were women fit to vote? Were the polls fit places for women? (The amendment went into effect August 26, 1920.) Other discussions—government operations of railroads, the "hands off" policy in Mexico, government grants to small businesses—all were fascinating subjects to this young girl in her mid-teens.

She was home in Killeen during her sixteenth and seventeeth years, when she was graduated from Temple High School and studied one year at Mary Hardin-Baylor College. But, by the time she was eighteen, her father was reelected to the house and she was back in Austin with him.

Then, however, she was making her own way. At twenty she had been asked by the speaker of the house to act as the parliamentarian. Her duties were to define and make clear the practices and procedures of the Texas House of Representatives. In a few more years she had rounded up a between-sessions job: legal clerk in the state banking department. By 1928, when she was twenty-three, she had completed the considerable task of codifying the state banking laws.

Oveta Culp Hobby

In 1931, 1939, and 1941 she again acted as parliamentarian. But after 1931 her home base was Houston. She had found a job there in the circulation department of the Houston *Post*. The publisher of this newspaper, a former governor of Texas, William Hobby, soon became aware of this newcomer, the daughter of his old friend Ike Culp. He liked the way her face would light up when she smiled. He liked the way she was always ready with good suggestions. He was later to tell her, "Anyone with as many ideas as you have is bound to hit a good one now and then." After several months of quiet courtship, they were married.

In the first ten years of their marriage the Hobbys were busy running the Houston *Post*, which they now owned. Their creative partnership became famous in newspaper circles. (Through the years Mrs. Hobby worked successively as research editor, literary editor, assistant editor, vice president and executive president.) Their home life was equally busy. Their son William and their daughter Jessica, born during this period, were their close companions. "Nothing gives one so widened a view of things," Mrs. Hobby once said, "as listening to a five-year-old tell about his school doings." She taught both her children horsemanship and she also taught them how to manage their allowances. It was while she was awaiting the birth of her daughter that she wrote *Mr. Chairman*, a book on parliamentary law. It was adopted as a school textbook in Texas and Louisiana.

Articles she prepared regularly for the Houston *Post* were widely read. In the summer of 1941 she was asked to come to Washington to set up a Women's Interest Section of the War Department's Bureau of Public Relations. The first peacetime draft had been set in motion the year before, and the department was receiving thousands of letters a day from all over the country, written by women who were worried about their men in service.

Oveta Culp Hobby

So in August 1941 this slight, soft-spoken indomitable woman went to Washington and took over Room 2840 of the War Department Building. Before the United States declared war in December 1941, she had to a large extent carried out her announced intention: to assemble a staff of women reporters to write Army news for the women's pages of leading newspapers. These writers would inform women across the country about their sons, husbands, sweethearts, brothers, fathers. They would give information on health, discipline, food, clothing, entertainment. "This is the public's Army," said Mrs. Hobby, "and the women have as much interest in it as the men." Also, through an organization made up of the presidents of the nation's large clubs and associations for women, she channeled pertinent information across the United States.

But with American troops deployed in widely separated zones, a manpower shortage became imminent. General George Marshall, then the Army's Chief of Staff, and Secretary of War Henry Stimson asked Mrs. Hobby to speak before Senate and House committees on behalf of a projected Women's Army Auxiliary Corps (WAAC). She was also asked to recommend a suitable woman to head such a corps. Mrs. Hobby suggested seven women, but in the end the legislators decided that she herself was the best choice. Her husband assured her "Go ahead—you can do it!" So, at the age of thirty-six, she became the first commander of the WAAC.

Now Jessica, aged seven, and William, aged eleven, came to live in Washington, and Mr. Hobby came there as often as wartime travel and Houston *Post* business permitted. "The team" kept in touch by telephone every evening.

Her job—the building of the nation's first women's army—was a tremendous one. She recruited officer candidates to be trained for administrative work. She crisscrossed the country, making speeches, wearing the only WAAC uniform then in existence, which she washed each night and ironed each morning.

Because of that word *auxiliary* the WAAC organization was hampered by many details and was barred from many valuable Army services. Director Hobby and her staff, for example, had to make up their own budget for presentation to Congress and check their own blueprints for the new housing for the women at every station. Finally, however, the term *auxiliary* was dropped. Now the organization, as the Women's Army Corps (WAC), became an integral part of the Army, and Director Hobby became Colonel Hobby.

Though the work went more swiftly, she still had multiple duties. Flying to England with Mrs. Franklin D. Roosevelt, she made a study of war work among the British women. She inspected units of the Women's Royal Naval Service and the Auxiliary Territorial Service. Back home again, she supervised the diet of the WAC—the young ladies were getting too fat on the regulation fare provided for men. She adjusted their marching pace—it must be shorter than that for men. She examined and in some cases revised the rules for leaves, recreation, inspections. At the beginning of the war Congress had drawn up a list of 54 Army jobs it considered suitable for women. By the end of the war Colonel Hobby had stretched that number to 239. Members of the WAC were working as boiler inspectors, clerks, riveters, interpreters, tractor mechanics, personnel officers, balloon gas chemists, laboratory technicians, surveyors, dieticians, photographers, and airplane plotters. They filled these roles in such distant points as North Africa, Egypt, India, and Australia.

By 1944 the demand for women of the WAC was exceeding by far the supply. Requests were coming in from all over the world for 600,000 women—three times more than the full complement of the corps. By 1945 the WAC, a full-fledged branch of the Army, was receiving soldiers' insurance benefits, pensions, dependency allowances, and overseas pay. On her resignation that year Colonel Hobby was awarded the Distinguished Service Medal, the first given to a woman. In 1947 the Philippine Military Medal of Honor was bestowed upon her.

Back in Houston Mrs. Hobby resumed her career with the Houston *Post* and its affiliate KPRC-AM-FM-TV. Again Mr. and Mrs. Hobby were sharing adjoining offices.

In 1948 she went to Geneva, Switzerland, with the United States delegation to the United Nations Conference on Freedom of Information and the Press. She also worked on the Hoover Commission Study. In 1949 she was elected president of the Southern Newspaper Publishers Association and vice-chairman of the American Cancer Society.

When General Dwight D. Eisenhower was elected president in 1952, he asked Mrs. Hobby to serve as head of the Federal Security Agency. When it was reorganized into a Department of Health, Education and Welfare, she, as its director, assumed Cabinet rank, taking the oath of office April 11, 1953.

This office was no easy job. The newly organized department administered old-age funds for sixty-seven million Americans. These pension and welfare funds totaled four billion dollars a year. Secretary Hobby broadened the base of social security to include all self-employed people. To her goes the credit that millions of self-employed people today enjoy social security benefits. Her responsibilities extended to the world's greatest medical research centers, hospitals for drug addicts and the mentally unsound, distribution of funds to land grant colleges, and teacher and student exchange programs with foreign countries. She got out up-to-date editions of such vital government information booklets as "Infant Care," which is published in eight languages and has sold millions of copies.

In 1955 her husband became seriously ill, and Mrs. Hobby resigned as Secretary of Health, Education and Welfare. She returned to Houston and took over as president of the *Post*.

But she continued her broad civic and cultural interests. In the late 1950's she was active in the fields of economic development, employment of the physically handicapped, graduate education, educational television, and the international exchange of students and scholars. Today she is editor and chairman of the board of the *Post*. Her husband died in 1964, and their son, William Hobby, Jr., is now the executive editor and president of the newspaper.

Under President Lyndon Johnson she became a member of the National Advisory Commission on Selective Service, a member of HEW's Vietnam Health Education Task Force, and a director of the Corporation for Public Broadcasting. But perhaps one of the most treasured honors came when the library of the new college in her home town of Killeen was named the Oveta Culp Hobby Library.

BIBLIOGRAPHY

ROOSEVELT, ANNA ELEANOR, and HICKOK, LORENA A., *Ladies of Courage*. New York: G. P. Putnam's Sons, 1954.
Time. May 4, 1953 (v. 61, No. 18, pp. 24–27).

MALVINA HOFFMAN

MALVINA HOFFMAN (GRIMSON): Born in New York, New York, June 15, 1885. Died in New York, New York, July 10, 1966. Father: Richard Hoffman; mother: Fidelia (Lamson) Hoffman; brothers: Charles, Richard; sisters: Helen, Elsie; husband: Samuel Bonarios Grimson.

✳

Malvina Hoffman, eminent sculptor, is known especially for her dancing figures and for her portrait busts of famous people. She won fame also when she was commissioned by the Field Museum of Chicago to make 110 bronze figures portraying the races of man, for the Hall of Man. A great service to anthropology, this vast work also stands as an enduring monument to this woman's perseverance, energy, and creative genius.

✳

EVEN in her childhood Malvina Hoffman was unconsciously preparing herself to be a sculptor, a profession that requires a great deal of constructional knowhow. She did not care for dolls. She favored mechanical toys, especially those she could take apart and put together again. Once she made harnesses for toy horses from leather straps. Another time, when her brother Richard was ill and confined to his bed, she rigged up wires along the ceiling and a little traveling basket with which they exchanged notes and gifts between their rooms.

Her father, a distinguished pianist, for thirty years soloist with the New York Philharmonic Orchestra, encouraged her to use her hands—and her head. He would take her to houses being built in the neighborhood and show her how roof beams were set up and how brick walls were constructed. He taught her how to break a brick, the way masons do, with a sharp blow of the trowel, making a clean cut, not on a slant.

By the time she was in her teens she was attending regular school and going two evenings a week to art school. She joined a class in painting and modeled in clay. On subways she would make rapid sketches of passengers, noting the folds in their clothing, the creases in their sleeves, the tilt of a hat, and the lines of a hand holding a newspaper. She learned to leave out the nonessentials and to draw rapid strokes that gave life to the sketches. When her parents realized how much in earnest she was about her art work they gave her a little room on the third floor, with windows facing north for steady lighting. Here she would work out her ideas. When a friend of hers died, she found comfort in creating a small standing figure of a woman with bowed head, the whole posture suggesting desolation.

She persuaded her father to let her mold a bust of him in clay while he played the piano. As the work progressed, she writes in her autobiography, *Yesterday Is Tomorrow*, she realized that "to make a likeness is not half the battle. I was interested in what went on behind the facial mask. What lines could show the inner character, the submerged struggle and patience of a man as dedicated as my father? Revealing this truth demanded an intensity of observation beyond just making the shape of his features. This probing for what lies beneath the surface has been the search of my whole life, and I confronted this high barrier on this first portrait, as well as on every one I have made since. I discovered that not one profile from the side, but countless profiles all around the head had to be modeled in the clay, and every one of these had to fit into the next one from front and back and sides, from above and below; every viewpoint was essential before the head would have living authority in its forms and entirety."

A friend brought the well-known sculptor Gutzon Borglum to the house to give his opinion on her work. The clay had "sagged," lowering the shoulders. Borglum asked her what she had used as an armature (the "skeleton" to hold a clay bust in shape) and she mentioned sticks of kindling, a tin can, and a short board. He showed her how to construct a proper armature, using a piece of pipe set into a larger pipe screwed to a wooden base, and several small bits of wood wired together to make "butterflies." He also encouraged her to reproduce the bust, once finished, in marble. The intense work required for this project she called her "salvation by self-obliteration." It made her decide once and for all to become a sculptor.

When the marble was finished she submitted it to the Annual Exhibition of the National Academy of Design in New York. It was accepted, and this strengthened her in her resolve.

Next she depicted a young violinist, Samuel Grimson. She had met him when he came from his native England to America on a concert tour. While the portrait of her father showed a mature artist, this one showed an ardent, sensitive young man at the dawn of his career. The heads of her father and Grimson, she says, "confirmed me in sculpture."

When she was twenty-four, Malvina's father died. She threw herself more than ever into her work, feeling this was what he would have wanted her to do. He had told her once, "My child, I'm afraid you're going to be an artist. It's a long hard road and you have to travel most of the time entirely alone . . . . Above all, you must *be* an artist; after that you may create art." Malvina Hoffman remembered that when he said this "a shock of courage" ran through her veins.

(227)

Malvina Hoffman

She went to Europe for further study. She learned how to chase (ornament by indenting with a blunt hammer) and finish her own bronzes, that is, cut off the little vents and pins and hammer the surface smooth. She began to realize what handicaps women suffer in the field of sculpture. Not only do they have to be on their feet from morning until night, lifting heavy weights, bending iron and sawing wood, but they must know how to use tools as the most expert carpenter would use them. In order to learn every element of her art, she went to the metal foundries to watch the men work. On these visits the workers would give her old pieces of twisted bronze to practice on and she would restore the surface to a smooth even finish. She also learned casting—making a mold from the clay figure, pouring in the molten metal, and seeing that it hardens evenly. Later in her life she cast twenty-seven small bronzes by a process called "lost-wax casting" in a fireplace in her own home.

In Paris she became a studio helper to the American sculptor Janet Scudder. She spent hours of intense study at the Louvre museum. Most important of all, she was accepted as a student of the great French sculptor Auguste Rodin. She watched him carve marble. He directed her in her own work. For sixteen months during this stay, and later for two summers more, she was guided by him. During this period she saw the great ballerina Pavlova dance. "Fireworks were set off in my mind," she said of this encounter. Thereafter she fashioned her *Russian Dancers*, which won first prize in a Paris exhibition.

When she returned to New York in late July 1911 Malvina Hoffman again worked on portrait busts. Becoming known for her accuracy of protrayal and for her sensitivity in projecting personality, she was soon swamped with orders. She needed more room, but in New York she had difficulty finding a studio with good lighting, plenty of space, and floors strong enough to support the heavy sculpture. After a less successful try she decided on a stable at 157 East Thirty-fifth Street. She had it cleaned out—it had seven horse stalls and an old-fashioned carriage room—and used it for both a studio and a place to entertain her many artist friends.

During this period Pavlova was touring America. Malvina came to know her well. She had her pose for the famous study *La Gavotte* wearing a poke bonnet with long streamers. The dancer also posed for a frieze of twenty-six panels—fifty-two figures, all representing her in her Bacchanale dance with Mikhail Mordkin.

During this time Miss Hoffman was improving her knowledge of anatomy by observing dissections at the Columbia University College of Physicians and Surgeons.

She had brought back from Paris a plaster cast of her group, *Russian Dancers*, and wished to have several copies done in bronze. But this is an expensive process, and she lacked funds. Then the master of a foundry made a sporting proposition: He would do the work on account, and she would pay him after the bronzes were sold. She resolved he must not lose out in this bargain and set herself to find a way to sell these pieces.

She took the first bronze casting to a prominent jeweler's shop on Fifth Avenue and asked if he would display it in the window. He agreed. Figures representing movements of the dance were a novel approach in those days, and he decided the group would be an eye-catcher. It was. She called this display her "debut." In three months the six bronze pieces had been sold and Malvina not only had paid the master founder his share but was on her way to fame.

The French government purchased another of her dancing groups, *Bacchanale*, and placed it in the Luxembourg Gardens in Paris. This sealed her success.

A quite different subject was her *The Sacrifice*, the study of a hooded grieving woman cradling the head of a fallen knight in her lap. It was commissioned for the War Memorial Chapel at Harvard University. It took her fifteen months to complete. One aspect of the work was the carving of a full suit of chain armor in stone by hand and chisel pressure, a tremendous undertaking.

After her mother's death in the early 1920's Malvina Hoffman returned to Europe. She visited Geneva, where the League of Nations was meeting, and sat where she could study Ignace Paderewski, the famous composer and pianist who was then Premier of Poland. She produced her bust of him, *The Statesman*. This was followed by portrait busts of Paderewski as *The Man*, as *The Artist*, and as *The Friend*, each giving a different aspect of that great man's personality.

Now she was commissioned to create a sculptured group symbolizing American and English friendship, to be placed over the Bush House, a nine-story office building in London. The pieces were assembled—male figures representing "America" and "England," holding between them a torch—under an arch at the top of the building. When this immense work was in place, she was dissatisfied with the way the faces of the figures dimmed out in the shadows under the arch. Nothing would do but she must climb out on the shoulder of one of the figures and, ninety feet above the street, chisel the lines deeper, while sharp winds blew about her and her hands became stiff with cold. It took her five weeks to complete the task.

In 1924 she married Samuel Grimson, the violinist. Two years later she and her husband bought a house in Paris, a "life-giving home," she called it, with a grand piano, walls warm with bright colors, and a studio large enough for her many projects. "My true center of work was not commissions," she stated. "It was an enormous capacity for falling in love with everything around me: every person, every man on the street, and every woman and child and cat and dog or any queer thing that happened in my path and became a sculptural idea . . . . I collected a group of varied types in Paris; as examples, the coal man, the mattress maker, and a 'witch' who lived on the other side of my high garden wall." Her sculptured figures of these persons have since become famous, and are now scattered with her other works in the great museums of the world.

Her first one-man exhibition was held in the Grand Central Art Gallery in Boston in the late twenties. Then for five years her "family of brain children" traveled to different art museums around the country.

From 1931 to 1936 she worked on a challenging commission, given her by the Field Museum of Chicago (now called the Chicago Natural History Museum). She was to travel all over the world, doing portrait sculptures from life, of persons from each of the world's racial groups. This project required months of preparation. She visited museums and libraries, consulted anthropologists and geographers. She made a small scale model of the Field Museum, Hall of Man area, indicating where pedestals should stand so that each full-length figure and bust might have a harmonious position in relation to the whole. In preparation for her travels she stored plaster in metal containers, packed rolls of lead pipe, wire, rope, and irons for armatures, as well as mechanics' soap, tins of oil, scrubbing brushes, tools, medical kits.

In the course of the journey she and her husband traveled in every type of ship, passed nights in all sorts of shelters, including thatched huts and tents, and on the seats of broken-down autos. They shared baths, diets, and customs with the local people. Tribesmen in remote places, lured by chocolates, beads, and medical advice, came to her improvised studios under cocoanut trees, on beaches, in swamp clearings. They would carry tools of their livelihood, such as fishnets and harpoons, for portrayal. Some brought gadgets—drums, shields, arrows, bells, and sometimes knives—to protect themselves from the evil spirits that might capture their souls in the act of being modeled. She portrayed a Hawaiian surfboard rider, a Chinese rickshaw coolie, a head-hunter of Africa, a Sicilian fisherman, a Mongolian dancer, a woman mud-carrier of Hong-Kong, a Kashmirian Brahman, a Maori of New Zealand, a Pigmy of the Malay Jungle tribes, a Solomon Islander. As she completed the busts and full figures, plaster casts were taken and then sent to Paris, where a master founder put his best craftsmen to work casting them into bronze.

After preliminary viewings in Paris the complete collection was assembled in Chicago. The exhibition was timed for the opening of the great Chicago "Century of Progress" World's Fair in 1933. More than two million people visited the new Hall of Man during its first year.

Her works figured in another world's fair: "The World of Tomorrow," held in 1938 in New York City. For this she created the *Fountain of Dancers*, depicting dancers from seven countries. A large drumlike shape with the outside carved in a sort of bronze lacework, this was set in the center of a round pool. It became one of the fair's chief attractions.

Miss Hoffman also found time to write of her life's activities. In her book *Heads and Tales* she told of circling the globe; in *Sculpture Inside and Out*, about her art; and in *Yesterday Is Tomorrow*, about her personal and artistic life.

Commissions led to important works. During World War II she was chosen by the Fine Arts Commission in Washington to model two large panels for a Memorial at the Epinal Cemetery for American Soldiers in the Vosges Mountains in France. In 1951 the Hall of Fame for Great Americans at New York University asked her to model a larger than life-size portrait of Thomas Paine, and again, in 1960, a portrait of Henry David Thoreau. In 1956 she depicted the History of

Medicine, in thirteen bas-relief panels on the facade of the Joslin Hospital in Boston.

In 1962 her figure *Mongolian Archer* won a gold medal of honor from Allied Artists of America. In 1964 the Gold Medal of the National Sculpture Society, given only a few times in the society's long history, became hers. She was made a member of the French Legion of Honor. It was good, she said, to have recognition while she could enjoy it, but "at heart we are really working for the angels. . . . What counts is the lasting integrity of the artist and the enduring quality of his work."

She died of a heart attack in her sleep when she was eighty-one years old.

BIBLIOGRAPHY

ALEXANDRE, ARSÈNE, *Malvina Hoffman*. Paris: J. E. Pouterman, 1930.
HOFFMAN, MALVINA, *Heads and Tales* (autobiography). New York: Charles Scribner's Sons, 1936.
———, *Yesterday Is Tomorrow: a Personal History*. New York: Crown Publishers, Inc., 1965.
Malvina Hoffman (American Sculptors Series No. 5). New York: W. W. Norton & Company, Inc., 1948.

HELEN KELLER AND ANNE SULLIVAN

HELEN (ADAMS) KELLER: Born in Tuscumbia, Alabama, June 27, 1880. Died in Westport, Connecticut, June 1, 1968. Father: Arthur H. Keller; mother: Kate (Adams) Keller; sister: Mildred; brother: Phillips.

ANNE (MANSFIELD) SULLIVAN (MACY): Born in Feeding Hills, Massachusetts, April 14, 1866. Died in Forest Hills, New York, October 20, 1936. Husband: John Albert Macy.

*

Helen Keller, stricken blind and deaf by an illness in the second year of her life, triumphed over her handicaps to be graduated from Radcliffe College and to become a skilled and subtle writer. A humanitarian, she stimulated movements to help the blind and the deaf. Her emergence from a childhood of deafness and silence to a rich maturity as a gifted and contributing adult was to a great extent the work of her teacher, Anne Mansfield Sullivan. The communication between teacher and pupil was the talk of doctors' conventions, educational institutions, and periodicals from coast to coast. Albert Einstein in 1929 told Miss Sullivan, "Your work has interested me more than any other achievement in modern education; not only did you impart language to Helen Keller; you unfolded her personality, and such work has in it an element of the superhuman."

Helen Keller

*

WHAT is perhaps the most remarkable teacher-pupil relationship on record began on March 3, 1887. On that day Miss Sullivan, a twenty-one-year-old graduate of the Perkins Institution for the Blind, in Boston, arrived at the home of Captain and Mrs. Keller in Tuscumbia, Alabama. She had come to teach their six-year-old daughter, who was blind, deaf, and mute. Anne Sullivan saw standing on the porch "an untidy, ruddy child," her brown hair tumbled, her dress soiled. Small Helen lunged at the newcomer, jerked her suitcase from her, tried to open it, failed, then darted upstairs with it. Miss Sullivan followed. And so began a human struggle as dramatic as it was poignant.

Miss Sullivan's life before coming to Tuscumbia had been unsettled at best, brutal at worst. Her parents, potato famine refugees from Ireland, had never gained a real foothold in the New World. The mother, worn down by the drudgery of her life, had died when Anne was eight, and two years later the father had abandoned the children. Anne and her seven-year-old brother, Jimmie, were sent to an almshouse in Tewksbury, Massachusetts, where homeless children mingled with the diseased and the demented, and all were neglected. Jimmie died there, but Anne, after enduring the hardships for four years, won, in a way, her own release. She flung herself into the midst of a group investigating the almshouse, crying, "I want to go to school!"

She was half blind; so she was taken to the Perkins Institution to begin her education by learning to read with her fingers. She was mothered by the matron there, and this human relationship, together with improvement in her sight after two operations, helped her to be graduated in 1886 at the head of her class. She was an impetuous young woman, relished the unusual, was bored with the commonplace. Every encounter was an adventure. So when Helen's father applied at the Perkins Institution for a teacher, she was eager to undertake the obviously difficult task.

The Perkins Institution had pioneered in work with the deaf-blind. Some fifty years before, its director, Dr. Samuel Gridley Howe, and the teachers under him, had managed to impart to Laura Bridgman, a deaf-blind girl, the manual alphabet, in which the teacher's fingers "spell out" words into the pupil's hand. Later attempts to teach the deaf-blind at Perkins Institution had been unsuccessful. However, Laura Bridgman was still living at the school, a cloistered person who spent much of her time making unbelievably delicate lace and occasionally giving instruction in the manual alphabet. It was she who had taught this system to Anne Sullivan. So it was natural the school authorities should think of Anne Sullivan first when Captain Keller inquired for a teacher for his daughter.

In her first few weeks at the Kellers', all of Miss Sullivan's resources were put to the test. Because of her disabilities, Helen had been indulged, and the family had no way of disciplining her because they had no way of communicating with her. As a result she was as unrestrained as a young colt. In letters to the matron at the Perkins Institution Miss Sullivan told of Helen's quick temper, her destructive habits—"her untaught, unsatisfied hands destroy whatever they touch"; of her atrocious table manners—"she puts her hands into our plates and helps herself"; of her absolute fury when restrained —"she kicks and screams" if "I try . . . to get her to do the simplest thing such as combing her hair or washing her hands." No wonder an uncle of Helen's had said to her mother, "You really ought to put that child away, Kate. She is mentally defective, and it is not pleasant to see her about." Helen Keller as a grown woman was to describe herself during this period as "a phantom living in a 'no' world .... I had neither will nor intellect. I was carried along to objects and acts by a certain blind animal impetus .... I never viewed anything beforehand or chose it."

Words, conceptions, should be taught the child, Miss Sullivan knew. But how? From the first day she would spell out with her fingers into Helen's hands the words *doll, mug, cake,* giving her each time the object to touch. The child would spell them back. But it was only a sort of game. Helen did not seem to get the idea that the word *stood for* the object. When she wanted anything, therefore, she would revert to unruly motions. Then one day, when Helen had persisted in confusing the words *mug* and *water,* and had moreover savagely broken a new doll, Miss Sullivan took her for a walk. She led her to a water pump—but let her tell it: "I let the mug overflow and go over Helen's hand, as I spelled 'water' into her free hand. The word, coming so close upon the sensation of cold water rushing over her hand, seemed to startle her. She dropped the mug and stood as one transfixed .... A new light came over her face .... She spelled 'water' several times. Then she dropped on the ground and asked for its name ... pointed to the pump and the trellis, and suddenly turned around and asked (by pointing) for my name. I spelled, 'Teacher.' All the way back to the house she was highly excited and learned the name of every object she touched so that in a few hours she had added thirty new words to her vocabulary—'door,' 'open,' 'shut,' 'give,' 'go,' 'come.'" She had discovered that words were the key to the outside world.

Helen herself later described the event: "Suddenly I felt a misty consciousness as of something forgotten—a thrill of returning thought ... and somehow the mystery of language was revealed to me." When the two returned to the house, Helen Keller felt her way to the doll she had broken. She picked up the pieces and tried to put them together. Then she started crying. "For the first time I felt repentance and sorrow."

This episode was a high point in a play by William Gibson, *The Miracle Worker*, based on a book by Nella Braddy. It had a long and exciting run on Broadway, beginning in 1959, and was later made into a movie.

Helen had this experience at the pump on April 5, 1887. Soon she had mastered some one hundred words. Miss Sullivan listed them and had each word printed in large embossed letters on cards. Helen would play with these cards; would place D O L L on the bed, and lay her doll on it, then arrange I S, O N and B E D beside the doll. Her vocabulary rapidly increased. By the end of that August she was using 625 words. She was learning meanwhile to read raised print books with her fingers, and to write, using thin rulers to keep her hand in alignment.

Miss Sullivan taught her to be self-reliant. She did not help Helen when she bumped her head against the laundry basket or stumbled on the stairs in finding her way. The child must learn how to contend with obstacles. She taught her to play, swing, jump, hop, tumble. She taught her to laugh by gently tickling her ribs, meanwhile laughing herself, and holding Helen's hand up to her face so that she could "feel" the laughter. She also taught the child to stick to a task until she had finished it. Soon Miss Sullivan was writing to the matron: "I know she has remarkable powers. I believe that I shall be able to develop and mould them . . . . I seem to divine Helen's peculiar needs. It is wonderful." And again, "I know the education of this child will be the distinguishing event of my life, if I have the brains and perseverance to accomplish it."

Helen for her part was all eagerness. "I wish to write about things I do not understand," she wrote in one of her notes to Miss Sullivan. "Who made the earth and the seas, and everything? What makes the sun hot? Where was I before I came to mother? I know that plants grow from seeds which are in the ground, but I am sure people do not grow that way. I never saw a child-plant. Little birds and chickens come out of eggs. I have seen them. What was the egg before it was an egg? Why does not the earth fall, it is so very large and heavy? Tell me something that Father Nature does. May I read the book called the Bible? Please tell your little pupil many things when you have much time."

Now she could communicate with her whole family. Her parents, as well as her younger sister, Mildred, had mastered the manual alphabet. She had many friends. She wrote letters by typewriter. There was talk in the family of Miss Sullivan's tutorship coming to an end. Even Anne Sullivan might have had cause to consider ending the relationship. As early as 1889 her own eyesight had begun to worsen. But wise advisers, among them Mark Twain and Alexander Graham Bell, both staunch friends of the Kellers and Miss Sullivan, counseled that here was a special case: a constantly questing mind, closed to ordinary channels of communication, yet reaching out for information. She needed such an intermediary as Miss Sullivan.

So when Helen took lessons in oral speech from Sarah Fuller at the Horace Mann School in New York City in 1890, Miss Sullivan went with her. As Helen Keller explained Miss Fuller's method later: "She [Miss Fuller] passed my hand lightly over her face, and let me feel the position of her tongue and lips when she made a sound." Miss Keller imitated the motions and within an hour had learned the sounds M, P, A, S, T, I. She was delighted when she could form her first sentence: "It is warm."

Miss Sullivan was also with Helen Keller when she attended the Wright-Humason School for the Deaf, for advanced lessons in oral speech and lip reading, and with her at the Cambridge, Massachusetts, School for Young Ladies. When Helen entered Radcliffe College, Miss Sullivan sat beside her, spelling the lectures into her fingers. By now the teacher's eyes had become so much worse that she had to hold the books close to her face. Still she sometimes read to Helen for five hours daily. When in 1904 Helen Keller was graduated from Radcliffe, *cum laude,* Miss Sullivan, at Helen's request, mounted the platform with her and stood beside her as she received the diploma.

Shortly after her graduation Miss Keller's first book, *The Story of My Life,* came off the press. A best seller, it was ultimately translated into fifty languages. Mark Twain wrote her, "I am charmed with your book—enchanted. You are a wonderful creature, the most wonderful in the world—you and your other half together—Miss Sullivan, I mean, for it took the pair of you to make and complete a perfect whole." It was Mark Twain, incidentally, who had put in motion the fund-raising that had helped to send Helen through college.

Miss Keller's book, which had first appeared serially in the *Ladies' Home Journal,* not only served to make Helen and her teacher famous but also acquainted Miss Sullivan with her future husband, John Macy. A writer himself and a social critic, Mr. Macy helped edit the book. Miss Sullivan and Mr. Macy were married in 1905. They went to New Orleans on their honeymoon. Helen Keller was still to have the services of her teacher—that had been discussed before the marriage.

Miss Keller's father had died a few years before. She knew from now on she would have to make her own way. During the following decade she published widely in leading magazines and went on lecture tours. Miss Keller's speech, always "breathy," was never well modulated. So Miss Sullivan was needed sometimes to supplement her comments. During these trips Mr. Macy remained in New York, engaged in his literary work. Miss Keller, tall, handsome, gracious, poised, talked not only on the problems of the handicapped, but on woman suffrage, and, as World War I loomed, on disarmament. Her audiences, however, were not ready for peace talks, and her lecture assignments gradually dwindled.

In 1914, in Bath, Maine, Miss Sullivan was taken ill suddenly, and Miss Keller was unable to use the telephone or to find her way downstairs to get help. It became clear that there should be an additional member of the party. They chose Polly Thomson, a Scotswoman who had a gift for organization—could plan the itinerary, balance the budget, and politely refuse interviews to importunate time-wasters. She was to be with Miss Keller for forty-five years.

In 1918 Helen Keller portrayed the highlights of her career in a motion picture, parts of which were used again in 1954 in a fine film documentary, *The Unconquered*. Also, for two years Helen Keller and Miss Sullivan toured on the vaudeville circuit in a twenty-minute demonstration of the teaching methods of Miss Sullivan, and of Miss Keller's means of communication with the outside world. She enjoyed it all hugely, though the questions from the audience were sometimes trying: Could she tell time without a watch? Did she close her eyes when she went to sleep? (Her stock answer to this was, "I never stayed awake to find out.") Did she dream? Had she ever thought of getting married? She threw off the last question with a whimsical shrug, but she might, under other circumstances, have answered by telling about "a brief love," which her mother had opposed, and which "will remain in my life a little island of joy surrounded by dark waters . . . . The fault was not in the loving but in the circumstances."

In 1921 Helen Keller decided her life work was henceforth to be raising funds for the American Foundation for the Blind. She gave hundreds of lectures—in churches, synagogues, town halls. She lobbied for legislation to finance talking books (books on phonograph records) and pensions for the blind. In three years alone she talked to more than 250,000 people at 249 meetings in 123 cities, and raised more than one million dollars. She was also appointed a member of the Massachusetts Commission for the Blind. In this capacity she helped to better conditions for the adult blind, increasing their opportunities for training and employment. In those days the blind were frequently ill-educated and kept in asylums. She was a major influence in changing these conditions.

In the twenties she, Miss Sullivan, Mr. Macy, and Miss Thomson moved from Wrentham, Massachusetts, to Forest Hills, New York. Miss Keller was to use Forest Hills as her base of operations from then on.

Miss Sullivan's sight was failing rapidly now. She underwent several operations but they only drained her strength. She had to relinquish one after another of her activities. When she died, in 1936, the Bishop of Washington called her "one of the great teachers of all time," and radio commentator Alexander Woollcott broadcast a moving memorial to "one of the great women of our time—or any time . . . . She started a work which has been recognized the world around as one of the heartening triumphs of the human spirit."

After the teacher's death the pupil was left to go the course alone. "Every hour I long for the thousand bright signals from her vital, beautiful hand," Miss Keller wrote in her *Journal*. "My fingers will cry for her descriptive touches which were nuggets of gold, her exquisite tenderness, her bright summaries of conversations or books not in raised print . . . . [She was] the creative flame from which sprang the joy of communication, the power of love binding me to my kind, and the intelligence that quickened new senses within my limitations."

Helen Keller now worked harder than ever. On March 19, 1937, she and Polly Thomson sailed for Japan. En route she spoke before the legislators at Honolulu, urging them to provide a bureau of welfare for the blind of Hawaii. In Japan she roused great interest in the care and training of the blind. In a trip around the world, traveling through India, Australia, Egypt, Siam, and a dozen other countries, hospitals and schools for the blind began to spring up in her wake. The *Pictorial Review* gave her their five-thousand-dollar annual achievement award, which she immediately turned over to the Fund for the Blind. She was honored by universities and institutions throughout the world—Harvard, Glasgow, Berlin, Delhi, among them. In the latter part of her life she made six worldwide trips.

In 1955 her book *Teacher*, a monument to her lifelong friend, was published. Other of her books are *Optimism, The World I Live In, The Song of the Stone Wall, Out of the Dark, My Religion, Midstream—My Later Life, Peace at Eventide, Helen Keller's Journal, Let Us Have Faith,* and *The Open Door.*

On June 23, 1960, just before her eightieth birthday, the Senate passed a resolution citing her work for the blind and the "countless new friends" she had made for the country. She was received in the White House by every President from Grover Cleveland to John Kennedy.

In 1960 Polly Thomson died, and Winifred Corbally became Miss Keller's companion. Helen Keller never forgot her first great teacher, Anne Sullivan. She wrote, "How much of my delight in all beautiful things is innate and how much is due to her influence, I can never tell. I feel that her being is inseparable from my own, and that the footsteps of my life are in hers . . . . There is not a talent, or an aspiration or a joy in me that has not been awakened by her loving touch."

Helen Keller passed away quietly in her sleep shortly before her eighty-eighth birthday.

BIBLIOGRAPHY

HARRITY, RICHARD, and MARTIN, RALPH G., *The Three Lives of Helen Keller*. New York: Doubleday & Company, Inc., 1962.
KELLER, HELEN ADAMS, *Journal, 1936–1937*. New York: Doubleday & Company, Inc., 1938.
———, *The Story of My Life*, New School Edition with Teaching and Study Helps by Eleonore Pollak-Ottendorff. Boston: Houghton Mifflin Company, 1928.
———, *Teacher: Anne Sullivan Macy; a Tribute by the Foster-Child of Her Mind*, Introduction by Nella Braddy Henney. New York: Doubleday & Company, Inc., 1955.

DOROTHEA LANGE

DOROTHEA LANGE: Born in Hoboken, New Jersey, May 26, 1895. Died in San Francisco, California, October 11, 1965. Father: Henry Nutzhorn; mother: Joanna Lange; brother: Martin; marriages: Maynard Dixon; Paul Schuster Taylor; sons: Daniel Rhodes Dixon and John Eaglefeather Dixon.

✻

Dorothea Lange's work is a significant part of the history of photography. Edward Steichen called her "without doubt our greatest documentary photographer." But her influence extends far beyond the field of photography. Her portrayals of the suffering of a segment of our population helped change the national outlook toward the underprivileged and led Congress to pass laws to protect and aid them.

✻

GRANDDAUGHTER of German immigrants, young Dorothea lived in her early years in Hoboken, New Jersey, a city largely settled by German-Americans. From her porch she would watch the workers heading homeward after a busy day downtown. Or she would go down to the docks with her brother to see the great ships being unloaded. Already her sharp eyes and her keen insight were taking in the human aspects of the scenes about her. But it was not until she had moved with her mother to New York City and had become a student at Wadleigh High School there that she came to a decision regarding her life work. "I was seventeen years old and a poor child," she wrote later. "I made up my mind to be a photographer. This came slowly. I had no camera. I had made no pictures. My mind made up itself, it was more like that."

She was fascinated by photographs of Isadora Duncan displayed in newspapers when that sensational dancer was making headlines in New York City in 1914. She saw the originals on display in a photographic studio at 562 Fifth Avenue. She was so impressed with the way they caught this dancer's personality that she went inside the shop and confided to its owner, Arnold Genthe, her aspiration to become a photographer. Mr. Genthe was struck with the young girl's earnestness, and helped her in various ways—gave her her first camera, watched over her progress, and even had her working briefly in his studio. It was at his suggestion that she took a basic photographic course with Clarence H. White at Columbia University. She found White a good teacher. "There was an atmosphere of photographic excellence in his work—no taint of vulgarity." For a darkroom, she rented a chicken coop in the Palisades of New Jersey, where she could go weekends to develop her pictures.

But she was restless. After a year or two she started out with her friend, Florence Ahlstrom, to travel around the world and take pictures en route. Their money gave out in San Francisco, however, and Dorothea Lange took a position in a photo supply house in that city. Later she opened her own photographic studio.

In 1920 she married the painter Maynard Dixon. During the next ten years, while she worked in her studio, she and her husband became part of an enterprising group of artists, sculptors, musicians, and photographers. The family—two sons, Daniel and John, were born during this period—spent vacations in the mountains of California, near Indian villages in New Mexico, or traveling through Utah, Nevada, and Arizona.

Dorothea Lange

But the Depression of the 1930's brought the American scene and her own thoughts into a new focus. She watched the unemployed standing in long rows before the free soup kitchens, old men huddled on park benches, ragged figures begging at street corners. Back in her studio she would turn from taking the portraits of complacent citizens to gaze out of the window at the homeless men drifting past. It came to her gradually that she must be "out there." One day she simply picked up her camera and made her way into the center of San Francisco's trouble spots. She photographed sidewalk orators, picket lines, street demonstrations, the waterfront. She had no assignment, no idea where to place her photographs. She only knew that here was life and that she must record it.

One of her photographs of this period was "White Angel Breadline," showing a hunched-up, unshaven old man, his back to the other men in the soup-kitchen line-up, his battered hat pulled down over his face to reveal only the grim lines of his mouth. He is leaning against a railing and his arms, resting along the top, are circling an empty tin cup. This photograph caught the eye of photographer Willard Van Dyke. He asked to see others of her pictures. He put on a special exhibition of them in his Oakland studio. He also wrote about them in the magazine *Camera Craft*.

One of the visitors to the studio, Paul Taylor, an economics professor at the University of California, saw the value of the photographs as human documents. He telephoned Miss Lange to ask if he could use one to illustrate an article he had written for the *Survey Graphic* magazine on "San Francisco and the General Strike." She gave her permission.

Shortly after this she became a member of Taylor's staff. He was field director of the division of rural rehabilitation of the state Emergency Relief Administration. His project was to make a study of the poverty-stricken farm laborers who had been victimized by the Depression, by drought, and by

Dorothea Lange

the machine-drawn tractor, with its disk ploughs. (These pulverized the soil so that the rich top layers were literally "thrown to the winds" in gigantic dust storms.) Since no provision had been made in the budget for a photographer, Miss Lange was designated on the payroll as a "typist."

The first rehabilitation report combined text and photographs. It showed migrant laborers and their families "squatting" (huddling overnight or for longer periods with their meager household goods piled around them) on roadsides, ditch banks, river bottoms, and in the brush. The report called for the establishment of government camps where these workers could find decent living facilities.

Mr. Taylor and Miss Lange continued to work together. The project was expanded to become, in 1935, a part of the Resettlement Administration. Mr. Taylor was transferred to the Research Division of the Social Security Board, assigned to study labor in agriculture throughout the United States. Now Miss Lange's work acquired a nationwide scope.

Her marriage to Maynard Dixon had ended in divorce. On December 6, 1935, Miss Lange and Paul Taylor were married. Their teaming up as social analyst and photographer not only made dramatic new use of photography, but also presented the problems of migrant workers so effectively that legislation was enacted to protect the workers' rights.

This particular Resettlement Administration project, in fact, proved to be the greatest photographic undertaking ever launched in this country. A group of a dozen photographers recorded a period of great upheaval between 1935 and 1939, when a full 300,000 emigrants headed toward California. Land owners were shifting from farming their land through tenant farmers to farming by wage labor employed by the day. Great areas in the southwest were plowed by tractor. The tenant farmers, "tractored out," as they put it, went on relief or became migrants, constantly traveling to do seasonal farm work. More than 6,000 people a month were counted crossing the borders of California by automobile. All of them were native-born Americans. They came from Oklahoma, Texas, Arkansas, and Missouri. The treeless landscape was strewn with abandoned tenant houses. The some 270,000 photographs the group took brought to notice these "invisible" members of the society, those overlooked in the scheme of things.

Miss Lange, one of the most active of these photographers, was soon traveling over most of the country. In one summer alone she ran up 17,000 miles on her speedometer. She documented the lives and backgrounds of the migrant workers. She photographed families in old cars loaded with bedding and stoves; hitchhiking families; pea pickers; carrot bundlers; workers sleeping in field furrows to hold their places for the next day; migrants packed in trucks like sardines to be hauled to the next work site. She photographed the treeless landscapes, the empty lurching shacks, the abandoned schools, the tent villages, the dazed faces, the scrawny children.

Those photographed did not resent her picture taking or her questions. They were willing to talk to this slight, intent woman with the soft voice, the generous mouth, and the compassionate eyes. So she asked questions and listened to the answers. Her ear was as good as her eye, as the captions on the photographs show: "No, I didn't *sell* out back there. I *give* out!" "What bothers us travellin' people is we cain't get no place to stay still." "When they get through working you they want you out of the way."

She drove up and down in her station wagon. In March 1936 she produced the photograph "Migrant Mother," a picture that has been published in hundreds of periodicals the world over. It shows a gaunt woman, her brow lined, her eyes perplexed, two ragged children at her shoulders, a baby, its small face splotched with mud, asleep in her lap. Miss Lange described how the picture was taken. "It was the end of a cold miserable winter. I had been travelling in the field alone for a month, photographing the migratory farm labor of California—the ways of life, and the conditions of these people who serve and produce our great crops. My work was done. Time was up and I was worked out . . . . I was on my way home . . . when out of the corner of my eye I saw a sign, 'Pea Pickers' Camp.'"

She drove about twenty miles farther, arguing with herself, then headed back and turned down the road. "I drove into that wet and soggy camp. I saw and approached the hungry and desperate mother, as if drawn by a magnet. She told me she was thirty-two, said they had been living on frozen vegetables from the surrounding fields, and birds that the children killed. She had just sold the tires from her car to buy food. She sat in a lean-to tent with her children huddled around her."

The picture's impact was explosive. Papers throughout the United States printed it. Editorials commented on it. This picture more than any other led President Franklin D. Roosevelt to get help from Congress, with the result that a chain of sanitary government camps with medical services was finally built for the migrant workers.

A further joint effort of Dorothea Lange and Paul Taylor was their book *An American Exodus: a Record of Human Erosion*. It was a volume of 115 photographs with running commentary. It sold widely, was bought not only by connoisseurs and camera fans but by thousands of people concerned about bettering human conditions.

With World War II new miseries had to be recorded. Miss Lange relinquished temporarily a Guggenheim Fellowship ("to make a study of the American scene") in order to fulfill a wartime duty: to photograph, under government auspices,

Dorothea Lange

the Japanese-Americans being taken to relocation camps for the war's duration.

From 1943 to 1945 Miss Lange worked for the Office of War Information, interpreting the American spirit to European peoples via photographs.

In 1944–1945 she did work for *Fortune* magazine, on the war shipyard boom town Richmond, California. In 1945, under the auspices of the State Department, she photographed the United Nations Conference in San Francisco. In the 1950's she shared her skills by conducting seminars at the San Francisco Art Institute and by participating in a photo conference at Aspen, Colorado. Also in the 1950's she worked on two assignments for *Life* magazine: "Three Mormon Towns" and "The Irish Country People." She photographed the devastation of the Berryessa Valley in California, a region cleared of homes, trees, brush, and fences to make way for a reservoir site, and produced "Death of a Valley," published in *Aperture* in 1960. In several of these projects her son Daniel Dixon, as well as Ansel Adams and Pirkle Jones, collaborated.

In 1958 Dorothea Lange accompanied her husband when he went as a government consultant to Korea, the Philippines, Vietnam, India, Pakistan, and Indonesia. Here again she took photographs which caught the innate character of the peoples. Ecuador and Venezuela were her bases for still more photographic studies, during 1960, when her husband had assignments there. Photographs of Egypt followed, when Dr. Taylor became a professor at the University of Alexandria.

Miss Lange's work has had five exhibits in the Museum of Modern Art in New York City, as well as exhibits in Boston, San Francisco, Chicago, Louisville, and other key cities. In 1960 the Biblioteca Communale in Milan, Italy, gave a showing of her photographs of farm women. Several of her published "essays"—bound collections of her photographs—have been very popular: *The Public Defender, On Security, On Justice,* and *Death of a Valley.*

In 1962 the Portrait Photographers of America presented her with their national award for her "international contributions to humanity through photography." In 1963 she was placed on the Honor Roll of the American Society of Magazine Photographers.

For many years her studio was about twenty-five yards from her home in Berkeley, California, on a slope covered with live oaks, shrubbery, and fruit trees, overlooking a creek running through the ravine. It held only a narrow couch, a couple of work tables, and a pair of canvas-backed chairs. In later years, when her health was failing, she moved her darkroom to the main house, and the living room there became her workroom. Characteristic of her way of thinking was the motto tacked on her darkroom door, one she had chosen when she was still in her twenties:

> The contemplation of things as they are
> Without error or confusion
> Without substitution or imposture
> Is in itself a nobler thing
> Than a whole harvest of invention—Francis Bacon

In August of 1964 she was told she had a malignant cancer. She was working with KQED (San Francisco) on two 30-minute films for the National Educational Television and Radio Center. This she continued. But most of the next year she devoted to printing and arranging the photographs that represented her life's work. These were to be shown in a one-man exhibit for the Museum of Modern Art: two hundred photographs dating from 1920 to 1965, documenting the Depression, the war, travels in Asia, Ireland, and Egypt, the new California, country women, and her own home and family. She had Irwin Welcher, an expert in preparing such exhibits, come to her Berkeley home. With prints strewn across the living room floor, they discussed print quality, cropping, layout, placement and general presentation. A "burning desire to have people know one another's problems" drove her on. Her son Daniel said, "Around her circled a complex kinship of lives— lives that shared nothing so much in common as that each was in some way shaped and enlightened by this extraordinary woman."

She died only a few days after Welcher's last visit, and only a few months before the opening of her one-man exhibition. And she died in the knowledge that she had completed, according to her exacting standards, this, her last great project. During her last hours she said to her husband, "This is the right time. Isn't it a miracle that it comes at the *right* time?"

In a letter sent at the opening of the exhibit, President Lyndon B. Johnson said, "All of us who lived through the Depression remember the special contribution of this gifted artist. The magic of her camera turned mere statistics into compelling human truth. Without retouching our blemishes, she showed the strength and gallantry of the American people under severe adversity."

BIBLIOGRAPHY

LANGE, DOROTHEA, *Dorothea Lange Looks at the American Country Woman; a Photographic Essay;* with a Commentary by Beaumont Newhall. Fort Worth, Texas: Amon Carter Museum, 1967.

LANGE, DOROTHEA, and TAYLOR, PAUL, *An American Exodus; a*

Dorothea Lange

Record of Human Erosion. New York: Reynal & Hitchcock, 1940.

Museum of Modern Art, New York City, *Dorothea Lange;* with an Introductory Essay by George P. Elliott. Distributed by New York Graphic Society Ltd., Greenwich, Connecticut.

SUSANNE LANGER

SUSANNE (KATHERINA) LANGER: Born in New York, New York, December 20, 1895. Father: Antonio Knauth; mother: Else M. (Uhlich) Knauth; brothers: Berthold, Peter; sisters: Ilse, Ursula; husband: William Leonard Langer (divorced); sons: Leonard Charles Rudolph, Bertrand Walter.

✳

Susanne Langer, one of the few women to win wide recognition in the field of philosophy, has extended the boundaries of twentieth-century thinking by bringing into the realm of philosophy the "non-discursive" means of expressing ideas, namely music, painting, sculpture, dancing, and the other arts.

✳

HER family spent their summers at Lake George in upstate New York. Here as a child Susanne would wander in the woods alone or with her childhood friend Helen Sewell. The girls would notice the way squirrels, when startled, sit up and put their paws to their hearts, in what appears an almost human gesture, and the way frogs, croaking, seem to answer each other from pond to pond. When she was twelve, Susanne was given a book on frogs and was so fascinated reading it that she gathered her family together and spoke for forty minutes about the habits of these small amphibians. Later she began to ask, "How are animals different from us?" "How is the way human beings think different from the way squirrels and frogs think?"

Susanne Langer

Her winters in New York City were filled with different sorts of activities. Her father, a well-to-do lawyer, with an amateur's love for music, would have his friends in every other Monday for chamber music. He himself would play the cello. Often Susanne, when she was supposed to be in bed, would creep to the head of the stairs to listen.

From her mother she acquired a love of poetry—she made up poems before she could write. In fact, she learned to write in order to set them down. In most of these indoor pursuits, her sister Ilse was her companion. Susanne was later to dedicate her book *Philosophical Sketches* to Ilse: "a student of nature, musician, and my truest friend."

Her father encouraged her in her reading. She read Louisa May Alcott's *Little Women* and philosopher Immanuel Kant's *Critique of Pure Reason* simultaneously, when she was fourteen. However, her father did not especially like higher education for women. But her sister started college, and before his death her father agreed that she could go too.

At college she acquired the mental discipline a philosopher must possess. She learned to hold many ideas simultaneously in her mind, to search out relationships between ideas, to entertain a proposition without having to believe it or disbelieve it, and to set aside unsolved problems in such a way as to be able to recall them when some new idea or finding made their solution possible.

Her marriage to William Langer, the historian, took place after both he and she received their B.A. degrees, hers from Radcliffe in 1920, his from Harvard in 1915. The couple spent one semester in graduate study at the University of Vienna in Austria, then returned to Massachusetts. Her husband taught history, first at Clark University, then at Harvard. Meanwhile Susanne Langer received her M.A. and Ph.D. degrees and tutored in philosophy at Radcliffe. Her two sons were born during this period.

Susanne Langer

Her writing career began about this same time. Her first book was one for children: *The Cruise of the Little Dipper and Other Fairy Tales*.

In the books that followed she went deeply into philosophical problems: *The Practice of Philosophy*, *Introduction to Symbolic Logic*, and *Philosophy in a New Key*. She developed her main thesis: that symbol-making is what has led to human development.

Symbols, as Dr. Langer considers them, are convenient "handles" for thought. All words are symbols, as well as such designations as $, %, &, and @. Used in talking and writing, symbols make possible the transmission of thoughts from one person to another. She believes that it is the ability to use symbols that distinguishes human beings from lower animals. Human beings alone have symbol-making minds.

Her book *Philosophy in a New Key* explores the matter of symbol-making further. Words and mathematical signs are not the only symbols we have, Dr. Langer says. She believes there are still other symbols, which she calls "non-discursive symbols." In painting, music, sculpture, the dance, and architecture, the artist, composer, sculptor, and choreographer "communicate" with others without using words. They have no vocabulary, but they get their message across nevertheless, and they get it across by the use of symbols, nonverbal yet communicable. By bringing these "unspeakable" areas of communication into the realm of philosophy, Dr. Langer opens up new worlds. She is the first philosopher who has sought to explain man's absorption in rhythms, rituals, and pictures. He is at his favorite activity of symbol-making. *Philosophy in a New Key* has been printed in paperback and has been translated into eight languages.

After leaving Radcliffe in 1942—her divorce occurred during this period—Dr. Langer taught for a year at the University of Delaware. From 1945 to 1950 she was a lecturer at

Columbia University in New York City. She also wrote her book *Feeling and Form*. A Rockefeller grant allowed her to devote her whole time to this project.

In 1954 Dr. Langer became chairman of the department of philosophy at Connecticut College in New London. She has also conducted seminars or lectured as visiting professor at New York University, the New School for Social Research in New York, Northwestern University, Ohio University, and the universities of Washington and Michigan, as well as giving courses at Wellesley and Smith.

In 1956 Dr. Langer continued her research and writing on a grant from the Edgar J. Kaufmann Charitable Trust of Pittsburgh. The results have been her books *Problems of Art: Ten Philosophical Lectures*, *Philosophical Sketches*, and the first volume of *Mind: an Essay on Human Feeling*. In *Problems of Art* she presents a new idea: "A work of art," she says, "possesses a conception of life, emotion, inward reality. But it is neither a confessional nor a frozen tantrum; it is developed metaphor, a nondiscursive symbol that articulates what is verbally ineffable—the logic of consciousness itself." It is such statements as these that cause her book to be so enthusiastically discussed wherever painters, musicians, and other artists come together. In *Mind: an Essay on Human Feeling*, she puts forward a further idea. Feeling, she believes —that is, any feeling, even a sensation of pain as evinced in the lowliest of animals—is the beginning of mind as it is manifested in human beings. "It is a turning-point . . . leads . . . upward to the purely human sphere known as 'culture.'" And she seeks to answer such questions as "Why can only man be properly said to have a mind, though all the higher animals . . . have mental functions?" and "Why does the mind appear so forcibly as a separate entity, a 'being' independent of physical organism?"

In 1960 Dr. Langer was elected to the American Academy

of Arts and Sciences. In 1964 she received the Honorary Doctor of Laws degree conferred by Columbia University. She has been awarded honorary degrees from six other universities.

Though her time is now devoted to her studies and her writings, Dr. Langer on occasion used to appear on the lecture platform. In the 1960's she lectured at Pittsburgh University, Brown University, Syracuse University, and Vassar. She read a paper at Cooper Union in New York City on "Man and Animal: The City and the Hive" and presented the speech "Scientific Civilization and Cultural Crisis" at a meeting of the Japanese Association for Philosophy and Science, at Nikko, Japan.

In these lectures she sometimes talked of current problems. "Many people are aware that humanity is on the edge of destruction for lack of social concepts to match the physical powers," she says. She maintains "that scientific production has outrun our imagination, and the change in our civilization—in the practical means and techniques of life—has advanced with a gathered momentum of its own and outstripped the advance of our thinking." She feels that "the danger of civilization to cultural life is more acute in our own world than in any previous era," that the modern spirit has taken from us old values, "state religion, marriage, paternal authority, deference to the aged, piety toward the dead, holiness and rank and royalty," and often has provided nothing in their place. She feels that "the time is ripe for entirely new forms of conception, a radical reinterpretation of the major facts, in short, for a philosophical advance in the field of baffled science." These lectures have been assembled to make up her book *Philosophical Sketches*.

Susanne Langer, however, must be thought of not as a public figure but as the eternal student, trying in isolation to come to grips with basic concepts. One must picture her in her Connecticut farmhouse built on a hillside above the road: a slim woman with clear blue eyes and close-trimmed gray hair, writing at a huge desk. She wears denim slacks and low-heeled shoes. Papers are spread before her and the back of the desk is bordered with some twelve card-index file boxes. A chameleon scurries about in a small cage at one side of the desk. In another cage on the desk two tree-toads chirp. The light through the windows shows the contents of jars and aquariums on the ledges: fish, tadpoles, and turtles.

She writes a few sentences, then pauses to search for a card. Over the years she has recorded items that have interested her in her work. The most important part of the card file is her reading notes, often whole abstracts of books, that she keeps alphabetically by the author's name. Today, she can put her hand on everything she has read since her junior year in college. The card she selects this time may be about dynamic forms in music, about the impulses behind laughter, about flower motifs in primitive art, or about the habits of small creatures. One card may read: "In centipedes each segment has a partly individual life. Kill the beast with a broom and segments squirm all over the floor . . . . When does the centipede die?" The cards deal with the whole realm of the animal-to-human transition, and of subsequent human development. And so she works hour after hour.

Hers is the philosopher's search—the search for underlying meanings. Words, she says, are changing their meanings. With present-day trips outside the earth's field of gravitation, and instantaneous worldwide communication systems, such words as "infinity" and "community" do not mean what they once did. But what do they mean? The search for exact meanings, she believes, should be encouraged "as a precise instrument for a high imagination to work with." She fears that, if it is not, "the most daring new ideas may be lost for lack of precision instruments to carry them out. Words are the instruments of thought."

Susanne Langer

So here in her cottage she wrestles with problems of basic reality. If one asks her if she is lonely, she smiles quickly. "Well, there's the canoe and the woods, when I need a change —and there's my music." One side of her large L-shaped living room holds a grand piano, violins, and a cello, all in readiness for the chamber music evenings once a week when her friends drop in. And she mentions her "Creek Mouse," a canoe she takes off in when she comes to a crisis in her thinking. She has learned the knack of lifting this canoe onto her hip and carrying it "like a fair-sized child" for short distances from her car to the shore. When she needs absolute quiet and solitude, she goes to a hideaway in the woods of Ulster County, New York, where there is no telephone, no postman to ring the doorbell, and only the sounds of a waterfall and the wind in the pine trees as background for her thoughts.

Her excitements, she explains in a *New York Times* interview, are those of mental discoveries. "All of a sudden a light dawns on something which I've been wrestling with for a long time. This happens every few weeks. Then I'm very excited. I know I should stay and work it out completely, but I can't. I get out my canoe or drive to Scarsdale to see my son and his family. I know I have the idea under control but my excitement has to settle down before I can return to my desk. Whenever you know that you've broken through a difficult problem it gives you a great feeling of security. The greatest security in this tumultuous world is faith in your own mind."

But the months and years crowd in on her. She feels time is pressing. "I'd like to be a cat and have nine lives," she says. "As it is I have to hurry." Still she is hopeful. She dedicated her book *Mind: An Essay on Human Feeling* "to them in whom I hope to live even to the great World Peace—my children and their children."

BIBLIOGRAPHY

LANGER, SUSANNE K., "Adventures of the Mind: Why Philosophy?" *Saturday Evening Post*, May 13, 1961.
———, *The Practice of Philosophy*. New York: Henry Holt & Company, Inc., 1930.
———, *Philosophy in a New Key*. Cambridge: Harvard University Press, 1942, Penguin, 1948.
———, *Feeling and Form*. New York: Charles Scribner's Sons, 1953.
———, *Mind: An Essay on Human Feeling*. Baltimore: The Johns Hopkins Press, 1967.
———, *Problems of Art*. New York: Charles Scribner's Sons, 1957.
———, *Philosophical Sketches*. Baltimore: The Johns Hopkins Press, 1962.
LORD, JAMES, "A Lady Seeking Answers," *The New York Times*, May 26, 1968.
SARGEANT, WINTHROP, "Susanne K. Langer, Profile," *The New Yorker*, December 3, 1960.

MARY LYON

MARY LYON: Born in Buckland, Massachusetts, February 28, 1797. Died in South Hadley, Massachusetts, March 5, 1849. Father: Aaron Lyon; mother: Jemima (Shepard) Lyon; brothers: Ezra (died young), Aaron; sisters: Electa, Jemima, Lovina, Freelove, Rosina.

*

Mary Lyon, famous educator, founder of Mount Holyoke College, established in her lifetime a means whereby young women might obtain an advanced academic education comparable to that previously available only to young men. She raised the status of women in the teaching profession to one of dignity and wide usefulness.

*

HER father had died before she was six, but her mother frugally managed to bring up seven children, relying largely on the produce of their small farm. Mary's weekday dress came from flax grown in their own garden and was spun, woven, and dyed at home. Her shoes, and those of her brothers and sisters, were made from the hide of calves they had raised themselves. The family had a small flock of sheep and the tasks of sheep shearing and wool carding produced "the rare gift of a Sunday suit." Coverlets on their five beds and one trundle bed were hand spun, hand woven, and hand dyed.

Time was precious in this household. The story goes that Mary in her early childhood once climbed on a chair and

Mary Lyon

tilted the hourglass so that the sand ran more slowly. "I think I have found a way of making more time," she told her mother. Throughout her life Mary Lyon was to be guided by a sense of the worth of every moment and every object she dealt with. "Never destroy any thing that God has made or given skill to," she would tell her pupils, "not even a kernel of corn, nor a pin. Never think any thing worthless until it has done all the good it can."

As busy as the members of the family were, the mother saw that the children attended the one-room district school. At home Mary would read the religious books left by her father, who had been active in the Baptist Church.

On Sundays the family would go in an "orderly group" to the Baptist Meeting House in nearby Ashfield, Massachusetts, the mother at the head on a pony, the seven children walking decorously behind. One day a group of people "under conviction of sin" came to Mary's grandfather, the Baptist minister, and were assured of God's great mercy. Mary, who had witnessed this interchange, left the church with a sense "of God's love and His goodness, and of an answering love for Him." His goodness, she believed, was behind "the rivulet [that] found its way among rocks and cliffs and hillocks and deep craggy dells . . . the apple [that] came fresh in the spring and the maple sugar [that] was never known to fail." She was to remember throughout her life her mother's garden and the orchard with its apple and peach and plum trees, and she was to remember "the far-off mountains" she could see from the top of the hill.

Mary's childhood ended when she was thirteen. Then her mother remarried and moved with the younger daughters to her new husband's home. Mary's twenty-one-year-old brother, Aaron, stayed on to run the family farm, and Mary kept house for him until she was seventeen. Then she started teaching in various district schools, boarding out with the families of her small pupils. She admits herself that at first she was not much of a success. She laughed too much with her pupils.

When Mary was twenty, the Sanderson Academy was opened in Ashfield. Higher education in those days was intended primarily for young men, but occasionally an ambitious young lady was allowed to share its benefits. So Mary herself became a student in this one-story school made over from a store. She earned her tuition by selling her household linens and spinning two coverlets. A prodigious learner, she memorized the assigned portions of Adams' *Latin Grammar* —an entire term's work—between a Friday afternoon and the close of school on the following Monday. She got along with about four hours of sleep a night, pored over books the rest of the time. She was always ready with her beaming smile when her schoolmates asked her for help in their studies. And she could take advice. When her deskmate, Amanda White, would give her some suggestions on improving her appearance —she was apt to dress carelessly—Mary would put her hands on Amanda's shoulders saying, "Oh, was there ever a poor erring mortal that had such fine friends!"

When in the second term the supply of Mary's coverlets gave out, it was Amanda's father, Thomas White, a trustee at the Sanderson Academy, who took her into his own home and who persuaded his fellow trustees to allow her free tuition. In fact, this good man was to help her at difficult times throughout her career. She called him her "second father."

After two terms at Sanderson, Mary went back to her teaching. But she had set her heart on studying at the highly reputed Academy at Amherst, and as soon as she had saved enough money, off she went. There she studied grammar and geography, rhetoric and logic, and took a course in chemistry, a subject she was later to teach with skill. Noah Webster, of dictionary fame, was a sponsor of the Amherst Academy. He occasionally addressed the students and also invited groups of them over to his house. Such contacts sent her back to Buckland—she could afford to stay at Amherst only one term—a more poised and comprehending person. She was "full of talk on subjects started in school and questions so that she could hardly take time to eat even when she came to the table . . . ." Her "adopted home" was still at Mr. White's in Ashfield, and it was Mr. White who in 1821 took her with his daughter Amanda in a "roomy carry-all" across the state of Massachusetts to attend an advanced school run by Rev. Joseph Emerson in the town of Byfield. She would tell her pupils years later about the trip, exclaiming, "It was like going to Europe now. Why, it took me three long days to go."

Joseph Emerson, an early advocate of "female education," believed that "Nature had peculiarly formed and designed the softer sex for the noble and delightful though arduous and trying office of teaching." He would thriftily add that such instruction was "at once more excellent and less expensive."

In the large hall at Byfield, made over from a former religious meeting house, some fifty or sixty young ladies sat on long benches at unpainted desks and learned geometry, geography, and calculus. When classes were over, they took turns sweeping the floors. Tuition was twenty-five cents a week, a sum made up in Mary Lyon's case by a loan from Mr. White.

At the Byfield school she made friends with a young teacher, Zilpah Polly Grant. They were to be associated in many later activities.

After her term at Byfield, Mary Lyon became an assistant to the head of her former school, the Sanderson Academy. The trustees had had some difficulty making up their minds about employing her (she was the first woman ever to teach there) but Mr. White put an end to their discussion with a brief, "Try her."

The experiment worked out to everyone's satisfaction. But

Mary Lyon

Mary Lyon was especially interested in teaching girls, and after a few terms she took a position at the Adams Female Academy in Londonderry (now called "Derry"), New Hampshire. Her friend, Polly Grant, was the principal of this forward-looking school. The sixty or so young ladies were taught by women, and taught not only the usual spelling, defining, reading, arithmetic, chirography (penmanship), and English grammar, but also natural philosophy, chemistry, astronomy, and—this was a true innovation—pedagogy, or the art of teaching.

So unusual was the school that it was called to the attention of the aged General Lafayette, who visited America in 1825. The girls received him—he arrived late, they had to wait most of the day—in white dresses "with bunches of natural flowers fastened to their pink belts." When he rode away in his four-horse carriage, with its escort of horsemen, the church bells ringing, everyone felt that the Adams Academy had won a proud place in the community and indeed in the nation.

Summer school sessions were common in those days of impassable winter roads and no railroads. Because the school at Londonderry held classes from the middle of April to the middle of November, Miss Lyon was able during the winter months to start a small school of her own in Buckland, her home town. She coached young ladies there at a modest price, and kept expenses down by teaching in any available location at any available time.

In 1827 Mary Lyon became acting head of the Adams Academy—Miss Grant had injured her leg and for two years could not move without crutches. The school was using, as well as elements of the Pestalozzi system (combining manual training with other instruction), the Lancastrian teaching system. That is, Miss Lyon had members of the senior class teach the students in the lower classes. She would pass from one class to another, assisting the monitors or listening to the recitations. A student of hers was to recall, fifty years later, "Even now the firm clear tones of her voice echo through my memory, and I see her earnest face, her keen hazel eyes, her auburn hair, and strongly marked features; the austere simplicity of her dress, and the brusque decision in every movement." That winter she taught again at the Sanderson Academy at Ashfield, the trustees having allowed her to transform the school at least temporarily into a girls' academy.

In late 1828 Miss Lyon gave up her other teaching work and put all her energies into a school Miss Grant had started in Ipswich, Massachusetts. This was an experimental station for new ideas. The "honor system" was put into action, with each student reporting on her own activities: "I have kept my chamber in reasonable order"; "I have called at others' rooms and doors only at the time specified"; "I have neither lingered nor made unnecessary noise in spaceways nor in the family rooms"; "I have walked out but once without Miss Farley's apprehension, and with the exception of laughing once at table, have behaved with propriety." Other rules included not leaving pasture bars down when crossing fields and never going to the post office without permission.

As the school grew, it became difficult to find places to board the pupils. A large house a quarter of a mile from the school building was taken over as a dormitory. In 1831 three hundred girls applied for entrance, and only half of them could be accommodated. Miss Lyon became convinced a school of higher education, to succeed, must have permanent facilities for boarding its students. By summertime she and Miss Grant presented a prospectus to the treasurer of the Ipswich school for a "New England Female Seminary for Teachers," its purposes: (1) to increase the number of well-qualified teachers; (2) to induce teachers already employed to improve themselves; (3) to bring teaching, especially in the higher subjects, into the hands of women; and (4) to "lead the way toward the establishment of permanent female seminaries in our land."

In 1833 she made a summer trip through Pennsylvania, Ohio, Michigan, and western New York State. She called on other educators, purchased science equipment, and visited "cooperative" schools, in which students helped in household tasks. This latter gave her her ideas for domestic work, later to be tried out at the new seminary.

On her return, at a meeting called at the Ipswich school and attended by trustees, ministers, professors, lawyers, and other prominent citizens, she presented her ideas for the education of women through permanent colleges. She had noticed, she told them, that schools, no matter how high their level of learning and how well-rounded their teaching, closed down upon the deaths of their founders. The reason? The schools had no permanent buildings and no means of support aside from student tuition. She offered a plan: a seminary building big enough to seat 175 scholars, with a laboratory and reading room containing the necessary apparatus and books; and, in close connection, a boarding house capable of accommodating 150 students, with rooms "so finished and furnished as to give ladies as favorable a situation while pursuing their studies as is afforded to young men at our colleges or other seminaries."

The money for this project was to come through voluntary contributions from ordinary citizens. Farmers, artisans, and professional people would, she argued, be willing to contribute, once they were convinced of the worth of the institution and once it was made clear to them that the school would be run with a minimum of expense: teachers working with missionary spirit at moderate salaries; the domestic work done by the pupils themselves; the board and tuition fees placed at cost. Dedication, simplicity of living, and rigor in administration would persuade even people in moderate circumstances to open their purse strings. This meeting, held in September 1834, marked the ideological birth of Mary Lyon's brain child, Mount Holyoke Seminary.

Her method of raising money was just as advanced as her ideas on education. An initial sum of about one thousand dollars was to be collected first. This sum was to finance the raising of the main fund. The donors to the main fund could thus be assured that no part of their contributions would be used in advertising or "fringe" expenses.

For this initial one thousand dollars Mary Lyon approached the ladies living in Ipswich and its surroundings, in a house to house canvass. "If you wanted a new shawl or a carpet you would find a way to get it . . . . But here is a benevolence that will go much further, will aid your own daughter and her daughters and *their* daughters." Some of the women gave the few dollars they had earned from sewing or other chores; some asked for money from their husbands and fathers. Sometimes it was Mary Lyon who spoke to the husbands to ask them "to cut off one little corner of their estates and give it to their wives."

Once the first thousand was collected, she set about raising money for the actual building. Up and down New England she went. A pupil of hers, Eunice Caldwell, wrote, "Traveling the road from Boston to Connecticut often, she could scarce ride any ten miles of the route without being recognized by some fellow traveler . . . . She would soon be invited to detail the progress of the enterprise . . . . She could make herself heard easily, although the road might be a little uneven, and would expatiate on the subject so freely as in her own parlor . . . . Many a man can say, 'I saw Miss Lyon once; I met her in the stage coach; an original character, quite.'" When some shook their heads, implying this was not "ladylike," she answered, "My heart is sick, my soul is pained, with this empty gentility, this genteel nothingness. I am doing a great work. I cannot come down."

Through her sheer earnestness and conviction she won people over. The wealthy farmer Joseph Avery, after listening to her, looked across to his wife: "I had set aside a sum of money for shingling the house this year." His wife replied, "I can set the milk pails under the leaky places another year." The Seminary trustees, Andrew W. Porter and Daniel Safford, threw themselves into the venture, too, and worked as if they had thought it up themselves, as indeed Miss Lyon wisely made them think they had.

On February 10, 1836, the act of incorporation of the Seminary passed both houses of the Massachusetts legislature. The charter was granted the following day. Three weeks later the trustees met and called for estimates and architects' plans. The popular press might lampoon the enterprise as a "Protestant nunnery" or a "rib factory," but the solid sense behind it could not be denied. Soon hundreds of individuals in more than sixty different towns had subscribed to Mount Holyoke Seminary.

On October 3, 1836, the cornerstone was laid. "This will be an era in female education," Miss Lyon rejoiced. "The work will not stop with this institution." By the autumn of 1837 the main building was ready for occupancy.

The financial panic in 1837 had swept many fortunes away, and the day for the opening drew near with some of the money pledges still unredeemed. Hasty notes from Mary Lyon reached the ladies thereabouts: "Some of the bedding which I hoped we should receive has not yet arrived . . . any kind of blankets, a little worn, if more convenient, as in that case some lady may give a pair of blankets"; "If you can borrow any tablespoons . . . and bring (them) with you, I should consider it a great favor"; "several of our chambers remain unoccupied for want of furnishing." When there was a windfall of fifty dollars, Mary Lyon made a quick trip to Boston to shop for "knives and forks and crockery."

Opening day of Mount Holyoke Female Seminary, November 8, 1837, brought 80 young ladies (later in the year augmented to 116) to the plain but charming brick building set on a bare patch of ground. They came from all along the East Coast. No trees, no fence, and not a blade of grass gave the place a homelike look. No matter. As one of the girls wrote, "In the absence of front steps we alighted on the back side of the basement at a door opening into the dining room. At one end of the room a group were at work on unfinished comfortables. At the other, tables were spread for hungry travelers. Mrs. Deacon Safford, a royal woman with a lovely face, and Mrs. Deacon Porter, of no less princely gifts, were washing crockery in the great kitchen. Presently Miss Lyon appeared, her face all aglow under the traditional turban, and gave us the welcome of a mother to her daughters. 'Come right up stairs,' she said, 'You have come to help us,' in a voice that had the true home ring. Heart met heart, teacher and pupil were one, and we followed her to the Seminary Hall. Deacon Safford, with his coat off, was on his knees tacking straw matting on the platform. Looking up with a bright smile he said, 'We are in glorious confusion now, but shall soon be in order' . . . At four o'clock the matting was down, the bell was rung, and Mount Holyoke Seminary opened. Though the sound of the hammer, the plane, and the lathe was still heard about the house, no other day could be thought of, for this was the one appointed."

So began the twelve best years of Mary Lyon's life.

She impressed on the young ladies that their hour-a-day housework stint should be only a stimulus to their real work: their studies. These included chemistry, botany, geology, history, geography, logic, and composition. As in modern colleges, visiting professors supplemented the instruction of the resident faculty. Even lectures on such a daring subject as human anatomy were given, by a professor from Amherst College.

When the first class was graduated in August 1838, visitors noticed "the radiance of Miss Lyon's face." The soft color of her lavender silk dress brought out the flush in her cheeks. Usually her walk was rapid, with quick steps, elbows thrust out, and cap strings flying, but on this occasion she moved with great dignity.

By the 1840's she had become a widely known educator, a public figure. She was swamped with requests for young graduates to fill school positions as a community service. But she kept her feet on the ground. When Catherine Beecher, another pioneer in education, wrote from Cincinnati, Ohio, asking for teachers, Miss Lyon wrote back that her graduates must be assured of at least one hundred dollars a year and expenses before they would be allowed to travel so far.

In 1846 increasing deafness and occasional bouts with pulmonary illnesses slowed Miss Lyon's activities. But she was on her feet and jubilant when in 1847, on her fiftieth birthday, nearly forty young ladies from the classes of 1844 and 1845 attended a Mount Holyoke reunion. Many others of her former students, now laboring in foreign countries as missionaries, wrote letters of felicitation.

Early in February 1849 she contracted influenza, but continued in spite of this to do her daily work. On February 23 she gave her last talk in Seminary Hall. That very evening one of her students, who had been ill with erysipelas, passed away. Mary Lyon, who had been at the girl's side in her illness, contracted the disease. Her health was so weakened that on March 5 she died.

She was buried on the grounds of the college, and on her

tombstone was inscribed "Founder of Mount Holyoke Female Seminary, a teacher for thirty-five years of more than three thousand pupils . . ." and her own words, "There is nothing in the universe that I fear, but that I shall not know all my duty, or shall fail to do it."

BIBLIOGRAPHY

BRADFORD, GAMALIEL, *Portraits of American Women*. Boston: Houghton Mifflin Company, 1919.

DOUGLAS, ELIZABETH BRONSON, *Life Story of Mary Lyon, Founder of Mount Holyoke College*. Minneapolis: The Beard Art and Stationery Company, 1897.

GILCHRIST, BETH BRADFORD, *The Life of Mary Lyon*. Boston: Houghton Mifflin Company, 1910.

LYON, MARY, *A Missionary Offering*. Boston: Crocker and Brewster, 1843.

WILLIAMS, SHERMAN, *Some Successful Americans*. Boston: Ginn and Company, 1904.

MARGARET MEAD

MARGARET MEAD: Born in Philadelphia, Pennsylvania, December 16, 1901. Father: Edward Sherwood Mead; mother: Emily (Fogg) Mead; brother: Richard; sisters: Elizabeth, Priscilla; marriages: Reo F. Fortune, Gregory Bateson; daughter: Mary Catherine Bateson Kassarjian.

*

Margaret Mead, one of America's foremost anthropologists, brought about major modifications in once accepted conclusions regarding primitive life. She was one of the first to go directly to existing primitive cultures and bring back eyewitness reports. A lecturer, columnist, and writer of widely read books, she is also a keen critic of modern America. There is scarcely a concern in civic or national life—juvenile delinquency, abortion laws, drug addiction, world peace, family planning, careers for women, campus riots, the population explosion—which has not been brought into clearer focus through her endeavors.

*

DR. Mead's childhood was well suited to give her an awareness of the social and cultural forces in her environment. Her father was a professor of economics at the University of Pennsylvania and wrote books on contemporary economic problems. Her mother was a social scientist, carrying on sociological studies of immigrant groups who had settled near Philadelphia. Her paternal grandmother, who lived with the family, had been a school principal. She played a major part in training Margaret and Margaret's younger brother and sisters.

Both her grandmother and her mother taught Margaret to be a "notebook child." Just as Margaret's mother had made psychological observations on her eldest daughter's progress, so Margaret was taught to make notes on the progress of her younger sisters. The child loved this way of observing and recording.

Hers was a highly cooperative family, and this habit was to carry over into Margaret's later life. Her father would bring home the manuscripts of his books for her mother to go over for suggestions and additions. Later, when Margaret wrote books herself, her mother put together the indexes. On Margaret's first field trip to far-off Samoa, her father provided one thousand dollars for her transportation, because he believed that "adding to the sum of exact knowledge in the world was one of the things in life most worth doing."

Her mother and grandmother were both fully able to give the child an education that related book knowledge to the world around her. Both women were critical of the existing educational system. Margaret was taught largely at home and had little experience of formal schooling. When it was time to go to college she first tried DePauw University, her father's alma mater. Finally, however, she settled on Barnard College in New York City. It turned out to be just the right place for a young girl eager to be in the midst of an intellectual world throbbing with new ideas. In her senior year there she took a course in anthropology under Dr. Franz Boas, and this determined her in her life's work.

Dr. Boas' idea of anthropology was to study man, not by delving into the ruins of ancient civilizations but by going directly to remote peoples still living out their lives in primitive cultures. In this type of study the anthropologist sees the sub-

Culver Pictures, Inc.

EDNA ST.
VINCENT MILLAY

The Public Service of the State of New York, 1882
New York Public Library Picture Collection

MARIA MITCHELL

HARRIET MONROE

Courtesy Chicago Historical Society

United Press International Photo

CONSTANCE
BAKER MOTLEY

LUCRETIA MOTT

*Engraved by G. E. Perine & Co.
New York Public Library Picture Collection*

ROSA PONSELLE
in costume for the title role in Bellini's Norma

Metropolitan Opera Archives

Library of Congress

ELEANOR ROOSEVELT

FLORENCE SABIN

Doris Ulmann © 1922
New York Public Library Picture Collection

MARGARET
SANGER *with her
sons* GRANT *(left)*
and STUART

MARGARET
CHASE SMITH

GERTRUDE STEIN

HARRIET BEECHER STOWE

HARRIET
TUBMAN

"BABE"
DIDRIKSON
ZAHARIAS

jects in "real life" situations and does not have to slice through thousands of years of civilization to get at the facts.

With spreading industrialization and commercial exploitation, however, existing primitive societies were becoming few and far between. If they were to be studied, it must be done quickly. Margaret Mead writes that she remembers waking up at night during her period of preparation "with the dreadful thought that the last man on Rarotonga might be dying this very minute."

How does one prepare for a trip to a primitive culture? After receiving her bachelor's degree at Barnard in 1923, she went on to Columbia University, supporting herself with jobs on campus. She took training in languages that had sounds similar to those she would be using in primitive groups. She studied intensively all available information on primitive peoples: their housing, their food, their ceremonials, their taboos. Then, on the recommendations of Dr. Boas and Dr. Ruth Benedict, another of her teachers, she applied for and received a fellowship from the National Research Council. She was to make a trip to the Samoan Islands, situated just south of the equator and inhabited by a Polynesian people. Her project was to study the role of the adolescent girl in this primitive Polynesian society.

In 1925 Margaret Mead boarded a steamer in San Francisco with her typewriter, a flashlight, a few clothes, and a metal strongbox to hold her notes. She stopped off in Honolulu to take some lessons in Polynesian grammar, and then boarded another steamer bearing southwest for the Samoan Islands. When she disembarked she was 7,500 miles from her Pennsylvania home. She had never before traveled outside her own country, never so much as stayed at a hotel overnight. She was to be gone nine months.

For the first six weeks in Samoa she put up at a ramshackle hotel in the port of Pago Pago, where she studied the language with a Samoan nurse attached to the medical station. Then she went to live in a little village on the coast of the island of Tutuila, where the chief had agreed to receive her. For the first few months she found herself repeating, "I can't do it. I can't do it." Then one day she noticed she was saying it in Samoan, and she knew she had a chance.

Being a woman is an asset in this type of anthropological field work. One can live in the home group, come close to the children, make friends with the adolescents and the mothers. Margaret Mead herself is small in stature and looked so young that the Samoan teen-agers accepted her as one of themselves. She became a companion of the chief's daughter and was called "Makelita." She learned to sleep on a springy pile of mats spread on the pebble floor, to carry on most indoor occupations sitting cross-legged, to eat raw fish with her fingers. Because the oval house was no more than a high thatched roof resting on a large circle of poles, with neither outside walls nor inner partitions, privacy was a luxury she had to forego. She had to become accustomed, for instance, to washing in the village shower and changing clothes from wet to dry before a group of watching children. However, all this had its positive side. She was fully accepted as one of the group. "I was never homesick in a Samoan house," she writes. "I know and cherish the knowledge that if I were ill or disabled, I could go back thirty years later and the children of Ufuti, my 'brothers and sisters,' would take me in."

Meanwhile she got on with her work. She explains it: "Equipped principally with a way of looking at things, the field worker is expected somehow to seize on all the essentials of a strange way of life and bring back a record that will make this comprehensible as a whole to others who very likely never will see this people in their living reality . . . . He must learn the culture without embodying it, in order to become its accurate chronicler . . . must learn to do something correctly and not to become absorbed in the doing . . . must live all day in a maze of relationships without being caught in the maze." So, while going fishing by torchlight, walking barefoot over the reefs, helping with the basket-making and the weaving, she talked with the girls, heard their gossip and their jokes, listened to their growing-up problems, their plans, and their prospects. Sometimes it was not easy. "It is very trying to kneel beside a village fire for four hours with smoke in your eyes and take notes while thinking up the right questions and judging the personality of your primitive informants—but it's part of the job."

The notes she took on this field trip she transformed, on her return to New York in 1926, into a book, *Coming of Age in Samoa*. The book's message was that human nature is remarkably malleable; that customs can alter it widely. *The New York Times* called it "a remarkable contribution to our knowledge of humanity." Dr. Boas said of it, "The results of her painstaking investigation confirm the suspicion long held by anthropologists, that much of what we ascribe to human nature is no more than a reaction at the restraints put upon us by our civilization." The book became a best seller and made Margaret Mead famous at the age of twenty-seven.

She spent the next two years in New York City, during which time she became a member of the Department of Anthropology at the American Museum of Natural History. She resumed field work in 1928, again among tribes in the South Pacific. This time she had as coworker Dr. Reo Fortune. Dr. Fortune "made it possible for me to work with people more savage and more inaccessibly located than I would have been able to reach alone." (She and Dr. Fortune were married during this period; five field trips later they were divorced.) Over the next eleven years she made expeditions to six different tribal groups, mastering their languages, participating in their social and religious activities, respecting their taboos, learning what gestures to make and when.

The first trip in this series was to the Manus, a fishing and trading tribe of about two thousand people settled along the south coast of the Great Admiralty Island off New Guinea. There for six months she lived as the Manus did, in a house with a thatched roof, set on stilts directly over the broad waters of a lagoon. One of the beliefs of the Manus was that the ghost of a recently dead male relative protected each household against the ghosts of other households. She learned to ask, when informed of a misfortune, "Which ghost is responsible?"

She went more fully equipped on this field trip—with beads, toys, balloons, paper flowers, and large amounts of rice and tobacco. Children would swarm into her house, sleep on the floor. With the paper and pencils she gave them they would delightedly draw ships, houses, and people; would have to be restrained from waking her at sunup with a plea for "papya." Through the children she reached into the homes, learning details of ceremonials, family conflicts, reconciliations. The book *Growing up in New Guinea* was the result of this expedition.

In 1930 she made a field trip nearer home, studied an American Indian tribe and recorded her findings in the book *The Changing Culture of an Indian Tribe*.

During seven months in 1931 she and Dr. Fortune made a trip to the mountain-dwelling Arapesh, a peaceable, unacquisitive tribe occupying territory on the northwest coast of New Guinea. They lived in tiny hamlets, the largest numbering some eighty-five inhabitants, and engaged in group activities —gardening, tending sago palms, hunting, building houses. The Arapesh were content except when one of their number failed to conform to their beliefs: namely "that all people are good and gentle, that men and women alike are neither strongly nor aggressively sexed, that no one has any other motive except to grow yams and children."

Beginning in the autumn of 1932 Dr. Mead and Dr. Fortune worked among the Mundugumor of New Guinea, a deeply hostile people—cannibals, head-hunters, despisers of gentleness. Unlike other tribes who build their villages around hospitable central plazas, each Mundugumor family group lived apart from the other groups. The family group would have a fenced-in enclosure of several huts, each accommodating one or two wives. The dominant men—about one in every twenty-five—maintained these large polygamous households. The tribe continually raided the miserable, ill-fed people of the neighboring grasslands for goods, for head-hunting victims, and for additional wives.

In 1933 they studied another small New Guinea tribe, the Tchambuli, who at the time were building a series of elaborately decorated houses. The men in this tribe normally busied themselves with artistic activities—elaborating their costumes, painting their masks, playing flutes, acting in plays. The women worked at making useful articles: mats, baskets, rain capes, mosquito baskets. These women were easygoing, good executives, and dominated their husbands and children.

Sex and Temperament was the book based on these field trips to the Arapesh, the Mundugumor, and the Tchambuli. Dr. Mead calls it her "most misunderstood book." In it she discusses the man-woman relationships in these varying communities and contends that the differences occur, not because of inherent differences between the sexes, but because of the differing cultural backgrounds of the three tribes, and the innate differences in human temperaments. But critics misinterpreted these contentions to mean that she denied altogether the role sex differentiations play as arbiters of personality. The book may have been misunderstood, but it was certainly popular. Dr. Ruth Benedict, writing in the New York *Herald Tribune* found it "as fresh and unhackneyed as an exploration in Mars."

From 1936 to 1938 and again in 1939 Dr. Mead and the English anthropologist Gregory Bateson, whom she married in 1936, did field work in Bali. This is a highly developed civilization of nearly one million people, living on a tiny island east of Java. Their findings here resulted in their book *Balinese Character*, illustrated with some of the 28,000 photographs taken by Professor Bateson on the trip. The book points out that the concept of the Balinese as a completely contented people, happy in their arts of music and the dance, is erroneous. On the contrary the Balinese society is one of deep tensions from which their music and art are a necessary emotional release.

In 1938 the couple made a field trip to the Iatmul of New Guinea, a people living in river-bank villages where sago culture and fishing—both the responsibility of the women—are the main support. In 1939 they returned to the United States, where in December their daughter, Mary Catherine, was born. World War II began and this meant Dr. Mead's confining her work to civilization for the next few years. However, it did not mean a curtailment of her activities. She believes that "women should not be forced to sacrifice all their talents as individuals in rearing children," and that "it is unrealistic to expect that professional men and professional women can do their exacting work and at the same time carry out the daily unremembered acts of kindness and love of which homemaking consists." She organized her own family life by a sort of communal adjustment. When her daughter was about two and a half years old and war work kept Dr. Mead busy away from home, the Batesons moved in with friends, who themselves had six children. The two families made a lively and congenial group.

Margaret Mead

From 1942 to 1945 Dr. Mead was executive secretary of the Committee on Food Habits of the National Research Council. She made a study of American food preferences, how they are formed and how they might be maintained in spite of food shortages. Another wartime job was lecturing in Great Britain on behalf of the Office of War Information. During this period she wrote the book *And Keep Your Powder Dry*, a searching analysis of America's weaknesses and strengths.

Next came her book *Male and Female*. In it Dr. Mead lashes out at our national shortcomings. In the preface of a later edition (1962) she writes, "We face a period when the individual contribution of both men and women, as initiating, innovating, inventing, creating beings, was never more needed, but where this individual contribution is being smothered by a competing style of immoderate biological self-replication," and adds, "we end up with the contradiction of a society that appears to throw the doors open to women, but translates her every step toward success as having been damaging."

Always in great demand as a teacher and speaker—she delivers as many as eighty talks a year in the United States, Europe, and Australia—Dr. Mead has taught anthropology at Columbia, Vassar, New York University, and Emory, and has been visiting lecturer at Yale University, at Teachers College, New York, and at the New School for Social Research. In 1968 she was named chairman of the social sciences division of Fordham University's new liberal arts college in New York City.

As an example of her busy life: during nine months in 1961–1962 she gave more than a hundred speeches in the United States and abroad; participated in almost fifty radio and television programs; discussed, in Montreal, women's plans for an International Cooperation Year; gave a paper on "violence" in Philadelphia at the American Association for the Advancement of Science; went to Geneva, Switzerland, for a United Nations Conference; and wrote prefaces for new editions of some of her books—all this, of course, in addition to her regular work at the American Museum of Natural History and Columbia University.

Dr. Mead's magazine articles are provocative and trend-setting. True to her belief that "the anthropologist's one special area of competence is the ability to think about a whole society and everything in it," she includes all human problems in her range of considerations. Her monthly column in *Redbook*, the magazine for young adults, is run largely on a question and answer basis and has an astonishing scope: *Should we change the abortion laws?* "Yes, there should be 'optimum medical protection' for any woman who undergoes an abortion." *Why must Americans limit their families?* "We run the risk of suffocating the next three or four generations." *Can we achieve world peace through world laws?* "We need a high level of organization on a worldwide scale and a higher sense of respect among world peoples."

The most explosive suggestion she has put forward in *Redbook* has been that of a two-marriage system: "individual marriage" and "marriage for parenthood," whereby a sort of childless arrangement, fully legalized, could (but would not have to) lead up to a "parental" marriage, in which children could be promised stability.

In the 1950's and '60's Dr. Mead resumed her anthropological field trips. Old cultures in many cases had given way to technological civilizations. She now revisited some places she had been before, for purposes of comparison. In 1953, and again in 1964, 1965, and 1967, she found the Manus people living no longer over water, but in villages neatly set out in streets, with modern houses and simple versions of modern institutions—a bank, a school. The Manus women, who formerly wore only small aprons of shredded grass, welcomed her at the boat in well-fitted cotton dresses. The very people who once quarreled about the sale of war prisoners to neighboring cannibal tribes were now arguing about what should be done with the sixteen dollars left over from the purchase of school uniforms for the village children. Her rare chronicling of this twenty-five-year transformation would have been impossible without her earlier field work. She had not been overapprehensive, after all, when she used to wake up in those early years wondering, "Am I too late?"

Margaret Mead still has her sights set far ahead. She was chairman (1967–1969) of the committee on "Science in the Promotion of Human Welfare," of the American Association for the Advancement of Science. She is involved in two New Guinea field projects: "A Study of Cultural Systematics in New Guinea" and "Cultural Structure of Imagery."

At her office at the American Museum of Natural History in New York City, where she is curator of ethnology, one sees her sitting squarely at a well-arranged desk, reading, writing, and directing activities of multiple import. A Columbia University student, one of several hundred "on strike" for fuller representation on the campus, comes in jubilant at the student group having held its own in a recent controversy. Dr. Mead presents straightforwardly and without a hint of paternalism the professor's point of view. There is a quick give and take, a healthy sparring, and the young lady leaves with Dr. Mead's "Think it over." Now a photographer arrives to get a photograph for a forthcoming lecture tour. Next a museum preparator consults her on the planning of the future exhibition hall of Peoples of the Pacific. Here she directs, coordinates, proposes.

But it is as an astute commentator on the American scene, with a gift for prophecy, that hundreds on hundreds of people in America know Margaret Mead. "Today," she says, "one can no longer save a society by dying for it . . . there wouldn't be anything left to save. The big issue now is the survival of mankind."

BIBLIOGRAPHY

CLYMER, ELEANOR, and ERLICH, LILLIAN, *Modern American Career Women.* New York: Dodd, Mead & Company, 1959.

MEAD, MARGARET, *And Keep Your Powder Dry; an Anthropologist Looks at America.* New York: William Morrow & Company, Inc., 1942.

———, Margaret Mead's Column, *Redbook,* December, 1961 (v. 118, No. 2, p. 29) to 1968.

———, *Coming of Age in Samoa; a Psychological Study of Primitive Youth for Western Civilization*; Foreword by Franz Boas. New York: William Morrow & Company, Inc., 1928.

———, *Continuities in Cultural Evolution* (Yale University Dwight Harrington Terry Foundation. Lectures on Religion in the Light of Science and Philosophy, v. 34). New Haven: Yale University Press, 1964.

———, *Male and Female; a Study of the Sexes in a Changing World.* New York: William Morrow & Company, Inc., 1949.

———, *Sex and Temperament in Three Primitive Societies.* New York: William Morrow & Company, Inc., 1935.

———, "Return of the Cave Woman," *Saturday Evening Post,* March 3, 1962, p. 6.

NATHAN, DOROTHY, *Women of Courage.* New York: Random House, Inc., 1964.

SARGEANT, WINTHROP, "Profile." *The New Yorker,* December 30, 1961, pp. 31-4.

YOST, EDNA, *American Women of Science.* Philadelphia: Frederick A. Stokes Company, 1943.

EDNA ST. VINCENT MILLAY

EDNA ST. VINCENT MILLAY: Born in Rockland, Maine, February 22, 1892. Died in Austerlitz, New York, October 19, 1950. Father: Henry Tolman Millay; mother: Cora (Buzzelle) Millay; sisters: Norma and Kathleen; husband: Eugen Jan Boissevain.

*

In Greenwich Village, New York, during the crucial years following World War I the poet Edna St. Vincent Millay became the spokesman for the younger generation, a generation looking for "the brave new world," one of limitless opportunities, vast areas of exploration and inexhaustible joys. Her finely wrought sonnets expressed woman's love as the twentieth century conceived it—full, passionate, and free.

*

E<small>DNA</small> St. Vincent Millay lived during her childhood in seacoast towns where the distinction between heaven and earth was barely perceptible on the misty horizon. Camden, Maine, was her home after her eleventh year. Her mother, who was divorced from Edna's father, a teacher, supported the family by nursing. "Vincent," as she was called, was often left in charge of her younger sisters. She made a game of it—pick-up lunches, impromptu picnics, gay dramatics. At school as well as at home she was a leading spirit. She edited the student publication, *The Megunticook*, and acted in school plays. She had poems accepted by a children's magazine, *St. Nicholas*. But with graduation her school activities came to an end, and she was faced with the problem of what to make of her life.

She worked awhile in a law office. Next she did typing for tourists. She toyed with the idea of becoming a concert pianist—she could play well—but gave that up. Then came an unexpected opportunity. She had written a poem—a cry of adolescence sensing the infinite possibilities of life—and her mother suggested that she submit it to the *Lyric Year*, an annual anthology of one hundred poems written during the previous twelve months. Out of the one thousand entries, her poem, "Renascence," was awarded fourth place. But when the anthology was published, the readers wrote in such numbers saying "Renascence" deserved first place that the editors had to agree it had won by popular vote. Now Vincent began to see her way more clearly ahead.

The poem opened up the future for her in another way. She read it at a party put on in 1912 at Camden's Whitehall Inn. It aroused such interest in one of the audience, Caroline B. Dow, head of the National Training School of the YWCA, that she arranged a college scholarship for the young poet. Vincent went first to New York City for a preparatory course at Barnard College. Then, in the fall of 1913, when she was twenty-one, she entered Vassar College.

She entered Vassar as a poet—the furor over "Renascence" had preceded her—and a poet she was determined to be, in her actions as well as in her writing. She would be "free" she decided, free of mundane rules and petty disciplines. So she cut some of her classes. She missed chapel. She overstepped visiting hours. But she was also an enthusiastic participant in college plays and was closely involved in a campus-centered movement for the emancipation of women. Vassar's president, Henry N. MacCracken, when he heard of her deflections, decided not to curtail her activities any more than was absolutely necessary. He called her to his office. He made it clear to her that colleges had to operate along certain lines, that if they did not there would be no instruction at all. He said he knew that she, as a poet, might feel as if she were an exception to all rules, but wouldn't she try to think of the disruption she might cause among the others?

Vincent, it seems, did not change her ways to any appreciable extent. But she did complete her college courses with good ratings, and a few years after graduation, as a sort of goodwill gesture, wrote the play *The Lamp and the Bell* for the fiftieth anniversary of the Vassar College Alumnae Association.

After she was graduated from college, she went to the Greenwich Village section of New York City. By 1919 the first World War had come to an end and the world had been made, so the posters said, "Safe for Democracy." Democracy, to the youth of the day, meant freedom—freedom from taboos, from clichés, from the strictures of Puritanism. The liquor prohibition amendment, which went into effect in 1920, was known more in the breach than in the observance, and only accentuated the spirit of unrestraint. Widespread unemployment sent many aimlessly searching for amusement. Young men, multitudes of them just returned from overseas, streamed along city streets and found their way onto campuses. Young women, with a new assurance acquired from work in offices and wartime factories, mingled in the general flow. Possibilities, if not opportunities, seemed limitless. Greenwich Village was the center of this movement toward "freedom." Here Edna St. Vincent Millay began her career as the poet of the emancipated.

At first, though, she faced the problem of making ends meet. She tried to get work as an actress, but found few openings. She gave readings of her poems and wrote short stories under the pseudonym Nancy Boyd. In December 1917 the publication of her first book, *Renascence and Other Poems*, had established her as poet-laureate of the "brave new world." Her next book, *A Few Figs from Thistles*, gave her further claim to the title.

Her poems were revolutionary. Women, she believed and wrote, should be allowed the same sexual freedom, the same breadth of choice, as men. She also had pacifist ideas. With the United States freshly basking in victory, she directed the Provincetown players in a Greenwich Village production of her *Aria da Capo*, an antiwar play.

The critic and poet Harriet Monroe described her at this time as "a wild cardinal-flower of the woods transplanted to Greenwich Village in wartime and resentfully hammering at Mars with bitter blows of genius . . . . She was slender and lovely, would have had 'style' even in rags, untamable as an egret trailing long plumes in the upper air."

Miss Monroe also spoke of Miss Millay "living through love affairs." These were the subject of burning discussions wherever youth gathered. "My candle burns at both ends;/ It will not last the night!/ But ah, my foes, and oh, my friends—/ It gives a lovely light!" was a poem recited in speakeasies and on campuses from coast to coast.

She set the pattern almost single-handedly for today's Greenwich Village. Mature and sober writers of the present still speak of her pervasive influence. Author Edmund Wilson relates how, in his youth, he fell "irretrievably" in love with her, as most of his friends were doing right and left, an "almost inevitable consequence of knowing her in those days." It was not just that she was beautiful, not just that she was eloquent as few are eloquent. It was rather that she stood for what they all—all the ardent youth of the land—stood for: the right as they considered it, to live, to love, to be happy.

But Edna St. Vincent Millay found working out her theories harder than writing about them. In the late 1920's, she sent word to a friend "I'm having a sort of nervous breakdown." She decided she must get away, and on January 4, 1921, on the strength of some advance payments on her Nancy Boyd stories, set sail for Europe and was soon getting her first taste of Paris.

She traveled to England, to Rome, made a trip through Albania and part of Yugoslavia on horseback, returned to Rome, moved on to Vienna, next went to Budapest. Then it was Paris again, where her mother joined her. The two spent the summer and fall in England, then returned to France. After a sojourn in Italy they came back to America early in 1923. She was ill when she returned, but this fact in no way diminished her "high, bright gaiety."

Her book of poems *Second April*, which represented her most thoughtful and serious side, had been published in America while she was still abroad, as well as a collection of three of her plays: *The Lamp and the Bell, The Slatterns*, and *Aria da Capo*. In Paris she had written her poem *The Ballad of the Harp-Weaver*.

Now artists and society members vied for a chance to entertain her. At one party at Croton-on-Hudson she was cast in a charade with Eugen Boissevain, a Dutch importer who had made America his home. The two fell in love there and then. But Boissevain, unlike most of her former admirers, thought of her health before anything else. He saw to it that she had a complete rest. After their marriage, on July 18, 1923, he took her to a hospital for a needed operation. He watched over her faithfully then, as he was to watch over her for the twenty-four years of their marriage.

She had shortly before received the Pulitzer Prize for her *The Ballad of the Harp-Weaver and Other Poems*. She was the first woman poet to receive such recognition. With royalties from her books she could now pay off old debts. It was too bad, she wrote her mother, that she had not been able to do this earlier because now "everybody thinks it is my rich husband who has done it."

In January 1924, her health much improved, she spent a few months on a poetry reading tour. She was henceforth to go on regular tours—people jammed the halls to hear her—as well as give a series of radio broadcasts over national hookups. Later she and her husband went on a pleasure trip around the world, arriving home in the fall. The following spring they bought a farm in Austerlitz, New York. In June they moved to "Steepletop," as they had named their new home. A few years later they also bought an island off the Maine coast where they spent many summers.

During these years others of her books appeared, as well as a libretto she wrote in 1926 for Deems Taylor's opera *The King's Henchman*. Her book *Buck in the Snow* (1928) was one of her best. Max Eastman called the title poem "one of the perfect lyrics in our language, a painting of life and death unexcelled, indeed anywhere." Then came other collections of finely wrought sonnets: *Fatal Interview* (1931), *Wine from These Grapes* (1934), *Conversations at Midnight* (1937), *Huntsman, What Quarry?* (1939), *Make Bright the Arrow* (1940), and *Collected Sonnets* (1941). These sonnets were compared by critics to those of Keats. Included in *Wine from These Grapes* was her astonishing "Epitaph for the Race of Man," a work particularly pertinent for today's readers.

Gradually, however, Miss Millay's work underwent a change—and not for the better. She became involved in social problems, and as her way of contributing to the World War II effort, started writing propaganda in the form of verse. "I have one thing to give in the service of my country, my reputation as a poet," she said. Unfortunately she did not remember that loss of reputation enriches no one. When she wrote propaganda poems which were "faulty and unpolished," as she herself said, not even her purchase of a Red Cross ambulance with the proceeds could excuse the deterioration in her artistic standards. However, her narrative poem *The Murder of Lidice* was broadcast over NBC in 1942, with distinguished commentators and actors taking part. It was shortwaved to England. And in 1943 the Poetry Society of America awarded her its Gold Medal "for meritorious work and abiding interest in humanity."

The critics, however, became harsh. She confessed she agreed with them. She wrote Edmund Wilson: "For five years I had been writing almost nothing but propaganda, and I can tell you from my own experience that there is nothing on this earth which can so much get on the nerves of a good poet as the writing of bad poetry."

Her following among the youth of the land had by now dwindled. For one thing, this poet of flaming youth was no longer young herself. The boys and the girls of the 1940's could not respond to the spirit of the '20's.

The Boissevains secluded themselves at Steepletop, seeing little company. Then in the late summer of 1949 her husband suffered a lung ailment, was hospitalized, and died after undergoing an emergency operation. Next, she herself was hospitalized for a long time. Finally, however, she was able to return to Steepletop. She lived there alone for many months, even spending Christmas Eve alone, as she said, "singing carols to myself."

On October 18, 1950, she read through the night on proofs of Rolfe Humphries' translation of the *Aeneid*, intending to write a critique of it. Just before dawn she started upstairs. She climbed a few steps; then, ill and weak, sat down, leaned forward, bowed her head, and died. A worker on the farm found her body the next day.

BIBLIOGRAPHY

EASTMAN, MAX, *Great Companions; Critical Memoirs of Some Famous Friends.* New York: Farrar, Straus & Cudahy, Inc., 1959.
GOULD, JEAN, *The Poet and Her Book, a Biography of Edna St. Vincent Millay.* New York: Dodd Mead and Company, 1969.
GURKO, MIRIAM, *Restless Spirit; the Life of Edna St. Vincent Millay.* New York: Thomas Y. Crowell Company, 1962.
SHEEAN, VINCENT, *Indigo Bunting; a Memoir of Edna St. Vincent Millay.* New York: Harper & Brothers, 1951.

MARIA MITCHELL

MARIA MITCHELL: Born on Nantucket Island, Massachusetts, August 1, 1818. Died in Lynn, Massachusetts, June 28, 1889. Father: William Mitchell; mother: Lydia (Coleman) Mitchell; brothers: Andrew, William Forster, Francis, Henry; sisters: Sally, Ann, Phebe, Eliza, Eliza Catherine.

*

Maria Mitchell, astronomer and educator, discovered a comet by telescope in 1847, the first woman in the world to do so. She received the King of Denmark's Gold Medal for the feat. She was also the first woman to be admitted to the American Academy of Arts and Sciences. She was a teacher of astronomy at Vassar College for twenty-three years.

*

AT the long wooden table in the kitchen of their gray-shingled home in Nantucket, the Mitchell children sat evenings studying their school lessons. Maria was glad to be helped by her older sisters and brothers. The sentences didn't seem clear until they were explained to her phrase by phrase, and she couldn't recite them until she knew what they meant. However, if she was slow in her early studies, she began to make better progress when her teacher father became head of his own school and she became his pupil. Then, when she went on to the school of Cyrus Peirce (later to become head of the first normal school in America and a famous educator), and he insisted that everything be "wholly precisely right," she made even greater progress. At home she was given her own little study place—a yard-square roomlet at the foot of the garret stairs. Here she would spread out her papers, her log book, her compasses and rules, and, under the circle of light from a whale-oil lamp, would solve the complicated trigonometry problems Peirce had given her.

On Nantucket, an island fifty miles out from the Massachusetts mainland, the tightly knit Quaker community of which the Mitchell family was a part lived mostly from the sea. As good sailors and fishermen the men were in the habit of observing the sky. Maria's father was an amateur astronomer. Far from being considered an eccentric, with his telescope and his stargazing, he was consulted by sea captains about the weather, and about favorable days and positions at sea. After each whaling voyage the seamen brought their chronometers (exceedingly accurate timepieces) to him to have them adjusted. Before she was in her teens, Maria had learned to "rate" the seamen's chronometers in her father's absence.

Like all her sisters she was taught sewing and cooking. Her mother, an energetic and practical woman, believed in introducing her children early to the disciplines of housekeeping. On her days for cleaning the rooms, Maria would go about it in a special way. She would put bottles, jars, spice boxes, in straight rows on the kitchen shelves with their labels neatly outward; would square the ladder-back chairs and her mother's rocker with the walls; would put the rugs at proper angles with the furniture. All her life such things as a line off the perpendicular or a picture the least bit on a slant—would annoy her. She took great delight not only in orderliness but in colors. Her father, in his experiments on the polarization of light, had suspended a glass ball filled with water from the sitting room ceiling. Maria loved to watch the flashing rainbow lights when it moved in the sun.

Maria's nights were for "sweeping the skies." In this her

father was her guide. At the time of an eclipse of the sun in 1831 they removed the whole window frame from the parlor and mounted their little telescope in the space. The eclipse was observed through the telescope by her father while Maria, aged twelve, stood at his side "giving the count," that is, counting the seconds steadily by the clock, so that the exact time of the eclipse could be recorded. It was at this moment, as she said later, that she first felt a sense of being a part of an orderly universe.

When she was sixteen, Maria became an assistant teacher in Mr. Peirce's school. Then, briefly, she ran a school of her own. When she was eighteen, she took a post she was to occupy for twenty years. She became librarian of Nantucket's subscription library, the Atheneum. This was a fine neo-Greek structure with Doric columns. Here lectures were given on animal magnetism, mnemonics, phrenology, hydrostatics, optics—all the scientific interests of the day. Because the building was open only afternoons and Saturday evenings, she could still help with the housework and devote her evenings to stargazing.

Also when she was in her teens, her father became cashier at the Pacific Bank in Nantucket. The bank building was a large brick structure at the head of the square on Main Street. It had space on the second floor for the family to live. Soon she and her father had built a little wooden shed on the roof to shelter their astronomical equipment. Here they kept the four-inch telescope owned by the director of the Coast Survey. It had been loaned them so that they could send in observations from Nantucket, as one of the "stations" along the coast. West Point Academy loaned them other instruments. William C. Bond, the great American astronomer and director of the Harvard Observatory, paid them a visit to show them how to use the new instruments to greater advantage.

For the next ten years the pattern of Maria's life was constant: housework, library work, sky work. With enthusiasm and sometimes plain doggedness, she and her father jotted down in their records thousands of observations. Then, on October 1, 1847, something happened that changed the course of Maria's life.

She had as usual dressed herself against the cold—put on her gray woolen hood, her great coat, and her heavy socks—had taken her whale-oil lamp in one hand and her chronometer in the other and climbed the steps to the roof. This particular evening she went alone, because her father was entertaining guests. Then, at half-past ten, as she sat with her eye to the telescope, she saw something which she had not seen in all her years of observation. There, just above the star Polaris, a faint light shone. She had viewed that portion of the sky time and again, and always it had been blank. Now here was a light—and moreover it was moving, if ever so slowly. She watched, motionless and absorbed.

Ten minutes later down in the parlor her father felt a slight nudge at his arm and saw his daughter standing beside him. Surprised to see her back so early, he was more surprised when she told him the news. He was soon up on the roof, too, looking through the telescope.

Even today comets are not common spectacles. In the mid-nineteenth century, however, when telescopes were much less developed, to see a comet was a most unusual event. In fact, the King of Denmark, Frederick VI, had in 1831 made a standing offer to present a gold medal to anyone who first sighted an unknown comet through a telescope.

So the news that Maria had sighted a comet was well worth leaving a party for. On the roof Mr. Mitchell checked the point Maria indicated. In his notebook he recorded: "10 mo.1,1847: This evening at half past ten Maria discovered a telescopic comet five degrees above Polaris. Persuaded that no nebulae could occupy that position unnoticed, it scarcely needed the evidence of motion to give it the character of a comet."

It took some time for the astounding fact to emerge—transatlantic communications were not what they are today. But at last scientists throughout the world became aware that a young lady on a tiny island off the coast of North America had discovered a comet and this in advance of all the great astronomers of Europe.

When the King of Denmark's medal arrived—she was the first woman to receive this award—she was as pleased with the Latin inscription on it as with the gold piece itself. Translated it read: "Not in vain do we watch the setting and the rising of the stars."

The King of Denmark's recognition made Maria Mitchell famous throughout the world. In America notices about the "lady astronomer" were published in papers across the nation. An entire chapter in the book *The Recent Progress of Astronomy Especially in the United States* (1848), by Elias Loomis, was devoted to "Miss Mitchell's Comet." In 1848 she was elected to membership in the American Academy of Arts and Sciences, the first woman to be admitted. In 1850 she became a member of the Association for the Advancement of Science, here again the first woman to attain this distinction. The director of the Smithsonian Institution, Joseph Henry, considered the foremost physicist in America, sent her a prize of one hundred dollars. She later spoke of this gesture as one of the most encouraging of her life. She bought books with the money.

Another who appreciated her talents was George Bond, son of the Harvard astronomer and himself a promising astronomy student. These two not only had a mutual interest in astronomy, they also shared an almost painful sense of the brevity of life. Maria would write, "I feel constantly hurried because of the shortness of life," and George, when his physicians told him he would have to take a rest (he suffered from what proved to be a fatal illness), answered, "This is the only remedy I cannot use; I have work to do, and must do it if I can, whether I am to live or die."

In 1849 Maria Mitchell began to work for the *Nautical Almanac*. This booklet, by predicting the movements of the stars one or more years in advance, helped seamen to find their way on the open seas. Her special assignment was to give information on the planet Venus.

Still, with all these developments, Miss Mitchell's day-by-day world remained about the same: up at six, get breakfast, do the housework, have dinner, go to the Atheneum; and at night lose herself in the stars. On September 25, 1854, when she was thirty-six, she wrote in her diary: "The best that can be said of me is that I have not pretended to what I was not."

Then, with money she had carefully saved, she took a trip to Europe, where she met some of the great people of the day, writers Thomas Carlyle, Nathaniel Hawthorne, William Cullen Bryant, and Charles Dickens, and astronomer Mary Somerville.

When she returned home she received two happy surprises. The association Women of America presented her with a wonderful new telescope, and an offer came which started her on an entirely new career.

The philanthropist Matthew Vassar held what was in those times a preposterous notion: that women should have an education equal to that of men. He was in the course of founding a college for women. Then he had the even more preposterous notion that the teaching staff of such a college should be made up at least partly of women. And so it happened that Maria Mitchell received a visitor at her home in Lynn, Massachusetts, where she and her father had moved on her mother's death. It was Rufus Babcock, a trustee of the newly founded Vassar College. He had a long talk with her, and reported back to Mr. Vassar: "Few of our manly sort are anywhere near her equals in her loved and chosen pursuits." Thus it was that on September 20, 1865, the opening day at Vassar Female College, Maria Mitchell stood, gray curls, dark eyes, in her best black dress and white kerchief, in the front parlor of the main building, receiving incoming students. Her professorship of astronomy at Vassar was to continue for twenty-three years. She retired just a few months before her seventieth birthday, only a little more than a year before her death.

Her teaching methods were in advance of the time. She disliked the marking system. When marks were demanded she would say, "You cannot mark a human mind because there is no intellectual unit." She believed in learning by doing. She taught her students to recognize the constellations not as the "Crab" or "Pegasus" or the "Great Bear" but by visualizing them in abstract patterns made by one group of stars against another—quadrangles slightly off angle, squares, semicircles. "When the sun sets," she would say, "watch for the first star that shimmers in the blue. See if you can connect this star with other stars, so as to make a triangle or a square. Learn to know a few of the leading stars by name and place, and then make constellations to suit yourselves." She asked them stimulating questions: "Do heavenly bodies ever exactly retrace their footsteps?"; "Are sun spots giant vortices originating in the sun's depths?"; "Is Jupiter icy?"; "Might not nebulae revolve around each other?" She told them, "I should have more hope of a girl who questions if three angles of a triangle equaled the sum of two right angles than of one who learned the demonstration and accepted it in a few minutes."

She could be stern: "You are neglecting infinities for infinitesimals," she would tell a student. She could be crusty. When a faculty member's wife ostentatiously removed a loose thread from her dress, she said, "Please put that thread back where it came from." But she could also weave delightful fantasies, compare the sinuous edge of a sunspot to waves on a shore, or the solar discs to the corrugations of coral. The Milky Way was the "tiara of the skies." She would say, "There is something of the same pleasure in noticing the hues of the stars that there is in looking at a flower garden in autumn."

She was firm. Her students quickly found out that such astronomical events as a meteor shower, a brilliant comet, a flaming aurora, were "unavoidable necessities," and must take priority over eating, sleeping, or anything else. Miss Mitchell would knock at their doors in the middle of the night to arouse them, when any of these phenomena was in evidence. There was the memorable night in 1869 when, with the thermometer registering below zero, she and her girls climbed the stairs to the roof of the dormitory to watch and count falling meteors by the hundreds, their cries of delight descending to the sluggish sleepers below. Then with teeth chattering and frost on the observation books, the girls came trooping down and Maria Mitchell had them sip steaming coffee before a glowing wood fire. Sometimes she gave "dome breakfast parties," with little tables clustered around the big telescope on the roof of the main building.

She was as firm with herself as she was with her students. In June 1881 she was on a stern-wheel steamer, headed for home after a hard semester, when through the porthole she spotted a comet. Back she must go to Vassar, the nearest point for observation by telescope. She stationed herself in the tower room and, as she tells it, "As it (the comet) approached the meridian, I saw that it would go behind a scraggly apple tree. I sent for the watchman, Mr. Crumb, to come with the saw and cut off the upper limbs. He came back with an axe and chopped vigorously, but, as one limb after another fell, and I said, 'I need more,' he said, 'I think I must cut the whole tree.' I said, 'Cut it down.'" The next morning the campus was rife with a new version of the George Washington story.

Maria Mitchell

There were special difficulties. The telescope at Vassar was faulty—"I labor under disadvantages such as no other astronomer knows in any other college in the country." It took twenty years, but finally she got the school to improve it. Then, after Mr. Vassar passed away in 1868, the question of employing women teachers was raised again. Women on the faculty were discriminated against. Their names were left out when faculty committees were formed. Their salaries were far less than those of the men. They were not allowed to lecture outside the campus. In this latter ruling Maria Mitchell won out. She lectured at Swarthmore College in Pennsylvania, and before women's clubs in New York, Newport, and as far west as Indianapolis and Chicago. She talked to her audiences not only about the miracles of the skies but about the social discrepancies on earth. Women, she said, should be admitted to all colleges. She would insist, "I believe in women even more than I do in astronomy." In 1873 she was elected vice president of the Association for the Advancement of Women, and in 1874 became its president.

Though solicitous for the proper recognition of women in general, she was indifferent to honors bestowed on herself. When in 1887 she received an honorary doctorate from Columbia University, the president had to write her over and over to confirm if she had received the notice. She was astonished that her name was included among the names of great Americans carved on the front of the Boston Public Library. It gave her the greatest amazement to hear that a crater on the moon had been named after her.

She retired as professor in 1888. Before she left the college she had been instrumental in collecting thirty thousand dollars toward an endowment fund for the school observatory. Known as the Maria Mitchell Fund, it was later augmented to fifty thousand dollars. When she retired she was offered a home at Vassar for life. This she did not accept. She returned to the town of Lynn, where some of her family still lived. As long as her health permitted, she continued to sweep the skies, charting and mapping the stars, noting the varied tints of the distant ones, watching for another comet. Even when she could no longer climb the stairs or see clearly through the telescope, she kept her capacity for wonder. When she was near the end, she commented in amused surprise: "Well, if this is dying, there is nothing very unpleasant about it."

An observatory in Nantucket was dedicated to her memory in 1910.

BIBLIOGRAPHY

KENDAL, PHEBE MITCHELL, editor, *Maria Mitchell, Life, Letters and Journals.* Boston: Lee and Shepard, 1896.

WRIGHT, HELEN, *Sweeper in the Sky; the Life of Maria Mitchell, First Woman Astronomer in America.* New York: The Macmillan Company, 1949.

HARRIET MONROE

HARRIET MONROE: *Born in Chicago, Illinois, December 23, 1860. Died in Arequipa, Peru, September 26, 1936. Father: Henry Stanton Monroe; mother: Martha (Mitchell) Monroe; sisters: Dora Louise, Lucy; brother: William Stanton.*

*

Through a quarter of a century Harriet Monroe championed the poet's cause, not only by the poems she included in her magazine, *Poetry: a Magazine of Verse*, but by her editorials and reviews. She battled for a "new movement" in poetry, "for freer technique, for stripped modern diction, for a more vital relation with the poet's own time and place, and especially for recognition of new talent." It was a one-woman championship of what seemed to many at the time a quixotic enterprise. But the simple fact remains: Harriet Monroe changed poetry in America from a historical study to a current event.

*

IN Harriet Monroe's childhood cows were driven to pasture past the Monroe place on Michigan Avenue, in what is now downtown Chicago. Harriet and her older sister, Dora Louise, played in and around their barn and sheds, rode the pony, romped with the dogs, and petted the horses. When she was six, her lawyer father took her for buggy rides outside the town along the new railroad tracks. Once they raced a train. As the buggy gained on the train, the passengers waved their handkerchiefs through the windows. That experience caused Harriet "divine excitement," as she was to write later. But another experience, seeing the huge red harvest moon rise slowly from Lake Michigan, "trailing the little waves with flame," filled her with a sort of terror.

Indoors she would pore over old volumes her father had collected, among them Cervantes' *Don Quixote*. Until she was twelve she walked a block and a half daily to the Moseley School. Then she transferred to Dearborn Seminary. Here, however, she had a worry. Wouldn't it be hard for her father to pay the tuition? His law library and law office records had been destroyed in the Great Chicago Fire of October 9, 1871, and replacing the books had been a drain on the family finances. Her parents were given to extravagant expenditures —loved a good table, fine furnishings, plenty of servants, and travel. Her father and mother would criticize each other for their extravagances, but neither one did much about it. Harriet was the only one who really worried. However, she continued at the seminary and finally decided the family's resources were able to stand the strain of her education. She was always sensitive, however, in her later enterprises to the need for sound financial backing.

When Harriet was sixteen, the family decided she should have a change of scene and her father took her to the Visitation Convent Boarding School in Georgetown (D.C.), where both Catholics, and Protestants like herself, were accepted. Here she encountered a "great inspirational teacher," Sister Paulina, who led her into the world of mysticism. When Harriet returned to Chicago two years later, her mind was made up: "I was to be a great poet," she wrote in her autobiography, *A Poet's Life*, "a great playwright . . . . I would prefer art to life."

Her first step into the world of letters was taken in the winter of 1888–1889. On a visit to New York City with her sister

Harriet Monroe

Lucy she paid part of her own expenses by sending back reviews of plays, art, and music to the Chicago *Tribune*. These were so well received that after her return to Chicago she became art critic on this newspaper. Then she was commissioned to write an ode for the dedication ceremonies of the Chicago Auditorium, December 9, 1889. Three years later she wrote another ode for the "Dedication of Buildings" ceremony at the World's Columbian Exposition in Chicago. For this ode she received a thousand dollars—an enormous amount for a poem in that day, or indeed in any day. She later wrote that only her innocence of the facts of poetic life in America led her to demand such a price. And it was probably their sheer astonishment that led the committee to grant it. In the end, curiously, the poem brought her even more than this amount. It was printed without her authorization in the New York Sunday *World*. She sued the newspaper for five thousand dollars and won the suit.

The same year, 1892, saw the printing of her first book, *Valeria and Other Poems*, in a special limited edition. The second edition, which came out the following year, contained the much discussed "Columbian Ode" and sold a heartening seven hundred copies.

She seemed to be progressing in her career with encouraging speed. But then came a series of setbacks. She loved to visit new places and spent several years traveling in Europe and in the American Great West. She returned hoping to take up in Chicago where she had left off. She hired a hall, sent out several hundred invitations for two poetry readings—and found herself speaking to rows on rows of empty seats. She had learned something about the public's capacity to forget.

Then came another shock—the complete lack of response to the publication of her book *Five Modern Plays in Verse*. One of the plays, called "The Thunderstorm," was, appropriately, about the frustrations of genius. She tried some plays in prose with no better results. Then she wrote plays in a lighter vein. But, though she consulted with actors, managers, and publishers, she had no offers to produce these works. Finally, after years of indifference, she gave up writing for the professional stage.

During the lean years, from the mid-nineties to about 1909, she tried to earn a living in various ways—a little private tutoring, a few lectures. Some of her essays appeared in *The Atlantic Monthly* and the *Century* magazines. A few articles were published in the Chicago newspapers. But as for her poetry, it seemed impossible to place. In 1906, a fairly typical year, her income from the material submitted to magazines was only five dollars, although she had sent out twenty-five poems and a few prose articles. One of her poems received only rejection slips, this in spite of the fact that it was sent over a considerable period to nearly every reputable magazine. It was her lyric "I Love My Life," which has since appeared in numerous anthologies. In 1909 *The Atlantic Monthly* published a poem of hers, and a year later, another. But mostly these years were a blank.

In 1909 a slight lift came when the Chicago *Tribune* again took her on as an art critic, a job she held for five years. When she returned from a trip abroad in January 1911, on leave from the newspaper, she found Chicago surging with every type of artistic activity except poetry. So she continued her work on the *Tribune* and her four hours a week teaching, and bided her time. But now she had come to a decision.

She had been forced to conclude that poetry was the stepchild of the arts. Large endowments, partly derived from taxation, went to the support of the Art Institute of Chicago. Painters and sculptors were given large prizes. A fine symphony orchestra flourished in Chicago. But the poets, major and minor, were given mere sops by way of recognition. Their poems were used as fillers and paid for at the whim of the publishers. Was it because poems couldn't be "exhibited," couldn't be brought into private collections or museums? The real reason, she finally concluded, was that "poetry had no one to speak for it, to plead its cause with a planned and efficient program of propaganda." She decided she would be its champion, its pleader.

She had long, serious talks with some of her influential poetry-loving friends. They decided that a small monthly magazine of new poems, with editorials and reviews, would be one way to help. They worked out a plan to finance it: She would go personally to one hundred prominent men in Chicago, asking each to pledge fifty dollars a year for five years. The five thousand dollars a year thus realized would pay for the magazine's printing and office expenses. The poets themselves would be paid with money received from subscriptions. The aim was to have the magazine, at the end of the five years, so widely accepted that its support would be assured through subscriptions alone.

Starting in September 1911, a slight woman of fifty with purposeful eyes and a determined air began to call at the offices of Chicago business leaders. She would enter "with a smile . . . as the idea of such a magazine seemed a bit amusing even to me . . . and laugh with the magnate if he thought my scheme ridiculous . . . . I never resented refusals . . . feeling they had a perfect right to encourage their own hobbies and disregard mine. But I was not stopped by secretaries. I felt I should be well enough known in my home town to have won a hearing."

What she told them was: "Great ages of art come only when a widespread creative impulse meets an equally widespread impulse of sympathy . . . . The people must grant a hearing to the best poets they have else they will never have better." She pointed out to them: "You enjoy reading Shelley's poems. Well, pay your debt to Shelley." She urged them: "Put Chicago on the cultural map."

By early June 1912 more than a hundred of the little printed five-year pledges had been signed. Altogether the contributors guaranteed $5,200 a year for five years for the upkeep of the magazine. Meanwhile she managed to keep the project before the public through the press. She was interviewed. Her statement calling poetry "The Cinderella of the Arts" was given front page placement in the Chicago *Tribune*. The New York *World* praised her efforts: "O unexpected boon! At last there'll be a publication that will accept, publish, and—most important—pay real money for poetry."

Now Harriet Monroe turned her attention to the poets. Through June and July she sat in the public library reading all the recently published books on poetry. She thumbed through magazines of the past five years, and made notes on the poets she thought interesting. In August she sent these poets a circular which explained the magazine's financial setup, its "open door" policy—no limitations as to length, style, or subject matter; the only test, *quality*. All poems published would be paid for. "The magazine," she explained, "is not intended as a money-maker but as a public-spirited effort to gather together and enlarge the poet's public and to increase his earnings." At this time she got in touch with, among others, poets Vachel Lindsay, Amy Lowell, Edwin Markham, James Oppenheim, Ezra Pound (then living in England), Edwin Arlington Robinson, Louis Untermeyer, Edith Wharton, John Masefield, Alice Meynell, Harold Munro, Alfred Noyes, and William Butler Yeats.

On September 23, 1912, Vol. I, No. 1, of *Poetry: a Magazine of Verse* came off the press—a thousand copies the first run, another thousand shortly after. More than fifty years later a person glancing over a current copy sees the same format, the same flying Pegasus on the cover, the same type face, the same layout, the same editorial breadth, the same pertinency, above all, the same high quality of poems. Few magazines can boast such continuity and stamina.

One of the first editorials proclaimed: "Poetry has been left to herself and blamed for inefficiency, a process as unreasonable as blaming the desert for barrenness . . . . The present volume is an effort to give to poetry her own place, her own voice." The "Open Door" policy was again underlined: "May the great poet we are looking for never find it shut, or half-shut, against its ample genius!"

To the headquarters of *Poetry* at 543 Cass Street came hordes of aspiring youngsters with armloads of manuscripts; came recognized poets at the heights of their careers: Rabindranath Tagore, in his Bengali robe; Vachel Lindsay, big, breezy, booming; Carl Sandburg, "a face cut out of stone"; Sara Teasdale, "delicate as a lily"; Edgar Lee Masters, "middle-aged, dark-haired, stocky"; John Gould Fletcher, William Butler Yeats, Padraic Colum, Bliss Carmen. Exciting poetry séances would take place. Once Robert Frost and Harriet Monroe argued about poetic rhythms till three in the morning "against a background of cheers and jeers."

The magazine *Poetry* was in those days almost the only vehicle for serious poets in America, almost the only standard for them to gauge their progress by. Robert Frost received the *Poetry* magazine prize of two hundred dollars, one of the earliest signals of his success in America, for his "Witch of Coös." T. S. Eliot's work first saw publication in its pages, with his poem "The Love Song of J. Alfred Prufrock." *Poetry* gave Vachel Lindsay the only prizes he ever received. Amy Lowell got her start in its pages. Edgar Lee Masters was so inspired after reading it that he left off old habits of versifying and conceived his *Spoon River Anthology*. William Carlos Williams wrote to Harriet Monroe, after having had some of his poems published in *Poetry*, of his face "shining very delightfully in your excellent mirror." Carl Sandburg, in his *Smoke and Steel* poems, introduced Chicago to the world through its pages.

The magazine's influence extended to England. For its first six years, Ezra Pound was *Poetry*'s very able British correspondent.

During World War I ghosts stalked the editorial rooms. The August 1918 issue contained the dark news that young Joyce Kilmer (his poem "Trees" had first appeared in *Poetry*) had been killed on the Picardy front. The check in payment for Rupert Brookes's "War Sonnets" came back with "Deceased" scrawled on the envelope.

The postwar spirit of "anything goes" was contrary to Miss Monroe's nature. "Too much of the vital strength of the nation is now being frittered away in Gopher Prairie banalities," she stated in the October 1922 editorial. She added the ominous warning of a "danger that poetry might become the fashion—a real danger, because the poets need an audience not fitful and superficial, but loyal and sincere."

Then came a time during the Depression in the 1930's when it seemed all interest in poetry—at least in financing a magazine devoted to poetry—was dead. Three generous grants from the Carnegie Corporation of New York saw the magazine through this dark period.

In 1936 Miss Monroe was chosen as the delegate of the Chicago Chapter of P.E.N. (the literary society representing poets, playwrights, editors, essayists, and novelists) to go to its congress at Buenos Aires, Argentina. She was seventy-five now, but both her love of travel and her pleasure in associating with her literary comrades made her discount personal difficulties. Soon she was writing home of her fascination at watching "the clash of nations and personalities" and of her own "spurt of speech" when it was suggested that a P.E.N.

magazine might be started on a shoestring. She said this might be true—with large reservations.

After the conference she made a trip to see the Inca ruins in Peru. She went by auto, train, and ship to the city of Arequipa, and then ascended the mountains by railway to a height of 7,500 feet to view the ruins. But the trip was too strenuous for her. She returned to Arequipa in a state of exhaustion. A few days later she died of a cerebral hemorrhage.

Less than two weeks before she had given an address at the P.E.N. Congress at Buenos Aires. "Our poets have a grand story to tell, and they are telling it in song and rhythmic words with gusto, power, and beauty," she said. She might have been speaking of her own life.

BIBLIOGRAPHY

MONROE, HARRIET, *A Poet's Life; Seventy Years in a Changing World.* New York: The Macmillan Company, 1938.

MONROE, HARRIET, and HENDERSON, ALICE CORBIN, editors, *The New Poetry, an Anthology of Twentieth Century Verse in English,* new and enlarged edition. New York: The Macmillan Company, 1923.

CONSTANCE BAKER MOTLEY

CONSTANCE BAKER MOTLEY: Born in New Haven, Connecticut, September 14, 1921, the sixth of nine children. Father: Willoughby Alva Baker; mother: Rachel (Huggins) Baker; husband: Joel Wilson Motley; son: Joel.

✳

Constance Baker Motley became a United States District Judge in New York City in 1966. In her earlier career she was associated with the NAACP Legal Defense and Educational Fund, Inc. Through twenty years she helped to frame most of the civil rights cases that gave "teeth" to what had previously been unenforced generalities in the Constitution of the United States. She was a key figure in the nation's campaign for desegregation in public schools. Many of her cases —she has argued and won nine before the United States Supreme Court—are now part of the fabric of our legal structure.

✳

WHILE she was growing up, her eight brothers and sisters provided plenty of family doings, plenty of improvised games in the back yard, plenty of exciting discussions around the dinner table. Constance Baker developed the habits of thinking in the midst of activity, and of thinking in terms of benefit to the group. One day the gateman at a fenced-in Milford,

Connecticut, beach told her that she and her friends weren't allowed inside. After that she did some particularly hard thinking. Why were Negro people barred from so-called "private" places where white people came and went freely? Why did the color of one's skin make such a difference? Her father and mother, who had come to Connecticut from the island of Nevis in the British West Indies, knew little about the patterns of American segregation. She had to find out for herself, as she encountered such practices, why they were allowed to exist in the United States.

So even as a young child she began watching people about her. She saw black and white standing together in line for busses, going into stores, buying across the counter, all seemingly without rules or regulations. But there were certain curious exceptions. The clerks in the downtown stores, she noticed, were all white, and so were nearly all of the teachers in the schools she attended. A small area of New Haven, around Dixwell Avenue, was peopled almost entirely by Negroes; but even here the persons in positions of authority were usually white.

At the age of fifteen, she began to study American history seriously—to read about the Civil War, about Abraham Lincoln, about the Emancipation Proclamation. She learned that, before the Civil War, Negroes in many states had been slaves, the "property" of white people. The Emancipation Proclamation, a wartime measure, had not made these people free—not in the way white people were free. It hadn't given them the opportunity to get a good education, hadn't given them access to responsible jobs, hadn't given them the right to go where they pleased, to live where they pleased.

She began attending adult community meetings at the local Dixwell community center. One of the lecturers, a prominent Negro lawyer, told about a recent decision of the United States Supreme Court. A Negro student named Lloyd Gaines had applied for admission to the University of Missouri Law School. The University Board refused him admission there, but offered to pay for his education outside the state. Mr. Gaines, however, wanted to study in his home state. He went to court about it. His case was carried right up to the Supreme Court. The final decision was that the State of Missouri must provide this student with an education equal to that given white students and that it must provide it *within the borders of the state.*

This decision, the lecturer had pointed out, was based on the Supreme Court's interpretation of the "equal protection" clause in the Fourteenth Amendment to the Constitution. So, when Constance Baker got home, she looked up this Amendment in her history book. "All persons," it read, "born or naturalized in the United States, and subject to the jurisdiction thereof, are citizens of the United States and of the State wherein they reside. No State shall make or enforce any law which shall abridge the privileges or immunities of citizens of the United States; nor shall any State deprive any person of life, liberty, or property, without the due process of law; nor deny to any person within its jurisdiction the equal protection of the laws."

From that night on, Constance Baker knew what she wanted to be: a lawyer. That would be a way to serve her people. She told her father of her decision. "Abraham Lincoln said law is difficult and I want to do something difficult," she explained.

Her father liked her spirit, but he was trying to bring up a large family on his income as a chef in a Yale fraternity house. Already he was making sacrifices to send an older sister of hers to college. His wages couldn't be stretched any further.

After she was graduated from high school, Constance Baker tried to get work, ruling out going into service as a domestic.

She met with defeat at every turn. For instance, answering an "ad" for a dental assistant over the telephone, she was told to come right around, the dentist could use her. He assured her she didn't need to have any experience. But when she got there—and it was only a few short blocks away—he gave her one hasty glance and told her the job had already been filled. She did manage to get a job paying fifty dollars a month with the National Youth Administration in New Haven, but this was all.

A year and a half went by. Then one evening at the Dixwell center a special meeting was called to discuss why so few of the local residents showed an interest in the activities of this, their community house. Constance Baker, who had opinions of her own on the subject, stood up and gave them. Negroes were nothing but guests at the center, she said. It was run by white people. Negroes couldn't be expected to take an interest in something they had no control over. Her speech brought some shaking of heads from older members of the audience. After all, Clarence Blakeslee, one of the principal white sponsors of the center, was sitting right there. It wasn't polite for her to speak out like that before him.

But Mr. Blakeslee thought differently. He admired her independence and forthrightness. That week he looked up her high school record and found she had been an honor student. He also learned she had a keen desire to become a lawyer. Impressed, he called her to his office and told her he was prepared to pay her way through college and through whatever law school she wished to attend.

That day, going home, her thoughts were busy with plans and prospects. She would study to become a lawyer. She would help her people. She would see they got equal protection under the law.

She first chose to attend Fisk University, in Nashville, Tennessee, one of the best Negro colleges in the country. Here she was brought in touch with other serious-minded and gifted students. She had lost a year and a half since her high school graduation, and to make them up she attended classes winter and summer. She began at Fisk in February 1941 and a year later transferred to New York University. She was graduated in the fall of 1943; then, in February 1944, she entered Columbia University Law School.

At Columbia University she became acquainted with the prominent lawyer Thurgood Marshall. He was later to become Associate Justice of the United States Supreme Court, but was then chief counsel of the Legal Defense Fund, a group working in close connection with NAACP (National Association for the Advancement of Colored People) and other organizations. Mr. Marshall found Constance Baker not only a clear-sighted and highly intelligent young woman, but a dedicated one as well. In October 1945 he asked her to join the staff of the Legal Defense Fund as a law clerk. She was then in her senior year.

Another person to recognize her abilities was lawyer Charles Houston, who worked with the NAACP in an advisory capacity. Through Mr. Houston she got her first courtroom experience in a civil rights case. She sat in on a trial in which a Negro girl, who had sought and been denied admission to the nursing school of the University of Maryland, brought suit. The successful outcome of the case was an opening wedge in ending the policy of racial segregation in such schools.

While at law school, she met Joel Motley who was attending New York University Law School. Their interests lay along similar lines, and after her graduation in 1946 they were married. Today she and her husband and their son, Joel, live in New York City, where Mr. Motley heads his own real estate and insurance business.

By 1949 Mrs. Motley, promoted to the position of assistant

counsel on the Legal Defense Fund, was deeply involved in school and college segregation cases. One especially significant case was that of *Herman Sweatt v. the University of Texas.* Mr. Sweatt, a Negro, applied to the University of Texas Law School and was accepted. But he was given all the requisite courses in a separate "school"—in a basement room of a building in Austin—a situation which left him without any campus contacts, without even the stimulus of classmates. He brought suit against the university, maintaining that he had not been given the full advantages accorded the other students. The case was carried to the Supreme Court. The final decision was that the University of Texas Law School *with all its facilities* "obviously possesses to a far greater degree those qualities which are incapable of measurement but which make for greatness in a law school." This being so, Sweatt could not get an "equal education" in a one-room law school set up for him alone. This decision challenged the "separate-but-equal" doctrine which had been maintained in virtually every southern school system up to that time.

Mrs. Motley assisted in preparing arguments for the Supreme Court decision that followed on May 17, 1954. The court ruled that our Constitution forbids any state or school district to separate students according to their race. This decision, though it did not immediately end such discrimination, did make it illegal and thus subject to prosecution. It was a landmark in the civil rights movement.

Then came another crucial case: *James Meredith v. Mississippi State University.*

It is instructive to note that in the Mississippi state capital in the mid-twentieth century, Negroes, who formed almost half of the population of the state, were excluded from the city auditorium, from downtown movie theaters, from the main libraries, from "public" parks, playgrounds, and other facilities. They were refused service in "white" restaurants and at lunch counters. Employment opportunities for Negroes were severely limited. There were white schools and Negro schools, but none instructing both races. During the sixteen months she worked on the case in Jackson, Mississippi, Mrs. Motley had difficulty finding places to eat and to sleep. Only because local Negroes opened their homes to her, often to their own inconvenience if not downright danger, did her stay in Jackson become possible. James Meredith in his book, *Three Years in Mississippi*, says of Mrs. Motley, "I do not believe anyone else could have survived two and a half years of Mississippi courts."

The resistance this seemingly clear-cut case aroused was intense and bitter. Mountains of legal briefs, thousands of dollars, and the dispatch of federal troops to the area were necessary before it was brought to a successful conclusion. After the storm cleared and James Meredith was enrolled at the University on September 30, 1962, Mrs. Motley summed up in the magazine *Crisis:* "The world watched intently as our national government sent 10,000 troops into one of our states to subdue open, physical resistance to the enforcement of the lawful orders of our federal courts. The point at question? Whether the State of Mississippi could forcefully prevent one of its own citizens from securing a college education in the State University solely because of the color of his skin." She commented that the moment James Meredith, at his graduation, reached out and received his diploma, was the most thrilling one in her life.

The James Meredith case was only one of many precedent-setting lawsuits on which Mrs. Motley worked. For ten years she labored tirelessly not only opening elementary and high schools to Negroes, but helping to end restrictive practices in housing, transportation, and recreational facilities. Her comment on a career in law is: "You win by preparation and experience—that's all. Preparation and experience."

Constance Baker Motley

In the case of *Hamilton v. Alabama* she argued successfully in the Supreme Court that a person who is tried for a crime carrying the death penalty has a right to have a lawyer at the time of his arraignment. She thus saved Hamilton from an impending death sentence. In 1962 another Supreme Court case which she argued, *Turner v. City of Memphis,* brought an end to segregation in a restaurant in the Memphis airport terminal. In 1963 she traveled some seventy thousand miles to argue not only segregation cases but charges arising from sit-in and protest demonstrations. As *The New York Times* once put it, she was "in the eye of the hurricane surrounding the struggle for civil rights throughout the South."

She was keenly aware of the responsibilities entailed by these advances. "The more successful we are," she said, "the greater the danger becomes . . . to the whole civil rights movement. Before 1954, no one down South really took us seriously. But after the Supreme Court desegregation decision you had massive resistance, you had actual outlawry."

By the mid-sixties her attention began to focus on abuses in our great cities—inadequate schooling for Negro children coupled with segregation practices, slum conditions, chronic unemployment. Such abuses, she felt, called for new laws. So in January 1964, when the state senator from her New York City district resigned and Mrs. Motley was suggested for the post, she accepted the challenge. Winning the special election in February, she became the first Negro woman ever to serve in the New York State Senate. In November of that year she was reelected to a full two-year term.

But New York City needed and wanted her. In early 1965 she relinquished her senate post and was elected president of the Borough of Manhattan, the first woman, white or black, to hold this office. Under her, the borough presidency assumed greater significance. She chose reliable and constructive members for Manhattan's twelve community planning boards, and stood behind them in their decisions. She arbitrated the rival factions in the Columbia University area during the 1966 Morningside Urban Renewal dispute and created a compromise plan. She worked for the physical revitalization of Harlem and the location of new municipal projects there. She barred the construction of a cement plant on the Harlem River. "I have not become President of the Borough of Manhattan to preside over the destruction of the Harlem waterfront by cement mixing plants unwanted in other communities." In her public talks she struck out at construction unions and other labor organizations for their discriminatory practices.

In 1966 she was nominated by President Lyndon B. Johnson to be a judge in the federal district court for the southern district of New York, a jurisdiction including Manhattan, the Bronx, and nine lower New York State counties. The Senate confirmed the nomination.

Holding this office is both a great honor and a great responsibility. The New York federal court is the busiest one in the nation, with 10,000 pending civil cases alone, to say nothing of the pending criminal cases. Federal district judges—there are 316 of them in the eighty-eight courts of the fifty states—must be residents of the districts from which they are appointed. They must have a capacity for hard work and intensive research, because they rule on matters of national import: antitrust cases; commercial transactions; income tax evasion; labor relations; federal constitutional questions; federal offenses in such fields as narcotics traffic, stolen goods in interstate commerce, immigration, and civil rights.

When Judge Motley assumed this office, many people voiced regret at her leaving the borough presidency. Wasn't she limiting her chances to help the civil rights movement? But she was firm in her decision: "It will help overcome discrimination if the majority of the community has an opportunity to see Negroes in positions of power and responsibility. So in that sense, I think I serve the civil rights movement."

She continues to serve it in other ways, too. As a federal judge she is in a position to see that the laws are just to all. In her very first year on the bench a case came up concerning a fourteen-year-old school boy who was suspended from school because of alleged "maladjustment." The boy's parents applied to Mobilization for Youth, Inc., and received the services of a lawyer. But this lawyer was not allowed to be present at the boy's hearing before the Board of Education, because of a ruling that school children may not have counsel to represent them. The *Madera v. the Board of Education* case came before Judge Motley. She realized that children were often excluded from school for months, even years, after a "guidance conference," while they awaited admittance to New York's special schools for problem children. Sometimes they were even institutionalized for treatment—all without due process of law. So she ruled that school children have the right to be represented by a lawyer, that to withhold "proper safe-guards of procedural fairness" in situations in which "serious consequences flow for the juvenile involved" is "constitutionally repugnant."

So she continues to work toward a just and true interpretation of the Constitution, the privileges it grants, and the immunities it declares; to insist on its provisions for "equal protection under the law."

To see her presiding in court in the Federal Building on Foley Square in New York City is to witness judiciousness of a high order. Seated on the bench, she follows the details of each case with logic and patience. She confronts and resolves complex issues with composure. She meets arguments with firmness and force. She senses unerringly where justice lies and sees that it is achieved. "We all have a stake in the fair and impartial administration of justice," she has said.

BIBLIOGRAPHY

Lamson, Peggy, *Few Are Chosen: American Women in Political Life Today*. Boston: Houghton Mifflin Company, 1968.
Crisis, official publication of the National Association for the Advancement of Colored People, issues from 1949 to 1965.

LUCRETIA MOTT

LUCRETIA (COFFIN) MOTT: Born the second of seven children, on Nantucket Island, Massachusetts, January 3, 1793. Died near Philadelphia, Pennsylvania, November 11, 1880. Father: Thomas Coffin; mother: Anna (Folger) Coffin; husband: James Mott; children: Anna, Thomas (died young), Maria, Thomas (2nd), Elizabeth, Martha.

*

Lucretia Mott, a leader in the antislavery movement, won her chief fame by being the first American to publicly advocate equal rights for women. She was considered the greatest woman preacher of her time. She was one of the organizers of a convention at Seneca Falls, New York, in 1848, which was the formal beginning of the woman's rights movement.

*

THE Coffins kept a "Shop of Goods" in their home on Nantucket Island. When her mother was off on a trip to Boston to stock up on materials and her father was away on a whaling expedition, the steady-eyed, poised little girl Lucretia would wait on customers. But when her mother returned with her yards of cloth, her spools, and her packages of needles, the household reverted to its usual routine: each morning Sarah, Lucretia's older sister, would dress the younger children and Lucretia would set the table, bring a bucket of water from the neighboring pump, and after breakfast help do the dishes.

Then she would rush off to the "dame school," where each student would put a penny on the teacher's desk as the day's tuition. At home after school she would do some mending, cut rags for rugs, or help with the supper. Once in a while she would go down to the wharf with her younger sister Elizabeth to see the great fish nets being knotted. The wind would sweep a salt smell around every corner. The gulls would swoop down, screeching, for morsels of food. A whaling vessel would come in heavy with its cargo. The freshness, the daring spirit of this wave-tossed island, were to stay with Lucretia all her life. In the home outside Philadelphia where she lived after her marriage, a picture of Nantucket Island always hung in a conspicuous place. She often took her children to visit the island.

When she was still a child her father gave up his maritime life. The family kept store for several years in Nantucket, and then moved to Boston. There, under the sign of "Sumner and Coffin," her father sold candles, oil, cotton, linen, carpets, rosin, turpentine, indigo, and other commodities, and as a side line "boat passage to Nantucket."

When Lucretia reached her teens, her parents, both staunch Quakers, decided on a Quaker boarding school for their daughter: the Friend's Academy in southeastern New York State. There "the teachers appealed to the reason of children and taught by example." Boys and girls were given instruction in separate classes and were forbidden to talk together at any time.

By the end of two years Lucretia stood at the head of the class of advanced girls. She was quick to learn not only from books but from things around her. She noted, for instance, that, though tuition was the same for girls and boys, the girls who grew up and became teachers received only half as much salary as the men teachers. When she was appointed an assistant teacher at the school, this discrepancy became even more pertinent. But now at least she was allowed to talk with the men teachers.

In a French class made up of teachers, male and female, she became acquainted with a tall young man, James Mott. He was drawn to her by her dark appealing eyes, by her gentle mouth, and by her intelligence. He, too, was keenly concerned at the discrepancy in the teachers' salaries, and just as eager to do something to put things on a fair basis. They had long talks together on the subject.

After four years at the academy Lucretia rejoined her family, now living in Philadelphia. Soon after, James Mott gave up his teaching career and followed her to that city. On April 10, 1811, the two young people were married in the Quaker fashion: by joining hands before a congregation of friends and relatives and declaring themselves, in the eyes of God, husband and wife. This simple ceremony was to hold them in perfect union until the death of the husband fifty-seven years later.

By now James Mott had gone into business with Lucretia's father: "Thomas Coffin, commission merchant." Lucretia became a housewife and mother. Six children were born between 1812 and 1828. She wove rags into carpets, sewed her own and the children's clothes, darned their stockings. She "kept a clean hearth," welcomed guests with a cheery open fire. She was a great reader and a voluminous letter writer. A letter to her sister gives an account of a day's activities: "We had a large wash and I hurried to get the ironing away before the people flocked in. Five came before dinner. I prepared mince for forty pies, doing every part myself, even to meat chopping; picked over some lots of apples, stewed a quantity, chopped some more, and made apple pudding."

She would put the reddest apples on the fence rail so that children on their way to school could pick them up.

During these years she became more and more active in the

Quaker community. In 1821, when she was barely twenty-eight, she was raised to the status of minister. Ministers in the Society of Friends (Quakers) do not come to their duties through ordination, but are selected as the ones best qualified to be responsible for the other members' spiritual welfare.

Long before the Civil War the cause of abolishing slavery was of paramount interest to all Quakers and particularly to Lucretia and her husband. Mr. Mott, as an act of conscience, transferred his stock-in-trade from cotton (a product of slave labor) to woolens. Lucretia began preaching against slavery in other communities. By the 1830's her influence had spread far beyond her own Meeting House.

To take up the cause of abolition in those days required courage. Arson, pillage, maulings, mob violence, were frequent measures of the opposition. William Lloyd Garrison, founder and editor of the antislavery weekly the *Liberator*, was tied to a rope and dragged through the streets of Boston. At Concord, the abolitionist poet John Greenleaf Whittier was set upon by a mob throwing mud and stones. The gatherings of the abolitionists were often broken up. However, Lucretia Mott was staunch: "If our principles are right, why should we be cowards?"

In 1833 an abolition convention was held in Philadelphia. She attended and sat in the balcony with the other women. It was the custom then at such gatherings for the men to sit in the main hall and carry on the business of the meeting. However, Lucretia had something to say. She laid aside her knitting, stood up, and said it. Slaveholders were men stealers, she told the hall. They committed a crime against God and man. At the end of the meeting she went below where the men were gathered around the platform to sign a "declaration of freedom." Her husband seemed to hesitate. "James, put down thy name," she told him.

As a result of this convention a "Philadelphia Female Anti-

Slavery Society" was formed, and Lucretia Mott became its first secretary. It sent petitions to Congress, established a school for Negro children, and instituted money-making "fairs." In 1837, at another antislavery convention, she was one of the leading speakers.

Opposition was becoming more violent, however. A hall was erected in Philadelphia in 1838 as a forum "wherein the principles of Liberty and Equality of Civil Rights can be freely discussed and the evils of slavery fearlessly portrayed." During the opening week rioters burned the building to the ground. Then the mob started out to find the Mott house and burn it down, too. The house was saved only by the quick thinking of one of the Motts' friends. He shouted, "On to the Motts!" then headed the rioters off in the opposite direction.

Such events only made Lucretia's resolve stronger. When in 1839 the Anti-Slavery Convention of American Women met in Philadelphia, she refused police protection. The mayor of the city suggested she avoid "unnecessary walking with colored people." She told him that she expected to have house guests "of that complexion" and that she would "in all probability accompany them to and from the Convention." She did. Neither she nor the meetings were molested.

Meanwhile she was traveling over the whole country, even to the South, giving her quiet, balanced talks, showing slavery to be a "curse to the master and a stain upon the honor of the Republic." Her clear sweet voice, her logical mind, her dignified manner were everywhere effective. The writer Ralph Waldo Emerson pointed out the basis for her success: "She brings domesticity and common sense, and that propriety which every man loves, directly into this hurly-burly, and makes every bully ashamed. Her courage is no merit, one almost says, where triumph is so sure."

But attending abolitionist meetings was a revelation to Lucretia, too. It became plain to her that though women did most of the detailed work—the listing of names, the checking of addresses, the writing of appeals—it was the men who presided over the meetings, regulated the procedures, and held the power. A meeting called in London, England, in 1840 brought the situation into even clearer focus. The women delegates to this world antislavery convention, Lucretia Mott at their head, were refused a place in the meeting by the London contingent. As a grudging concession, however, they allowed the women to observe from the balcony. From there Mrs. Mott heard the case of the women argued by the men. Despite her husband's protest against their exclusion, the matter was shelved. She realized that this meeting, held to end human inequities on the basis of race, was in itself denying human equality on the basis of sex.

This frustrating experience, however, led to one of the most fruitful friendships in the history of woman's rights. At a London dinner party, several male members of the convention began to ridicule the ladies for their woman's rights stand. Elizabeth Cady Stanton, a young American bride attending the convention with her husband, was later to remember that evening. She described what took place: "Mrs. Mott calmly and skillfully parried all their attacks, now by her quiet humor, turning the laugh on them, and then by her earnestness and dignity silencing their ridicule and sneers . . . . I shall never forget the look of recognition she gave me when she saw by my remarks that I fully comprehended the problem of women's rights and wrongs."

From then on, during the London stay, Mrs. Stanton—she later was to become one of the chief leaders in the woman's rights movement in America—sought every opportunity to talk to Lucretia Mott. She wrote, "I continually plied her with questions and I shall never cease to be grateful for the patience and seeming pleasure, with which she fed my hungering soul . . . . I felt at once a new-born sense of dignity and freedom; it was like suddenly coming into the rays of the noonday sun after wandering with a rushlight in the caves of the earth." And she added, "I had never heard a woman talk what, as a Scotch Presbyterian, I had scarcely dared to think."

After three months of visiting and speaking in England, Ireland, and Scotland, Lucretia Mott returned to America. Now she began speaking not only for abolition but for equal rights for women. In May 1845, while attending a yearly meeting of Friends in Ohio, she held a special session for women. There she voiced what was for those days an amazing set of theories: Women should have the right to hold property even after marriage; young women should have the right to an education equal to that of young men; women should have the right to sue and to execute legal documents. Some of the male listeners simply could not take what she said. During one midwestern speaking trip she had an attack of neuralgia and appealed for help to a physician, a fellow boarder at the Quaker home where she was staying. "Lucretia," he said, "I am so deeply afflicted by thy rebellious spirit, that I do not feel that I can prescribe for thee." However, others liked her courage. The author Henry David Thoreau heard her at the Hester Street (Friends) Meetinghouse in New York: "Mrs. Mott rose, took off her bonnet and began to utter very deliberately what the spirit suggested. Her self-possession was something to see, if all else failed, but it did not. Her subject was 'The abuse of the Bible,' and thence she straightway digressed to slavery and the degradation of women. It was a good speech . . . ."

When in July 1848 Mrs. Mott went to Waterloo, New York, to visit a sister and speak at the Meetinghouse there, Mrs. Stanton, who lived ten miles away at Seneca Falls, decided this was the time to hold a woman's rights convention. Lucretia Mott agreed to be the principal speaker. A "Declaration of Sentiments" was drawn up, patterned after the Declaration of Independence but so paraphrased as to voice women's grievances. Men monopolized the well-paying professions, it emphasized; they closed institutions of higher learning to women; they taxed her to support a government in which she had no voice; they deprived her of property earned by her own efforts; they considered her "dead to the law" at marriage. Women, the document demanded, should be admitted to all the rights and privileges that belong to them as citizens of the United States.

This Woman's Rights Meeting was held on July 19 and 20, 1848, in the Wesleyan Chapel at Seneca Falls, New York. They had printed a brief notice of it in the local paper, and this, to their surprise, brought out the curious, some three hundred of them rumbling up in farm wagons and buggies from miles around. The very fact of women speaking in public at all was amazing, but speaking of their *rights*—it was unheard of. The Wesleyan Chapel was found locked—the minister had probably regretted his generosity in making it available for such a cause—but a small boy obligingly crawled in through a window and unlocked it from the inside.

Once assembled, the women were at a loss how to begin, because no one had the slightest idea about parliamentary procedure. They asked James Mott, because he was familiar with such procedure, to preside. Lucretia Mott gave the opening address. Her clear, calm voice stated that "the speedy success of our cause depends upon the zealous and untiring efforts of both men and women for . . . securing to women an equal participation with men in the various trades, professions, and commerce." Her words brought courage and determination to the timid group. The only resolution she did not at first agree with was one advocating votes for women. "Lizzie, thee will make us ridiculous," she is said to have warned Mrs. Stanton. However, she came to accept this, too. Her name headed the one hundred signatures appended to the convention's resolutions.

Lucretia Mott

Newspaper reporters had a field day, writing about this meeting and those that followed. "Hen conventions" where women "try to crow like roosters"; "Time to put men in petticoats and set them at the washing tubs." But Lucretia Mott's speeches—and before long she was traveling across the country speaking for women—gave the cause dignity and plausibility.

In the fall of 1852 she was elected president of the Woman's Rights Convention at Syracuse. On September 5 and 6, 1853, she presided at the fifth annual meeting in New York—under difficulties this time, for a mob stormed the evening session, and hissed, stamped, and screamed from the gallery. This convention was moved to Cleveland, Ohio, where it was concluded peacefully.

The Motts' home on Arch Street in Philadelphia was a meeting place for the great thinkers and reformers of the day: John Quincy Adams, Ralph Waldo Emerson, John Greenleaf Whittier, the Negro agitator Sojourner Truth. In the mid-fifties Susan B. Anthony was a guest there, with William Lloyd Garrison sitting at Lucretia's right at the long table accommodating twenty-four guests. At the end of the meal a "little cedar tub filled with hot soapy water was brought in and set before Lucretia so that she could wash the silver, glass, and fine china at the table . . . while the interesting conversation continued.

As the Civil War loomed, abolition became a burning national issue. Here Mrs. Mott again was the subject of journalistic attacks. In 1853, when she spoke in Kentucky, a slaveholder, writing in the local newspaper, called her "a brazen infidel" engaged in "treason against God and her country." When, shortly after the election of Lincoln in 1860, Mrs. Mott, Mrs. Stanton, and Susan B. Anthony toured New York State calling for "immediate and unconditional emancipation" for slaves, mobs pursued them in the street. At a Syracuse meeting men rushed down the aisles brandishing knives and pistols. Mrs. Mott went on with her speech as if nothing was happening.

Once the President had issued the Emancipation Proclamation, however, the public attitude changed. Mrs. Mott became a popular figure, was flooded by appeals for her autograph and for "original anti-slavery sentiments."

Now Mrs. Stanton with Mrs. Mott formed the National Woman Suffrage Association, its aim to get full rights both for the freedmen and for women. In 1866 Lucretia Mott, now a seventy-three-year-old woman, was escorted to the seat of honor at the association's first meeting held in New York City.

After the death of her husband in 1868, she took his place as president of the Pennsylvania Peace Society. Later she addressed a New York meeting called in behalf of international peace, advocating settlement of differences by an international court. In January 1869 she was in Washington, D.C., for an equal rights convention and for a meeting of the Universal Peace Union. In the summer of 1878 she attended the thirtieth anniversary of the Woman's Rights Movement and appealed again for the right of women to hold property, to receive equal wages for equal work, and to enjoy higher education. Her last public appearance was at the executive committee of the Peace Society in Philadelphia, in 1880, when she was eighty-seven.

But now she preferred to stay at her quiet home with her children and grandchildren about her. She loved to get up early and pick blackberries or gather the early peas and currants. Nothing, she said, refreshed her so much as the smell of moist earth in the early morning.

She must have looked back on her life with satisfaction. "Christendom needs to be shocked," she once said. In her time, she had shocked it as much as any one person could.

BIBLIOGRAPHY

CROMWELL, OTELIA, *Lucretia Mott*. Cambridge: Harvard University Press, 1958.
HALLOWELL, ANNA (DAVIS), ed., *James and Lucretia Mott, Life and Letters*. Boston: Houghton Mifflin Company, 1884.
HARE, LLOYD CUSTER MAYHEW, *The Greatest American Woman, Lucretia Mott*. New York: American Historical Society, Inc., 1937.
LUTZ, ALMA, *Susan B. Anthony; Rebel, Crusader, Humanitarian*. Boston: Beacon Press, 1959.

ROSA PONSELLE

ROSA PONSELLE: Born in Meriden, Connecticut, January 22, 1897. Father: Beniamino Ponzillo; mother: Maddalena Conti Ponzillo; sister: Carmela; brother: Antonio; husband: Carle Jackson (divorced).

✳

One of the leading sopranos of the twentieth century, Rosa Ponselle was the first American singer to become a Metropolitan prima donna without previous European training. Through her immediate and unqualified success at the Metropolitan Opera House, she helped open those doors to other young American singers.

✳

EVEN as a young girl in Meriden, Connecticut, Rosa possessed a "natural" voice. Filled with the joy of life, she would sing as she ran out to feed the chickens and ducks, would sing as she dusted the rooms. "The more work I did," she says, "the more I sang; the harder the work, the harder I sang." When her older sister, Carmela, made beds or washed dishes with her, the singing became a duet.

In 1908 Carmela decided she and her sister Rosa should be singing professionally—for pay. It happened to be the very year the great Italian opera manager Giulio Gatti-Casazza crossed the ocean to direct the Metropolitan Opera Company. If the sisters could have foretold their future, they would have considered this a good omen. Work was found for Rosa in a silent movie theater. She played piano during the pictures and sang to her own accompaniment during the intermissions. (She had received some piano instruction from her church organist.) At the end of a year Carmela rounded up another job for her sister, this time in nearby New Haven, at the Cafe Malone. But singing in restaurants wasn't Carmela's idea of success. At the end of three years she told Rosa, "Now you are ready for vaudeville."

Carmela, meanwhile, had been singing in New York theaters. She told Rosa to come down to New York City over a weekend. There the two sisters concocted a plan. Carmela invited a vaudeville producer, Mr. Hughes, to their home for a spaghetti supper. "Home" was really the house of Carmela's Irish landlady. Falling in with their scheme, the landlady let the sisters use the whole downstairs, including the kitchen, for the evening. After a steaming Italian dinner and some good wine, Mr. Hughes settled back comfortably in his chair. Then Carmela laid their plan before him. Would he promote the two of them in a sister act, singing duets? At first Mr. Hughes shook his head. "Too fat," he said, meaning Rosa. (They had to agree with him there. This was before Rosa went into her dieting regime and became beautifully slim.) But when he heard her sing, he decided her size didn't matter. In fact, he had them both sign a contract that very evening. Four days later they opened at the Star Theater in the Bronx as "The Ponzillo Sisters—Those Tailored Girls," "tailored" because they wore street clothes. Rosa had not had time to send home for an evening gown.

Their singing during this period won them a contract in the B. F. Keith Vaudeville Circuit. Performing on Keith's Circuit or being a member of one of the few minor opera companies was in those days the only way a young singer could get operatic experience in America. One "act" in each Keith show was put in the "cultural" category and was listened to with the greatest respect. This was the status of "The Ponzillo Sisters" act.

They were a great success. The Pittsburgh *Leader* pronounced the ovation at their local debut "thoroughly deserved." In Atlanta, Georgia, their "flexibility" and "unusual range" were noted. In New York their "excellent taste" was underlined.

Still, after three seasons of Keith, they decided that a life of sister acts in vaudeville was not for them. What they needed was a voice teacher who would not only coach them but would help them meet people in the professional operatic world. They chose William Thorner, who was then at the very center of operatic life in New York City.

Thorner was quick to recognize the caliber of his new pupils. One day when Rosa was to have her lesson, he had the great tenor Enrico Caruso drop in, as if for a casual visit. Then Thorner had Rosa sing arias in which she had been carefully coached. As she sang, she suddenly realized Caruso was singing along with her. When she had finished, he spoke to her in her parents' Neapolitan dialect, calling her *Schugnizza*—Little Street Urchin. Later Rosa recalled that first meeting: "I had listened to him, a god on the big Metropolitan stage, and now here he was in the same room. It seemed like some crazy joke. I thought for a moment I was going to laugh."

As Caruso left the studio he said to her, "You, little girl, are going to sing with me at the Metropolitan one day." Rosa asked, "I sing with *you*? How? When?" "That is in the laps of the gods," Caruso answered. "You have it here [pointing to her throat], and you have it here [pointing to her heart], but the rest depends on what you have up here [pointing to her head]. But I don't think it will be long."

While the sisters were still excitedly going over every moment of that fabulous interview, they learned that Caruso had told Metropolitan director Gatti-Casazza that he wanted Rosa to sing the part of Leonora in the Verdi opera *La Forza del destino*. Caruso had been waiting to sing this opera for some time, but had not found the right Leonora to sing opposite his Don Alvaro.

Rosa was asked to come to Gatti-Casazza's office. The interview ended in an assignment: "How soon can you learn 'Pace, pace mio dio!' and 'Casta diva'?" Gatti asked her.

Now the aria "Pace, pace," Leonora's tragic outburst in the last act of *La Forza*, when she learns her lover (Don Alvaro) has mortally wounded her brother (Don Carlo), is difficult enough to sing, but "Casta diva," the celebrated apostrophe to the moon in the Bellini opera *Norma*, is the one of the most difficult arias in the whole operatic repertoire. "If I had known what I know now," Rosa Ponselle reminisces, "I would have fainted. But I didn't. I simply said, 'All right, Mr. Gatti,' thanked him profusely, and left the house." That week she worked night and day, forgetting her meals, forgetting her sleep. At the second audition, she got through the "Pace" all right, but "in the middle of that terrible allegro of 'Casta diva,' my breath stopped and I fainted. Sister rushed out from the wings with smelling salts, and revived me."

But Gatti-Casazza was able to see beyond the fright and the fainting. Much later he gave his opinion of her voice: "Signorina Ponselle has a voice like Caruso's. It is like velvet. It is without holes. Most voices are like a garment, thick in one place, thin in others. Hers is strong and even." On the very day of this second audition she left his office with a contract signed to debut in Verdi's *La Forza del destino*. The date was only five months away.

That summer, under the famous teacher Romano Romani, Rosa worked harder than she had ever worked before. She learned the whole score of *Forza*, that opera of star-crossed lovers, where death seems to stalk in every shadow. She learned, that is, not just the arias, then afterward filled in the recitatives, but learned her part right through from the beginning to the end. She was to use this difficult method through her whole career. She felt it was the only way she could get a proper perspective on the mood and progress of the story. Once the score had been memorized, she tackled problems of interpretation, phrasing, and voice placement.

All this time an idea having nothing to do with her debut, yet having everything to do with it, kept running through her head. It was Gatti-Casazza's parting message to her at her second audition with him: "You will be the first American to appear at the Metropolitan without having been to Europe first," he had told her. "If you make good, I will open the door to all American talent as long as I am here. If you fail, the doors are closed forever. The future of the others depends on you." What made this a fearsome challenge was the fact that it was the first production of *Forza* in the history of the Metropolitan Opera Company. Rosa had never heard the role of Leonora sung on any stage. She had to create the part entirely from her own imagination.

At the end of the summer rehearsals began on the actual Metropolitan Opera stage. Rosa Ponselle said that on that great stage she felt "like a bird trying to fly for the first time."

Her debut occurred on November 15, 1918. The old Metropolitan Opera House, razed in 1967, probably saw as many tragedies turning on the debuts of young artists as tragedies written into the opera plots themselves. That evening Miss Ponselle thought she was heading for one herself. Trying to vocalize in her heavily carpeted dressing room, where sounds were muffled, she thought she had lost her voice. Drenched with perspiration she went for a word of comfort to Caruso. She found him behind the flats nervously gargling his famous salt-water gargle. "Never again!" he was muttering to himself. "It's too much to ask of a man! I'll never sing again." Then she saw her mother with her rosary beads, and her sister with her smelling salts, and thought to herself, "I'm going to die. Oh, my poor mother!"

But—and here her strength of character showed itself—even under the stress of that first night, she would not allow herself to get out of control, to overemphasize, either in voice or in gesture, a single phrase. For she knew if she did, it would be harder to keep within bounds the next time. "I cultivated restraint until I felt that I was using no more voice or dramatic action than was suited to each situation." That night she had still another problem to cope with, this one special to *Forza*. The soprano voice range of this opera is pitched unusually high. As she sang, Miss Ponselle had constantly to remind herself, "Top, top, top—up, up." She says that, in later years, whenever she was confronted with difficulties in her portrayals, she would think back to that first night. Since she had lived through that, she could live through anything.

By the time she had sung the "Addio" in Act I, the audience realized that it was witnessing the debut of a great singer. From then on all was triumph. The next day the critics vied with each other in praising her: "A voice of natural beauty"; "splendid potentialities"; "luscious lower and middle tones"; "voice of exceptional sweetness"; "evenness throughout its entire register"; "fine stage presence."

When an opera company acquires a great singer who has special abilities, it uses the opportunity to bring back old operas that have been shelved because there was no one who could sing certain parts adequately. This naturally makes the task of the gifted new singer doubly difficult. She must not only exercise her voice in unusual ways, but she must create anew parts that she has never heard sung. Miss Ponselle, however, was equal to the challenge. In her first season Weber's *Oberon*, a story of true love tested, was given its first Metropolitan performance in ninety years. It was a success because of the force and fervor with which Rosa Ponselle sang the part of the beautiful maiden, Rezia. In her second season she sang the title role in Halévy's grim tragedy *La Juive,* with Caruso singing the part of the father, Eléazar. This opera had been dropped for thirty years. Also in her second season she took the part of Elisabeth in Verdi's *Don Carlos,* an opera about Philip II of Spain and his hapless son, Don Carlos, both in love with Elisabeth. This was the first performance of this work at the Metropolitan. Here the critics praised her for her fine interpretation of a complex role. A few months later she sang the part of Elvira in Verdi's *Ernani,* revived especially for her after an eighteen-year silence. Here she displayed her remarkable coloratura. In Meyerbeer's *L'Africaine,* revived in 1923, she was a magnificent Sélika, the captured African queen who dies of thwarted love.

In the 1924–1925 season Miss Ponselle took over the title role in Ponchielli's *La Gioconda* (The Ballad Singer), to become one of the great Giocondas in the history of opera. Violent and melodramatic, this story of intrigue in medieval Venice brought out Ponselle's ability to produce startling vocal effects in the midst of a rich melodic flow. Later that season her sister, Carmela, by that time also a member of the Metropolitan, appeared with Rosa, in *La Gioconda,* singing the role of Laura. In this opera La Gioconda (Rosa) and Laura (Carmela) are in love with the same man, Enzo. Nevertheless, Laura at one point saves La Gioconda's mother from death, and later in the opera La Gioconda not only saves Laura from death but brings her safely into the arms of Enzo—a sort of "sister act" transported to the stage of the Metropolitan.

The two most celebrated events in Miss Ponselle's career were her appearances as Giulia in Spontini's *La Vestale* and as Norma in Bellini's opera of that name.

Rosa Ponselle

The *La Vestale* was given eight times in the 1925-1926 season with Ponselle heading the cast. Set in ancient Roman times, this opera is the story of a vestal virgin who is pledged to attend the sacred flame but who allows it to go out—with dire results. This role affords the singer long grave melodies which Ponselle sang with a fine sense of vocal line and with great dignity of style. She soon became completely identified with the part.

In *Norma*, revived after thirty-five years, she was the Druid priestess who goes to her sacrificial death after renouncing her love. Here the critics noted that her words and tones merged into "absolute oneness." In the task of preparing herself for these operas, Miss Ponselle speaks warmly of the aid given her by the opera conductor Tullio Serafin. "Serafin," she says, "was a singer's conductor; he knew just how to give a singer support and how the orchestra should sound."

From 1929 to 1932 she sang three seasons in London, at the great opera house Covent Garden. An English critic wrote in the London Sunday *Times* about her role of Violetta in Verdi's *La Traviata:* "Nothing finer has been heard in London this season . . . . Miss Ponselle proves to us once more that the finest singing, given a good voice to begin with, comes from the constant play of a fine mind upon the inner meaning of the music . . . even coloratura, as she sings it, ceases to suggest the aviary and becomes the revelation of human character." In 1933 she sang at the Florence Music Festival in that Italian city.

Her audience in America was growing. By the end of the 1920's she was reaching, through the Metropolitan-on-tour performances, not only nearby Brooklyn and Philadelphia, but also Atlanta, Cleveland, Baltimore, Washington, D.C., and Richmond. On rare occasions ambitious entrepreneurs lured her west of the Mississippi and into Canada. In 1934-1937 she made a series of radio broadcasts.

Rosa Ponselle

Miss Ponselle's whole Metropolitan career lasted a little over nineteen years. But these were years of such intense activity that they might well have been several lifetimes. Once in a while the public would catch a glimpse of her living her life like an ordinary citizen: walking the several miles from her apartment on Riverside Drive to the opera house on Broadway for exercise; gaily cutting the first slice of her birthday cake at a backstage party; singing at a memorial service, which she gave on the death of her friend Enrico Caruso. But mostly it was the Ponselle of the stage one saw—one woman being a hundred women, living lives which, projected beyond the footlights, became more real to her millions of devotees than her own personal life.

After the death of her mother in 1933 Rosa Ponselle relinquished the role of Norma, this against the protests of her devoted followers. Then Gatti-Casazza announced his retirement. There was some doubt that she would care to return for the following season. In the end she not only returned but on December 17, 1935, added another individualistic interpretation to her long list: that of Carmen, in the Bizet opera.

At the end of the 1937–1938 season she retired. In December 1936 she had married Carle A. Jackson of Baltimore, and a period of rest seemed in order. But many thought her retirement was simply another proof of her innate good judgment. Rare among singers, she had the will power and wisdom to end her singing career while her voice was still in its prime.

Now she showed another of her special qualities: the ability to retire into a happy and fruitful life. Her home is the beautiful Villa Pace in Green Spring Valley, Maryland. She is the busy artistic director of the Baltimore Civic Opera. In this capacity she coaches singers, readies them for appearances in the company. She allows them to use her own historic costumes, accessories, and jewels. Before she took over the directorial duties, the Baltimore Opera Company was in financial straits.

Rosa Ponselle

After she took over, it began to engage the whole Baltimore Symphony Orchestra for its performances and began consistently selling out the 2,600-seat Lyric Theater.

In 1951 she presented a significant series of phonograph recordings of her chief operatic arias to the Library of Congress. In 1954 she made recordings for RCA Victor, which attested to the enduring beauty of her voice. In June 1965 she was awarded an honorary Doctor of Music Degree from the Peabody Conservatory in Baltimore. In 1967 she became the first woman to receive Baltimore's Metropolitan Civic Association's Achievement Award.

On February 27, 1969, Rosa Ponselle was named "Commander of the Order of Merit of the Republic of Italy." Conferred upon her by President Saragat of Italy, it is that nation's highest civilian honor, and only three women had been so honored before. Rosa Ponselle was the first American-born woman to be decorated for her great contribution in the field of Italian operatic music.

Then always there is that fabulous life behind her. The *Concise Oxford Dictionary of Opera* sums it up: "Her rich dramatic soprano voice, perfectly covered and even in scale throughout its range, of a dark, exciting quality, made her one of the greatest singers of the century."

BIBLIOGRAPHY

EBY, GORDON M., *From the Beauty of Embers (a Musical Aftermath)*, Introduction by Milton J. Cross. New York: Robert Speller & Sons, Publishers, Inc., 1961.

THOMPSON, OSCAR, *The American Singer; a Hundred Years of Success in Opera*. New York: Dial Press, Inc., 1937.

Rosa Ponselle

"From the Villa Pace; Rosa Ponselle Describes the Forces of Destiny in Her Meteoric Career to Charles and Mary Jane Matz." in *Opera News,* November 24, 1952 (v. 17, No. 4, p. 9).

ELEANOR ROOSEVELT

(ANNA) ELEANOR ROOSEVELT: Born in New York, New York, October 11, 1884. Died in New York, New York, November 7, 1962. Father: Elliott Roosevelt; mother: Anna Eleanor (Hall) Roosevelt; brothers: Elliott (died young), and Hall "Josh"; husband: Franklin Delano Roosevelt; children: Anna Eleanor, James, Franklin Delano, Jr. (died at eight months), Elliott, Franklin, Jr., and John Aspinwall.

*

Eleanor Roosevelt, during her years as America's First Lady, worked to overcome discriminatory practices against minority groups. After her White House stay she continued to champion these groups. A delegate to the first session of the United Nations, she defended the right of war refugees to choose whether or not to return to their homelands. As first chairman of the United Nations' Human Rights Commission, she played a leading role in formulating and passing the historic Declaration of Human Rights. Of all American women up to her time, she played the greatest role in national and international affairs.

*

HER father was a big-game hunter and sportsman like his brother, President Theodore Roosevelt. When Eleanor was small, he would whirl her around in a dance, then toss her in the air. He took her for carriage rides in Central Park. Once he took her to a newsboys' clubhouse to help serve Thanksgiving dinner. He drew her attention to the boys' ragged clothes and told her how many of them were homeless and had to sleep in the vestibules of apartment houses.

Her mother was a society "belle" of the era. Eleanor called her "the most beautiful woman I have ever seen." The child loved to watch her mother dress to go out in the evening. But she did not like meeting her mother's visitors. Speaking of Eleanor, her mother would tell them, "She's so old-fashioned I call her 'Granny' "—and Eleanor would be ready to sink through the floor for shame. She became intensely shy—and afraid of many things: dark rooms, loneliness, strange people.

When Eleanor was eight her mother died of diphtheria, and when she was nine, her father was thrown from a horse and killed. After that the children were cared for by governesses, French maids, and German maids. Eleanor would sometimes walk fast "to get away from them." Or she would take a book away somewhere and read. She lived in a dream world, in which her father still seemed to be present. She wrote later: "I have a curious feeling that as long as he remains to me the vivid, living person that he is, he will . . . be alive to continue to exert his influence which was always a gentle, kindly one."

By the time she was in her teens, she had moved with her brother Josh to her maternal grandmother's palatial house on West 37th Street, New York City. Her grandmother believed in Spartan discipline for children. She had Eleanor walk with a stick held at her elbow crooks and across her back to give her better posture. She had her take a cold bath in the morning. She did not allow her to have any sweets. She must never, never complain of upsets and illnesses.

One course her grandmother decided on made Eleanor forever grateful to her. She sent Eleanor to the Allenswood

School in England for three years. There she was a schoolgirl with other schoolgirls, made the hockey team, chattered in French and Italian with her classmates, and during vacations traveled on the Continent with the school's director, Mademoiselle Souvestre.

On her return to America at the age of eighteen Eleanor's shyness took possession of her again. At her own "coming out" party, she was rescued from being a wallflower only when an acquaintance from Europe rounded up some dancing partners for her. At another, later dance she was saved from the same situation when her distant cousin Franklin D. Roosevelt, then a student at Harvard, asked her to dance. She begged her grandmother to let her go to college, but was told, "No, all you need, child, are a few of the social graces to see you through life."

Eleanor Roosevelt taught some classes for little girls at the Rivington Street Settlement House. Franklin Roosevelt began coming down from Harvard to see her on weekends. After a year or so of taking her to theaters or restaurants or just on long walks, he asked her to marry him. She said yes. It seemed a natural thing.

They were married on March 17, 1905, in New York City. Theodore Roosevelt, then President of the United States, as the uncle of the bride, gave her away. It was the social event of the season. So many spectators had gathered to see "Teddy" that the whole block had to be roped off and seventy-five policemen called to keep order. When the wedding was over, the newly married couple found themselves on the sidelines, with the President, in grinning prominence, absorbing the attention of the reception guests.

Eleanor Roosevelt had entered into the marriage, she wrote, "Still timid, still afraid . . . of making mistakes . . . of failing to do what was expected of me." Then the babies started coming—"for twelve years I was either having a baby or getting over having one"—and she found her days so filled that she ceased to worry about her possible drawbacks.

Her husband was elected a New York State Senator and the family moved to the city of Albany. She fought off her shyness and called on the wives of his colleagues. She invited them to the house. In 1913 Mr. Roosevelt became Assistant Secretary of the Navy, and the couple and their three children went to Washington, D.C., to live. This was the pattern of Mrs. Roosevelt's early years there: she made ten to thirty calls a day, dined out almost every evening, entertained at home at least once a week. During this period her two younger sons, Franklin, Jr., and John, were born.

But World War I brought her social life to an abrupt halt. Like most of her friends in Washington she threw herself into the war effort. Thousands of soldiers were streaming through the city. Eleanor Roosevelt made sandwiches and coffee in a cook-shack in the Washington railroad yards, distributed food to the soldiers, and mopped floors, sometimes for sixteen hours a day. She visited the wounded in nearby Naval hospitals. She knitted woolies and sweaters for the men in the service. She got the Red Cross to build a recreation center for soldiers and sailors.

All over the United States women were furthering the war effort. Their work became essential to the successful outcome of the war. Duly noting this, President Woodrow Wilson consented to have the Woman Suffrage Amendment to the Constitution put up for ratification by the states. It was finally declared in effect August 26, 1920. Now Eleanor Roosevelt had a chance to prove her long-held belief: "If you want to institute any kind of reform you can get far more attention if you have a vote than if you lack one."

In June of 1920 her husband had resigned his Navy post to become the vice presidential running mate of presidential candidate James M. Cox. When Cox lost the election to Warren G. Harding, Franklin Roosevelt was out of public office for the first time in ten years.

He returned to his law practice. Now he had more time to spend with his family. In August 1921 he went on a vacation with them to Campobello Island, New Brunswick, Canada, where the Roosevelts had a summer place.

One day he took Eleanor and their sons for a sail in a small boat. He was teaching the boys how to handle it. On the way home they saw a forest fire and stopped off to help put it out. Afterward, to cool off, Franklin Roosevelt took a swim. He and the children then jogged home one and a half miles. There he was confronted with a great batch of mail and sat down to read it in his wet bathing suit. Later that night he had a chill. When Mr. Roosevelt began to run a high fever, doctors were called. His case was diagnosed as polio (poliomyelitis). His legs were completely immobilized, and remained so for the rest of his life.

It is hard now to realize the havoc wrought by polio in the days before immunization with Salk's vaccine had become possible. Epidemics swept the country periodically. Children were forbidden access to beaches and other places of public gatherings. Adults were rarely affected. But when they did contract the disease, they often suffered more severely than children.

It seemed for a time that Mr. Roosevelt would be a permanent invalid. His wife saw the danger he was in. She knew he would be happy only in an active life. So she built a world of politics about him. She stepped up her work in the League of Women Voters, joined the Woman's Trade Union League, became an effective public speaker, edited the paper of the Women's Division of the Democratic party, drove all over New York State organizing women voters for the Democratic party. As she introduced activity after activity into her own life, she got her husband back into his. She brought her colleagues—teachers, social workers, research students, editors, intellectuals—home to dinner. They carried on spirited discussions on issues of the day. Her husband entered into these discussions with zest.

Finally, with braces fitted to his legs and crutches making walking possible, Franklin Roosevelt began going regularly again to his law office. In 1924 in New York City he reentered active politics by making his famous "Happy Warrior" speech, nominating Al Smith as candidate for President of the United States at the Democratic National Convention. The crowd stood and cheered for almost five minutes.

Eleanor Roosevelt also was increasing her sphere of activities. At the same Democratic convention she presented planks in the party platform concerning woman's rights. To relieve local unemployment at Hyde Park, New York, she started a furniture factory there. In New York City she bought part interest in a private school, the Todhunter, and became a history teacher on its faculty.

In 1928 Franklin Delano Roosevelt was elected governor of New York State. Now Eleanor again became a familiar figure in Albany, hurrying along the streets in a white dress and flat-heeled shoes, a velvet band about her brown hair. She substituted for her husband at fairs, at cornerstone layings. She attended charity balls, horse shows, political gatherings. She donated blood regularly to the Red Cross. She handed printed cards to beggars, giving them instructions that free meals awaited them at her home. She continued to teach in New York at the Todhunter School for two and a half days a week, leaving Albany Sunday evenings and returning on Wednesday afternoons.

Once every summer she and her husband went on an automobile tour of the state, visiting prisons, hospitals, and institutions for the blind, deaf, insane, and aged. He would drive about the grounds while she would inspect the interiors. She learned "to look into the cooking pots on the stove . . . and to notice whether the beds were folded up and put in closets, which would mean they filled the corridors at night." She made speeches—on politics, on social reform, on reducing unemployment. With her simple clothes, loosely fitted, in the days of tight corseting; with an old-fashioned watch (her husband's wedding present) pinned to her blouse; with her genuine manner and her telling sincerity, she captivated her audiences.

On March 4, 1933, Franklin Delano Roosevelt became the thirty-second President of the United States. In the election he had carried all but six of the forty-eight states. She was glad for him, but as for herself—"I had watched Mrs. Theodore Roosevelt and had seen what it meant to be the wife of a President, and I cannot say that I was pleased at the prospect." As the President's wife she never became a "social" figure. But with a war in the offing and a Depression to be weathered, the American people were not too concerned that the new First Lady ran the White House elevator herself, often answered the front door, and dictated letters with a grandchild on each knee.

Soon after they moved into the White House, Mrs. Roosevelt found she was answering hundreds of letters sent personally to her—over 300,000 in a single nine-month period—from office seekers, estranged couples, school children with themes to write, fund-raisers, politicians with irons in the fire, "lonely hearts," pen pals, and plain beggars. Besides this, Mrs. Roosevelt inspected ships, police stations, and slum houses. She wrote syndicated columns. She crisscrossed the country, visiting a girls' camp at Bear Mountain, New York; shipyards in Portsmouth, Maine; miners' homes in West Virginia; rural schools in Puerto Rico; a SAC training center in Des Moines; a women's Methodist Convention in North Carolina; International Flower Shows; and dinners for the National League of Women Voters. She lectured throughout the West, laid wreaths on myriad monuments, opened innumerable bridges —this besides shaking thousands of hands, serving oceans of tea and coffee, *and* personally monogramming her husband's handkerchiefs.

Many of her activities were directed toward widening women's participation in public life. She called regular press conferences for women reporters, conducted them on a personal inspection tour of a controversial government housing project, held an annual garden party for women in executive positions in the government, reminded the President (when a new organization was set up with no women administrators) to remind the Cabinet "that women were in existence, that they were a factor in the life of the nation and increasingly important politically." She fought for equal pay for women in industries under the National Recovery Act. She was instrumental in having four thousand jobs in fourth-class post offices throughout the country filled by women. She got Henry Hopkins, head of the Works Progress Administration, to hire more women in the administrative offices. Perhaps more than any other individual, she made women politically conscious. Needless to say, she changed the public's concept of First Ladies for all time.

By her example she helped diminish racial, age-group, and other prejudices. When the great Negro singer Marian Anderson was refused permission to use the D.A.R.'s Constitution Hall, Mrs. Roosevelt immediately resigned from the Daughters of the American Revolution. She personally investigated alleged discriminatory practices in war plants. When, during her travels, she entered a hall where whites and Negroes were separated by an aisle or a rope, she sat with the Negroes. She agitated for improvements in homes for the aged.

Eleanor Roosevelt

From her own personal funds she gave substantial financial aid to the Women's Trade Union League to pay off the mortgage on its clubhouse; she contributed money to build cottages in poverty-stricken mining areas. She responded to innumerable personal appeals. It is said she gave away more than a half-million dollars from her own resources during her first eight years in the White House.

She had direct influence on the public through her lectures, her radio appearances, and her two columns: "My Day," which ran regularly in some 140 key newspapers, and another, which ran monthly, first in the *Ladies' Home Journal* through the 1940's and then in *McCall's* magazine. These carried, besides personal items, her opinions on the pros and cons of United States neutrality, emerging international issues, and problems arising at home.

During World War II she went on goodwill missions for her husband. In 1942 he sent her to England during the blitz to check on the work of British women in wartime. She went to the South Pacific, flew 23,145 miles, clattered over another thousand miles in old trains, and bounced along jungle roads in jeeps, to get firsthand information on the soldiers there. The film record of this trip was later distributed to nine thousand theaters. In 1943 she went with her husband to inspect war plants in Mexico, and in 1944 accompanied him to a war conference in Quebec, Canada. As *The New York Times* editorialized, "No First Lady could touch her for causes espoused, opinions expressed, distance spanned, people spoken to, words printed, precedents shattered, honors conferred, degrees garnered."

Because of her husband's physical handicap, Eleanor Roosevelt was often the liaison between the President and his public. She brought his attention to the causes she supported. She herself said of her role, "He might have been happier with a wife who was completely uncritical. That I was never able to be, and he had to find it in other people. Nevertheless, I think I sometimes acted as a spur, even though the spurring was not always wanted or welcome. I was one of those who served his purpose."

Franklin D. Roosevelt, by the time he ran for his fourth term, was a tired, if not a sick, man. For a while special calls on his strength seemed to buoy him up. He returned from an international conference at Casablanca in better health than when he left. But the conference at Yalta, Crimea, in February 1945 left him physically spent. When on the first of March he reported on this trip to Congress he remained seated while he spoke. "I knew," wrote his wife, that by doing this "he had accepted a certain degree of invalidism."

On the morning of April 12, 1945, when she was holding her regular press conference for women reporters, word came over the telephone that the President, who had gone to Warm Springs, Georgia, for a rest, had "fainted." She surmised then that the facts must be worse than given. However, she "observed the amenities," saw the meeting to a graceful end, and boarded a plane for Warm Springs. She wrote of the period later, "We know that death is inevitable. You have to be able to bear the inevitable. You're not given any other choice."

Even after she ceased to be mistress of the White House, Eleanor Roosevelt's influence continued to grow. In December 1945 President Truman appointed her a delegate to the General Assembly of the United Nations. These important UN sessions were held in London in 1946. Mrs. Roosevelt wrote, "I walked on eggs. I knew that, as the only woman on the (U.S.) delegation, I was not very welcome. Moreover, if I failed to be a useful member, it would not be considered merely that I as an individual had failed, but that all women had failed, and there would be little chance for others to serve in the near future."

But Eleanor Roosevelt didn't fail. The question arose, what

was to be done with war refugees (many of whom were Jews, survivors of German death camps) who did not wish to return to their country of origin. The Soviet bloc named them traitors, said they should be forced to return. The western countries maintained they should be guaranteed the right of choice. The United States had to appoint a speaker to present its position. This, she wrote, "threw our delegation into a dither . . . . When the huddle broke up, John Foster Dulles approached me rather uncertainly. 'Mrs. Roosevelt,' he began lamely, 'Since you are the one who has carried on the controversy in the committee, do you think you could say a few words in the Assembly? Nobody else is really familiar with the subject.' " She told him she would do her best.

Her task involved more than merely presenting the subject. It involved getting the requisite number of votes. In order to hold the South American delegates at the meeting—their vote might decide the issue—she talked about Simón Bolívar and what he had done for the freedom of the people of Latin America. (Her strategy worked—they stayed.) But she also talked about the United Nations itself: "We are trying to frame things which will consider first the rights of man and what makes men more free—not governments but man!" The upshot was that right of choice was given the war refugees. International Refugee Organizations were established to help solve the problem of these people. *The New York Times* called her presentation "the most dramatic event of the session."

On her return to America, Eleanor Roosevelt was appointed one of nine members of the United Nations' Human Rights Commission. This commission was to outline a program for drafting an international bill of rights. The three aims were to define human rights, formulate a legally binding covenant, and create a system for the implementation of the covenant. As first chairman of the commission she presided over meeting after meeting in country after country, for eleven weeks of feverish debate. The climactic moment came in Paris in December 1948, when the final draft of the Declaration of Human Rights was approved by a vote of 48 to 0, the Soviet bloc abstaining. All eyes turned toward Mrs. Roosevelt. "It is particularly fitting," said the Australian statesman Herbert V. Evatt, "that there should be present on this occasion the person who, with the assistance of many others, has played a leading role in the work, a person who has raised to greater heights even so great a name—Mrs. Roosevelt, the representative of the United States of America." The delegates broke into cheers. Today the concepts of the declaration have worked their way into many legal documents, have been used as a measuring rod for United Nations accomplishments in many fields. Statesman Adlai Stevenson said of her work then and later, "By candor, by simplicity, by utter dedication to the work at hand, by her fabulous inability even to see herself doing it, she created for a whole world the ideal of the dedicated and selfless human being."

It was this year, 1948, that a national magazine poll indicated she was the most popular living American of either sex.

Eleanor Roosevelt relinquished her work at the United Nations in 1952. Then heads of foreign nations vied for the honor of playing host to her. Premier Nehru invited her to address the Indian Parliament. She visited Morocco on the invitation of the Sultan. But everywhere it was the people themselves who clamored loudest for her. Londoners shouted themselves hoarse whenever she appeared in that city. When she visited Luxembourg and called on the Grand Duchess, thousands stood in the pouring rain outside the palace calling, "Mees-ess Roose-felt!" In Oslo, Norway, at the dedication of a monument to Franklin D. Roosevelt, a crowd of forty thousand thronged the square to see her. In Bombay, India, a textile worker unrolled more than one hundred yards of silk along the path she was walking into a tenement. A Japanese newspaper editorialized, "Mrs. Roosevelt represents the conscience of America."

In her own column, "My Day," she wrote of her travels and reminded her readers that "in many countries, particularly in Asia and Africa, the freedom that is uppermost in the minds of the people is freedom to eat." She expanded her reading public through her many books: *The Autobiography of Eleanor Roosevelt, Eleanor Roosevelt's Book of Commonsense Etiquette, If You Ask Me, India and the Awakening East, It Seems to Me, It's Up to the Women, Ladies of Courage* (with Lorena A. Hickok), *The Moral Basis of Democracy, This I Remember, This Is My Story, On My Own, You Can Learn by Living, When You Grow Up to Vote, Tomorrow Is Now,* and *UN: Today and Tomorrow* (with William DeWitt).

At her seventieth birthday celebration in New York City a thousand guests, among them some of the world's most notable citizens, turned out to greet her. Said author Clare Boothe Luce, "Mrs. Roosevelt has done more good deeds on a bigger scale for a longer time than any woman who ever appeared on our public scene. No woman has ever so comforted the distressed or so distressed the comfortable."

In 1959 she gave ten television programs on the need for understanding other countries, and in 1960–1961 she introduced a radio program of anecdotes about refugees, with the purpose of bettering conditions in refugee camps in Europe. In 1961 President Kennedy appointed her as one of the five members of the United States delegation to the fifteenth session of the General Assembly of the United Nations.

But her health was deteriorating, and she was told she must slow down. (She was still beginning her day at seven-thirty, taking two or three vigorous walks a day, and signing the last of her mail at two or three o'clock in the morning.) One morning she got as far as her desk in the living room, tottered, and said, "I can't work." She had shortly before finished dictating the last draft of her book *Tomorrow Is Now*, forcing herself to sit upright in her chair, but with her voice coming so low it was difficult to hear her.

Today, this message of her old age comes through strong and clear, however: "It is deeply important that you develop the quality of stamina. Without it you are beaten. With it, you may wring victory out of countless defeats."

BIBLIOGRAPHY

ASBELL, BERNARD, *When F.D.R. Died*. New York: Holt, Rinehart and Winston, Inc., 1961.

GUNTHER, JOHN, *Roosevelt in Retrospect; a Profile in History*. New York: Harper & Brothers, 1950.

HICKOK, LORENA A., *Reluctant First Lady*. New York: Dodd, Mead & Company, 1962.

ROOSEVELT, ANNA ELEANOR, *The Autobiography of Eleanor Roosevelt*. New York: Harper & Row, Publishers, Inc., 1961.

———, *Tomorrow Is Now*. New York: Harper & Row, Publishers, Inc., 1963.

STEINBERG, ALFRED, *Mrs. R, the Life of Eleanor Roosevelt*. New York: G. P. Putnam's Sons, Inc., 1958.

FLORENCE SABIN

FLORENCE (RENA) SABIN: *Born in Central City, Colorado, November 9, 1871. Died in Denver, Colorado, October 3, 1953. Father: George Kimball Sabin; mother: Serena (Miner) Sabin; sister: Mary; brothers (both of whom died in infancy): Richman and Albert.*

*

Florence Sabin, eminent scientist, was noted for her studies of the lymphatic system, of the blood vessels, and of tuberculosis. She was the first woman to teach at the Johns Hopkins Medical College. She is ranked as one of the great teachers of medical science. She was a key figure in the twentieth-century movement to change the aim of medical study from the cure of disease to the maintenance of health.

*

WHEN her mother took Florence to school the first day, they saw the other school children drinking one after the other from a common drinking cup. "All your life I want you to remember not to drink out of anyone else's cup no matter how clean it looks," her mother told her. This impressed the child. Why should one care so much about a little thing like that? It impressed her, too, when her father told her he had wanted to be a doctor, had even studied medicine for two years before he had been caught up in the Gold Rush fever and left his native Vermont for Colorado. Then he had given up the idea.

Her mother died after the birth of her fourth child. Her

Florence Sabin

father could not care for young Florence. For a while he tried. Florence remembered he once took her down into a mine in a big bucket. She was wearing red boots and a slicker and a red hat. But before long she was sent to Chicago to live with her Uncle Albert's family. There music was the center of attraction. The family would gather around her cousin Stewart at the piano and they would all sing. Her uncle took her to concerts. She decided to study the piano herself. But this ambition gave way to another when she went to live with her grandparents near Saxton's River in Vermont and attended the academy there. Then she became absorbed in books on science. She read them over and over. She marveled at the construction of the human body—its blood vessels, its cells, its glands. She wondered at the efficient way the body has of getting things done—absorbing food and air and turning them into body materials and energy, and detecting sights and sounds and smells. She decided she would study every moment she could. After her graduation from the Vermont academy, she went to Smith College and majored in science.

In the midst of studying she would often scribble absent-mindedly on her note paper: "Florence Sabin, M.D." One day she looked long and steadily at this signature. That is what I shall be—a doctor, she decided. When she wrote her sister, Mary, of her decision, however, Mary tried to dissuade her. Their father wasn't well, Mary said. He wouldn't be able to send the money for a medical course. Besides, women just didn't study to be doctors. Mary suggested Florence put the whole thing out of her head.

But Florence Sabin wasn't that easily discouraged. News had reached the campus that now was just the time for a girl student to think of becoming a doctor. Plans were being made to establish a medical school at Johns Hopkins University in Baltimore, Maryland. A group of Baltimore women had promised to finance the erection of a Medical School building at the university on the precise stipulation that women be admitted to study there on the same terms as men. Florence realized she would have to earn the money for her tuition. Well, that could be managed by teaching for a year or two, before beginning her medical studies.

After receiving her Bachelor of Science degree from Smith, Miss Sabin taught mathematics and history for a year at Wolfe Hall, the school in Denver that she had attended as a young girl. The following summer she tutored the children of a friend. Then she worked as a substitute instructor at Smith College and an assistant in the college library. By the early fall of 1897 she had saved enough to enter Johns Hopkins as a student in the new Medical College. Her Uncle Albert wrote her from Chicago, "I think you are grand. You have sized up the problem in all its dimensions and are not appalled. You will do your whole duty, as you see it. You will be serene through it all."

She entered Johns Hopkins at a fortunate time. The group of women who had donated the sum for the Medical School Building were particularly interested in this eager young student. They proved a stimulus to Florence Sabin, helped her overcome difficulties from time to time, chorused their approval of her achievements. Another fortunate circumstance: From the very start she came under the instruction of the eminent anatomist Dr. Franklin Paine Mall. He not only guided her into independent research but stood as a model for her when she became a teacher. Moreover, she was welcomed by him and his wife, Mabel, as a protégée and friend, a situation that meant much to a young lady in a strange city. She would always plan to return from her vacations early, to see that the Malls' house was in order, the milkman posted, provisions in, everything ready for their arrival. When the elder Malls had to be away, she stayed with the children. In a biography she wrote of Dr. Mall on his death in 1917, she mentions that she "worked for twenty years on his staff," and owed "wholly to him" her start in research as a medical student and her opportunity for a career in scientific medicine.

Dr. Mall valued independent research above all else, and chose for his assistants those students he believed most capable of it. When he stopped by Florence Sabin's table one day and casually said, "I am looking for someone to make a study of the fibre tracts of the brain as they are medullated at birth," she knew she had arrived at an important turn in her career. The head of the department of anatomy had entrusted her with a research project.

Dr. Mall had not made a mistake in choosing her. When she was in her senior year she made a three-dimensional model of the brain. It was so precisely done that it led to new understanding about the structure of the lower part of the brain. Later she took her model to Germany and had it reproduced by a firm specializing in such work. Copies of her model are still in use today in medical colleges all over the world.

On June 12, 1900, she received the degree of Doctor of Medicine from Johns Hopkins Medical College. Then began her year of internship. One doctor closely associated with her did not approve of women interns. He gave her orders, then countermanded them. He set her impossible tasks. She was glad when, at the end of the year, she was made a member of the research staff of the College Department of Anatomy, an appointment made possible through a scholarship given by the Baltimore Association for the Promotion of University Education of Women.

Then Dr. Sabin was free to devote her full time to scientific studies, using as her chief tool the microscope. In 1901 came her first published work—a laboratory manual to go with her model of the brain, *An Atlas of the Medulla and Midbrain*. For many years it was considered the most authoritative textbook on the subject.

Next, at the suggestion of Dr. Mall, she began to study the lymphatic system. The lymphatic system is one of the most complex and vital systems in the human body. It is made up of a very large number of thin-walled fine vessels. These start blindly in the tissues, then unite to form progressively larger vessels as they go from the periphery to the central part of the body. This vast network of vessels carries a colorless fluid called *lymph*. Lymph brings food to every cell of the body and carries wastes and toxic substances away. It acts as an intermediary substance between the blood and the other tissue cells.

The lymphatic system is essential to the body's ability to resist infection and also to the digestion of fats. As vital as it is, in Dr. Sabin's time some of the anatomy of the lymphatic system was still unknown. For example, there were conflicting opinions as to how, precisely, the smallest lymphatic vessels start to grow in the body tissues. This was one of the questions Dr. Sabin set out to answer.

Through an ingenious series of experiments, using the embryos of pigs obtained from a nearby abattoir, Dr. Sabin traced the system's origin and development. A paper giving the results of her investigations brought her the Naples Table Association prize of one thousand dollars for "the best scientific thesis written by a woman embodying new observations and new conclusions based on independent laboratory research." Between 1902 and 1911 she published seven papers on the origin of the lymphatics, and in 1913 brought them all together in one monograph, *The Method and Growth of the Lymphatic System*. Many consider this work her most significant contribution to science.

The origin of the blood vessels and of the red blood cells also commanded her attention. During one night of investigation via the microscope, she witnessed, as she described it, "the birth of a blood stream." In a live chick embryo she saw the blood vessels form, traced the appearance of the cells, and then witnessed the actual beginning of the heartbeat. "The most exciting experience of my life," she later called it.

She developed a method of studying living cells by placing drops of blood, often drawn from her own arm, within a warm box and analyzing their reactions to various stimuli. By such means she found that a normal person's white corpuscles may vary from five thousand to ten thousand in a cubic millimeter of blood in the course of a day.

In 1913 she made a trip to Germany and learned new methods of preparing specimens for microscope study. In 1916 she pleased the Baltimore ladies again when she was asked to give the Harvey Memorial Lecture. Her subject was "The Method and Growth of the Lymphatic System." In 1921 she went to China to deliver an address at the opening of the Peking Union Medical College and while there was awarded a medal. The same year at a huge gathering in Carnegie Hall, New York, she welcomed Madame Marie Curie on a visit to America on behalf of the women of science.

Through these years she was also teaching. She had become associate professor in anatomy in 1905, and held this position until the death of the head of that department, Dr. Mall, in 1917. In the usual order of advancement, she should then have taken his place. But a man was chosen over her for the post. Her pupils got up a petition. The group of Baltimore ladies who had backed her all along voiced indignation. When she was offered instead the position of professor of histology—anatomy that deals with the minute structure of animal and plant tissues, as shown under the microscope—her supporters urged her not to take it, but rather to resign in protest. "I'll stay, of course," Dr. Sabin answered them. "I have research in progress." As it was, she was the first full time woman professor ever appointed at Johns Hopkins.

In her courses, students had to work very hard. She lec-

Florence Sabin

tured with machine-gun rapidity. She refused to repeat her statements. In the work with a microscope, she insisted on checks and rechecks. All this kept them constantly alert. For one final examination she presented the students each with a stained cross-section of the belly of a mouse and asked them to identify the tissues—a test that only the most observant could pass. By methods such as this she led them to discover for themselves the wonders under the microscope and to reach their own conclusions from what they saw. From the year 1902 to 1925 every freshman medical student at Johns Hopkins took anatomy under her as a required course. The extent of her influence may be imagined.

Each day, when her classes ended, her own laboratory work began. Students going to their dormitories late at night would catch a glimpse of her through the laboratory window, bending over her microscope.

Meanwhile Dr. Sabin's professional prestige was growing. She was elected president of the American Association of Anatomists (the first woman to hold that office) and was awarded membership in the highly reputed National Academy of Sciences. Her work had repeatedly won the admiration of Dr. Simon Flexner, the scientific director of the Rockefeller Institute in New York City. In 1925 he invited her to join the institute's scientific staff and set up a new department of cellular studies. She was to begin intensive investigations of blood cells and their relation to disease. She was the first woman to be invited into full membership in the institute.

She accepted and, after saying farewell to her beloved laboratory in Baltimore, to the loyal Baltimore ladies, and to her hordes of devoted students, went into a new phase of her career, this one to extend through the next thirteen years.

At her new post she again made thoroughness the keynote. She assembled a staff of laboratory assistants, technicians, and secretaries, each of whom had the equivalent of a Bachelor of

Science degree. Her workers at the microscopes were to "count, repeat, observe, over and over again, and finally to draw conclusions." But, as Dr. Flexner later wrote, her success "was not scientific only. It was something more. She never ceased being a teacher, and she not only inspired young men to work at scientific problems but she imbued them with high ideals of achievement." He added, "No one, I suspect, of her pupils left her without carrying away a sense of her rare generosity and her valuation of honest work, and I believe that whenever subsequently these pupils did work of their own they always thought of the good opinion that Dr. Sabin would have of it." Her "pupils" graduated from the laboratory to teach, to become medical practitioners, administrators of scientific research, and deans of medical schools.

During the years at Rockefeller Institute she worked at eleven different scientific investigations. Her study centered on the tubercle, the characteristic lesion of "tuberculosis," which she had traced down while still at Johns Hopkins. She went deeply into the cause and mechanism of tuberculosis infection. She became a member of the Committee of Medical Research of the National Tuberculosis Association and was thus part of a long-term research program in which universities, research institutes, and research divisions of pharmaceutical companies pooled their resources to advance the knowledge of tuberculosis along all fronts simultaneously.

In 1928 the *Pictorial Review* magazine presented her with an award of five thousand dollars for "the most distinctive contribution made by an American woman to American life in the fields of art, science and letters." In 1929 she was received at the White House by President Herbert Hoover. In 1931 she became the twenty-fifth member of the Guggenheim Foundation Advisory Board. On her retirement from Rockefeller Institute in December 1938 she was given the title of "Member Emeritus of the Institute."

Florence Sabin

Now Dr. Sabin went back to her home state, Colorado—to Denver where her sister lived. Her activities there even increased. She was appointed a member of the Colorado State Post-War Planning Committee, as head of the subcommittee on health. It was a sort of gesture of recognition to a returning native daughter who had made good. This seventy-three-year-old little lady with the friendly smile would be happy, they thought, just to hold the title, without stirring up undue activity. Instead, Dr. Sabin went into her work like a whirlwind. She led the people of Denver—of all Colorado—in a health campaign that made the state and city models of achievement.

First she concentrated on statewide legislation. The bills that she fought for and brought into being stand as patterns for health legislation everywhere. And she watched over the bills' progress through the legislature, from their introduction to their successful passage. While they were up for the vote she would sit listening in the senate chambers, as one of the senators later put it, "like my own mother."

But to get these bills passed took active agitation, too. She would hold a banquet for the "milk people" and talk on pasteurization. She would invite sanitary engineers and talk on sewage disposal. She got health planks introduced into both the Republican and Democratic party platforms; she distributed leaflets ("Health to Match the Mountains"); she spoke before Parent-Teacher Associations, Service Clubs, the American Association of University Women, the League of Women Voters, chambers of commerce, church congregations, doctors' and lawyers' clubs. She would tell her audiences, "We think of our state as a health resort, but we're dying faster than people in most states." Touring the state, she would ask to be taken to a town's sewage disposal system. "You'll have to show her the river," the jittery officials would say.

She rounded up influential citizens to work in health projects. An ex-state senator recalled that a corner drugstore conversation between himself and this "little bump of a woman with a twinkly sort of smile that made her eyeglasses seem to light up" got him on one of the committees, and that after that, "I spend half my time at health meetings in Denver and half the rest rooting things up elsewhere for the little lady."

When Colorado had passed health laws that put it ahead of the rest of the country, Dr. Sabin turned her attention to Denver itself. She was named manager of Health and Charities and worked for proper sewage disposal, garbage collection, dump elimination, rat riddance, and restaurant sanitation. It is said that the sale of hairnets and of double sinks for restaurants went up during her campaign.

In 1948 (she was seventy-six then) at a mass tuberculosis X-ray survey, which she initiated, a news photographer snapped her picture, standing in line with the mayor, waiting to be X-rayed. Within two years Denver's death rate from tuberculosis was cut in half. The National Tuberculosis Association awarded her the Trudeau Medal for "meritorious contribution to the cause, treatment and prevention of tuberculosis." She won the Jane Addams medal for "untiring achievement in Colorado public health work."

But her sister Mary was ill and needed her care. In 1951 she gave up most of her campaigning activities. She had by then accomplished more for health in Denver than had been accomplished in all the city's previous history. In 1952 the Business and Professional Women's Club of Colorado made her an honorary member and established the Sabin Award in Public Health in her name. (Her accumulated salary as Manager of Health and Charities went to the Colorado University for medical research.)

On her eightieth birthday a letter from Dr. Alfred Cohn, member of the Rockefeller Institute and author of medical books, voiced the sentiments of thousands. He wrote of the several lives she had lived "each of singular distinction, in each of which you have advanced far." He asked, "How came you to possess these many skills and virtues? . . . It has been, I think, because of your great humanity. You have cared deeply for your kind. And men have come to recognize in you that rare total person—of wisdom and of sentiment—heart and mind in just and balanced union."

BIBLIOGRAPHY

BLUEMEL, ELINOR, *Florence Sabin; Colorado Woman of the Century*. Boulder: University of Colorado Press, 1959.

PHELAN, MARY KAY, *Probing the Unknown: The Story of Dr. Florence Sabin*. New York: Thomas Y. Crowell Company, 1969.

SABIN, FLORENCE RENA, *Franklin Paine Mall; the Story of a Mind*. Baltimore: The Johns Hopkins Press, 1934.

YOST, EDNA, *American Women of Science*. Philadelphia: Frederick A. Stokes Company, 1943.

MARGARET SANGER

MARGARET SANGER (SLEE): *Born in Corning, New York, September 14, 1883. Died in Tucson, Arizona, September 6, 1966. Father: Michael Hennessy Higgins; mother: Anne (Purcell) Higgins; ten brothers and sisters; marriages: William Sanger; J. Noah H. Slee; children: Stuart, Grant, and Peggy Sanger.*

*

The initiator of the birth control movement in America, Margaret Sanger opened the first birth control clinic in this country in New York in October 1916. Her book *Family Limitation* was the spearhead of the movement, and a second book, *Woman and the New Race*, contending that control of conception is a basic human right, became the "bible" of the movement. When she was editing the periodical *Birth Control Review*, the advertisers used to say to her, "Lighten up your subject." "I always resented this," Margaret Sanger commented in her autobiography. "I am the protagonist of women who have nothing to laugh at."

*

MARGARET was eight when she helped wash the newborn baby, her brother. He weighed fourteen and one half pounds. "A terrible hard time!" her father said. But her father had a midwife's skills and had somehow managed to pull her mother through the birth, as he had done with all the previous births. Each of the eleven Higgins children was large at birth, at least ten pounds. The situation was complicated by the fact that Margaret's mother was tubercular. A few weeks after each birth, however, she would be going about her household tasks again, tired and coughing harder than ever, but happy in the thought of her new baby.

Margaret's father and mother loved each other—were concerned for each other's welfare. But her father told Margaret years later, when she was in the midst of the birth control movement, "Your mother would have been alive today if we had known all this then."

Margaret Sanger's father was a stonecutter who chiseled angels and saints for the tombstones in cemeteries. He had a mind of his own and believed in using it. Once the local hall, where the agnostic Robert Ingersoll was scheduled to speak, was closed by the town authorities. Mr. Higgins directed the people to an open place in the woods near his home to hear the lecture. Even if this meant he would no longer be hired to make tombstones for the church cemeteries, he held to the conviction that everyone had a right to speak his opinions. He would tell young Margaret, "Leave the world better because you, my child, have dwelt in it." She was always to say that he was the strongest influence in her life.

After attending Claverack College and teaching briefly in southern New Jersey, Margaret went into nurse's training at the White Plains Hospital in New York. When she went out on maternity cases, labor would often terminate before the doctor arrived, and she would have to perform the delivery herself. She never got over her wonder at seeing a newborn baby. In her autobiography she called it "one of the greatest experiences that a human being can have . . . . Birth to me has always been more awe-inspiring than death. As often as I have witnessed the miracle, held the perfect creature with its tiny hands and tiny feet, each time I have felt as though I were entering a cathedral with prayer in my heart."

But as her training progressed, she was forced to notice that sometimes parents were too overworked and too poor to afford or enjoy the many children they had. For the most part her patients were the wives of small shopkeepers, truck drivers, pushcart vendors, and peddlers on the impoverished lower East Side of New York City. She saw many mothers in their twenties and thirties worn out and hopeless, distraught at seeing their children undernourished and poorly clad. Sometimes they would be so desperate that they would resort to self-induced abortions, which frequently ended in their own deaths.

While she was nursing one mother back to health after such an abortion, the doctor came one day to examine the patient. The young mother asked him for something to prevent further pregnancies. "Tell your husband to sleep on the roof," he briskly told her as he gathered up his instruments. Margaret Sanger glanced quickly at the woman. "Even through my sudden tears," she wrote in her autobiography, "I could see stamped on her face an expression of absolute despair." When three months later the woman died after another self-inflicted abortion, "I came to a sudden realization that my work as a nurse and my activities in social service were entirely palliative and consequently futile and useless to relieve the misery I saw about me."

While she was in training she met and married William Sanger, an artist and architect. Their three children were born during the next seven years. Their apartment in New York City became a meeting place for artists and writers. One of these, Anita Block, editor for the "Woman's Page" of the magazine *Call*, suggested Mrs. Sanger write a series of health articles. The result was two series, "What Every Mother Should Know" and "What Every Girl Should Know." Then suddenly publication of Mrs. Sanger's articles ceased. They had been banned as "obscene" material "by order of the Post

Office Department." The censorship of Margaret Sanger had begun.

Now she tried to discover a method of contraception that could be made available to mothers in poverty-stricken areas. She searched the libraries, she read medical reports, inquired among her friends. One friend told her, "The women of France have been limiting their families for a hundred years. Go to France and get your answers." Since her artist husband himself liked the idea of living in Paris, the Sangers wound up their affairs in America, and in October 1913 sailed with their three children for Europe.

In Paris Margaret Sanger talked with doctors, midwives, druggists, and mothers. She found the mothers were as proud of their contraceptive recipes as of their culinary skills. She wrote down their formulas. Later she was to use this information in her book *Family Limitation*. After two and a half months of gathering material, she was ready to return to America. Her husband, however, was deep in his art work, and said he would come later. So on December 31, she and the children sailed for New York.

Back in America Mrs. Sanger started a monthly magazine, *The Woman Rebel*. It dealt "with the conditions which enslave woman and the manner in which she is enslaved." The first issue (March 1914) listed seven circumstances in which birth control should be practiced: when either spouse has a transmittable disease; when the wife suffers a temporary infection of the lungs, heart, or kidneys, the cure of which might be retarded in pregnancy; when a mother is physically unfit; when parents have subnormal children; if the parents are adolescents; if their income is inadequate; and during the first year of marriage.

The Woman Rebel soon had a mailing list of two thousand. During the eight months of its existence Margaret Sanger received ten thousand letters. It made many friends for her in

America. In Great Britain the feminists Ellen Kay, Olive Schreiner, and Emmeline Pankhurst became aware of her through its pages.

From the start she faced opposition. When the first issue had been mailed out as far as the *M*'s, the remainder was confiscated by the postal authorities. Mrs. Sanger and her friends continued to distribute it through personal means. When this was discovered, she was called before a New York court on August 25, 1914. Her trial was postponed till the fall—six weeks off. She used this time to hunt for a printer for the book she had recently completed, *Family Limitation*. This book explained in simple language (with diagrams) how to use contraceptives. She went to printer after printer with the manuscript. Most of them called it a "Sing-Sing job"—wouldn't touch it. At last she found a linotype operator who agreed to set the type. (He did it behind drawn blinds, at night.) Once printed, the book was hidden away in spare rooms and closets in the houses of friends in a dozen different cities. She arranged a code with them so that when she gave the word, even if she were in jail at the time, the book would be distributed.

On October 20, 1914, she was again called into court: *The People v. Margaret Sanger*. The case was set for trial at ten the next morning. With the trial so close, she began to consider closely what it might entail. She knew if she were pronounced guilty, as she was almost certain to be, she would be sentenced to a long prison term. Imprisonment didn't frighten her—later events were to prove that—but to be imprisoned on false charges of obscenity without having time to prepare her case, this would weaken her whole position. At that time she had no society or group to back her in her project. Feminists of the day were more interested in getting the vote than in championing what seemed then a bizarre cause.

That afternoon she took a hotel room away from her children, away from phone calls and telegrams. Here she carefully thought the matter out. She decided she must have time and freedom to assemble her facts. She could not get either time or freedom in America. She must go to Europe and prepare her case there; and she must act quickly and quietly.

From her hotel room she telephoned the station. She learned that a train was leaving within a few hours for Montreal, Canada. She arranged for her children to stay with their father weekdays—he had now returned to America, but was living at a separate address—and with her sister on evenings and weekends. Then she hastily packed a few things, hurried to the station, and boarded the train. From Montreal she took passage on a ship bound for Europe.

This period of decision, she wrote later, was the most crucial and painful of her life. Years later she spoke of it as her "Gethsemane." "How could I do it? How could I leave three adorable children? It sickens me even forty years later to think of that struggle within me. But there was no turning back. I had to fight this through even if it meant leaving children, home, friends, everything I held dear."

When she was three days out at sea, she sent word to release the copies of her book *Family Limitation*. She did this knowing that it would be considered a true violation of the law, liable to a stiff prison term. "I had to be the protagonist of American mothers. I wanted to express their longings, ambitions, and thwarted lives . . . . I could no more stop than I could change the color of my eyes." In a short time there came a reply to her cable, saying that the ten thousand copies of *Family Limitation* were in the mail. She could not know then that in the course of time ten million copies were to be distributed and it was to be translated into thirteen languages.

Mrs. Sanger's trip abroad brought her invaluable allies. In London she looked up the leaders of a birth control movement there, Dr. C. V. Drysdale and his wife, Bessie. They had become acquainted with her work through *The Woman Rebel*, and welcomed her to their home. Now at last she found herself in a group that "instead of heaping criticism and fears upon me, offered all the force of an international organization as well as their encyclopedic minds to back me up." Authors Olive Schreiner, Marie Stopes, and Havelock Ellis, an innovator himself with his books on *Studies in the Psychology of Sex*, became staunch allies of hers.

A trip to Holland—then the most advanced nation in contraceptive knowledge—crystallized her plans. At the Rutgers clinic at The Hague—in Holland birth control clinics were looked on as public benefactions—she was told about the role of the "Councillors." These professionally trained people were sent out by the clinics, to the homes where a child had recently died, and gave sympathetic advice regarding the mother's health and the prospects for future offspring. From talks with these advisers Mrs. Sanger developed a plan for the proper spacing of children as a means toward both family and national health. At the Rutgers clinic she also studied the fifteen types of contraceptives being used. She advised patients herself. She noted that in Holland the lower birth rate had improved the financial status of the poor, had allowed more children to go to school, and had advanced the general health of the people.

Having gathered her information, she returned at the end of September 1915 to America, ready to face whatever it had in store for her. One welcoming note: the *Pictorial Review* magazine ran a leading article on birth control.

On home soil she informed the authorities of her arrival. But the government now dismissed her case. She guessed it might have been because of the influence exerted by her English friends. They had written, calling the case to President Woodrow Wilson's attention. They had pointed out the absurdity of her being subjected to criminal prosecution "for circulating a pamphlet on birth control, which was allowed in every civilized country except the United States." Whatever the reason for the case's dismissal, it left her with an uneasy sensation. "I felt the danger of having a privilege under a law rather than a right."

Now Margaret Sanger went on a lecture tour of cities across the nation. "The first right of every child," she would tell her audiences, "is to be wanted, to be desired, to be planned for with an intensity of love that gives it its title to being." She insisted, "The greatest issue is to raise the question of birth control out of the gutter of obscenity . . . into the light of intelligence and human understanding."

About this time a fine photograph was taken, showing Mrs. Sanger and her two young sons. Reproduced in magazines across the nation, it probably won more sympathy for her than anything else could have done.

However, most of the people were still not ready to accept her beliefs. Demonstrations were staged against her in various cities. The ensuing publicity, however, actually helped her cause. In Hagerstown, Maryland, when the regular meeting hall was closed to her, she hired a dance hall to speak in. In St. Louis, when they locked her out of the theater where she was scheduled to speak, she announced she was suing the manager for five thousand dollars for breach of contract. (The Men's City Club invited her to speak at a luncheon the next day and the club was jammed to capacity.) When she was jailed in Portland, Oregon, other women insisted on being jailed with her, and four of them spent the night locked up, refusing to ask for bail.

In Denver, on the other hand, she was received by the city's high-ranking officials. In Beaumont, Texas, a cowboy folk singer added the theme of birth control and its pioneer to his repertoire—and she was sung into folklore. Her visit to Indianapolis, Indiana, coincided with the National Social Workers Conference, and the social workers turned out full force to hear her. Newspaper commentator Walter Lippmann wrote, "This will kick the football of birth control straight across to the Pacific."

Margaret Sanger felt people should be made aware of all the issues involved in birth control. But she finally came to the conclusion that the quickest and surest way to change reactionary laws was to challenge them, not just by talk but by actions. She returned to New York and laid her plans carefully.

She and her associates—her sister Ethel Byrne and a friend, Fania Mindell—had five thousand notices printed, in English, Italian, and Yiddish. These they crammed in mailboxes and beneath doors in the underprivileged areas of the city. "Can you afford to have a large family?" the pamphlets read. "Do you want any more children? If not, why do you have them? . . . Safe, harmless information can be obtained from trained nurses at 46 Amboy Street . . . . All mothers welcome."

On the morning of October 16, 1916, Margaret Sanger opened a birth control clinic in the Brownsville section of Brooklyn. Mrs. Sanger wrote in her autobiography, "Before we could get the place dusted and ourselves ready for the official reception, Fania called, 'Do come outside and look.' Halfway to the corner they were standing in line, at least one hundred and fifty, some shawled, some hatless, their red hands clasping the cold, chapped, smaller ones of their children."

For nine days the clinic served its patrons unmolested. On the tenth day a woman came in and bought a copy of the book *What Every Girl Should Know* and insisted on paying two dollars rather than the usual ten-cent fee for it. The following day she was back. "I'm a police officer," she said. "You are under arrest."

Margaret Sanger and her companions spent the night in jail.

The next morning they were let out on bail. They went straight to the clinic and reopened it, only to be told by the landlord that he was forced to evict them on the grounds of "maintaining a public nuisance." After several postponements the court decided Mrs. Sanger's sister Mrs. Byrne was to be tried first. (She was the one who sold the book to the policewoman.) Ethel Byrne was sentenced to thirty days in jail. In jail she went on a hunger strike. As she weakened dangerously, she was finally pardoned by the governor and released a few days short of the thirty. She had become so ill that it was two weeks before the doctors declared her out of danger and two years before she regained her full health.

But this affair had made headlines throughout the nation. On January 29, 1917, while Mrs. Byrne was still in prison, a giant rally in support of birth control was held in Carnegie Hall in New York City. The hall was jammed to the doors. Margaret Sanger, coming directly from hearing of her sister's plight, told those who crowded the auditorium—among them the famous dancer Isadora Duncan—"I come not from the stake at Salem, where women were once burned for blasphemy, but from the shadow of Blackwell's Island, where women are tortured for obscenity."

At Margaret Sanger's own trial at the end of January the climax came when the judge insisted she give a straight *yes* or *no* to his question as to whether she would, in the future, obey the law. The small woman in a dark dress answered in a low voice, "I can't respect the law as it stands today." The judge's gavel pounded down to drown out the applause. "The judgment of the Court," he declared, "is that you be confined to the Workhouse for a period of thirty days."

During her stay at Queens County Penitentiary Mrs. Sanger kept busy. She gave information on birth control to the thirty-seven women in her cell block. (She noted that these women averaged seven brothers and sisters each.) When she left, friends met her at the gate, singing the "Marseillaise." From the upper windows behind her, her new friends joined in the singing.

Her second magazine, the *Birth Control Review*, began printing while she was still in prison. She had planned for it carefully. She arranged with H. G. Wells and Havelock Ellis to contribute articles. The magazine gave information on the development and growth of the movement. It soon had over three thousand subscribers.

In the winter of 1917–1918 she wrote her book *Woman and the New Race*. "When motherhood becomes the fruit of deep yearning," she stated in it, "not the result of ignorance or accident, its children will become the foundation of a new race." In one year alone this book sold 250,000 copies in the United States plus many thousands more abroad.

Now she called a birth control conference under the auspices of the newly launched American Birth Control League. The first meeting was called on November 14, 1921, at Town Hall, New York. When Mrs. Sanger arrived, she found a pushing, shouting crowd collected and the doors guarded by burly policemen, who had received last-minute instructions to bar the hall to all comers. The early arrivals were already inside, however. Mrs. Sanger managed to slip in under the officer's outstretched arms. Inside, lawyers, doctors, judges, dignified citizens all, with their families and guests, were milling about or standing in obvious bewilderment at the commotion outside and inside. Someone gave Mrs. Sanger a lift onto the speakers' platform—the police had barred the stairs to that, too. She shouted, "Don't leave—we're going to hold the meeting!" But when she started to speak, a policeman took her arm. "You can't talk here," he said. "Why not?" someone shouted. "An indecent, immoral subject is to be discussed," he answered. "This meeting must be closed."

Mrs. Sanger was put under arrest and marched through the

streets, the crowd pressing around her in "one of the wildest parades New York had ever seen." The *Tribune* reported, "The police broke up the meeting without waiting for an expression of opinion which would warrant repressing . . . . It was arbitrary and Prussian to the last degree."

This raid of a public lecture hall by city authorities brought the cause of birth control more favorable publicity than had years of campaigning. Hundreds of letters demanded court action for false arrest. The American Civil Liberties Union offered Mrs. Sanger its legal facilities. When, the next day, the disorderly conduct charge against her was dismissed, she immediately called together the board members of the American Birth Control League and announced another meeting. Held a few days later at Park Theater, this meeting was packed to the doors. The discussions went forward without interruption.

Mrs. Sanger and her husband had long since gone their separate ways, and in 1921 they were divorced. In 1922 she went on a round-the-world lecture tour to Japan, China, India, and arrived in London in July, in time for another conference on birth control. That same year she met the industrialist J. Noah H. Slee, who became her second husband. During the twenty years of their life together he was a generous contributor to the birth control movement.

In January 1923 she opened another birth control clinic, in the same building as the Birth Control League's office, at 104 Fifth Avenue, New York. This time she was unmolested. The law, by now, had been reinterpreted to allow birth control information to be conveyed by word of mouth from physician to patient "for the patient's health." The Chicago chapter of the Birth Control League next opened a clinic in that city.

Eighteen hundred delegates from eighteen countries registered for the Sixth International Birth Control Conference, which convened in New York City in March 1925. Contraceptive information was given at a special session, presided over by Dr. Hannah Stone, physician in charge at the clinic, and Dr. James Cooper, medical director. Almost a thousand doctors who tried to gain admission could not be accommodated, and another session had to be held for the overflow.

For some time the idea of birth control had become linked with population planning, a combination that brought the movement a wider significance. In 1927, in Geneva, Switzerland, Mrs. Sanger helped organize the First International Conference on Population Planning. However, she records, at the meeting the phrase "birth control" was "edged about like a bomb which might explode any moment."

Back in America the work of the clinic again came under attack. In March 1929 the police entered her clinic without ceremony, went through her papers, and made some arrests. This time, though, there were no imprisonments. The defendants were discharged after the magistrate summed up: "The law is plain that if the doctor in good faith believes that the patient is a married woman and that her health requires prevention of conception, it is no crime to so advise and instruct therein." The clinic was shortly thereafter moved into a building at 17 West Sixteenth Street, where it still operates today.

From 1928 on, the birth control movement gradually took on the dignity accorded any other legitimate medical procedure. In response to a report prepared by Margaret Sanger, Dr. Robert L. Dickinson, dean of American gynecologists, stated, "I believe this to be the first considerable and detailed study of the efficacy of contraceptive measures combined with reliable follow-up that has ever been made . . . . This report constitutes a pioneer contribution." In 1930 he joined the advisory board of the Birth Control Clinic.

The last thirty years of Margaret Sanger's life saw the realization of many of her most cherished dreams. On a trip to India (1935) she was the key speaker at the All-Indian Obstetrical and Gynecological Congress. In 1936 she and her associates won a notable victory when on January 6, in the case of *The United States v. One Package,* U.S. District Court Judge Grover Moscowitz decided that Dr. Hannah Stone, a physician, could legally receive a contraceptive device sent to her in the mail by a physician in Japan. This meant an end to the law forbidding the distribution by mail of contraceptive devices. Not long thereafter the American Medical Association formally recognized birth control as a part of legitimate medical practice. Mrs. Sanger received the Town Hall Club Award of Honor for "contribution to the enlargement and enrichment of life," in the very hall where fifteen years before she had been forcibly removed by the police.

In 1942 Mrs. Sanger became honorary chairman of the Planned Parenthood Federation of America. Today the movement is worldwide, with at least 250 Planned Parenthood Centers in 150 American cities and many others throughout 88 foreign countries.

In the early 1940's she and her husband bought a home in the Santa Catalina foothills of Tucson, Arizona. From there she kept in touch with developments by phone and was consulted on important issues. She enjoyed being with her children—both her sons became doctors—and with her grandchildren.

In 1949 she received an honorary doctorate from Smith College as a "leader in the world-wide study of population problems and pioneer in the American birth control movement." On a trip to Japan in April 1954 she was received like a national hero. She was asked to address that country's legislature. The World Population Conference held in Rome in 1954, unlike the one held in 1927, made fertility-control a central issue.

At Margaret Sanger's death an editorial in *The New York Times* called her "one of history's great rebels and a monumental figure of the first half of the twentieth century." She herself, in an even more vivid way, commented on her life: "I found myself in the position of one who had discovered a house was on fire and it was up to me to shout out the warning."

BIBLIOGRAPHY

BARTLETT, ROBERT MERRILL, *They Did Something About It.* New York: Association Press, 1939.
LADER, LAWRENCE, *The Margaret Sanger Story, and the Fight for Birth Control.* New York: Doubleday & Company, Inc., 1955.
LADER, LAWRENCE, and MELTZER, MILTON, *Margaret Sanger, Pioneer of Birth Control.* New York: Thomas Y. Crowell Company, 1969.
SANGER, MARGARET, *Margaret Sanger; an Autobiography.* New York: W. W. Norton & Company, Inc., 1938.
———, *My Fight for Birth Control.* New York: Farrar & Rinehart, Inc., 1931.

MARGARET CHASE SMITH

MARGARET CHASE SMITH: Born in Skowhegan, Maine, December 14, 1897. Father: George Emery Chase; mother: Carrie (Murray) Chase; three brothers, of whom only one, Wilbur, survived to maturity; sisters: Laura and Evelyn; husband: Clyde H. Smith.

*

Margaret Chase Smith is the first woman to serve in both Houses of Congress: in the House of Representatives for four consecutive (two-year) terms and in the Senate for four consecutive (six-year) terms. She is also the first woman elected to a leadership post in the Senate: In 1967 she was elected chairman of the Conference of All Republican Senators. In addition she is the first woman to be placed in nomination for the presidency of the United States at the national convention of a major political party.

*

YOUNG Margaret grew up in the white frame house on North Avenue, in Skowhegan, Maine, with her parents and her younger brother and sisters, enjoying the activities of the community. In her father's barber shop, next door to their house, she would listen as yarns were swapped and political opinions aired. On weekends in the summer her whole family would pile into the family buggy filled with provisions—sandwiches, homemade cookies, a jug of lemonade—and be jogged by the family horse to Smithfield East Pond, where they had rented a cabin. There they would go swimming, picnicking, and fishing. Her father would sometimes get Margaret up at four o'clock in the morning to go with him to troll for white perch. By the time the rest of the family was ready for breakfast, the fish would be caught, cleaned, fried, and on the table.

At home, she helped her mother with the housework. Starting when she was thirteen, she took late afternoon and Saturday work at the Green Brothers Five-and-Ten-Cent Store. Her pay was $3.50 a week.

She entered high school in 1912. She made the basketball team and soon became the center, and by her senior year, the manager. That same year the team won the state championship. The trips the team made were a useful experience for this girl who later was to tour the state many times on vote-getting campaigns.

While she was still a high school student Margaret Chase got a job at the telephone company as an evening switchboard operator. The town's first selectman, Clyde Smith, made many telephone calls—a selectman in a New England town must keep up with state and local affairs—and the dispatch with which Margaret put his calls through, and if he wanted to have the time, gave it to the minute, made him think of her when he was interviewing for a job. It was a temporary one —as recorder of tax payments in the town's books—but she found she could combine it with her senior year studies at high school and gladly accepted it.

After graduation she was successively a teacher, again a telephone operator, a circulation manager of the newspaper, *Independent Reporter*—here she wrote advertising—and office manager for Willard Cummings' woolen mill.

Clyde Smith was a co-owner of the *Independent Reporter*, and her association there brought them together again. He began to call regularly at the white house on North Avenue.

As her friendship with Mr. Smith grew, Margaret became more interested in politics. He had now become a state senator. The two were married in the spring of 1930—he a man of fifty-four, deep in politics, and she a woman of thirty-two, ready to take her place at his side.

From 1930 to 1936 Margaret Chase Smith served on the Republican State Committee. Mr. Smith was a member of the Governor's Council in Augusta, and the couple spent much of their time at the state capital. Next he was up for election to the United States House of Representatives, and she campaigned with him throughout Maine's Second District. After he was elected, they moved to Washington, D.C. She became his full time secretary, handled his mail and did research on the various bills introduced in the House. She also became treasurer of the Congressional Club, made up of the wives of Congressmen and Cabinet members. At their home in the Washington suburb Chevy Chase, and between sessions in their old-fashioned thirty-room house in Skowhegan, she was the gracious hostess.

In 1940 her husband suffered a fatal heart attack. Congressman Smith's last public act had been to send a message back to Maine: "Elect my partner in public life" to assure a "continuance of recent aims." Thus, in a special election on June 1, 1940, Margaret Chase Smith was voted to her late husband's seat in the House of Representatives.

To elect the widow of a Congressman to fill out the husband's term is not unusual. Twenty or so congressional seats through the years have been filled by part-term wives. Politicians figure the wife of the deceased is the one most likely to get the sympathy vote and feel, moreover, that she will be easy to put into retirement, once the proper (male) candidate is found.

Margaret Smith's election, however, did not follow the

usual pattern. Serving out her husband's term, she worked for her own reelection, driving between sessions up and down her district in Maine, talking before small and large gatherings, referring everyone to the way she had continued her husband's policies. She won hands down.

Thus on January 6, 1941, this five-foot-two-inch, clear-eyed, straightforward woman, who always wears a red rose at her shoulder, was sworn in as a Representative "on her own."

This wasn't the only surprise this woman was to give the politicians. The early 1940's was a time of great tension. World War II had begun in Europe in 1939, and what with Europe about to be overrun by Hitler and the Nazi forces, Americans were vehemently taking sides for and against involvement. Margaret Chase Smith, a woman and a Republican, voted for the extension of the Draft Act. "My hardest decision," she said of it later. Then, too, she voted for the then unpopular Lend-Lease Bill to send a shipment of arms, food, and supplies to Britain. For that vote, "I got some black looks," she said.

She didn't forget the women of America. One of her first acts was to be a co-leader with Representative Melvin J. Maas on a bill that authorized the WAVES to serve in hospitals and offices overseas. She also put through a bill that made the WAVES, at first called merely Women's Reserve of the United States Navy, regular military personnel, with pay equivalent to other branches. She also piloted a bill through the House providing for regular military status for Army and Navy nurses.

Even more important than debating and voting on legislation, however, is a Congressman's committee work, for it is the committees that prepare bills for the vote. When Margaret Smith first came to Congress, she asked to be put on the Labor Committee, of which her husband had been a member. Maine's sawmills, shoe factories, paper and textile plants, make it a highly industrial state. A Labor Committee appointment would help her to help her constituents back home. However, she was politely turned down—was appointed instead to several lesser committees. But in 1943, when she had been voted in for a second full term, she asked for and received a place on the House Naval Affairs Committee. (In 1947 this, merged with the Military Affairs Committee, became the important Armed Services Committee.) For a Representative from Maine, a seaboard state dotted with Navy Yards and interested in Naval expansion, this was an especially strategic post.

By the early 1940's Margaret Smith had a reputation for being an independent voter, adhering to party lines only when she saw this as beneficial to her state and to the nation. Whether a bill concerned Labor, Social Security, or the budget of the United States President, she thought long and hard, then cast her vote with honesty and courage.

In late 1947, after an inspection tour at the request of the Armed Services Committee through Asia, Africa, and Europe, she began campaigning again in her home state. Such campaigns, whether an election is due or not, are annual fall affairs with Margaret Smith. She wants to find out what her constituents like and what they don't like. She wants to learn their reactions to recent developments.

This particular fall, however, her tour had a new aspect. For now her goal was the Senate. She had no party machine, no large campaign funds to back her. But she had her past record in the House. Moreover, her name was now nationally known, and what she said was being picked up by newspapers from coast to coast. So, often driving her Ford through snowdrifts in subzero weather, she went from Fort Kent at the northern end of Maine to Kittery at the southern point, and from Calais in the far east, to Fryeburg in the west. Often she spent the night at farmhouses in remote spots. She spoke not only in cities but in towns and hamlets hardly a dot on the map. In February 1948 her right arm was fractured when she slipped on the ice. With her arm in a sling she continued her tour. She was billed as the "Can-Do Candidate with the Can-Did Record." Sometimes she would hold meetings especially for women. "This is how I think about things," she would say to women gathered at P.T.A. meetings, in grange halls, in churches: "I represent you. If you want to see a woman in office, vote for me." On September 13, 1948, she won the Senate seat by the biggest majority and the greatest total vote ever given a candidate in Maine, polling over 71 percent of the vote. She was sworn in January 3, 1949.

She made her aim clear from the start: She had worked her way to the Senate, not as a widow filling out a husband's term, not as a lady responding to a chivalrous gesture, but as a working lawmaker.

For five of her early years in the Senate she was a nationally syndicated columnist. Her "Washington and You" column appeared in thirty newspapers in major cities. She feels this sort of publicity is worthwhile. She once pointed out, when she was seeking to bring greater attention to juvenile delinquency, "It's the squeaking wheel that gets the grease."

At first she was an almost silent figure in the Senate. Then, on June 1, 1950, she stood up and made a speech.

In the early 1950's the United States came very close to launching a nationwide "witchhunt." Communists, real and imaginary, were the focus of the hunt. The chief witchhunter was Joseph McCarthy, senator from Wisconsin. He came to wield such power that a new word was coined for it: *McCarthyism*. He made most of his accusations in the Senate, where he was accorded "Senatorial immunity," that is, where he could not be sued for libel or otherwise legally dealt with. As for the senators—that dignified group of "ambassadors from the states to the central government"—they were held in the vise of an "inquisition," an investigating subcommittee superintended by McCarthy. Resorting to "police state" tactics, insinuations, blackmail, Senator McCarthy made increasingly reckless accusations. The government was being infiltrated by Communists. They were right here in the Senate. Anyone who in any way seemed to oppose him became the subject of these attacks. Some Republicans went along with him because they felt this witchhunt would put the Democratic administration in a bad light, and bring the Republicans back into power. But Margaret Smith refused to be a part of this fear-ridden complex, with its contradictions, evasions, and doubletalk. Having always gone about her work independently, she was able to look objectively at the situation. She knew the value of a solid front, however, and now she spoke to other senators who she believed opposed McCarthy's tactics. Everyone of the six whom she approached was glad to give her his backing.

On that June 1 she stood up on the Republican side, a cool, immaculate lady, her aquamarine suit etched against the green-carpeted floor. A narrow aisle divides the two sections of the Senate, Democrats and Republicans. Just a few feet behind her was the desk of Joseph McCarthy. In a clear, firm voice she began her "Declaration of Conscience."

"I should like to speak briefly and simply," she said, "about a serious national condition . . . . The United States Senate has long enjoyed world-wide respect as the greatest deliberative body in the world. But recently that deliberative character has too often been debased to the level of a forum of hate and character assassination sheltered by the shield of congressional immunity." Then she spoke of the rights that all citizens should enjoy: the right to hold unpopular beliefs; the right to protest; the right of independent thought. She maintained that "the exercise of these should not cost one single American citizen his reputation or his right to a livelihood." She decried the "know nothing, suspect everything" attitude.

"I don't like the way the Senate has been made a rendezvous for vilification, for selfish political gain at the sacrifice of individual reputations and national unity." She spoke of her shame at the way many of the accusers hid behind the cloak of congressional immunity. She ended with, "It is high time that we all stopped being tools and victims of totalitarian techniques—techniques that, if continued here unchecked, will surely end what we have come to cherish as the American way of life."

Throughout this address reporters in the gallery kept their eyes fixed on Senator McCarthy, who alternately scowled and put his forehead in his hand. When it ended, he got up and strode out without saying a word. Senators crowded around Margaret Smith with congratulations.

By being the first senator to publicly criticize "McCarthyism," Margaret Chase Smith had broken the ice of fear. She suffered the consequences of her bravery. She was later removed from the McCarthy controlled Republican Policy Committee (she was subsequently reinstated) and put on a lesser committee. McCarthy passed off objections to this shift with a blustering, "She wasn't dumped—she was promoted."

It would be a matter of years before McCarthy was actually brought to justice. When he was, it was partly through the work of a subcommittee of which Margaret Smith was a member. In 1954 Senator McCarthy was formally censured by the Senate, and his political life came to a virtual end.

On July 17, 1950, Margaret Smith was appointed a lieutenant colonel in the Air Force Reserve, her commission including active tours at Air Force bases. This military work was useful to her in her capacities as a member of the Armed Services Committee (1953) and of the Space Committee (1958). Also because, as she says, "Maine is just one big air base, one of the most important advance fortresses within the continental limits of the United States," the appointment fell in naturally with her duties as a senator from Maine.

One of her most important duties during this period was serving as chairman of the Armed Services Sub-Committee investigating General Van Fleet's charge of an ammunition shortage in Korea. This study revealed that the shortage had caused "needless loss of American lives." The thoroughness and impartiality of her work at this time, her scrupulous investigation of the smallest details, made her one of the most valued armaments advisers in the Senate. She has consistently favored a strong military program and a sound space program.

By now many awards and honors were coming her way: "Woman of the Year," "Most Admired Woman." She was cited for "Distinguished Service" by the Reserve Officers Association and by the National Federation of Business and Professional Women's Clubs. The Freedom Foundation gave her its Freedom Award; the Women's National Press Club, the Politics Achievement Award.

In 1954 a global tour—the first such trip by a United States senator to be reported on television—increased her popularity. Viewers saw her chat with England's Prime Minister, Sir Winston Churchill, Premiere of France, Pierre Mendès-France, Generalissimo Franco of Spain, Soviet Foreign Minister Molotov in Moscow, and General Chiang Kai-shek on Formosa. She had a five-hour interview with a typical London family, discussing British employment, food, housing, children.

Senator Smith conducts herself in Senate committee work with dignity and poise, and when occasion demands, with searching directness. When in 1957 Congressman Dewey Short was nominated Assistant Secretary of the Navy, he appeared, as is usual before such appointments, for questioning by the Armed Services Committee. Things were proceeding methodically, when Margaret Smith inquired if he had changed his opinions since 1948 when he had opposed giving women regular status in the armed forces. Momentarily flustered, he pulled himself together and assured her that he had "become reconciled" to the situation. His appointment was then confirmed.

Senator Smith can be counted on to be present when a vote is to be taken in the Senate, that is, when each senator is called on to give his *yes* or *no* to a bill up for passage. Indeed she holds the all-time consecutive roll call voting record in the entire history of the United States Senate, with 2,941 consecutive roll call votes. When Senator Dirksen once praised her from the floor—"No one excels her in diligence and sustained attention to duty"—she answered him simply with, "I made a pledge when I first ran for office. I said I would stay on the job." She is equally meticulous in answering letters. She sees that every constituent's letter received at her office gets a response the very day it arrives.

But it is not only in these more obvious ways she shows her scrupulousness. Her fellow legislators know that when they speak on issues in which they oppose her, they must construct airtight cases. She is not only well prepared down to the last detail but fearless in defending her own convictions.

She has moved quietly yet persistently into fields that have heretofore been barred to women. In July 1964 Senator George Aiken placed her name in nomination for the United States presidency at the National Republican Convention in San Francisco. He said, "My candidate has common sense. She does not panic. I have watched her keep her head when others lose theirs." (In the final ballot, she polled the second highest number of votes.)

The reason few women hold high political offices, she realizes, lies in the very nature of politics. "There is nothing subtle about being a candidate for office," she says. "In politics the old prejudice of men against women is given full warning for resistance. Immediately when a woman candidate announces her candidacy, the male cry is that 'public office' is no place for a woman or 'the State is not quite ready for a woman in that office.'" The method of selecting governmental candidates is also to women's disadvantage: "Because candidates, for instance for the presidency and vice presidency, are picked in the smoke-filled rooms by party bosses, it is practically impossible for a woman to have a chance to be considered, much less to be nominated." Senator Smith has on several occasions made proposals to change the nomination methods, but so far with little success. It seems that the Halls of Congress are themselves to some extent "smoke-filled."

If she is aware of the obstacles in woman's path in politics, she is also determined not to accept favors because of her sex. When Senator Aiken made the speech nominating her for President, he had to do so without once referring to her as a woman.

She looks forward to women's greater participation in government. She says, "If they have sufficient desire and determination to hold not only public office but to organize politically and vote in blocks and elect qualified women candidates, then there is most definitely a future in politics for women. The inescapable fact is that they hold the control of the public office with their majority vote power. It is only a question of time."

BIBLIOGRAPHY

FLEMING, ALICE, *The Senator from Maine: Margaret Chase Smith.* New York: Thomas Y. Crowell Company, 1969.

GRAHAM, FRANK, *Margaret Chase Smith; Woman of Courage.* New York: The John Day Company, 1964.

LAMSON, PEGGY, *Few Are Chosen: American Women in Political Life Today.* Boston: Houghton Mifflin Company, 1968.

ROOSEVELT, ANNA ELEANOR, and HICKOK, LORENA A., *Ladies of Courage.* New York: G. P. Putnam's Sons, 1954.

GERTRUDE STEIN

GERTRUDE STEIN: Born in Allegheny, Pennsylvania, February 3, 1874. Died in Neuilly-sur-Seine, near Paris, July 27, 1946. Father: Daniel Stein; mother: Amelia (Keyser) Stein; brothers: Michael, Simon, Leo; sister: Bertha.

*

Gertrude Stein, a "stream of consciousness" writer, was a central figure in a war between literary factions in the early decades of the twentieth century. In her writing, she put aside the traditional functions of verbs and nouns and other parts of speech in the sentence context, and instead made words a sound flow comparable to the flow of subconscious thought. Her fame rests also on her genius for recognizing great oncoming talents in the art world and in surrounding herself with their masterworks. Her apartment in Paris has been called "the first museum of modern art." Through her famous "Saturday evenings" there, when notables gathered to discuss the modern trends, she undoubtedly helped to shape the era of modern art.

*

BEFORE she was six years old, Gertrude Stein had lived in Allegheny, Pennsylvania; in Vienna, in Paris, and in Baltimore. Her father tested business possibilities in each of these cities and finally settled the family in East Oakland, California. They had a house with ten acres of land around it and an avenue of eucalyptus trees leading up to it. Here Gertrude and her brother Leo would stock up on crusts of bread from the pantry and wander along California's dusty roads, munching them. They would talk about evolution—"as exciting," Gertrude later wrote, "as the discovery of America"—about the poetry of Wordsworth and Crabbe, about their resentment of their domineering father, and about the way a clump of live oaks at the bend in the road became beautiful just by its placement in the landscape.

Gertrude was stimulated by these exchanges of thought. But when she tried to think things out by herself, she became depressed. It worried her, for instance, that she could not define herself. Was the real "she" the same person others thought her? Was she the same person she thought herself? It worried her that she was part of an earth in limited space and yet she could look up into a sky that seemed limitless. She was shocked to discover that civilizations, once flourishing, had disappeared leaving scarcely a trace. Could that happen to her? Death, loss of identity—such thoughts would disturb her all her life. Perhaps she could circumvent death by becoming famous. "I always wanted to be historical," she was later to say. "From almost a baby on, I felt that way about it."

During this Oakland period her mother was ill and gradually dying of cancer. The household was disorganized. The table was not even laid for meals. Each member of the family, when he got hungry, helped himself to whatever was there. Her mother died when Gertrude was fourteen. Then, three years later, her father followed her mother in death, and her eldest brother, Michael, took over the family affairs. He managed things so well that he was able to see that each of his brothers and sisters received a small independent income for life.

The five orphans moved for a short time to San Francisco; then Gertrude, Leo, and Bertha were sent to live in Baltimore with their mother's sister, Mrs. Fannie Bachrach. Here, as

Gertrude Stein

Gertrude said, she "fairly lived" in her favorite library. But she had time also to enjoy the "solid good riches" with which her aunt's family was surrounded and the solicitude of "a whole group of lively little aunts." Her cousin, Helen Bachrach, who was seven years old when Gertrude came, remembered her as "quick-thinking and speaking, original in ideas and manner, with a capacity of humor so deep, kindly, and embracing that you found yourself laughing at everything she found extremely amusing, even yourself . . . . Everybody was attracted to Gertrude—men, women, and children, our German maids, the Negro laundresses, even casual acquaintances. . . ." Gertrude summed up this period: "There you are, you are privileged, nobody can do anything but take care of you, that is the way I was and that is the way I still am, and anyone who is like that necessarily liked it. I did and I do."

But she also felt, during "wild moods" in these Baltimore days, that she must have a change. Leo was now at Harvard. She enrolled at Radcliffe College and took a miscellany of courses, among them morphology of animals, embryology in vertebrates, and the study of cloud formations. She read more than ever, filled her room with books. She rode a bicycle, took long walks, swung along the corridors full of zest and humor.

The real excitement of her college days was William James, the philosopher and psychologist, then teaching at Harvard and Radcliffe. "Is life worth living? A thousand times yes when the world holds such spirits as Prof. James," she wrote in an English composition course. James's statement, "An idea is 'true' so long as to believe it is profitable in our lives," must have seemed exactly right to her. William James, impressed with the young student's perceptiveness, advised her to adopt a career in philosophy or psychology. About this time she made experiments in automatic writing and found that she was able to write without reference to anything but the words that had been just previously written.

On the morning of her final examination in James's course, she arrived at the classroom and ran her eyes over the list of questions. "Dear Professor James," she wrote across the top of her examination book, "I am so sorry but really I do not feel like an examination paper in philosophy today," and left the room. The next morning she received a note from James: "I understand perfectly how you feel. I often feel like that myself." He gave her the highest mark in his course. In the end she did take all the required examinations and was graduated *magna cum laude*.

She was well liked on the campus, for her naturalness, her forthrightness. She joined the Idler Club, a drama group, and was secretary of the Philosophy Club. She dressed mannishly, wore her hair short, and did nothing about her stoutness. Her college mates thought her ungainly. But Hutchins Hapgood, a journalist friend of her brother's, who met her about this time, called her "an extraordinary person: powerful, a beautiful head, a sense of something granite. I felt in Gertrude Stein something wholly intense . . . a deep temperamental quality which was also inspiring . . . . She . . . was by an inner necessity compelled to be conscious of her essential superiority, but at that time her extraordinary life-quality and her beauty were what struck the eye and the imagination."

When she returned from a European trip in the fall of 1897, she decided to take a medical course and matriculated at Johns Hopkins Medical College. But after two years she became bored, neglected her studies, and flunked one of the examinations. She was offered a chance to make it up during the summer but decided against it. Instead she thanked the professor who had failed her for showing her, in time, that medicine was not her field. Then off she went to Europe again to join her brother, who had settled there. She and Leo lived for a while in Italy, then in London. In 1903 they took an apartment at 27 Rue de Fleurus in Paris. There Gertrude was to live for thirty-four years, was to become a famous art connoisseur, was to preside over a salon of celebrities, and was to write a new-style prose.

Now she and Leo began to assemble their collection of art works, a collection that would become famous. They were largely the paintings of artists as yet unknown except in their own circles. Therefore the paintings were inexpensive. But even so, brother Michael sometimes had to help Leo and Gertrude out, giving them the money for purchases. As they bought paintings, they became acquainted with the artists. They visited Matisse's top floor studio-apartment when he was working on his canvas *La Bonheur de Vivre.* Finding the picture too large to hang in his own apartment, he handed it over to the Steins, and it became one of their choice paintings. So, in the course of time were assembled Cézanne oils and watercolors, early pictures by Matisse and Picasso, paintings by Renoir, Manet, Gauguin, and Toulouse-Lautrec.

Leo suggested they buy Picasso's painting *Jeune Fille aux Fleurs,* and Gertrude Stein attended an art exhibition to have a look at it. There Picasso's attention was attracted by her massive figure and her fine head. He asked a mutual friend who she was and would she pose for him. She would and did. During the winter of 1905–1906 she traveled across Paris daily for eighty or more days to sit for her portrait in Picasso's jumbled quarters. There an old stove held together with wires kept them warm, and the clutter of the painter's studio furthered their conversations into the whys of modern art. When the painting was finished, Picasso made her a present of it. Gertrude Stein liked the picture. "For me, it is I," she said, "and it is the only reproduction of me which is always I, for me." (On her death she left it to the Metropolitan Museum in New York.) Art historians consider it an important transitional work, one of the pictures marking the end of Picasso's Rose Period and the beginning of cubism.

It was in 1907 that Alice B. Toklas, who became famous as Gertrude's satellite, arrived in Paris from San Francisco, a refugee from the earthquake and fire there. For the rest of Gertrude Stein's life this slight, decisive woman was to relieve her of all the arduous details of daily living: do her typing for her, read proofs of her books, knit her stockings, keep her wardrobe in order, make the apartment comfortable, manage trips, protect her from undesirable contacts, and in wartime unravel miles of red tape. Without Alice Toklas' behind-the-scenes organizational ability, Gertrude Stein could not have lived her life either as comfortably or as creatively as she did.

Gertrude Stein gave her nights to writing, going to bed just before the birds started singing, and sleeping until noon. "Slowly and in a way it was not astonishing but slowly I was knowing that I was a genius," she commented. She worked on the theory that her writing was automatic, i.e., subconscious. The day after she had engaged in a bout of writing, according to her friend Mabel Dodge, she would give Miss Toklas the manuscript to type and "she and Gertrude would always be so surprised and delighted at what she had written, for it had been done so unconsciously she'd have no idea of what she'd said the night before." (Later, when asked about her style of writing, she was to answer, "I don't know anything about it. I take things in and they come out that way, independent of conscious processes.")

Leo Stein did not like the style of his sister's writing. As she put it, "He did not say it to me but he said it so that it would be true for me. And it did not trouble me and as it did not trouble me he knew it was not true . . . But it destroyed him for me and it destroyed me for him." Whatever the cause, Leo left the apartment in 1912 and brother and sister were never again to be closely associated.

Gertrude Stein

By this time the apartment had become a magnet for collectors, critics, musicians, writers, painters, sculptors, poets. Gertrude Stein would preside, sitting in a high-backed Renaissance chair, next to a big cast-iron stove. She would be dressed in brown corduroy, and with her high forehead and massive proportions would look not unlike an all-encompassing Buddha. Practically all of the greats and to-be greats of the day attended these Saturday evening soirées. They came to exchange ideas, to talk over new trends, to philosophize, and of course to gossip. Cliques and coteries, confidences and collaborations, were centered here. Here Hemingway told her of his terrible sense of inadequacy. Here author Carl Van Vechten listened spellbound to her deep velvet voice, more moving, he thought, than Sarah Bernhardt's. Here Sherwood Anderson saw her as the "very symbol of health and strength." Here the famous photographer Edward Steichen often stood near her just to hear her laugh. "She had the most infectious laugh I ever heard from a grown-up. Some children laugh like that, but it was good to hear from a grown woman."

Here some of the guests arrived as strangers and remained in her regard as friends for the rest of their lives. Others had the door firmly closed on them after a few visits. One of the latter was the poet William Carlos Williams. "Are you sure that writing is your métier?" he had asked Miss Stein. "Things that children write have seemed to me so Gertrude Steinish in their repetitions. Your quality is that of . . . slowly and innocently first recognizing sensations and experience." Said Gertrude Stein, "I told the maid I was not in if he came again. There is too much bombast in him."

But whatever her foibles, the fact remains that Gertrude Stein was a genius in personal relationships. Her passionate interest in human beings drew people from all over the world. They listened to her talk, poured out their troubles to her, followed her advice, spread her name abroad. It was in this sphere of human interchange that she achieved the glory she sought.

Gertrude Stein had brought out her book *Three Lives* in 1909, with scarcely a ripple returning from the outside world. This book could still be considered in the tradition of American writers interested in grass roots portrayals. However, with each successive book she made a wider break with the logic of language, using words as a vehicle of expression, but as expression divorced entirely from conscious meaning. In the books written between 1909 and 1912—*A Long Gay Book, Many, Many Women,* and *G.M.P.* (Gertrude, Matisse, and Picasso)—she rejected writers' ordinary standards and wrote as though words existed the way brooks gurgle, for their sounds only. Parts of the latter book were published in the magazine *Camera Work* in August 1912, Miss Stein's first appearance in a periodical. But all three books were not published in book form until a later date.

She had established no name for herself in her new writing genre until the publication of *Tender Buttons* in 1914. The advance brochure on this book tried to prepare the readers: "She [Gertrude Stein] is a ship that flies no flag and she is outside the law of art. But she descends on every port and leaves a memory of her visits . . . . The last shackle is struck from context and collation, and each unit of the sentence stands independent and has no commerce with its fellows. The effect produced on the first reading is something like terror." The effect on the literary world, in fact, was that of a cataclysmic jolt.

However, before she could fully relish the book's impact, World War I was declared. To get away from the bombing, Gertrude Stein with Alice Toklas set up residence on the island of Mallorca off the coast of Spain. But they returned to Paris in 1916, when Gertrude decided to get into the war—

after her own fashion. Aligning herself with the American Fund for French wounded, she had a cousin in America send over a Ford car, learned to drive it, and delivered supplies to hospitals in and around Paris. Miss Toklas attended to all the details. Later they opened a hospital supply distribution depot in the town of Perpignan in the south of France. When the Americans entered the war, they opened another depot serving much of southeastern France. Gertrude made an immediate hit with the doughboys, who relayed to her the latest American slang and told her their life stories. After the armistice she and Miss Toklas were assigned to the liberated Alsace province in northeast France, and through a cold winter, distributed supplies to the shelled cities.

The war over, she returned to her writing. She looked at the mass of her unpublished manuscripts and contrasted their neglect with the crowds of admirers who came to her apartment as to a shrine. She decided something would have to be done about it. So, amid writings deliberately divorced from meaning, appeared her book *The Autobiography of Alice B. Toklas*, written, in spite of the title, by Gertrude Stein and written clearly and simply. It was published in August 1933. A memoir of her Parisian years, it became a best seller and brought her not only fame but good solid royalty checks. "I love being rich," she said, "not as yet so awful rich but with prospects, it makes me all cheery inside . . . ."

But she wasn't so happy about the fact that "Nothing inside me needed to be written. Nothing needed any word and there was no word inside me that could not be spoken and so there was no word inside me. And I was not writing. I began to worry about identity."

One result of *The Autobiography of Alice B. Toklas* was an invitation to come to America to lecture. So, after some soul searching, off she and Miss Toklas went, arriving on October 24, 1934. Now her fears that she would never attain glory were once and for all put to rest. The reporters who crowded about this stout woman in a homespun skirt and flowered vest were delighted with her good humor and simplicity. When they asked, "Why don't you write the way you talk?" she asked them, "Why don't you read the way I write?" The people who stopped her on the street and in the shops, the news that raced in lights around the Times Building ("to suddenly see your name is upsetting . . . it is one of the things most worrying in the subject of identity"), all proclaimed the fact that Gertrude Stein not only had come home but had come home a famous figure. She flew between Massachusetts and California, giving lectures. People fought for tickets. In Chicago she saw her play, *Four Saints in Three Acts,* and liked the way her words sounded set to Virgil Thomson's music. She told the Signet Society of Harvard "A rose is a rose is a rose." She dined with Charlie Chaplin in Beverly Hills. She watched a marathon dance. She rode in a police car while it was on official duty. She took tea with Eleanor Roosevelt at the White House. She said, "It is very nice being a celebrity, a real celebrity."

But still there was that nagging matter of identity. She told a friend, "I want to write a novel about publicity, a novel where a person is so publicized that there isn't any personality left. I want to write about the effect on people of the Hollywood kind of publicity that takes away all identity. It's very curious, you know, very curious the way it does just that." She produced a touching couplet: "Why have they thought/ I sold what I bought?" Around this time journalistic take-offs of her style became better known than her own writings.

The rest of her life, back in France, is the story of a woman famous as an art connoisseur, a leader in the expatriate world of Paris, a phenomenon. "A summons to her home," said historian Lloyd Morris, "was an invitation to present oneself to Monte Blanc." At her new apartment in the Rue Christine, right after the liberation of Paris from German occupation,

Gertrude Stein

GI's crowded around her, bringing gifts, letters of introduction, and their own verses *à la Stein*. After the Second World War she toured occupied Germany in an American bomber and wrote about the American soldiers for *Life* magazine. One day a crowd of fifty GI's enthusiastically walked her home after a lecture at the Red Cross Center, a procession that forced motor traffic into side streets. When asked what to do about the Germans, she said, "Teach them disobedience."

In July 1946—the year she finished writing *The Mother of Us All*—she and Miss Toklas went off by car for a rest. On the way she was taken violently ill. She was rushed back to Paris by train and carried to the American hospital at nearby Neuilly. After the medical examination (cancerous growths were discovered) an operation was performed. When she had come out from under the anesthetic, she asked Miss Toklas at her bedside, "What is the answer?" Miss Toklas was silent. "In that case," Miss Stein said, "what is the question?" Soon after, she sank into a coma from which she never emerged.

BIBLIOGRAPHY

BRINNIN, JOHN MALCOLM, *The Third Rose; Gertrude Stein and Her World*. Boston: Little, Brown and Company, 1959.
STEIN, LEO, *Journey into the Self; Being the Letters, Papers and Journals*, edited by Edmund Fuller; Introduction by Van Wyck Brooks. New York: Crown Publishers, Inc., 1950.
UNTERMEYER, LOUIS, *Makers of the Modern World; the Lives of 92 Writers, Artists, Scientists, Statesmen, Inventors, Philosophers, Composers, and Other Creators Who Formed the Pattern of Our Century*. New York: Simon & Schuster, Inc., 1955.

HARRIET BEECHER STOWE

HARRIET BEECHER STOWE: Born in Litchfield, Connecticut, June 13, 1811. Died in Hartford, Connecticut, July 1, 1896. Father: Lyman Beecher; mother: Roxana (Foote) Beecher; eleven brothers and sisters; husband: Calvin Ellis Stowe; children: Harriet and Eliza (twins), Henry Ellis, Frederick William, Georgiana May, Samuel Charles, Charles Edward.

*

Harriet Beecher Stowe, in her book *Uncle Tom's Cabin*, startled America with a vivid portrayal of the sorrows and cruelties of slavery. She is credited with actually bringing the issue to the point of combat. President Lincoln is reported to have said to her, when she sought him out to test him on his promised Emancipation Proclamation, "So this is the little lady who made the big war."

*

THE Beecher children, their father and mother, *and* three or four theological students (boarders at the parsonage) made quite a gathering around the supper table. Harriet Beecher's father, a famous preacher of his time, dominated the group. He led them in debates. Sometimes he himself would switch to the weaker side to illustrate how to strengthen an argument. He encouraged his children to take part, to make telling points. "Now if you take this position you will be able to trip me up!"

Young Harriet adored her father. Besides his intellectual feats, he could easily vault over a rail fence (still could at the age of eighty). He played the violin. He would sometimes play while the children danced, and then would break the rhythm, just for the fun of it, throwing the group into a merry turmoil. Harriet found inspiration in his presence. "The very touch of his hand seemed to put strength into me."

Her mother died when she was five. In this busy and money-scarce household (even at the height of his fame Lyman Beecher made hardly more than a schoolboy today makes doing odd jobs after school) Harriet was expected to do her part. So she helped care for her younger brother and sister, and did some mending and crocheting besides. She also helped with the table setting and the dishwashing. There was fun mixed in with it all—the hayrides, the horseback excursions, the picnics, the games in the woodshed. It was a great day when they got a piano. Then with her father playing the violin, her brothers playing flutes, and others taking turns at the piano, they could hold evening "sings."

Next to her father, she adored her younger brother, Henry Ward, later to become an even more famous clergyman than his father. Brother and sister would walk hand in hand to the nearby dame school, would go together to pick berries and gather nuts, and in winter would coast down hills together on their sleds.

When she was six and a half, her father married again, but Harriet never felt very close to her stepmother. She was "so elegant, so delicate that we were afraid to go near her."

After the dame school, Harriet spent two years at the Litchfield Academy. At the "annual exhibition" she wrote a composition on the immortality of the soul, and her father praised it. "It was the proudest moment of my life," she wrote later. That was when it dawned on her she might become a writer.

When she was twelve going on thirteen, she packed her small carpetbag with her winter clothes and traveled to Hartford, Connecticut. There her older sister Catherine had started a school, the Hartford Female Seminary, in a large room over a harness shop. Harriet boarded with a family whose daughter received free instruction at the school. When Harriet was fifteen Catherine made her a part time teacher at the Hartford Seminary. All her life this older sister was interested in women's education, and often Harriet would be drawn into her sister's projects.

During her growing-up years Harriet would often sink into periods of deep introspection: "owling about," her brothers and sisters called the habit. Finally she found relief by mapping out ideals of behavior: love for God, for her friends, for humanity. In a schoolgirl letter she wrote she was "trying not to shrink in a corner . . . . I am holding out my hand."

When she was twenty-one, her father was called to Cincinnati, Ohio, to take on double duties as president of the Lane Theological Seminary and as pastor of the Second Presbyterian Church. She and eight other Beechers piled into a stagecoach, with the luggage on top. En route they made stops in New York, Philadelphia, Harrisburg, Wheeling, and other cities, so that Lyman Beecher could preach, hold prayer meetings, and collect funds for the seminary. Then they jogged on, the young Beecher boys throwing religious tracts out of the stagecoach windows.

These were the days before the Civil War, when the southern states were still slaveholding states. Cincinnati was a city in the free North, but it was on the border of a slave state, Kentucky. The Ohio River divided the two states. For eighteen years this area was to be Harriet's home. It was as if she had an observation post just right for watching the panorama of American slavery. A sign on a country store would read: "One hundred dollars reward . . . will be paid by the subscriber for the apprehension and delivery of Humphrey, a slave." A young woman fleeing slavery was rescued after a wild flight across the ice floes of the Ohio River. Once Harriet walked across the town to see the still smoking ruins of a hall where an antislavery convention had been held. The fire hose had even been cut so that no water would be available to put the fire out. Houses of free Negro people were burned. When the town newspaper tried to present both sides of the question, its office was broken into and its presses thrown into the river. Sometimes she went over into Kentucky and actually saw the slaves working on the plantations.

Once the family was settled in Cincinnati, the "Misses Beecher" started a school there. Harriet was not only a teacher but a cowriter with Catherine of a geography book—an unusually popular schoolbook for the day, because it was written as a continuous narrative. She joined the Semi-Colon Club, a local literary gathering. The club held a contest, and she wrote a story, "Uncle Lot," to be read at one of its meetings. The story not only won her a fifty-dollar prize but was published in April 1834 in the *Western Monthly Magazine*.

After she had been in Ohio two years she made a trip east to see her brother Henry Ward being graduated from Amherst College. On her return west she was saddened to learn of the death of a dear friend of hers, Eliza Stowe. The widower, Calvin Stowe, was a teacher of Biblical literature at Lane Theological Seminary. Harriet and Mr. Stowe were drawn together by their mutual sorrow. After two years Calvin Stowe and she were married. She wrote a friend that he was "rich in Greek and Hebrew, Latin and Arabic, and alas rich in nothing else." Nevertheless, he had good common sense and a critic's appreciation of his wife's ability to write. "My dear," he told her, "you must be a literary woman. It is so written in the book of fate. Make all your calculations accordingly. Get a good stroke of health and brush up your mind.... Write yourself fully and always 'Harriet Beecher Stowe.' Then, my word for it, your husband will lift up his head in the gate, and your children will rise up and call you blessed."

So the hardships of her marriage—unremitting housework and stringent poverty, as well as frequent separations from her husband while he was off on research projects for the seminary—were balanced by the benefits: a husband who wept and laughed over her writings and was an intelligent host to her literary friends; and children who made her days rich and varied.

Her first-born, the twins Eliza and Harriet, and the next baby, Henry, came very close together. She felt frustrated. "Indeed ... I am a mere drudge," she wrote a friend, "with few ideas beyond babies and housekeeping.... I start to cut out some little dresses, have just calculated the length and got one breadth torn off, when Master makes a doleful lip and falls to crying with might and main. I catch him up, and, turning round, see one of his sisters flourishing the things out of my workbox in style. Moving it away and looking the other side, I see the second little mischief seated by the hearth chewing coals...."

However, she kept to her writing—sold stories to several magazines. Her book *The Mayflower*, sketches and scenes among the descendants of the Puritans, was published in 1843.

Then in 1848, during a cholera epidemic in Cincinnati, her little son, Samuel Charles, died of the disease. In her grief Mrs. Stowe's thoughts turned longingly toward New England. A little later her husband was offered a professorship at Bowdoin College, Brunswick, Maine. The family decided their destiny lay in the East.

On their trip to Maine the Stowe family stopped off in

Brooklyn, New York, and she heard her brother Henry Ward preach an impassioned sermon against slavery. He had a young Negro girl, a slave, brought up to the pulpit, and called to the congregation, "What am I offered to buy this slave out of bondage?" Thus she was "auctioned off to freedom," the members of the congregation there and then pledging money enough to cover her purchase price.

By the time they were settled in Maine, it was 1850, a crucial year in the history of the United States. The fugitive slave act, which empowered masters to drag back their "property," no matter where the escaped slaves had established themselves, became a law in September. Official Boston decided it would collaborate with slave hunters, but humane citizens went into an uproar. At first Mrs. Stowe, immersed in the chores of housekeeping and caring for a newborn baby, ignored the controversy. Finally, however, she had to listen. "If I could use a pen as you can," wrote her sister-in-law, Mrs. Edward Beecher, from Boston, "I would write something that would make this whole nation feel what an accursed thing slavery is."

About that time Harriet Beecher Stowe had what she described as a "vision." While attending a commencement day service at Bowdoin College, she seemed to see before her the flogging to the death of an old Negro slave. When she got home and had a free moment, she jotted down her impressions on a piece of wrapping paper. Her husband happened to pick it up. "Hattie, you must go on with it," he told her. "You must make up a story with this as a climax!"

On June 5, 1851, the story that was to become the book *Uncle Tom's Cabin* started as a serial in the magazine *National Era*. Mrs. Stowe wrote at odd moments, anywhere. A neighbor saw her scribbling away on the back doorstep. However, as the demand for her articles increased, she became desperate for time. She finally took over a room assigned to her husband on the Bowdoin campus, and wrote there. The Bowdoin students grew accustomed to seeing the beshawled little woman trudging along the walks in the winter, only her head showing above the bordering banks of snow.

In 1852 Calvin Stowe took a new teaching post, at Andover, Massachusetts, and the family moved there. Here, too, the pay was pitifully small, and Harriet was glad she could help a little with her magazine writing. She faithfully sent off her weekly installments to the *National Era*. In writing the entire serial of "Uncle Tom's Cabin" she missed only one issue. It was after completing the chapter on little Eva's death. She herself was so moved that she took to her bed to recuperate.

Throughout the series she presented the problem of slavery as one for the North as well as the South. The fault lay, she pointed out, with the system: The North had its interest in buying slave products from the South; the whole country had laws to protect the system.

Uncle Tom's Cabin, first subtitled *A Man That Was a Thing*, and later *Life Among the Lowly*, came out in book form on March 20, 1852. In spite of its popularity in magazine form, Mrs. Stowe was dubious about its reception as a book. Her whole family was dubious. However, they hoped she would at least be able to buy herself a silk dress with the proceeds.

She got her silk dress. Two days after the book's publication the entire first edition of five thousand copies was sold out. Eight presses were run continuously, Sundays excepted, and one hundred book binders were kept steadily at work to keep up with the demand. A German language edition was put out for German immigrants. When it was published in England, Queen Victoria wrote Mrs. Stowe, thanking her for the good work done. The novelist Tolstoy called it one of the "great achievements of the human mind." It was translated into every written language from Finnish to Bengali. It was soon the world's best seller, outranked only by the Bible.

Stage presentations started in September 1852. One, a dramatization by George L. Aikens, drew enthusiastic audiences for 100 performances in Troy, New York, and went on to New York City for 350 performances there. At one time four different companies were presenting *Uncle Tom's Cabin* simultaneously in New York. For the next eighty years *Uncle Tom's Cabin* was to be a staple on the stage—one of the few American folk dramas. A card game called "Uncle Tom and Little Eva" was put on the market. Eight different "Uncle Tom" songs were peddled on Broadway.

Uncle Tom was published when Harriet Beecher Stowe was forty-one years old. The forty-four years she had yet to live were in effect a new life. During these years she would travel with her husband—he was given time off to accompany his famous wife—to speak in England and on the Continent. (With the money earned, she bought slaves into freedom, sent her daughters to fashionable schools abroad, and purchased for her son Charles a parsonage in Hartford.) She would become the author of some thirty more books, countless magazine articles, and commentaries in newspapers.

Before 1852 ended, urgent calls were already coming to her to speak before antislavery societies in Liverpool, in Glasgow, and in London. Yes, she would come, but first she must finish her *Key to Uncle Tom's Cabin*. This book brought together records of court decisions, newspaper clippings, notices posted for fugitive slaves—her "source material"—and silenced those who had questioned the authenticity of the brutal conditions she pictured in *Uncle Tom's Cabin*.

In the British Isles she was feted, dined, lionized. Cheers followed her from the station in Glasgow; streets were roped off in Edinburgh; in London, crowds followed her about. When she went by water, the river banks were lined with spectators. The London *Times* listed her daily schedule in its pages for the convenience of her devotees. She was a special guest of the Lord Mayor, sat at table with writers Charles Dickens and Thomas Carlyle. The ladies of London made her a gift of 130 gold sovereigns for the Negroes of America. Meanwhile her husband, patiently accompanying her, wrote home, "I would rather be at Andover about my business," but added, "Wife bears it very well. She is gaining in health. She is meek, pious, and loving, the same that she ever was."

When they returned to America, she began to write another abolitionist novel, *Dred: A Tale of the Great Dismal Swamp*. One hundred thousand copies sold in four weeks. In the late 1850's and early 1860's she finished two novels of New England manners: *The Minister's Wooing* (this book is considered autobiographical) and *The Pearl of Orr's Island*. These and her later *Oldtown Folks* and *Poganuc People*, as well as *Agnes of Sorrento*, *Pink and White Tyranny*, and *We and Our Neighbors*, were all successful books at the time. But she was never again to match the appeal or reach the heights of *Uncle Tom's Cabin*.

In the early months of the Civil War she saw her son Frederick William off to battle. (He was injured by a fragment of shell and never fully recovered.) In spirit she saw off thousands of other young men, brought to a horror of slavery by reading *Uncle Tom's Cabin*.

Then England, despite all its previous antislavery furor, proclaimed its neutrality in the American Civil War. Mrs Stowe decided to appeal to the women of that country. First, though, she was careful to learn whether President Lincoln meant to keep his promise to issue an Emancipation Proclamation on New Year's Day 1863. She asked for and was granted an interview with him. She came away completely convinced of his sincerity. Now she wrote an article. It was published in *Atlantic Monthly* magazine for November 27, 1862. It reminded British women of their former stand, rebuked them for their support of the South, and underlined the forthcoming Emancipation Proclamation. It was her ablest pronouncement on slavery and one of the chief influences in changing the minds of the English toward the Confederacy.

On January 1, 1863, the day assigned for the Proclamation, a "Jubilee" was held in the Music Hall of Boston. During the intermission the news was telegraphed that emancipation had indeed been proclaimed. The audience went wild—cheered, waved, kissed, wept. Somebody spotted Mrs. Stowe in the balcony. She was gently pushed toward the railing, where she could be seen by the whole audience. She leaned over, and looking down on the sea of upturned faces, bowed right and left while the audience cheered. Here was recognition, not in print, not by strangers on foreign soil, but by her own people, at home. Later she was to recall this as the crowning moment of her life.

In the 1870's Mrs. Stowe took on a new role, that of public reader. Dressed in black satin with black lace draped about her shoulders, and speaking in a soft, gentle voice as though she were talking to a friend, she read passages from the best loved of her works. Mostly she spoke in New England, but in 1873 she traveled to the Middle West. She was particularly well received in Cincinnati.

The *Atlantic Monthly* arranged a celebration for her on her seventieth birthday. (It was really her seventy-first, the editors had miscounted.) At this, a garden party held near Boston, authors Oliver Wendell Holmes and John Greenleaf Whittier contributed poems. Among the several hundred distinguished guests were the philosopher Bronson Alcott and the author Thomas Bailey Aldrich. Harriet Beecher Stowe made a short speech, ending with the words, "Everything that ought to happen is going to happen."

Her own life seemed to bear this out.

BIBLIOGRAPHY

ADAMS, JOHN R., *Harriet Beecher Stowe*. New York: Twayne Publishers, Inc., 1963.

BRADFORD, GAMALIEL, *Portraits of American Women*. Boston: Houghton Mifflin Company, 1919.

FIELDS, ANNIE, *Life and Letters of Harriet Beecher Stowe*. Boston, 1897.

GILBERTSON, CATHERINE, *Harriet Beecher Stowe*. New York: D. Appleton-Century Company, Inc., 1937.

JOHNSTON, JOHANNA, *Runaway to Heaven; the Story of Harriet Beecher Stowe*. New York: Doubleday & Company, Inc., 1963.

STOWE, CHARLES EDWARD, and STOWE, LYMAN BEECHER, *Harriet Beecher Stowe; the Story of Her Life*. Boston: Houghton Mifflin Company, 1911.

STOWE, HARRIET ELIZABETH (BEECHER), *Uncle Tom's Cabin*. New York: Coward-McCann, Inc., 1929.

WILSON, FORREST, *Crusader in Crinoline; the Life of Harriet Beecher Stowe*. Philadelphia: J. B. Lippincott Company, 1941.

HARRIET TUBMAN

HARRIET TUBMAN: Born in slavery in Bucktown, Dorchester County, Maryland, probably in 1820. Died in Auburn, New York, March 10, 1913. Father: Benjamin Ross; mother: Harriet Green; six brothers and four sisters; marriages: John Tubman; Nelson Davis.

*

Harriet Tubman, "the Moses of her people," led some three hundred Negro slaves out of the slave South to the free North by hazardous exploits. After her own escape she made nineteen trips back into the South—the "Land of Egypt," she called it. A price of $40,000 was placed on her head, and her capture in the South would probably have meant instant death.

*

AT the age of five Harriet Tubman was "farmed out" by her owner as a house helper and baby tender. By the age of nine, still with the same family, she was made a house-and-grounds worker. Her duties now included bringing in the kindling and setting muskrat traps. This out-of-door work, while it was harder, got her away from the quick whip that had lashed about her head at the least deflection, such as forgetting to put the sugar bowl on the table or neglecting to pat down the feather beds.

She worked outside for several months. But then, just as she was coming down with the measles, she was made to go on her usual round of muskrat-trap setting. She caught cold and became so ill she had to be taken home to her parents' cabin. There she was nursed lovingly by her mother. When she asked, why, why had she been treated so, her mother only answered, "Child, don't fret. Be as good as you best know how to be."

When she got better she was put out to do fieldwork on her owner's plantation. Now she could get a cool drink when she wanted it at her cabin, could look over the great sweep of fields, and could sing to the rhythm of her work. When she was fifteen, however, this too came to an end. One day a runaway slave darted past her. She tried to bar the way of the pursuers, and was hit on the forehead by a two-pound weight aimed at the runaway. It almost killed her. For three months she lay on a straw pallet in a corner of the cabin. Eager to get rid of the disabled young girl, her owner would kick the door open almost daily and, with a flourish, say to his companion, "Here she is. What am I offered?" ("I wasn't worth a penny," she later reminisced, with a wide smile. "I was too weak and scrawny.")

During this period she did some hard thinking. A few years before, the slave Nat Turner had waged his unsuccessful rebellion, and the cabins had been simmering with talk of it. Harriet had taken in every word. Now she decided God had a reason for letting her receive the blow meant for the runaway slave. The convex dent in her skull, scarring her for life, became her badge of faith. She had been singled out to come to the aid of her people.

Around this time her owner died. Her father had a responsible job as supervisor of the cutting and hauling of large quantities of wood, and through his recommendation she was put into the service of another master. She was now very strong. Working near her father, she drove oxen, carted, plowed, split rails.

When she was in her mid-twenties, she married a freed

Harriet Tubman

Negro, John Tubman. This did not exempt her from labor—she was still a slave herself—but it did set her to looking into the whys of freed Negroes. Her husband, she found out, had obtained his freedom when his former master died. The man had written in his will that all his slaves should be set free. Then Harriet found out that some years before, her own mother, on the death of a former master, had been freed in the same way. But her mother had never even been told of her free status. So, ironically, while having a free mother would legally have made Harriet Tubman free, too, she could now not claim the right. This unfairness led her to decide to help her people in ways outside the "mess of papers."

One day the grapevine carried the news that she and her brothers were to be sent away to a chain gang in the deep South. Two of her sisters had already "disappeared." Flight, she knew, was dangerous. But, she reasoned, "There's two things I've got a right to and these are death and liberty. One or the other I mean to have."

Her husband had no interest in emigrating to the North. She tried to persuade her brothers to escape with her, but they were afraid to take the risk. The Nat Turner rebellion had brought a wave of repressive measures. No Negro, for instance, was allowed to leave his master's territory without a pass signed by his master, and all Negroes taking a boat or railroad had to be weighed, measured, and certified by someone in the locality.

Well, if no one would go with her, Harriet Tubman would make her escape alone. One night the other slaves in their rows of shacks heard her strong, clear voice singing the spiritual:

> Ah'm gwine to leave ye
> Ah'm bound for de promised land.

They nodded knowingly to one another.

She had laid her plans carefully. A white woman in the vicinity had a reputation for being helpful to escaping slaves—for a consideration. Harriet Tubman sought her out. In exchange for a patchwork quilt she had worked on over the years, the woman gave her a slip of paper with two names on it. Harriet Tubman went to the first name and was asked by the mistress of the house to rake the leaves in the yard. (An idle Negro would be highly suspect anywhere.) Later the woman's husband casually remarked in Harriet Tubman's hearing that he had a load of vegetables to haul that evening "northward." She was shown the shed where the cart stood. When the load started on its way, she lay hidden beneath the vegetables.

When the cart was unloaded at the end of its journey, she was directed to a farmhouse. Here much of the same procedure was repeated. And so it went. Traveling mostly by foot and always at night, with the North Star constantly ahead of her, she arrived one early morning in 1849 on the free soil of Pennsylvania. "When I found I had crossed that line," she said later, "I looked at my hands to see if I was the same person. There was such a glory over everything; the sun came like gold through the trees, and over the fields, and I felt like I was in Heaven."

Harriet Tubman's history might simply have ended there, with her name to be found only on old lists of "slaves escaped." Instead it was just at this point that her life of service began. For even at this first moment of freedom she thought, as she said later, "I was a stranger in a strange land; my home, after all, was down in Maryland, because my father, my mother, my brothers, my sisters, and friends were there . . . . But I was *free* and *they should be free!* I would make a home in the North and bring them there!"

The first step was to get in touch with William Stillman, Negro chief "brakeman" on the Underground Railroad. This transport system was really neither "underground" nor "railroad." It was rather a vast network of escape devices, comprising false walls in attics, kitchen ceilings with bunklike rooms above, sliding panels by fireplaces, hidden alcoves beneath stairways. It was Quaker Meeting Houses, African Methodist Episcopal Zion Churches, tunnels from cellars to barns, spaces under store counters, haystacks, brush piles, hidden compartments in wagons, and closed carriages. For train and boat transportation, it provided false identification papers. The whole was superintended by skilled "agents" and "brakemen." The requisites for travel on this "railroad" were shrewdness in planning routes, skill in avoiding observation, quick thinking in emergencies, courage to face danger, and strength to endure hardship.

Mrs. Tubman made herself known to Mr. Stillman at his headquarters in Philadelphia. Stillman gave her directions on how to find a job. She became an employee at a hotel. She saved her money carefully. Finally she had enough to make her first trip South.

On this trip one of her sisters and her sister's two children were brought North. On a second trip shortly after this she brought back a brother and two other men.

She planned her "escapes" as if they were military maneuvers. She would start her groups on Saturdays, because on Sundays no posters advertising fleeing slaves were printed. If handbills did go up, she would hire a Negro to follow the sheriff at a safe distance and tear them down. To confound pursuers, she would make sudden changes in directions, sometimes redirecting her charges due South. She would use songs as signals. "Go Down, Moses!" was her fighting song; "Steal Away," was the song to summon the slaves for a meeting. Singing was a safe enough means. Who would listen to a slave woman chanting hymns along the roadway?

"Moses" got to be her second name. A slave would stop by

her father's cabin. "Tell me next time 'Moses' comes." Or another, sitting in his own dark cabin at night, would shiver, mutter something about "Moses," and start preparations. Sometimes she would just appear: "It's me. Time to go north."

She would hide her charges in haystacks, in potato holes, in pigpens, while she reconnoitered. On approaching a town, she would see that a baby was given paregoric to quiet it, and would slip it in a ticking bag to conceal it.

She did not lack firmness. If a faint-hearted runaway would beg to be left behind in the darkness of a swamp, she would put a pistol to his head. "Move or die. Dead men tell no tales." Once, to get her nervous charges across a guarded bridge, she waded the river herself to find help. Soon a wagon lumbered back over the bridge going southward. It carried a load of bricks. The Negro drivers were singing and shouting. On their return shortly thereafter, they were passed along without the usual inspection. ("Those same rowdy drivers!") The sentries did not guess that now, concealed under the bricks, were Harriet Tubman's people.

Once, when she had dozed off near a post office, she awoke to hear two white men talking about her—could she be the one who was wanted? They'd read a leaflet advertising such an old woman. Harriet Tubman pretended to be reading a book. "That can't be her—the one they want can't read or write." She prayed the book was right side up.

For twenty years Harriet Tubman led fugitives to freedom. Frederick Douglass, the Negro abolitionist leader, once wrote to her, "Most that I have done and suffered in the service of our cause has been in public, and I have received much encouragement at every step of the way. You on the other hand have labored in a private way . . . . I have had the applause of the crowd and the satisfaction that comes of being approved by the multitude, while the most that you have done has been witnessed by a few trembling, scarred, and footsore bondsmen and women . . . whose heartfelt 'God bless you' has been your only reward . . . ."

In 1850 the Fugitive Slave Law was reactivated, binding people north of the Mason-Dixon Line to return to southern masters any fugitives found in their territory. When the North became unsafe for refugees, Harriet led her charges clear through into Canada. In 1851 she arrived in the town of St. Catharines, in Ontario, with eleven fugitives, including another of her brothers and his wife. This town was to be her home base for the next six years. Here she collected clothes for her fugitives, boarded them, and found them work chopping wood in the forests. In time many educated themselves, bought property, became enterprising citizens.

From 1851 to 1857 she made eleven trips back into slave territory. In 1854 she got out three more of her brothers as well as her aged parents. Her husband had meanwhile married again and did not want to come north. By 1857 Mr. Stillman had listed sixty arrivals from Harriet's home region. Dorchester County, Maryland, was being "plucked of slaves like a chicken of its feathers."

While she was settling her parents in St. Catharines, the abolitionist leader John Brown came to consult her. It was shortly before he invaded Virginia and tried to start a general slave insurrection. She gave him information on the routes he was to follow and the allies he might count on in his Harpers Ferry raid. He always referred to her as "General Tubman." Mrs. Tubman called him "the true emancipator of my people."

In 1859 she settled in Auburn, New York, a prominent station on the Underground. It was to be her home for the rest of her life.

By 1860 Harriet Tubman's exploits had become known throughout the nation. She was much sought after by abolitionists as a speaker—sometimes under a false name for precautionary reasons—at antislavery events. She spoke movingly of the sufferings of her people. But whenever she was questioned about her attitude toward slaveholders, she would fix the questioner with her piercing eyes and answer that "They don't know no better. It's the way they was brought up." While she was in Boston she visited in the homes of the writer Ralph Waldo Emerson and the philosopher Bronson Alcott, father of Louisa May Alcott. Author Thomas Wentworth Higginson wrote his mother, "We have the greatest heroine of the age here, Harriet Tubman . . . . She has been in the habit of working in hotels all summer and laying up money for this crusade in the winter. She is jet black and cannot read or write, only *talk* . . . ."

During the Civil War Harriet Tubman operated for the Northern forces in a quasi-official position, working in hospitals and camps as a nurse, spy, scout, and intermediary between slaves and the Northern soldiers. After nursing the sick in the daytime, she would bake fifty or so pies in the evening, and next day put them up for sale. So she supported herself.

In her spy work she would make her way through Southern picket lines to get an idea of defenses. A sentry would scarcely notice the little old black woman trudging along in a coarse dress, a bandana on her head. She organized a scouting service, at one time had nine scouts and river pilots under her supervision. She provided information on inland areas—pointed out where Negroes were waiting, half-starved, for a chance to join the Northern forces. She was employed by Northern troops to act as scout in a raid up the Combahee River in South Carolina. When the gunboats advanced, the Negroes took to the swamps in fear. But she passed word around that these were "Lincoln's gunboats." Then down every road and across every field the slaves swarmed, until the boats were crowded to the point of sinking. Later she chuckled, "We took away 756 head of their most valuable livestock."

No wonder Colonel Montgomery, who was in charge of the raid, wrote to Brigadier General Gilmore: "I wish to commend to your attention Mrs. Harriet Tubman, a most remarkable woman and invaluable as a scout."

During this period she met Nelson Davis, an enlisted man from Philadelphia. They were married in 1864.

After the war Harriet Tubman returned to Auburn, New York. She was tired out, half sick. She had received only $200 for her three years of service. However, leading citizens of Auburn and friends everywhere saw that she was made comfortable. The Salvation Army sent funds. The proceeds ($1,200) accruing from a biography by Sarah Bradford, *Scenes in the Life of Harriet Tubman,* went for her support. The reformer Wendell Phillips saw her through one winter by providing money for fuel. The suffragists of Boston gave a benefit party for her.

But money given to her quickly evaporated. The needy were forever knocking at her door, and she could turn no one away. She was providing funds for two schools for freedmen in the South. Soon, to raise money, she was going from house to house, selling produce that she and her dependents raised on her bit of land.

Finally an appeal was made by Congressman Ray of New York before the House of Representatives: "She acted as a nurse in the hospitals, as a cook, as a courier messenger and spy during the whole period of the war," he told the congressmen. "She is old and very poor and an object of charity." This brought her a government pension of twenty dollars a month for the rest of her life. From this amount and from what she was given by others, she bought some twenty-five acres of land adjoining her house and in 1903 deeded it and her home to the African Methodist Episcopal Zion Church there for a community farm. In 1908 a center was opened on this property to house whoever was in need. Here Harriet Tubman spent her last days.

On June 12, 1914, the year after her death, a "Day of Demonstration" was organized in Auburn. The mayor issued the Proclamation: "Let all display flags . . . that the memory of faithful old slave Harriet Tubman may be honored." The Negro educator Booker T. Washington reminded those who gathered for the event that she had "brought the two races nearer together [and] made it possible for the white race to place a higher estimate upon the black race."

BIBLIOGRAPHY

BRADFORD, SARAH ELIZABETH (HOPKINS), *Harriet Tubman, the Moses of Her People.* New York: G. R. Lockwood & Son, 1886.

BUCKMASTER, HENRIETTA, *Let My People Go; the Story of the Underground Railroad and the Growth of the Abolition Movement.* New York: Harper & Brothers, 1941.

CONRAD, EARL, *Harriet Tubman, Negro Soldier and Abolitionist.* New York: International Publishers Co., Inc., 1942.

SILLEN, SAMUEL, *Women Against Slavery.* New York: Masses & Mainstream, 1955.

"BABE" DIDRIKSON ZAHARIAS

(*MILDRED ELLA*) *"BABE" DIDRIKSON ZAHARIAS: Born in Port Arthur, Texas, June 26, 1914. Died in Galveston, Texas, September 27, 1956. Father: Ole Didrikson; mother: Hannah Marie (Olson) Didrikson; brothers and sisters: Dora, Ole, Ester Nancy, Louis and Lillie (twins), and Arthur; husband: George Zaharias.*

*

Mildred (Babe) Didrikson Zaharias was the foremost all-round athlete in American sports history. In the Olympics of 1932 she excelled in three categories: javelin throwing; the hurdle race; and the high jump. She held the women's record for a baseball throw. She hit the longest drive of any woman golfer. She won every available golf title from 1940 to 1950. She was also outstanding in shot-put, discus throwing, tennis, billiards, diving, figure skating, and lacrosse. Sportswriter Grantland Rice said of her: "The Babe . . . is without any question the athletic phenomenon of all time, man or woman."

*

MILLY was born right into an athletic team—six brothers and sisters, all enthusiastic about sports. In Beaumont, Texas, where the family had moved when Milly was three and a half years old, they had a regular gymnasium in the back yard.

"Babe" Didrikson Zaharias

Their father had set it up, with bars for jumping, a weight for lifting (flat-irons suspended from the ends of a broomstick), and trapezes for doing acrobatic stunts. The children also played baseball in the yard. Their mother scolded them at first when they threw balls into her rose bushes. But after she had been invited to play herself and had thrown a few balls wild, she didn't complain anymore.

Soon the back yard wasn't big enough to hold the Didrikson athletes. They spread out into the whole neighborhood. The long smooth sidewalk in front of the grocery was just right for a roller-skating rink. (The grocer's children joined in the fun.) They raced the streetcars from stop to stop. A new house going up had a large sand pile and they flung themselves down it. Then there were lovely rows of hedges dividing the back yards of the block. These they used as hurdles. One hedge was a bit too high, but an obliging neighbor cut it down to size.

Indoors, life was one big athletic tryout, too. It was Milly's job to scrub the linoleum floor of the sleeping porch every other week. This was an area built around the back of the house by their father, one side for the boys, one for the girls. She would tie scrubbing brushes to her feet and skate around on the suds. When finances were low—her father couldn't always earn enough from his craft as cabinetmaker to meet the expenses of a growing family—her mother took in washing. Then the children would pitch in and help, make a race of it, see who could hang the most clothes on the lines in the shortest time.

Both Mr. and Mrs. Didrikson were in sympathy with their children's activities. Mrs. Didrikson had been an expert skier in her native Norway. In 1928, the year the Olympic Games were held in Switzerland, the whole family sat around the supper table and discussed the winners and how they came to win. Even then, at the age of fourteen, Milly vowed she

"Babe" Didrikson Zaharias

would somehow get into the Olympics in 1932, when they were to be held in the United States. And she'd come out ahead! She once wrote, "All my life I've always had the urge to do things better than anybody else. Even in school, if it was something like making up a current events booklet, I'd want mine to be the best in the class." At school she beat the typewriting speed record. She also designed a sports dress that won first prize.

At Beaumont High School Milly soon qualified for the basketball team. This team traveled around the state, competing with other high schools. She began to be singled out for her playing: "Beaumont Girl Stars in Basketball Game!"—her first newspaper notice. When the team played in Houston in 1930, M. J. McCombs, head of the women's athletic program in the Employers' Casualty Company in Dallas, Texas, went over to Houston to have a look at this crack basketball player. What he witnessed at the game interested him so much that he traveled to nearby Beaumont and had a talk with Milly's mother. The upshot was that Mildred Didrikson, after arranging to complete her high school work in the spring and be graduated with her class, went to Dallas as an employee of the Employers' Casualty Company. She got seventy-five dollars a month to start and sent forty-five of it home.

This move to Dallas meant more than just getting a job. Young women in the late 1920's were beginning to go in seriously for careers in athletics. The Dallas company had built up its athletic program to national importance. Its girls' basketball team, the Golden Cyclone Athletic Club, was the best amateur team in the country. In 1931, the year after she became a member, the team won the national championship. So in reality, when she took her first job, Mildred Didrikson began her athletic career.

The company had an expert coaching program. The "Babe" —they had begun to call Mildred that by now, because, like

(433)

the famous baseball star "Babe" Ruth, she was such a record-breaker—went in for every sort of training offered: discus and javelin throwing, broad and high jumps, fifty, one hundred, and two hundred yard dashes, fancy diving, motor-boat racing. She worked consistently and thoroughly. She found, for instance, that she couldn't beat the then-current record for high jump with her old-fashioned scissors jump. So, although it took her days, even weeks, to master it, she shifted to the western roll. (In this, the jumper, when he reaches the top of the bar, is in a horizontal position, with his feet a little ahead of the rest of his body. Then he just "rolls" over the bar.)

In 1932 the Employers' Casualty was one of the entrants in the National Amateur Athletic Union track and field meet held at Northwestern University in Evanston, Illinois. This meet served also as a tryout for the Olympics. So of course Mildred Didrikson had her heart set on competing in it.

On his side, McCombs had made a careful study of her abilities. Now, instead of sending a dozen or so girls to play in the different women's sports events, he decided that he would send just Mildred Didrikson—a "one-woman team." If she made her usual scorings, he reasoned, she would win enough points to bring home the banner.

On the opening day at the Dyche Stadium at Northwestern University, the various other teams, each with a dozen or so members, were presented. Finally the "team" of the Employers' Casualty was announced. Out sprinted the Babe, waving her arms and grinning her infectious grin. A roar went up that she was to remember for the rest of her life. She always thought of this as the beginning of her career.

She was busy enough that day. She would take a high jump, then run in the eighty-meter hurdles. Then she would go to another location and take the standing broad jump. Next she would do a baseball throw, then fling the javelin, then "put" an eight-pound shot. Out of eight events, she won five outright, and "placed" in two others. Altogether, she won thirty points, enough not only to win the Amateur Athletic Union national championship for Employers' Casualty but also to qualify for entrance in the Olympics. George Kirksey, who covered the meet for the United Press, called her work "the most amazing series of performances ever accomplished by an individual, male or female, in track or field history."

The Olympics were held in Los Angeles in July, a few weeks after the Evanston event. Even on the train going there Mildred Didrikson kept in condition. She jogged up and down the whole length of the train. She practiced hurdle bends in the aisles.

The Olympic Games of 1932 made her a national figure. Contestants in the Olympics were allowed to enter not more than three events each, but with her three events she set the world record in javelin throwing, won the eighty-meter hurdle race, and beat the world's record in the high jump. In the latter event a technicality prevented her from being awarded first place. The judges decided her feet did not precede her body over the bar. (Today this rule has been relaxed.) But, though she made only second place, in actuality she had set the high jump record.

A huge homecoming celebration awaited her in Dallas. The mayor and other dignitaries came to the airport to greet her. In a tickertape motorcade through the downtown streets of Dallas she sat in an open car, waving, and having, as she said, "a whale of a time."

This Olympic episode had another effect on her career: It introduced her to golf. While she was in Los Angeles, sportswriter Grantland Rice invited her out to a nearby course to see how she took to the game. Her performance showed that golf was to become another of her triumphs.

But in training for golf there were problems of financing to be considered. She would need at least a year of training to perfect herself. But how to save up enough money for this? She knew she could not accumulate enough working at the Employers' Casualty. So she took a leave of absence and went on the RKO vaudeville circuit. On stage, against a black velvet backdrop, she ran on a treadmill with a companion running competitively on another treadmill. A big clock marked the time. She drove imitation golf balls. She skimmed hurdles. When she had saved enough to pay for a training period, she flung herself into a regime of golf practice in Los Angeles. She drove a thousand golf balls a day. She drilled until there was "tape all over my hands and blood all over the tape."

When her money ran out, she would go on exhibition tours again. For a while she was the only girl member of The Babe Didrikson All-American Basketball Team and of the House of David baseball team. She pitched for the St. Louis Cardinals in an exhibition game. About her baseball record: She once hit three home runs in one game. She made a 313-foot throw from centerfield to the plate.

In November 1934 she entered her first golf tournament—the Fort Worth Women's Tournament. A newspaper report stated: "Wonder girl makes her debut in tournament golf; turns in 77 score."

She now had her sights set to win the Texas State Tournament, which was to be held in the spring of 1935. But again her finances were at a low ebb. She went back with Employers' Casualty. Weekends she put in twelve to sixteen hours a day on golf practice. Weekdays she got up at dawn, and practiced from 5:30 to 8:30 A.M. She was allowed to use one of the offices for lunchtime practice. When her workday ended at 3:30 P.M., she was ready for more links practice. Nights she absorbed the golf rule book.

She won the Texas State championship. Now a problem arose. Because she had put on exhibitions for the RKO circuit, the United States Golf Association decided (belatedly) that she was "professional." (All sports are divided into two categories, amateur and professional. Professionals get financial remuneration. Amateurs work for the sheer joy of engaging in the activities, and of course for the honors—prizes, medals, loving cups, and such. The amateur status is considered more in the spirit of sport, untainted by any hint of commercialism.) She was therefore disqualified from further amateur golf tournaments. Just starting her golf career, this was a terrible setback. "The bottom dropped out of everything," she said.

But she wouldn't give up. She was determined to get back her amateur standing. But how to get the money to keep herself in training? She solved the problem by turning professional in earnest—signed a contract with a sporting goods company, became namesake to a line of women's golf equipment, played exhibition matches. In 1936 she toured with leading male golfer Gene Sarazen, playing exhibitions with him in the United States and Australia.

During this period she could, of course, enter tournaments for professionals. At the Los Angeles Open Tournament she met George Zaharias, a husky young wrestler and an expert at golf. It was love at first sight. They were married December 23, 1938. They combined their wedding trip with a golf exhibition trip to Australia.

Back in California in the fall of 1939 they came to a decision. Now was the time for Mildred to get back her amateur standing. Her husband was happy to see her through the three-year waiting period required for such a reinstatement. At last, on January 21, 1944, she was declared an amateur.

A steady winning streak followed. She came out ahead in the Western Women's Open, the Women's Texas Open, and the Broadmoor Invitational Tournaments. In the annual Associated Press poll she was chosen the Woman Athlete of the Year. She was to win this award eight times.

In 1946 she played in the National Women's tournament, her goal for years, and won by the biggest margin in the history of the contest. With the opening of the 1947 golf season in Florida, she won six tournaments in six weeks. In Georgia on March 30 she took the Women's Titleholders Championship.

Her next try was even more daring. She entered the British Women's Amateur title. This meet was held in Edinburgh, Scotland, in June 1947. From the start of this series in 1893 no American woman had ever come back the winner. The feeling was that it couldn't be done. So of course the Babe did it. British golf writer Fred Pignon headlined an article about her "Our Girls Shaken by Golf Babe" and called her manner of crashing her way "over the hills and dales of this testing, undulating course . . . the most tremendous exhibition of long driving ever seen in women's golf." Mildred Zaharias' feat was even more remarkable when one considers that British links are much more difficult than ours. They are left in the rough, become tangled jungles, and bad shots are severely penalized.

Both the British and the American sports fans liked the Babe for her informality. She established empathy with her audiences. "Boy, don't you men wish you could hit a ball like that!"; "Watch this. My best shot of the day."

On her way back to America, when her boat was still two hours and forty minutes out of New York harbor, a convoy of seventy-two reporters and photographers came out to meet her. Her husband was with them. There was dancing on the deck that day.

Back in Denver—this city had become the Zaharias home after their marriage—the citizens put on a parade with floats, depicting the stages of the Babe's career: basketball, baseball, javelin throwing, hurdling, golf. Babe sat in an embankment of roses on the last float and threw flowers to the crowd. The mayor and governor welcomed her to City Hall and presented her with an enormous key to the city.

Now she had won every major amateur title. Her nieces and nephews needed help in their higher education. So she again went professional. Dress manufacturers, sporting goods companies, shoe companies, sought her endorsement. She brought out a golf instruction book, *Championship Golf*. She gave golf exhibitions. She taught professional golf at the Sky Crest Country Club outside Chicago, the first woman to hold such a key teaching job. She and her husband established The Ladies Professional Golf Association. In its second year she became its president.

In 1950 the Associated Press Club voted her The Woman Athlete of the Half Century. During her life she personally won ninety-two medals for sports feats.

It is this half-century mark that must be used as a dividing line between two distinct parts of Mildred Didrikson's life. She had won practically all the top golf tournaments. But now she had a setback. She began to experience severe pains in her left side. She consulted doctors. She was told that she had cancer. She took the news with the same courageous spirit that she had taken obstacles in her hurdle races. Somehow or other she would come out on top. "All my life I've been competing—and competing to win," she wrote in her autobiography. "I came to realize that in its way, this cancer was the toughest competition I'd faced yet. I made up my mind that I was going to lick it all the way. I not only wasn't going to let it kill me, I wasn't even going to let it put me on the shelf. I was determined to come back and win golf championships just the same as before."

At first it really seemed that she would do it. In a matter of months after her first operation she was back on the course. She won the five-thousand-dollar Serbin Women's Open Tournament of Miami Beach and the National Open Tournament. For her sheer grit she was awarded the Ben Hogan trophy (given by the Golf Writers) for overcoming a physical handicap. She was invited to the White House to meet President and Mrs. Eisenhower and officially to tee off a Cancer Crusade. She made personal appearances—spoke on radio and over television—in behalf of cancer projects.

But it became clear that she would have to undergo another operation. She withdrew from her golf and went with her husband to Florida, to a house they had in Tampa. She dictated her autobiography. She and her husband established the Babe Didrikson Zaharias Fund to support cancer clinics and treatment centers. They also established a trophy in her name to be awarded each year to the woman athlete who had done the most for amateur sports in the United States.

At her death President Eisenhower paid a tribute to her courage. He added, "Everyone of us feels sad that finally she had to lose."

BIBLIOGRAPHY

CLYMER, ELEANOR, and ERLICH, LILLIAN, *Modern American Career Women*. New York: Dodd, Mead & Company, Inc., 1959.

ZAHARIAS, MILDRED, *This Life I've Led; My Autobiography*, as told to Harry Paxton. New York: A. S. Barnes & Company, 1955.

INDEX

abolitionism, 36, 40-41, 426-429
  Mott and, 325, 328-330, 331, 333-334
  Stowe and, 413, 415-418
Adams, Ansel, 251
Adams, John Quincy, 182, 183, 333
Addams, Jane, 1-11, *foll.* 84
Addams, John H., 1; quoted, 2
African Methodist Episcopal Zion Churches, 425, 430
Aiken, Senator George, 397
  quoted, 396
Aikens, George L., 417
Alabama, 143, 234, 235, 321
Albert I, king of Belgium, 168
Alcott, Abigail, 12, 13-14, 18, 22
  quoted, 15, 16, 17
Alcott, Amos Bronson, 12, 13, 15, 16, 18, 20, 21, 419, 428
  quoted, 14, 17, 179
  death of, 23
  Temple School of, 184
Alcott, Louisa May, 12-23, *foll.* 84, 146, 179, 256, 428
American Academy of Arts and Letters, 57, 109, 216
American Academy of Arts and Sciences, 258-259, 295, 299
American Association for the Advancement of Science, 284, 285, 289
American Association of Anatomists, 367
American Ballet Theater, 116, 117-118, 120, 121
American Birth Control League, 282, 283
American Cancer Society, 223
American Civil Liberties Union, 10, 383
American Foundation for the Blind, 241
American Museum of Natural History, New York, 279, 284, 285
American National Theater and Academy (ANTA), 57, 121
Amherst College, 125, 265-266, 273, 413
Anderson, John and Anna, 24, 25, 26
Anderson, Marian, 24-35, *foll.* 84, 354
Anderson, Sherwood, quoted, 405
Andersonville National Cemetery, 64
animals: Langer study, 255, 257, 258, 260
  Sabin study, 365, 366
Anthony, Joseph, 116
Anthony, Susan B., 36-47, 64, 65, *foll.* 84, 333
anthropology, 225, 231-232, 275-286
Anti-Slavery Convention of American Women (1839), 329
Anti-Slavery Society, 40-41
Arizona, 372, 385
Arkansas, 249
art (*see also particular arts,* i.e., dance; music; painting; poetry; sculpture; theater), 35, 152, 156, 255, 257, 399, 403
  anthropology and, 281, 282
  at Hull House, 4, 6

Index

art (*continued*)
  philosophy and, 255, 257, 258, 260
  televised auction, 90
Arthur, Chester, 66, 67
astronomy, 295-304
athletics, 6, 388, 431-440
Atkinson, Brooks, quoted, 56
Atlantic Monthly, 19, 129, 308, 419
Austria, 81, 190
  Vienna, 30, 145, 153, 256, 291, 399
Avery, Joseph, 271
aviation, 162-172

Babcock, Rufus, 300-301
Bachrach, Helen, quoted, 401
Baker, Abigail, 173, 174, 175
Baker, Abigail Barnard, 173, 174
Baker, Rachel Higgins, 314
Baker, Willoughby, 314
Ballet Russe de Monte Carlo, 116-118
Ballet Theater, 116, 117-118, 120, 121
Baltimore, Maryland, 46, 146, 213, 343, 344-345
  Sabin and, 362-364, 366, 367
  Stein in, 399, 400-401
Bankhead, Tallulah, quoted, 57
Baptists, 264
Barnard College, 163, 276, 277, 288
Barnes, Clive, quoted, 201
Barrymore, Ethel, 48-58, *foll.* 84
Barrymore, Georgiana Drew, 48, 49, 50
Barrymore, John, 48, 49, 52, 53, 54
Barrymore, Lionel, 48, 49, 53, 56
  quoted, 52, 55
Barrymore, Maurice, 48, 49, 50, 52

Barton, Clara, 59-69, *foll.* 84
Barton, Capt. Stephen, 59, 60
Bateson, Gregory, 275, 282
Beecher, Catherine, 273, 412, 413
Beecher, Mrs. Edward, quoted, 415
Beecher, Henry Ward, 411, 413
Beecher, Lyman, 410-411
Beecher, Roxana Foote, 410, 411
Bell, Alexander Graham, 239
Bellini, Vincenzo, 339, 342, 343, 344
Benedict, Ruth, 277; quoted, 282
Bethune, Albertus, 71, 74
Bethune, Mary McLeod, 71-80, *foll.* 84
Bethune-Cookman College, 71, 77-78, 80
birth control:
  abortion laws and, 275, 284, 374
  Sanger and, 372-386
Birth Control Review, 372, 382
Blaine, James G., quoted, 66
Blakeslee, Clarence, 317
blindness, 234-244, 352
Block, Anita, 374
blood vessel study, 361, 365-366, 367
Bloomer, Amelia, 38
Boas, Dr. Franz, 276-277
Boghetti, Giuseppe, 26, 27-28
Bohemian immigrants, 102, 106, 107
Boissevain, Eugen Jan, 287, 291, 293
Bolm, Adolph, 114
Bond, George, 299-300
Bond, William C., 297
Borglum, Gutzon, 227
Boston, Massachusetts, 9, 53, 94, 98, 105, 159, 194, 231
  Alcott in, 14, 16, 17, 18, 19, 21, 22
  Dix in, 137, 138, 139, 140, 142

(*442*)

Index

Earhart in, 164, 166
Eddy in, 173, 176, 177, 178-180
Fuller in, 184-186, 187
Public Library, 303
slavery issue in, 328, 415, 419, 429
Sullivan in, 235
Bowdoin College, 414, 415, 416
Bowen, Louise de Koven, 10
Bowles, Samuel, 130
  quoted, 134
Braddy, Nella, 238
Bradford, Sarah, 429
Brahms, Johannes, 152
brain anatomy, 361, 364
Branhan, Grace, quoted, 214
Bridgman, Laura, 236
Britten, Benjamin, 121
Brooke, Rupert, 312
Broun, Heywood, quoted, 54
Brown, John, 427
Brown, John Mason, quoted, 217
Browning, Elizabeth Barrett, 41, 187, 189
Brownson, Orestes, quoted, 187
Bryant, William Cullen, 300
  quoted, 187
Bryn Mawr College, 212, 213, 214
Burne-Jones, Sir Edward, 104
Butler, Nicholas Murray, 10
Byrne, Ethel, 380, 381

Cabrini, Frances Xavier, saint, 81-89, *foll.* 84
Caldwell, Eunice, 270
California (*see also* San Francisco, Calif.), 50, 109, 163, 166, 201, 248-250, 253
  Hollywood, 48, 55, 57, 112, 115, 116, 118
  Los Angeles, 86, 87, 118, 169, 202, 435, 436, 437
  Oakland, 169, 170, 193, 247, 399-400
  University of, 113, 194, 247

Canada, 50, 107, 283, 343, 377
  Dix in, 142, 144
  Roosevelt in, 351, 355
  Tubman in, 427
cancer, 252, 400, 439, 440
Carlyle, Thomas, 103, 188-189, 300, 418
  quoted, 13
Cartier, Jacques, 114
Caruso, Enrico, 338-339, 340-341, 342, 344
Cassatt, Alexander, 91, 94, 95
Cassatt, Katherine K., 90, 93, 94, 95, 96, 97, 98
Cassatt, Lydia, 91, 95
Cassatt, Mary, *foll.* 84, 90-100
Cassatt, Robert Simpson, 90-91, 92, 93, 94, 97
Cather, Roscoe, 101, 103, 109
Cather, Willa, *foll.* 84, 101-110
Catholics, 81-89, 145, 150, 190, 306
Catt, Carrie Chapman, 9
Cézanne, Paul, 403
Channing, William Ellery, 15, 184
  Dix and, 138-139, 140, 141
Chase, George and Carrie, 387, 388
Chase, Lucia, 116
Chicago, Illinois, 45, 69, 97, 99, 151, 163, 232, 303, 383
  Addams and, 1, 4-11
  Bethune in, 81, 86, 87, 88
  Eddy in, 178
  Fire of 1871, 92, 306
  Monroe in, 305-306, 307-312
  Sabin in, 362
Chicago Columbian Exposition (1893), 45, 97, 307
Chicago Natural History Museum (Field Museum), 225, 231
Chicago *Tribune*, 217, 307, 308, 310

(443)

Index

children, 38, 41, 150, 189
  civil rights of, 314-321, 323
  labor of, 7-8, 71
  orphan, 81-88, 235
  slave, 421-423, 426
Chopin, Frédéric, 156
Chrissman, Mary, 72-73
Christian Science Monitor, The (newspaper), 173, 179
Church of Christ, Scientist, 173, 175-180
civil rights, 139, 392-394
  of children, 323
  of Negroes, 314-323, 329, 334
  of women, 43-44, 325, 330-334
Civil War, 91, 315
  Alcott and, 19-20
  Anthony and, 40, 41
  Barton and, 59, 62-64, 66, 69
  Dix, and, 145-146
  Mott and, 328, 333
  Stowe and, 410, 412, 418
  Tubman and, 428-429
Clarke, James Freeman, 182-183
Cleveland, Grover, 243
Coffin, Thomas, 325, 326, 327
Cohn, Dr. Alfred, quoted, 370-371
Colorado (*see also* Denver, Colo.), 361, 369-371
Colt, Ethel Barrymore, 48, 53, 55
Colt, Russell Griswold, 48, 53
Columbia University, 163, 164, 194, 229, 246, 303
  Earhart at, 163
  Langer at, 258, 259
  Mead and, 277, 283, 284, 285
  Motley and, 318, 322
Coolidge, Calvin, 166
Cooper, Dr. James, 384
Copland, Aaron, 35, 117
Corbally, Winifred, 243
Cornell, Katharine, 57, 205
Correggio, Antonio Allegri da, 92

Corrigan, Michael A., archbishop of New York, 84
Cox, James M., 351
Cox, Kenyon, 53
Crafts, Hiram S., 175-176
Craig, Gordon, 153-154
Culp, Isaac William, 218, 219, 220
Culver, Helen, 4
Cunningham, Merce, 204
Curie, Marie, 366

Damrosch, Walter, 32, 156
  quoted, 155
dance, 246, 255, 257
  de Mille and, 111-123
  Duncan and, 149-161
  Graham and, 201-210
  Hoffman sculpture themes from, 228, 229, 232
Dance Theater, 115, 118
Daughters of the American Revolution (DAR), 24, 31-32, 33, 354
Davis, George, 182
Davis, Nelson, 421, 429
Daytona Educational and Industrial Training School for Negro Girls, 75-78
"Declaration of Conscience" (Smith), 393-394
Declaration of Human Rights (United Nations), 347, 357-358
Declaration of Sentiments (Women's Rights), 331-332
Dégas, Edgar, Cassatt and, 93-94, 95, 96, 97, 99
Delaware, 27, 257
Dell, Floyd, quoted, 149
de Mille, Agnes, *foll.* 84, 111-123, 202, 207
de Mille, Anna George, 111, 112, 113, 116
de Mille, William Churchill, 111, 112, 113, 118

(*444*)

Index

Denham, Serge Ivanovitch, 116-117
Denishawn Company, 202, 203
Denmark, 28, 46, 114, 120, 160, 208
   King's Gold Medal, 295, 298, 299
Denver, Colorado, 72, 86, 87, 379, 438-439
   Sabin in, 361, 363, 369, 370
Depression, The (1930's), 198
   Lange and, 247-250, 252, 253
   Monroe and, 312
   Roosevelt (Eleanor) and, 352, 353
DeWitt, William, 359
Diaghilev, Sergei, 155
   quoted, 154
Dial, The (periodical), 15, 185-186
Dickens, Charles, 300, 418
Dickinson, Edward, 124, 125, 126, 127, 131
Dickinson, Emily, *foll.* 84, 124-135, 206
Dickinson, Lavinia Norcross, 124, 125, 126, 129, 130, 132, 134
Dickinson, Dr. Robert L., 384
Dickinson, Susan Gilbert, 127
Dickinson, William Austin, 124, 125, 126, 127
Didrikson, "Babe," 431-440
Didrikson, Ole and Hannah, 431, 432
Dirksen, Everett, quoted, 396
disaster relief services, 66, 67-68, 78, 219
disease (*see also* cancer; tuberculosis; yellow fever), 18, 20, 133, 142, 273, 348
   childbearing and, 373, 375
   Eddy view of, 174-176, 177, 178, 180
   mental, 136-137, 139, 140-147, 187
   sanitation and, 7, 146, 361, 369, 370
divorce, 38, 150, 175
Dix, Dorothea, *foll.* 84, 136-148
Dixon, Daniel Rhodes, 245, 246, 251, 253
Dixon, Maynard, 245, 246, 248
Dodd, Joseph, quoted, 143
Dodge, Mabel, quoted, 404
Douglass, Frederick, quoted, 426
Dow, Caroline B., 288
Drew, Mrs. John, 48, 49, 50, 52
   quoted, 51
drought, 66, 67, 219, 247-249
Drysdale, C. V., 377-378
Duke, Ashley, 115
Dulles, John Foster, quoted, 357
Dunant, Jean Henri, 65
Duncan, Elizabeth, 149, 150, 151, 154
Duncan, Irma, 158
   quoted, 152-153
Duncan, Isadora, *foll.* 84, 149-161, 246, 381
Duncan, Mary Dora, 149, 150, 151, 152
Duncan, Sarah Lynde, 137
Duse, Eleanora, 157

Earhart, Amelia, 162-172, 198, *foll.* 212
Earhart, Edwin Stanton, 162, 163-164
Eastman, Max, quoted, 150, 155, 292
Eddy, Asa Gilbert, 173, 177
Eddy, Mary Baker, 105, 173-180, *foll.* 212
education (*see also* teaching):
   Addams and, 3, 4, 5, 6, 8
   Cabrini and, 81-88
   Dix and, 137-139
   Lyon and, 263-274
   feminist movement and, 22, 37, 38, 185, 263-274, 300-301, 303,

Index

education (*continued*)
    332, 334, 362-363, 364, 366, 412
  free, 61
  of the handicapped, 234-243
  industrial, 198, 199
  Negro, 71-80, 314, 315-321, 329, 429
  night schools, 189
Einstein, Albert, quoted, 234
Eisenhower, Dwight David, 33, 218, 223
  quoted, 440
Elder, Louisine, 95, 98-99
Eliot, George, 150
Eliot, T. S., 311
Elliott, Edward G., 169
Ellis, Havelock, 378, 382
Emancipation Proclamation, the, 315, 334, 418-419
Emerson, Ellen, 16
Emerson, Rev. Joseph, 266
Emerson, Ralph Waldo, 126, 428
  Alcott and, 15, 19
  Fuller and, 183, 184, 185, 186, 187, 189
  Mott and, 329, 333
engineering, 193
  psychology and, 194-195, 198, 199
England (*see also* London, England), 43, 310, 312, 376, 390
  Addams in, 2, 9
  Anderson in, 28, 29
  Barrymore in, 49, 51-52, 53, 56
  Cabrini in, 86
  Cather in, 104, 105
  Civil War and, 418-419
  de Mille in, 114, 115
  Dix in, 139, 145
  Duncan in, 152, 155, 156, 158
  Earhart in, 165-166, 168
  Fuller in, 188-189
  Hobby in, 222
  Hoffman in, 230
  Mead in, 283
  Millay in, 291
  Mott in, 330-331
  Ponselle in, 343
  Roosevelt in, 349, 355, 358
  Smith in, 395
  Stowe in, 417
Esenin, Sergei, 149, 159, 160
Evatt, Herbert V., quoted, 358

Farrar, John, 183, 184
feminism, 22, 36-47
  Barton and, 61, 62, 64-65
  Bethune and, 79
  Cassatt and, 97
  Earhart and, 163, 164-165, 166, 167, 168, 169-170, 198
  Eddy and, 179
  Fuller and, 181-192
  Hamilton and, 212
  Lyon and, 263-274
  Mead and, 275, 282, 283
  Millay and, 288, 290
  Mott and, 325, 326-327, 329-334
  Roosevelt and, 350, 352, 354
  Sabin and, 362-363, 366
  Sanger and, 376
  Smith and, 392, 396-397
  Stowe and, 412
Fisher, Orpheus H., 24, 27
Fisk University, 79, 317-318
Flexner, Dr. Simon, 367
  quoted, 368
floods, 66, 67
Florida, 67, 170, 438, 440
  Bethune in, 71, 74-78
Fokine, Michel, 154
Fontanne, Lynn, quoted, 57
Fortune, Reo F., 275, 279, 280-281
France (*see also* Paris, France), 145, 168, 190, 375, 395
Frankenstein, Alfred, quoted, 118

(*446*)

Index

Frederick VI, king of Denmark, 298
Fremstad, Olive, 107
Frohman, Charles, 51, 53, 55
Frost, Robert, 108, 216, 311
Fugitive Slave Law (1850), 415, 427
Fuller, Loie, 153
Fuller, Margaret, 181-192, *foll.* 212
Fuller, Sarah, 239
Fuller, Timothy, 181-182, 183
Fuller-Maitland, J., quoted, 152

Gaines, Lloyd, 315-316
Gamble, James N., 76
Garfield, James, quoted, 66
Garibaldi, Giuseppe, 191
Garrison, William Lloyd, 328, 333
Gatti-Casazza, Giulio, 336, 339, 340, 344
Genthe, Arnold, 246
George, Henry, 112
Georgia, 68, 74, 356, 438
  Atlanta, 79, 338, 343
Germany, 29, 91, 157, 211, 409
  Addams and, 2-3, 9, 10
  Anderson in, 28, 30, 33
  Anthony in, 45-46
  Dix in, 145
  Duncan in, 153, 154
  Hamilton in, 210, 212
  immigrants from, 245, 357
  Sabin in, 364, 366
Gibson, William, 238
Gilbreth, Ernestine, 193, 196
Gilbreth, Frank Bunker, 193, 194-197
Gilbreth, Frank B., Jr., 193, 196
Gilbreth, Lillian, 193-200, *foll.* 212
Gillette, William, 51
Glover, George Washington, 173, 174

Goerner, Fred, cited, 171-172
Goethe, Johann Wolfgang von, 183, 185
golf, 435-440
Gordon, Louis, 165
Graham, George, 201-202
Graham, Jane Beers, 201, 202
Graham, Martha, 201-210, *foll.* 212
Grant, Zilpah Polly, 266, 267, 268
Gray, Diane, 210
Greece, 145, 153, 158
  Duncan in, 158
  Hamilton and, 211, 212, 214-215, 216-217
Greeley, Horace, 38, 186-187, 188
  quoted, 40
Grimson, Samuel Bonarios, 225, 227, 230
Grosz, Alexander, 153
Guest, Mrs. Frederick, 165, 166
Guggenheim Fellowship, 205
Gutelius, Phyllis, 210

Hale, Edward Everett, quoted, 179
Halévy, Jacques, 342
Hallé, Charles, 152
Hamilton, Alice, 211, 212-213
Hamilton, Edith, 211-217, *foll.* 212
Hamilton, Gertrude Bond, 211, 212
Hamilton, Montgomery, 211, 213
Hammerstein, Oscar, 118, 119
Hampden, Walter, 55
Hapgood, Hutchins, quoted, 402
Harding, Warren Gamaliel, 351
Harper, Ida Husted, quoted, 43
Harvard University, 137, 164, 182, 185, 198, 256, 349, 401
  Observatory, 297
  War Memorial Chapel, 230
Haskell, Arnold, quoted, 114

(447)

Index

Havemeyer, Mrs. Henry O., 95, 98-99
Hawaii, 31, 162, 169, 170, 243, 277
Hawkins, Erick, 201, 204, 207
Hawthorne, Nathaniel, 15, 187, 300
Hayes, Roland, 26, 32
Hayes, Rutherford B., quoted, 66
Heath, Ann, 138, 144
Hegel, Georg W. F., 175-176
Heine, Heinrich, 104
Hemingway, Ernest, 405
Henry, Joseph, 299
Hepburn, Katharine, quoted, 57
Hickok, Lorena A., 359
Higgins, Michael and Anne, 372-373
Higginson, Thomas Wentworth, 129-130, 132, 134
  quoted, 131, 428
Hobby, Oveta Culp, *foll.* 212, 218-224
Hobby, William Pettus, 218, 220, 223, 224
Hoffman, Fidelia L., 225, 230
Hoffman, Malvina, *foll.* 212, 225-233
Hoffman, Paul Grey, quoted, 208
Hoffman, Richard, 225-226, 227
Hogan, Judith, 210
Holland, 9, 46, 145, 154, 208
  birth control in, 378
Holmes, Oliver Wendell, 419
Hoover, Herbert, 57, 78, 168, 368
Hopkins, Henry, 354
Horst, Louis, 116, 202, 203, 204, 205
hospitals (*see also* nursing), 77, 243, 352
  Catholic, 81, 83, 84-85, 86, 88
  mental, 136, 139, 140-147
  military, 19-20, 59-69, 146, 157, 350, 407, 428
Housman, A. E., 104

Houston, Charles, 318
Howard University, 31, 79
Howe, Dr. Samuel Gridley, 140, 141, 236
  quoted, 142
Hubbell, Julian B., 66
Hull House, 1, 4-7, 9, 10-11
Humphries, Rolfe, 293
Hurok, Sol, 29-30, 31, 159
Huysmans, J. K., quoted, 97

Ickes, Harold Le Clair, quoted, 32
Illinois (*see also* Chicago, Illinois), 67, 143
immigrants, 1, 4, 17, 164, 235
  Addams and, 6
  Cabrini and, 83-84
  Cather and, 102, 106, 107
  Lange and, 245, 251
  Mead (Emily) and, 275
India, 34, 208, 243, 251, 358-359
  Sanger in, 383, 384-385
Indiana, 24, 379
Indians, 205, 246
Ingersoll, Robert, 373
insanity, treatment of, 136-137, 139, 140-147, 187, 352
International Birth Control Conference (1925), 383-384
International Conference of Population Planning (1927), 384
International Congress of Women (The Hague, 1915), 9
International Cooperation Year, 283
International Council of Women (Berlin, 1904), 45-46
International Management Congress (1924), 197
International Women's Suffrage Alliance, 46
Ireland, 167, 168, 235, 252, 331

Index

Italian Revolution of 1848, 190-191
Italy, 30, 81-83, 120, 139, 208, 251, 291, 385, 403
    American immigrants from, 83-88
    Cassatt in, 91, 92, 98
    Duncan in, 157, 158
    Fuller in, 189-191
    Ponselle in, 343, 345

Jackson, Andrew, 183
Jackson, Carle A., 336, 344
Jackson, Helen Hunt, quoted, 132, 133-134
James, Henry, 53, 105
James, William, 401-402
Japan, 171, 172, 208, 259, 359
    American immigrants from, 251
    Keller in, 242-243
    Sanger and, 383, 385
Jewett, Sarah Orne, 105
Jews, 357
Johns Hopkins Medical College, 361, 362-364, 366-367, 368, 402
Johnson, Lyndon B., 34, 35, 224, 322
    quoted, 253
journalism:
    Cather and, 103-106
    Dix and, 142
    Earhart and, 166
    Eddy and, 173, 174, 178, 179
    Fuller and, 181, 185-189, 190
    Hobby and, 218, 220, 221, 223, 224
    Mead and, 275, 284
    Monroe and, 308-309
    Roosevelt and, 351, 353, 354, 355, 356
    Sanger and, 372, 374-375

    Smith and, 388, 392
    Stowe and, 415-416

Kansas, 40, 44-45, 162
Kant, Immanuel, 176, 184, 256
Kassarjian, Mary Catherine Bateson, 275, 282
Kay, Ellen, 376
Keller, Helen, *foll.* 212, 234-244
Kennedy, John Fitzgerald, 33, 243, 359
Kennedy, Richard, 176
Kentucky, 207, 333, 412, 413
Kerr, Walter, quoted, 119
Kilmer, Joyce, 312
King, Billy, 26
King of Denmark's Gold Medal, 295, 298, 299
Knauth, Antonio and Else, 255, 256
Kosloff, Theodore, 113

labor, 9, 74, 390-391
    conditions, 3, 7-8
    crafts, 6
    dance theatre, 122
    domestic, 16, 73, 316
    factory, 41, 352
    farm, 71, 247-250
    of the handicapped, 199, 224
    mine, 86, 355
    Negro employment and, 315, 316-317, 320, 322, 354
    night schools and, 189
    scientific management and, 193, 194-195, 196, 197-199
    slave, 421-422, 423, 424
    social security and, 223
    of working mothers, 5, 26, 60, 189
    wage rights of women, 38, 42, 326, 332, 334, 354
Lafayette, Marie Joseph, marquis de, 267

(*449*)

Index

Lane, Charles, 13-14
Laney, Lucy, 74
Lange, Dorothea, *foll.* 212, 245-254
Lange, Joanna, 245
Langer, Susanne Katherina, *foll.* 212, 255-262
Langer, William Leonard, 255, 256
League of Nations, 219, 230
League of Women Voters, 351, 354
lecturing, 8, 16-17, 99, 107, 121
  of Addams, 8
  of Alcott (Bronson), 16-17
  of Anthony, 37, 40-42, 44-45
  of Barton, 64-65, 66
  of Bethune, 78, 79
  of Duncan, 152, 157-158
  of Eddy, 178
  of Gilbreth, 196, 198, 199
  of Hamilton, 216
  of Hobby, 221-222
  of Keller, 240-241, 242-243
  of Langer, 257-258, 259
  of Mead, 275, 283
  of Millay, 292
  of Mitchell, 303
  of Monroe, 308, 313
  of Mott, 328, 329, 330, 331, 332-333
  of Roosevelt, 351, 353, 354, 355
  of Sabin, 369
  of Sanger, 379, 382-383, 384-385
  of Stein, 407-408
  of Stowe, 417, 419
  of Tubman, 428
Lee, Vernon (Violet Paget) quoted, 98
legislation, 218
  on abortion, 275, 284, 374
  on aid for the blind, 241-242
  censorship, 374-375, 376, 379, 380-381, 382-383, 384-385
  on civil rights, 314-324
  on divorce, 38
  on health, 369-370
  on insane asylums, 141-142, 143-145
  on labor, 7-8, 354, 390-391
  on legal aid, 321, 323
  on liquor, 289
  on military service, 390
  on poor relief, 245, 250
  on property rights, 39, 41, 42
  on slavery, 423, 427
  on suffrage, 38, 42-43, 46, 219, 350
  on Sunday theater, 122
  on taxation, 219
Lend-Lease Bill, 390
Leo XIII, pope, 83
Leonard, Warren, 114
Lewis, Edith, 106, 107, 108
Lieven, Prince Peter, quoted, 154
Lincoln, Abraham, 32, 62, 64, 316, 333
  Emancipation Proclamation, 315, 334, 410, 418-419
Lindbergh, Charles A., 165
Lindsay, Vachel, 310, 311
Lippmann, Walter, quoted, 380
literature:
  Alcott and, 12-23
  Cather and, 101-110
  de Mille and, 122
  Dickinson and, 124-135
  Dix and, 137, 138
  Duncan and, 160
  Earhart and, 163, 165, 166, 169, 171
  Eddy and, 173, 176-177, 178, 179
  Fuller and, 181, 183, 184-185, 187
  Gilbreth and, 196, 198
  Hamilton and, 211-217
  Hoffman and, 226, 232

Index

Keller and, 234, 240, 242, 243
Langer and, 257, 258, 259, 260
Mead and, 275, 279, 280, 281, 283
Millay and, 287-294
Monroe and, 305-313
Roosevelt and, 359
Sabin and, 363-364
Sanger and, 372, 375-377
Stein and, 399, 403-409
Stowe and, 410-420
Zaharias and, 439, 440
Litz, Katherine, 116
London, England, 2, 3-4, 28, 29, 52, 90, 105, 168, 358, 403
 Mott in, 330
 Sanger in, 377-378, 383
 slavery issue in, 330-331, 417-418
 Stowe in, 417
 theatre in, 49, 51, 56, 114, 115, 120, 121, 152, 155, 343
Loomis, Elias, 299
Lord, Judge Otis, 133, 134
Louisiana, 85, 86, 87, 220, 240
Louis Napoleon, 91
Lowell, Amy, 310, 311
Luce, Clare Boothe, quoted, 359
Lunt, Alfred, 57
Lyon, Aaron and Jemima, 263, 264
Lyon, Mary, 125, *foll.* 212, 263-274

Maas, Melvin J., 390
McCarthy, Joseph, 392-394
McClelland, Robert, quoted, 61
McClung, Isabelle, 104
McClure, S. S., 105, 106
McCombs, M. J., 433, 434
MacCracken, Henry N., 288-289
McGehee, Helen, 210

McKayle, Donald, 204
McLeod, Samuel and Patsy, 71, 72
Macy, John Albert, 234, 240, 242
Maine, 105, 107, 136, 137, 214, 241, 414-415
 Eddy in, 175
 Millay in, 287-288, 292
 Smith and, 387-397
Mall, Dr. Franklin Paine, 363-364, 365, 366
Mann, Horace, 140, 141
 quoted, 142
Maracci, Carmalita, 115
marriage, 13, 19, 60
 childbearing and, 284, 372-386
 Duncan view of, 150, 154, 155, 159
 interfaith, 190
 occupational partnership in, 194-195, 196, 197, 220, 248, 250, 279-281, 282, 327, 351-356, 389
 Quaker rite, 327
 rights of women in, 37, 38, 40, 41, 42, 167, 186, 282, 332
Marshall, Gen. George, 221
Marshall, Thurgood, 318
Martha Graham Company, 204, 208, 209-210
Martin, John, 114
Maryland (*see also* Baltimore, Maryland), 78, 144, 379
 Barton in, 59, 68, 69
 Tubman in, 421-424, 427
Maslow, Sophia, 204
Mason, Judge Charles, 61
Massachusetts (*see also* Boston, Mass.), 36, 176, 234, 416, 418
 Alcotts in, 12, 13, 14, 15, 18, 19, 21, 22
 Barton in, 59-60, 62, 69
 care of the blind in, 235-236, 242

(*451*)

Index

Massachusetts (*continued*)
  care of the insane in, 140-141, 142
  Dickinson in, 124, 126, 130, 131, 132, 133, 134
  Fuller in, 181, 182, 183, 184
  Keller in, 240, 241-242
  Lyon in, 263, 264, 265, 266, 268, 269, 270
  Nantucket Island, 295, 296, 297, 304, 325-326
  slavery issue in, 328, 415, 416, 418, 419, 429
  state legislature, 141-142, 181, 271
Massine, Leonide, 204
Masters, Edgar Lee, 311
Matisse, Henri, 403
Mayo, Rev. A. D., quoted, 40
Mazzini, Giuseppe, 190
Mead, Edward and Emily, 275-276
Mead, Margaret, *foll.* 212, 275-286
medicine (*see also* disease; hospitals; nursing), 164, 212, 351, 402, 440
  contraceptive and, 372-386
  Sabin and, 361-371
Mellour, C. C., 77
Meredith, James, 319-320
Metropolitan Opera, 33-34, 118
  de Mille and, 118
  Duncan and, 155, 158
  Ponselle and, 336, 338-344
Michigan, 68, 258
Mickiewicz, Adam, quoted, 189
military service, 390
  women in, 79, 218, 221-223, 390, 396, 428-429
Millay, Edna St. Vincent, *foll.* 276, 287-294
Missionary Sisters of the Sacred Heart, 82-88

Mississippi, 143, 319-320
Mississippi, University of, 319-320
Missouri, 153, 249, 316, 379, 436
Mitchell, Maria, *foll.* 276, 295-304
Mitchell, William and Lydia, 295, 296-298, 300
Mitropoulos, Dimitri, 33
Moller, William, 193, 194
Monroe, Harriet, 155, *foll.* 276, 290, 305-313
Monroe, Henry and Martha, 305, 306
Morris, Lloyd, quoted, 408
Moscowitz, Judge Grover, 385
Motley, Constance Baker, *foll.* 276, 314-324
Motley, Joel Wilson, 314, 318
Mott, James, 325, 327, 328, 332
Mott, Lucretia, *foll.* 276, 325-335
Mount Holyoke College, 125, 263, 270-274
Mundelein, Cardinal George, quoted, 88
music, 6, 203, 292, 308, 362, 411
  Anderson and, 24-35
  Barrymore and, 50, 51
  Bethune, 77
  de Mille and, 117
  Duncan and, 150, 151, 152-153, 154, 155, 156-157, 158, 159
  fugitive slaves and, 423, 425
  Graham and, 204-205, 207
  Langer and, 255, 256, 257, 260, 261
  Millay and, 288
  Ponselle and, 336-346
  Sabin and, 362
mythology, 211, 212, 215

Nathan, James, 188
National Association for the Ad-

(*452*)

Index

vancement of Colored People, 33, 78, 314, 318-319
National Council of Negro Women, 79
National Recovery Act, 354
National Woman Suffrage Association, 8, 45, 46, 334
National Youth Administration, 71, 78-79, 317
Nebraska, 101-108
Negroes (see also slavery; and see individual names), 42, 116
  discrimination against, 24, 30, 31-32, 33, 34, 35, 71, 314-324, 354
  education and, 71-80, 314, 318, 319-321, 329
Nevin, Ethelbert, 151
New Guinea, 171, 280-281, 282, 285
New Hampshire, 18, 173, 174, 175, 267
New Jersey, 86, 114, 191, 195, 245, 246, 373
  Barton in, 60-61
  care of the insane in, 136, 143, 147
  Newark, 53, 85, 169, 198
New Mexico, 106, 107, 108, 246
  Graham in, 205
Newton, Benjamin Franklin, 126
New York City, 40-41, 90, 146
  Anderson in, 27, 30-31, 33-35
  art galleries, 251, 252, 253, 403
  Barrymore in, 50-51, 52, 54, 56
  Bethune in, 77
  Cabrini in, 83-85, 87
  Cather in, 101, 105, 106, 108
  de Mille in, 111, 112, 113-114, 115, 118-120
  Duncan in, 151, 155, 157-158, 159
  Earhart in, 163, 166
  Fuller in, 188

  Gilbreth in, 194, 195
  Graham in, 203, 204, 206-208
  Hamilton in, 214-216
  Hoffman in, 225-229, 232-233
  Keller in, 239
  Lange in, 245, 246
  Langer in, 255, 256, 258, 259
  Mead in, 276, 279, 283, 284, 285
  Millay in, 287, 288, 289, 290
  Mitchell in, 303
  Monroe in, 306-307
  Motley in, 318-319, 321-323
  Mott in, 331, 333, 334
  Ponselle in, 337, 338-344
  Rockefeller Institute, 367-368, 370
  Roosevelt in, 347-348, 349, 352, 359
  Sanger in, 374, 376, 380-384
  Stein in, 407-408
  Stowe and, 415, 417
New York *Daily Tribune*, 186-187, 188-189, 190-191, 383
New York *Evening Post*, 102, 187
New York *Herald Tribune*, 28, 171, 282
New York State (see also New York City), 54, 234, 242, 259, 261, 287-294, 372
  Constitutional Convention, 44, 45
  Legislature, 39, 41, 321, 322, 350, 352, 429
  Rochester, 36, 37, 38-39, 41, 42-43, 67, 203
  slavery issue in, 40-41, 333-334, 421, 427, 429-430
New York Times, The, 30, 34, 119, 261, 279, 321, 355, 357
  on Sanger, 385-386
New York University, 57, 232, 258, 283, 318
New York *World*, 161, 307, 310
Niles, Thomas, 20, 21, 133

(453)

Index

Nobel Peace Prize, 10
Noonan, Fred, 170-171, 172
North Carolina, 73, 143
nursing, 41, 77, 390, 428
   Alcott and, 17, 18, 19-20, 146
   Barton and, 59-69
   Cabrini and, 84, 85, 86
   Cassatt and, 93
   Dickinson and, 132
   Dix and, 137, 145-146
   Negro education in, 318
   Sanger and, 373, 374
Nutzhorn, Henry, 245

Ohio, 208, 258, 331
   Cincinnati, 204, 273, 412, 413
   Cleveland, 166, 333, 343
Oklahoma, 249
Olympic Games, The, 431, 432-433, 434, 435
Oregon, 379
orphanages, 81-83
Ossoli, Giovanni Angelo, marquis, 181, 189-190, 191
Ossoli, Sarah Margaret Fuller, marquise, 181-192
Owen, Robert, 15

Paderewski, Ignace, 230
Paine, Thomas, 232
painting, 184, 203, 255, 257, 308
   Cassatt and, 90-100
   dance and, 113
   Stein and, 399, 403
Panelka, Anna, 107
Pankhurst, Emmeline, 376
Paris, France, 20, 29, 65, 120
   Cassatt in, 91, 92, 93-97, 100
   Cather in, 107
   de Mille in, 114
   Duncan in, 149, 152, 153, 155-156, 157, 158, 160
   Fuller in, 189
   Graham in, 208
   Hoffman in, 228, 229, 230-232
   Millay in, 291
   Sanger in, 375
   Stein in, 399, 403-409
Paris Salón, 92, 93, 94
Parker, Theodore, 15, 18
Patterson, Daniel, 173, 174
Paul, king of Greece, 216
Pavlova, Anna, 112, 207, 228, 229
Peabody, Elizabeth, 15, 185
Peirce, Cyrus, 295-296, 297
P.E.N., 312-313
Pennsylvania (*see also* Philadelphia, Pa.), 67, 78, 90, 143, 275, 399
   Alcott in, 12, 14
   Pittsburgh, 77, 91, 103-104, 201, 258, 259, 338
   Tubman in, 424-425
Perkins, Frances, 218
Perkins, Francis, quoted, 28
Philadelphia, Pennsylvania, 14, 45, 127, 128, 131, 343
   Anderson in, 24, 26, 27, 28, 33
   Barrymore in, 48, 49-50
   Cassatt in, 91, 92, 98
   Earhart in, 163
   Mead in, 275, 284
   Mott in, 325, 326, 327, 328, 329, 333, 334
   Tubman in, 425, 429
philanthropy:
   Addams on, 1, 3-4, 6-7
   Alcott family and, 16, 17
   Bethune and, 74-76, 77
   Cabrini and, 84, 86, 87
   Monroe and, 309-310, 312
   Roosevelt and, 353-354, 355
Phillips, Wendell, 429
philosophy, 11, 13-14, 15
   Eddy and, 174-177, 178, 179, 180
   Fuller and, 181, 183, 184-185

(454)

Index

of Langer, 255-262
Stein and, 401, 402
photography, 245-254
Picasso, Pablo, 403
Pierce, Franklin, 144
Pignon, Fred, quoted, 438
Planned Parenthood Federation, 385
Plato, 217; quoted, 214
Pleasant, Richard, 116
Poe, Edgar Allan, quoted, 187, 188
poetry, 203
of Cather, 104
of Dickinson, 124-135
Duncan and, 151, 152, 156
Langer and, 255, 256
of Millay, 287-294
Monroe and, 305-313
Stein and, 400, 405
Poetry: A Magazine of Verse, 305, 309-312
politics, 321, 347-360, 387-398
Ponselle, Carmela, 336, 337-338, 341, 342
Ponselle, Rosa, *foll.* 276, 336-346
Ponzillo, Beniamino and Maddalena, 336, 341, 344
Porter, Andrew W., 271
Porter, Cole, 115
Pound, Ezra, 310, 312
poverty:
Addams and, 1, 2-3, 4, 11
Alcott family and, 13-14, 16-18, 20, 21
Anderson and, 25-27, 28, 35
Anthony and, 37
Barton and, 61, 65
Bethune and, 71-73, 74-76, 77, 78
Cabrini and, 82, 83-84, 85, 86, 88
Cassatt and, 98
Dix and, 138

Duncan and, 150, 151, 152, 159-160
Lange and, 245, 246, 247-253
Motley and, 316-317, 321
Roosevelt and, 348, 352, 353, 355, 359
Sabin and, 362, 363
Sanger and, 374, 375, 378, 380
Stowe and, 411, 414
Sullivan and, 235
Tubman and, 421-430
Powell, Robert, 210
Presbyterians, 72, 74, 127, 331
prisons, 8, 140-143, 187, 352
Sanger in, 376, 379, 380-382
property rights, 38, 39, 41, 42, 43, 332, 334
Protestants, 306
Puritanism and, 126, 173, 175, 289
Prude, Walter Foy, 111, 119
Pryor, Lucius, 116
psychology, 401
the arts and, 203, 209
industry and, 193, 194-195, 196, 197-199
Pulitzer Prize, 107, 291
Purdue University, 169-170, 198
Putnam, George Palmer, 162, 165, 166-167, 171
quoted, 163

Quakers, 1, 36, 38, 44, 425
education and, 72
marriage rite, 327
ministry of, 328
in Nantucket, 296, 326
women's rights and, 331-332
Quimby, Phinias P., 175

Radcliffe College, 234, 240, 256, 257, 401
Rambert, Marie, 115

(455)

Index

Rathbone, Dr. William, 139, 144, 145
Ray, Dr. Isaac, quoted, 146
Red Cross, The, 59, 65-69, 78, 157, 219, 350, 352
Reid, Doris Fielding, 214, 216, 217
religion, *see specific faiths*
Rhode Island, 138-139, 146, 184, 195
Rice, Grantland, 435
  quoted, 431
Rittmann, Trude, 116
Rodgers, Richard, 118
Rodin, Auguste, 228
Romani, Romano, 339
Roosevelt, Eleanor, *foll.* 276, 347-360
  Anderson and, 32, 354
  Barrymore and, 57
  Bethune and, 77-78
  Earhart and, 168-169
  Graham and, 206
  Hobby and, 222
  Stein and, 408
Roosevelt, Elliott and Anna Hall, 347-348
Roosevelt, Franklin Delano, 33, 78, 109, 206, 250
  marriage of, 347, 349
  migrant labor and, 250
  Navy post, 350
  poliomyelitis and, 351-352
  Presidency of, 353-356
Roosevelt, Theodore, 8, 155, 347, 349, 353
  Anthony and, 46
  Barton and, 68
Ross, Benjamin and Harriet Green, 421, 422, 423
Ross, Bertram, 210
Rubens, Peter Paul, 92-93
Rummel, Walter, 158
Russia, 31, 122, 145, 357, 358, 395
  Duncan in, 154, 156, 158-160

Sabin, Florence, *foll.* 276, 361-371
Sabin, George and Serena, 361, 362
Sabin, Mary, 361, 362, 370
Safford, Daniel, 271, 272
St. Denis, Ruth, 202
Salk, Jonas, 351
Sanborn, Mahala, 174
Sand, George, 189
Sandburg, Carl, 311, 312
San Francisco, California, 32, 118, 128, 161, 277, 396, 404
  Duncan in, 149-151
  Lange in, 245, 246, 247, 251, 252
  Stein in, 400
Sanger, Grant and Stuart, 372, 374, 377, 379, 385
Sanger, Margaret, *foll.* 276, 372-386
Sanger, William, 372, 374, 377, 383
Saragat, Giuseppe, 345
Sarazen, Gene, 437
Sargeant, Georgia Graham, 201, 208
Sargent, John Singer, 53
Schonberg, Harold, quoted, 34-35
Schreiner, Olive, 376, 378
Schuman, William, 207
Scotland, 145, 331, 417, 438
Scudder, Janet, 228
sculpture, 156, 255, 257, 308
  Hoffman and, 225-233
Seneca Falls Woman's Rights Convention (1848), 37-38, 325, 331-333
Serafin, Tullio, 343
Sergeant, Elizabeth Shepley, quoted, 105-106, 108
settlement house movement, 85, 349
  Addams and, 1, 3-7, 9, 10-11
Sewell, Helen, 255

(456)

Index

Shakespeare, William, 54, 55
Shawn, Ted, 114
    quoted, 202
Shearer, Sybil, 116
Short, Dewey, 395-396
Sibelius, Jean, 29
Singer, Paris Eugene, 156, 157, 158, 159
Skene, Hener, quoted, 157
slavery (*see also* abolitionism), 42, 174
    emancipation, 315, 334, 410, 418-419
    fugitives from, 41, 413, 415, 421, 422, 423-429
    Underground Railroad, 424-426
Slee, J. Noah H., 372, 383
Smith, Al, 352
Smith, Clyde H., 387, 388-390
Smith, Margaret Chase, *foll.* 276, 387-398
Smith College, 258, 362, 363, 385
social work, 164, 198, 199, 407
    Addams and, 1-11
    Cabrini and, 81-88
    in France, 189
    Keller and, 241-243
    Lange and, 247-253
    Mead and, 275, 284, 285-286
    Roosevelt and, 350, 352-353, 354-355
    Tubman and, 424-430
Sokolow, Anna, 204
Somerville, Mary, 300
South Carolina, 71-72, 74, 174, 428
Spain, 3, 86, 87, 92, 98, 406
    Smith in, 395
Spanish-American War, 59, 68
Spingarn, Joel, 33, 78
Spontini, Gasparo, 342-343
Stanton, Elizabeth Cady, 38, 185, 332, 333, 334
    quoted, 330-331
Starr, Ellen, 3, 4

Starrett, Mrs., quoted, 44
Steichen, Edward, quoted, 245, 405
Stein, Daniel and Amelia, 399, 400
Stein, Gertrude, *foll.* 276, 399-409
Stein, Leo, 399, 400, 401, 402-403, 404
Steloff, Frances, 204
Stevenson, Adlai, quoted, 358
Stillman, William, 424-425, 427
Stimson, Henry, 221
Stone, Dr. Hannah, 384, 385
Stopes, Marie, 378
Stowe, Calvin Ellis, 410, 416
    quoted, 413-414, 415, 418
Stowe, Harriet Beecher, *foll.* 276, 410-420
Strange, Michael, 54
Strauss, Richard, 204
Stravinsky, Igor, 204
Stultz, Wilmer, 165, 166
suffrage, *see* voting rights
Sullivan, Anne Mansfield, *foll.* 212, 234-242, 243
Sumner, Charles, 140, 142
Sweatt, Herman, 319
Sweet, Frederick, cited, 94
Switzerland, 10, 145, 158, 208, 432
    Geneva, 65, 67, 223, 230, 284, 384

Tamaris, Helen, quoted, 159
Taubman, Howard, quoted, 30-31
Taylor, Deems, 292
Taylor, Paul, 204
Taylor, Paul Schuster, 245, 247, 248, 250, 251, 253
teaching, 25, 104, 251, 283, 308, 373, 439
    Alcott family and, 14, 18, 19, 184
    Anthony and, 37, 38-39, 41
    Barton and, 60-61
    Bethune and, 73-80
    Cabrini and, 81, 82

(457)

Index

teaching (*continued*)
  Dix and, 137-139
  Duncan and, 149, 150-151, 152-153, 154-155, 156, 157, 158-159
  Earhart and, 164, 167-170
  Eddy and, 174, 177-178
  education for, 263, 266, 267, 268-269
  Fuller and, 183, 184
  Gilbreth and, 196, 197, 198
  Graham and, 202, 203, 204, 205, 207, 208
  Hamilton and, 213-214
  Langer and, 256, 257-259
  Lyon and, 263-274
  Mitchell and, 295, 297, 300-304
  Mott and, 326-327
  Negro employment in, 315
  Roosevelt and, 349, 352
  Sabin and, 361, 363, 366-367, 368
  Stowe and, 412, 413
  Sullivan and, 234-242, 243
temperance movement, 36, 37, 38
Tennessee, 143, 321
Terry, Ellen, 153
Tetley, Glen, 204
Texas, 32, 67, 68, 249, 319, 379
  Hobby and, 218-220, 221, 223, 224
  Zacharias in, 431-437
Texas, University of, 319
Thackeray, William Makepeace, 18
theater, 6, 319, 408, 417, 436
  acting and, 48-58
  dance and, 111-123, 149-161, 201-210
  poetry and, 288, 289, 290, 291, 293, 306, 307-308
  singing and, 24-35, 336-346
Thomson, Polly, 241, 242, 243
Thomson, Virgil, 408

Thoreau, Henry David, 15, 186, 232, 331
Thorner, William, 338
Tilton, Abigail Baker, 173, 174, 175
Todd, Mabel Loomis, 134
Toklas, Alice B., 404, 406-407, 408, 409
Tolstoy, Leo, 9
  quoted, 416-417
Toscanini, Arturo, 30
Tourny, Joseph, 93
Toynbee, Arnold, 216
Transcendentalism, 13, 15, 174, 176, 185
Truman, Harry S., 33, 57, 356
Truth, Sojourner, 333
tuberculosis, 8, 50, 86, 126, 373
  Sabin and, 361, 368, 370
Tubman, Harriet, 41, *foll.* 276, 421-430
Tubman, John, 421, 423
Tudor, Anthony, 115
Tuke, Samuel, 139
Turner, Nat, 422, 423
Turney, Matt, 210
Tuskegee Institute, 79
Twain, Mark, 105, 239; quoted, 240

Unitarians, 138
United Nations, 223, 251, 284
  Roosevelt and, 347, 356-357, 359
  Special Fund, 208
  Trusteeship Committee, 34
United States Air Force Reserve, 394-395
United States Army, 218, 222
United States Bureau of Missing Men, 64
United States Congress, 35, 44, 46, 67, 126, 219, 356
  Earhart and, 168

Index

migrant labor and, 250
slavery and, 329
Smith in, 387, 389-396, 397
state land grants, 144
WAC's and, 222
United States Constitution, 43, 289, 314, 323
   Fourteenth Amendment, 316, 323
   Fifteenth Amendment, 42
   Sixteenth Amendment, 219
   Nineteenth Amendment, 46, 219, 350
United States Department of Food Administration, 9
United States Department of Health, Education and Welfare, 218, 223, 224
United States Department of the Interior, 61
United States Department of the Navy, 66, 171, 350, 390, 395-396
United States Department of State, 34, 66, 120, 251
United States Department of the Treasury, 66
United States Department of War, 220-221
United States Distinguished Service Medal, 223
United States Fine Arts Commission, 232
United States Golf Association, 437
United States House of Representatives, 144, 387, 389
   Armed Services Committee, 391, 395, 396
United States Navy, 390, 391
United States Office of Patents, 61, 62
United States Office of War Information, 251, 283
United States Post Office, 66, 374-375, 376
United States President's Emergency Committee, 198
United States Resettlement Administration, 248
United States Senate, 67, 144, 219, 243, 387, 391-396
United States Social Security Board, 248
United States Supreme Court, 43, 318
   civil rights decisions, 314, 315-316, 319, 321
United States War Manpower Commission, 199
Universal Peace Congress (1904), 9
Universal Peace Union (1869), 334

Van Dyke, Willard, 247
Van Vechten, Carl, 405
Vassar, Matthew, 300-301, 303
Vassar College, 259, 283, 288-289, 295, 300-303
Vehanen, Kosti, 28, 29
Verdi, Giuseppe, 33, 339-340, 341, 342, 343
Vermont, 107, 205-206, 362
Victoria, queen of England, 416
Virginia, 62-63, 78, 101, 427
Vollard, Ambrose, quoted, 95
voting rights, 38, 40, 45-46, 219
   Anthony arrest and, 42-44
   Keller on, 241
   Mott on, 332
   Roosevelt on, 350

WAC (Women's Army Corps), 79, 218, 221-223
Wadsworth, Rev. Charles, 127, 128, 131, 132-133, 134
Wagner, Cosima, 153

Index

Wagner, Robert F., quoted, 32
WANDS (Women's Army for National Defense), 79
war:
　labor and, 199
　nursing and, 19-20, 59-69, 145-146
　pacifism and, 9-10, 241, 290
　refugee rights, 347, 357, 359
　Smith and, 395
　suffrage and, 40
　women army workers in, 220-223
Ward, Samuel, 184, 185
Washington, Booker T., quoted, 430
Washington, D. C., 19-20, 144
　Anderson in, 24, 31-33, 354
　Barton in, 61-62, 66-67, 68
　Dickinson in, 126-127
　Duncan in, 155
　Earhart in, 168-169
　Hamilton in, 210, 216
　Hobby in, 218, 220-224
　Monroe in, 306
　Mott in, 334
　Roosevelt in, 350
　Smith in, 387, 389-396
Washington State, 86, 87, 88, 258
Watteau, Jean Antoine, 113
WAVES (Women's Reserve of the United States Navy), 390
Wayne, "Mad Anthony," 60
Weber, Karl Maria von, 341-342
Webster, Noah, 265-266
Welcher, Irwin, 253
Wells, H. G., 382
Whicher, George Frisbie, 128
White, Amanda, 265, 266
White, Clarence H., 246
White, Thomas, 76
White, Thomas (of Massachusetts), 265, 266

Whittier, John Greenleaf, 328, 333, 419
　quoted, 147
Williams, William Carlos, quoted, 311-312, 405
Willis, Llewellyn, 17
Wilson, Edmund, 293
　quoted, 290
Wilson, Emma, 72, 73, 74
Wilson, Woodrow, 9, 219, 350, 378
　quoted, 54
Wisniewski, Ladislas, 20
Woman Rebel, The (periodical), 375-376, 378
Woman's Rights Convention, 37, 331-333
Woman's Rights Movement, *see* feminism
Women's Peace Conference (1919), 9-10
Women's Suffrage Amendment, *see* U. S. Constitution, Nineteenth Amendment
Women's Temperance Society, 38
Women's Trade Union League, 351, 355
Woollcott, Alexander, quoted, 242
Woolsey, Dr. Theodore D., quoted, 66
Wordsworth, William, 188, 400
World Population Conference (1954), 385
World's Columbian Exposition, 45, 97
World War I:
　Addams and, 9-10
　Bethune and, 78
　Cather and, 107
　Duncan and, 157
　Gilbreth and, 196
　Hobby and, 219

(460)

Index

Keller and, 241
Millay and, 287, 289, 290
Monroe and, 312
Roosevelt and, 350
Stein and, 406-407
World War II, 33, 79, 232, 250-251
  de Mille and, 115
  Earhart and, 171-172
  Gilbreth and, 198-199
  Hobby and, 218, 220-223
  Mead and, 282
  Millay and, 292-293
  Roosevelt and, 355

Smith and, 390
Stein and, 408-409
Wright-Humason School for the Deaf, 239-240

Yale University, 198, 216, 283
Yalta, Crimea, conference (1945), 356
yellow fever, 67, 86, 174

Zaharias, George, 431, 437, 438, 439
Zaharias, Mildred Ella ("Babe" Didrikson), *foll.* 276, 431-440

ABOUT THE AUTHOR

Hope Stoddard has two major interests: music and writing. In her childhood she studied to be a concert violinist. Before entering college, however, her second love won out and she decided to become a writer. She was graduated from the University of Michigan with a degree in journalism. Then she became interested in teaching English and, for two years, she lived and taught in Europe. When she returned to America she combined her talents to become a writer and editor for a music periodical. She was on the staff of *Étude* magazine and then she became an editor for *The International Musician*.

Hope Stoddard has long been concerned about woman's role in American society. Her interest was first aroused in her childhood when she listened to her mother tell about the achievements of the great women of history such as Susan B. Anthony and Clara Barton. In later years, when she saw more of the arbitrary limitations imposed on women in society and the business world, she began to study the question further. She wanted to write a book that would focus on the accomplishments of American women: "Simply set them down, not put forward any message or raise any questions. Only give the record and let that speak for itself."

In recent years Hope Stoddard has devoted full time to her writing. Her articles have appeared in several national magazines and she is the author of four books, including *From These Comes Music: Instruments of the Band and Orchestra*, a widely read book for music students, and *The Noon Answer*, a collection of her poetry. Hope Stoddard makes her home in New York City.